Additional Praise for *Civic and Moral Learning in America*:

"Don Warren and John Patrick have compiled a fascinating and provocative collection of readings on the history of civic and moral education in the United States. It conveys the diversity of thinking on the topic that has pervaded discussions throughout our history about the proper role of citizens in the American democratic republic and the responsibilities of our schools and other institutions in the preparation of young people for citizenship. This text is an invaluable resource for those concerned with the need to improve the civic and moral education of young people in America. It should also be found useful by those dedicated to advancing the cause of democracy in both advanced and emerging democracies throughout the world."

—Charles N. Quigley, Executive Director,
Center for Civic Education

"In a political climate where the debate over moral values appears to leave us only two choices—'traditional' or none at all—Warren and Patrick have compiled a fitting analysis that questions the need to find a moral center in our pluralistic democracy. The multiple historical perspectives offered by the scholars in this work not only explicate the turbulent history of moral and civic learning in America, but also offer feminist, multicultural, and global perspectives on the seemingly unending quest for the elusive moral center of civic life in our democracy."

—Gregory E. Hamot, Associate Professor of Social
Studies Education, The College of Education at
The University of Iowa

This page intentionally left blank

CIVIC AND MORAL LEARNING IN AMERICA

Edited by

Donald Warren

and

John J. Patrick

CIVIC AND MORAL LEARNING IN AMERICA
© Donald Warren and John J. Patrick, 2006.

Softcover reprint of the hardcover 1st edition 2006 978-1-4039-7395-5

All rights reserved. No part of this book may be used or reproduced in any manner whatsoever without written permission except in the case of brief quotations embodied in critical articles or reviews.

First published in 2006 by
PALGRAVE MACMILLAN™
175 Fifth Avenue, New York, N.Y. 10010 and
Houndmills, Basingstoke, Hampshire, England RG21 6XS
Companies and representatives throughout the world.

PALGRAVE MACMILLAN is the global academic imprint of the Palgrave Macmillan division of St. Martin's Press, LLC and of Palgrave Macmillan Ltd. Macmillan® is a registered trademark in the United States, United Kingdom and other countries. Palgrave is a registered trademark in the European Union and other countries.

ISBN 978-1-349-53462-3   ISBN 978-1-4039-8472-2 (eBook)
DOI 10.1057/9781403984722

Library of Congress Cataloging-in-Publication Data

   Civic and moral learning in America / edited by Donald Warren and John J. Patrick.
      p. cm.
   Includes bibliographical references and index.
   ISBN 978-1-4039-7396-2 (pbk.)
      1. Moral education—United States. 2. Character—Study and teaching (Elementary)—United States. 3. Civics—Study and teaching—United States.
   I. Warren, Donald R., 1933– II. Patrick, John J., 1935–

LC311.C483 2006
370.11′40973—dc22   2005044867

A catalogue record for this book is available from the British Library.

Design by Newgen Imaging Systems (P) Ltd., Chennai, India.

First edition: April 2006
10 9 8 7 6 5 4 3 2 1

To B. Edward McClellan, Professor Emeritus of Education, American Studies, and History, Indiana University Bloomington, and to Mary and their sons Doug and Robert.

Ed McClellan has produced foundational work for a long-established, growing, and contentious literature in the history of moral and civic education in America. Where some offered pronouncements and imperatives, he has searched for evidence and understanding, framing large, urgent questions and inviting others to add to the list. All along, he has insisted that the field's importance, particularly in the context of a democratic society, warranted rigorous, pointed curiosity. The editors and authors of this book have attempted to rise to his challenge. As readers will discover, the book pays tribute to Ed in ways that are consistent with his own contributions to the literature. This requires at minimum that we build on, expand, and argue with his work. If we had asked him, that is how he would have wanted us to proceed.

We know Ed as a disciplined scholar, colleague, teacher, mentor, and friend. He is known too for his wry and unerringly perceptive sense of humor. Here and there, that admirable human trait also intrudes on the following pages.

This page intentionally left blank

Contents

Acknowledgments	ix
List of Contributors	xi
Introduction: Civic and Moral Learning in Question *Donald Warren and John J. Patrick*	1
1 The Politics of Civic and Moral Education *R. Freeman Butts*	7
2 Can Civic and Moral Education Be Distinguished? *Barry L. Bull*	21
3 Cato's Resolve and the Revolutionary Spirit: Political Education, Civic Action, and the Democratic-Republican Societies of the 1790s *Brian W. Dotts*	33
4 Moral Educations on the Alaskan Frontier, 1794–1917 *Milton Gaither*	51
5 Social Capital and the Common Schools *John L. Rury*	69
6 Between Hogs and Horse-Trots: Searching for Civic Learning in 1850s Indiana *Glenn Lauzon*	87
7 Widening the Circle: African American Perspectives on Moral and Civic Learning *Paulette Patterson Dilworth*	103
8 Land, Law, and Education: The Troubled History of Indian Citizenship, 1871–1924 *David Wallace Adams*	119
9 "Let Virtue Be Thy Guide, and Truth Thy Beacon-Light": Moral and Civic Transformation in Indianapolis's Public Schools *Paul J. Ramsey*	135

10	Berkeley Women Economists, Public Policy, and Civic Sensibility *Mary Ann Dzuback*	153
11	Character and the Clinic: The Shift from Character to Personality in American Character Education, 1930–1940 *David P. Setran*	173
12	Sex, Drugs, and Right 'N' Wrong: Or, The Passion of Joycelyn Elders, M.D. *Jonathan Zimmerman*	191
13	Monuments and Morals: The Nationalization of Civic Instruction *John Bodnar*	207

Afterword   221
Donald Warren and John J. Patrick

Index   223

Acknowledgments

This book began as a student idea. Glenn Lauzon and a group of his colleagues argued that the literature on civic and moral education would be greatly enhanced by a collection of essays that built on the research agenda formulated by B. Edward McClellan, one of their most respected teachers. They also proposed (gleefully) that such a book would make Ed suitably uncomfortable.

Practical and collegial support came quickly from multiple sources. Barry Bull, David Labaree, Bill Reese, John Rury, and Jonathan Zimmerman generously gave time to formulating plans for the book, and their encouragement has continued throughout the project. The conceptual framework and several of the case studies emerged from faculty and student discussions during a doctoral seminar last year. Going far beyond any reasonable sense of duty as Ed's department chair, Barry Bull brought technical and editorial expertise to the pre-publication process. The reference staffs of the Indiana University Herman B Wells Library, the Education Library, and the Social Studies Development Center answered our questions with their usual competence and even did their own digging. The SSDC's Jane Henson was particularly helpful. Our dean, Gerardo Gonzalez, who faced numerous other claims on his attention, nevertheless kept informed about our progress. A grant from Kenneth R. R. Gros Louis, Vice President of Indiana University and Chancellor of the Bloomington campus, provided funding for research and preparation expenses.

It was John Rury who introduced us to Amanda Johnson at Palgrave Macmillan. She responded enthusiastically to our proposal and at every point subsequently proved to be the ideal editor. Elizabeth Sabo has been an attentive production editor, and Emily Leithauser developed marketing plans and materials. Christopher Cecot created the index. Maran Elancheran has overseen the copyediting and production processes. We are also indebted to Monica Halcomb and Nancy Novotny for typing seemingly countless drafts, Christopher Essex for transforming hard copies into electronic files, and Joshua B. Garrison for research assistance. Sandra Strain served as project manager at Indiana University Bloomington. Finally and notably, we are grateful to the chapter authors who worked against impossible deadlines to produce essays reflecting the high quality of inquiry the field of civic and moral learning warrants.

Donald Warren
John J. Patrick
Bloomington, Indiana
August 2005

This page intentionally left blank

Contributors

David Wallace Adams is Professor of Education and History at Cleveland State University.

John Bodnar is Chancellor's Professor and Chair of the Department of History at Indiana University Bloomington.

Barry L. Bull is Professor of Education and Chair of the Department of Educational Leadership and Policy Studies at Indiana University Bloomington.

R. Freeman Butts is William F. Russell Professor Emeritus in the Foundations of Education, Teachers College, Columbia University and member emeritus of the Board of Directors of the Center for Civic Education.

Paulette Patterson Dilworth is Assistant Professor of Education in the Department of Curriculum and Instruction at Indiana University Bloomington.

Brian W. Dotts is a Ph.D. candidate in the Department of Educational Leadership and Policy Studies at Indiana University Bloomington.

Mary Ann Dzuback is Associate Professor of Education and History at Washington University in St. Louis.

Milton Gaither is Assistant Professor of Education at Messiah College.

Glenn Lauzon is Visiting Instructor, Department of Secondary Education, School of Education and Professional Studies at State University of New York, College at Potsdam.

John J. Patrick is Professor Emeritus of Education and Director Emeritus of the Social Studies Development Center at Indiana University Bloomington.

Paul J. Ramsey is Associate Instructor and Ph.D. candidate in the Department of Educational Leadership and Policy Studies at Indiana University Bloomington.

John L. Rury is Professor of Education at the University of Kansas.

David P. Setran is Assistant Professor of Educational Ministries at Wheaton College.

Donald Warren is Professor and University Dean Emeritus of Education at Indiana University Bloomington.

Jonathan Zimmerman is Professor of Education and History in the Department of Humanities and Social Sciences, Steinhardt School of Education and Professor of History in the Department of History of the Graduate School of Arts and Sciences at New York University.

This page intentionally left blank

Introduction: Civic and Moral Learning in Question

Donald Warren and John J. Patrick

From its formative years to the present, advocates of various persuasions have written and spoken, often urgently, about the country's need for civic and moral renewal. The voices have been thoughtful or strident, occasionally both, and sometimes marked by an unambivalent certainty. Invariably, the last has proved fleeting. Debates have come and gone, leaving a vast, still expanding literature. As befits the American context, the literature has been hydra-headed, incorrigibly diverse, and contentious, even in wartimes when clarity of purpose might be expected.

As B. Edward McClellan has observed, no single voice has prevailed, although many have been undeniably distinguished. Thomas Jefferson deserves at least partial credit for starting the argument. He linked moral and civic education in the nation-to-be as a blended enterprise, giving the mixture experimental form, republican substance, and partisan flavor, notably in the Declaration of Independence. But no popular consensus on an American public philosophy followed in the wake of this iconic broadside. With independence won, almost the exact opposite occurred. Conflicts erupted over basic questions: What did it mean to be a citizen of the now launched United States, as against an individual state or community? Who qualified for the role? What did the Revolutionary War and the ideal of self-governing citizens mean for domestic political values and nascent systems of government, for diverse, often antagonistic, religious confessions and sensibilities, and by extension for Americans' European cousins still under monarchal rule?

Political nostalgia has tended to iron out the wrinkles of ambiguity, doubt, and disagreement evident in these beginnings, attributing to Jefferson and the other founders a fully wrought confidence in what the Union and a good, moral citizen should be. Later generations discovered that slavery was the most costly of the intractable civic and moral dilemmas left in their hands, but there were others. Jefferson, for one, placed his trust in citizens schooled to be engaged, upright, and independent by their attachments to land and to each other in communities and the states. As this agrarian vision lost its footing, the political experiment nonetheless continued, driven by changing social conditions, new questions, and recurring old ones. McClellan has restored the rough contours of the accumulated, sometimes incompatible answers, offering schools, colleges, and universities as a kind of composite prism through which light refracted across the country's political and moral landscape. In effect he outlined a research and education reform agenda.

The authors and editors of this book build from the foundation he has provided. Representing the differing perspectives of established and beginning scholars and professional educators, we pursue lines of thought exposed when familiar questions are turned inside out. Because the debate over civic and moral education has been routinely framed by intentions and imperatives, it has tended to ignore the places and processes through which Americans have learned, for good or ill, to perform civic roles and adopt moral stances. The traditional approach has placed great emphasis on teachings, programs, and requirements within educational institutions, on the assumption that the institutions themselves could guarantee essential learning. While affirming the potential of curricular purpose and planning, we prefer to clarify basic questions and to refrain from answering them before curiosity has had a say. On this road, a premature search for consensus may lead only to divisive moral and civic cul-de-sacs.

Why, for example, have adult generations regularly looked askance at the moral and civic tendencies of the young? If the latter display ignorance of historical facts and treasured documents, does it matter that large segments of the former have forgotten the history and civics lessons presented to them in school or college? Can we trace the declining learning curve to ineffective teaching, uninspired curricula, or additionally to more powerful learning acquired elsewhere? Are adult perceptions of youthful lapses misinformed or even wrong? Maybe any refusal of adolescents to mimic the civic and moral repertoires of their elders has signaled not only mental health, but also healthy potential for a democratic society.

The uncertainties suggest fresh analytical approaches. To the extent that school-based learning and adult socialization have occurred in separate domains, at different life stages, and under varying influences, any bridge seeming to span the experiences bears scrutiny. Among them may well be the lingering effects of formal curricula in civics and American values, but memories of these sorts tend to fade, shift, and regroup over time and in response to disruptions. Oral history research tells us adults fondly recall the moral and civic lessons they heard in school, the comradery of the clubs and teams they joined, and the warm satisfaction they felt as participants in social service projects; yet they also report finding their memories of schooling trumped by demands and interactions of the moment. The moral and civic mindedness they practice apparently reflects the processes and contexts through which they have earned livings more than any residues of formal instruction. If they lose their jobs or if an entire community must endure the closing of a major employer, the idealized social fabric can begin to unravel. Going to war may unify the nation, but battlefield casualties, grief, or spreading reservations about the competence of elected leaders can just as easily shatter the consensus locally. Although curriculum proposals by moral and civic educators may anticipate such vicissitudes in general, it is the subsequent particulars of public learning that threaten to ambush their plans.

The predictability cautions curriculum planners to hedge their bets by playing several hands simultaneously, as it were. They attend to the social and institutional contexts of their proposed reforms to avoid errors that can be likened to rearranging deck chairs on a doomed ship. They seek to promote a deepening literacy across the curriculum on the strong indications that the accumulating skills and values deliver more lasting potential than, say, a semester of civics. Expanded and altered to encompass, in this example, learning to read and to value analytical thinking, moral and civic education becomes a complicated project, with multiple dimensions, nuances, and implications that reach beyond adolescence and formal academic knowledge.

The experiential approach suggests other focused inquiries as well. By what means and in what settings have women in the United States prepared for and practiced citizenship? The question is germane historically and to current educational and policy issues. The architects of nineteenth-century public schools expected the emerging systems to ensure the nation's safe future by properly shaping the moral and political character of the young. Consider then the likely civics lessons offered in the person of their teachers. Well before the century's end, the great majority of these teachers were poorly paid women who could not vote in national or often state elections or perform other civic roles either. They may have been commonly regarded as a rural community's educated elite, but their low status in the policy environment was understood even by their own pupils. The historical record tells us these women, often no older than teenagers, viewed teaching, despite its hardships, as personally liberating and rewarding work they could perform on their own. It was one of the few available alternatives to the customary roles assigned to them by males. Liberation also seems to have been increasingly on the minds of twentieth-century women who pressed into the colleges, graduate schools, and faculties that would admit them. This was a time for women when moral and civic learning was in flux across the country. While needing a better grasp of the changes and their contexts, we already know that not all the lessons acquired by women along the way were intended within reigning social and legal conventions. Women may offer historical examples of civic and moral learning as subversive activity, which typically has not been among the explicit goals of curriculum reforms.

Similar ironies can be detected in African American history. Recent scholarship has underscored the accuracy of W.E.B. DuBois's prediction that the "color line" separating black and white people would haunt American experience pervasively in the twentieth century. His argument rested on an analysis of nineteenth-century U.S. history, a period dominated by the "moral stench" of slavery, the bloodiest war Americans ever fought, and de jure and de facto racial segregation. New research has paid belated attention to the civics lessons brought forward by African Americans from their cross-generational experiences. Equally relevant are the often starkly different civic and moral learnings drawn by blacks and whites from slavery, lynchings, race riots during wartimes, when patriotic unity was deemed essential, and racially inspired (and unequal) school funding allocations. As for the last point, African American history repeatedly documents why school district budgets and local tax referenda function as more revealing mirrors of a community's moral cohesiveness and civic resolve than formally enacted mission statements.

In addition to generational, gender, and racial differences, other fissures in the blended enterprise of moral and civic learning quickly come to mind. Consider the socializing experiences of immigrants and Native Americans, which varied widely across ethnicities, races, and tribes, and low-income people generally. Consider the school-based education offered outside classrooms and curricula by the workings of the institutions themselves, their policies, regulations, and cultures and even their architecture. As the country's demography shifted from rural to urban and became more racially and ethnically diverse, as practical applications of the scientific revolution reordered work on farms and in cities, fostering among other results widening income gaps and sharpening social class distinctions, and as the demands of a market economy penetrated even remote agricultural communities, where and how did ordinary Americans learn the virtues they practiced? What tangle of contexts, concepts, and experiences were in play? The questions imply a need for broad nets to capture reliable and valid answers, assuming our purposes owe less to a determined quest for where moral and civic education ought to have occurred and far more to curiosity about the footprints left by actual learning. The approach opens a wide gate onto the forming of American culture as a lived, changing social environment whose debts to the capabilities of diverse participants can easily go unnoticed, mismeasured, and unpaid.

Divisions among citizens and future citizens notwithstanding, the United States has more than survived. In the twentieth century the nation prospered economically, politically, and militarily, and now at the beginning of the twenty-first century, it dominates the world stage. To design effective curricula, we should want to understand the moral and civic trajectory of this success in explanatory detail. The chapters that follow offer case histories, policy analyses, conceptual inquiries, and curriculum studies as tools to unearth and examine varieties of lessons offered and accepted, unintended learnings, perilous missteps, generational memories, and the foundations laid as a consequence, whether by purpose or accident, that altogether seem to explain the moral and civic mold that has become the United States.

Admittedly unusual in the country's long history of moral and civic education, the approach invites analyses of claimed dysfunctions and proposed remedies. The authors emphasize contested transitions; tensions between formal academic goals and curricula, on one hand, and experiences in classrooms, schools, and communities, on the other; and cross-generational continuities and disruptions. In effect the chapters present case studies of cultural formation, suggesting these details also bring resources for educational planning and practice. Even so, the research and planning agenda they represent leaves untouched large, unexplored territories. The case studies are focused exclusively on the United States and nineteenth-century Alaska. We acknowledge at the outset that the relevant spheres of interest reach far across the American continents, Europe, Africa, the Middle East, Asia, and Australia. The need for historical and philosophical inquiries on indigenous civic and moral learning in these regions and for comparative analyses presses for attention that we admittedly do not provide.

Given the global surge of constitutional democracy during the past 25 years, the ideas and issues of this volume nonetheless have broad international relevance. Diverse peoples in various regions of our world express common concerns about the importance of civic and moral learning in the development and maintenance of democracy. They commonly recognize that if there would be fulfillment of Abraham Lincoln's pithy promise of democracy—"government of the people, by the people, and for the people"—then there must be effective civic and moral education of the people. So, educators in both nascent and mature democracies throughout the world are seeking challenging commentaries about how to improve the teaching and learning of democratic citizenship. They will find much to ponder within the chapters of this work.

Suggested Reading

Anderson, James D., *The Education of Blacks in the South, 1860–1935* (Chapel Hill, NC: University of North Carolina Press, 1988).
Berlin, Ira, *Generations of Captivity: A History of African-American Slaves* (Cambridge, MA: Belknap Press of Harvard University Press, 2003).
Dewey, John, *Interest and Effort in Education* (Carbondale, IL: Southern Illinois University Press, 1975 [1913]).
DuBois, W.E.B., *Souls of Black Folk* (New York: Modern Library, 2003 [1903]).
Ellis, Joseph J. *Founding Brothers: The Revolutionary Generation* (New York: Alfred A. Knopf, 2000).
Fujitani, T., *Splendid Monarchy: Power and Pageantry in Modern Japan* (Berkeley: University of California Press, 1998).
Hahn, Steven, *A Nation under Our Feet: Black Political Struggles in the Rural South from Slavery to the Great Migration* (Cambridge, MA: Belknap Press of Harvard University Press, 2003).
Jones, Edward P., *The Known World* (New York: HarperCollins, 2003).
McClellan, B. Edward, *Moral Education in America* (New York: Teachers College Press, 1999).
Menand, Louis, *The Metaphysical Club: A Story of Ideas in America* (New York: Farrar, Straus and Giroux, 2001).
Ogren, Christine A., *The American State Normal School: "An Instrument of Great Good"* (New York: Palgrave Macmillan, 2005).
Ostler, Jeffrey, *The Plains Sioux and U.S. Colonialism from Louis and Clark to Wounded Knee* (New York: Cambridge University Press, 2004).
Webber, Thomas L., *Deep Like the Rivers: Education in the Slave Quarter Community, 1831–1865* (New York: W.W. Norton & Company, Inc., 1978).

This page intentionally left blank

Chapter 1

The Politics of Civic and Moral Education

R. Freeman Butts

President Bush's Agenda for Education

In this chapter, relying in part on public media sources, I explore the present political context of civic and moral education in the schools of the United States. I write near the beginning of President George W. Bush's second term, with Republican control of both houses of Congress and a generally favorable Supreme Court. In his first inaugural address President Bush issued an eloquent call for all Americans to be good citizens, sounding themes the *New York Times* thought worthy of a front-page, six-column headline:

BUSH, TAKING OFFICE, CALLS FOR CIVILITY,
COMPASSION AND "NATION OF CHARACTER"
UNITY IS A THEME
In Inaugural Speech, He
Asks Citizens to Seek
"a Common Good"[1]

Listen again to some of his soaring rhetoric:

> America has never been united by blood or birth or soil. We are bound by ideals that move us beyond our backgrounds, lift us above our interests and *teach us what it means to be citizens. Every child must be taught these principles. Every citizen must uphold them,* And every immigrant, by embracing these ideals, makes our country more, not less, American.
>
> Today we affirm a new commitment to live out our nation's promise through civility, courage, compassion and character. . . .

> If we do not turn the hearts of children toward knowledge and character, we will lose their gifts and undermine their idealism. . . .
>
> Together, we will reclaim America's schools before ignorance and apathy claim more young lives. . . .
>
> Government has great responsibilities, for public safety and public health, for civil rights and common schools. . . .
>
> Our public interest depends on private character, on civic duty and family bonds and basic fairness, uncounted, unhonored acts of decency which give direction to our freedom. . . .
>
> *I ask you to be citizens. Citizens, not spectators. Citizens, not subjects. Responsible citizens, building communities of service and a nation of character.*[2]
>
> (Emphasis added)

As we read again this remarkable testament, we are struck by its attention to the twofold themes of this book. President Bush stressed moral and civic education in his campaign, and in the first weeks of his presidency, he said again and again that the reform of education was his top legislative priority. Nicholas Lemann summarized the promise and its power in a single sentence: "Education was the issue that made Bush president."[3]

I was heartened by those words in January 2001, but since then I have been looking mostly in vain at the specific educational proposals of the President and in legislation by Congress for what they thought the ideals of democracy are and what should be taught about them in the schools. On the positive side, their overriding emphasis on strengthening the federal role to aid underprivileged children to attain a better education, close the gap between the children of affluent families and low-income and minority families and thus to "leave no child behind" certainly represents the democratic ideals of equality of opportunity and justice desirable in American society. In strengthening the federal role and increasing the amount of federal funds for education, Bush's proposals abruptly depart from the approach of the Reagan administration and the Newt Gingrich "Republican Revolution" of 1994, which had tried to deflate the federal role in education and even to abolish the U.S. Department of Education. In this respect, Bush was redefining the conservative approach to education that had emphasized local control of schools as "the American Way." Instead, the federal government's role was to be greatly expanded, not only in the amount of federal funds but also in the federal control over "accountability" and over standards of achievement to be measured by required testing of students.

But I felt less reassured when I found that the education bills passed by the Senate and House gave primary emphasis to the annual measured achievement of students in reading and mathematics along with more federal accountability for states in meeting challenging standards but said nothing about civic education. While they would continue to increase federal aid for the P-8 education of poor and minority children, the enactments have scarcely confronted the need to stress education for democracy in the entire curriculum, in the student activities of public and private schools, or in the preparation of teachers. Instead they have tacitly posed a questionable dichotomy between academic and civic and moral learning.

In order to get a final education bill passed that he could sign, President Bush had to give up his promise to include provisions that would have encouraged federal funds to go to parents who wished to send their children to private and religious schools. The final bill did permit federal funds to be used by parents to send their children to other, presumably more suitable, public schools and to pay for private tutoring and for other after-school activities conducted by private agencies and faith-based religious institutions.

The No Child Left Behind Act that President Bush signed on January 8, 2002 not only highlighted the importance of improving achievement in reading and mathematics in every grade school level from 3rd through the 8th but also provided that science should be added in three grades to the preferred subjects to be tested beginning in the fall session of 2005. In the published reports of the law I found also that teaching of reading should be based on "scientifically-based" methods which presumably meant that phonics should be preferred over whole language. A potentially most important element provided that within four years all teachers should be qualified to teach their subject in order for districts and states to receive funds for training, hiring, and salary raises. What role schools of education should play in determining the qualifications teachers should have was surrounded with controversy. When, if ever, civic education should be a part of the core programs in schools or teacher education was not clearly stated. Moral or character education did find a strong place in Bush's pursuit of federal funds for his faith-based initiative.

To put the matter bluntly, school reform now seemed to reflect a political agenda, as Richard Rothstein warned at the time:

> The law has a new program for strengthening American history instruction by, for example, providing grants for training teachers. But dollars can be used only for "traditional" American history. Most historians now urge teachers to cover the experiences of minorities, women, and ordinary workers, not only political leaders. There is debate about how much the emphasis should shift, but virtually no respected educator wants a return to the traditional teaching of only facts about leaders. Yet this approach is a matter of law for schools that accept this federal money.[4]

I found no stress upon teaching civics or government at any grade level as a means of encouraging the development of the democratic citizenship that President Bush had emphasized in his first inaugural address. This was disappointing because the means were already at hand to promote this objective, namely, the *National Standards for Civics and Government*, a guideline that deals with the civic knowledge, civic values, and civic skills of participation that can and should be the core of education from kindergarten through high school and of teacher education for all qualified and certified teachers. This neglect was made all the more tragic in view of the resounding blows to American national stability hammered into our consciousness by the events of September 11, 2001. The war against illiteracy remained the paramount domestic aim of American education rather than strengthening the public's understanding of the meaning and values of democratic citizenship, as though the two priorities could be separated and ranked. The nation's need to respond wisely and effectively to acts of terrorism by antidemocratic forces, from whatever source they might come, advised otherwise. A single-focused war against illiteracy remained the major domestic purpose of the

No Child Left Behind Act until President Bush's first State of the Union address on January 29, 2002.

At this point, national security understandably became his top priority and the federal role in promoting good schools was treated in three or four sentences as primarily important to assure good jobs and economic security for the people:

> Good jobs begin with good schools, and here we've made a good start.... There is more to do. We need to prepare our children to read and succeed in school with improved Head Start and early childhood development programs. We must upgrade our teacher colleges and teacher training and launch a major recruiting drive with a great goal for America: a quality teacher in every classroom.[5]

Later as budgets for teacher training scholarships were cut, Arthur Levine, president of Teachers College, argued forcefully that the definition of teacher quality by Secretary of Education Rod Paige was hopelessly inadequate because it assumed that new teachers did not need any knowledge of teaching and child development or student teaching experience. Instead, Paige called these "burdensome education requirements" that should be eliminated. Levine concluded that this means that low-wealth inner-city school districts will be the recipients of poorly trained "rookie" teachers and will fall still farther behind affluent suburban school districts: "Teachers who know only subject matter are not qualified to enter our classrooms, nor are teachers who know only pedagogy. Our children need teachers who know both. This kind of dual qualification cannot be reserved only for the affluent."[6]

President Bush gave much more attention to his call "for every American to commit at least two years, 4,000 hours over the rest of your lifetime, to the service of your neighbors and your nation." His plan for voluntary service involved not only an expansion of the Peace Corps, AmeriCorps, and Senior Corps but also a new Freedom Corps to aid volunteers to respond to crises at home, rebuilding communities, and "extending American compassion throughout the world . . . and lead the world toward the values that will bring lasting peace." Again, the President's recital of the pertinent values to be achieved go to the heart of democracy: "liberty and justice . . . and the nonnegotiable demands of human dignity; the rule of law, limits on the power of the state, respect for women, private property, free speech, equal justice and religious toleration."[7] But there was no indication that teaching and learning these values should be at the core of the curriculum of American schools, colleges, and teacher education rather than being left solely to volunteer activities and community service by interested citizens.

Officials of the National Council for the Social Studies (NCSS) soon began to echo fears that the high priority of testing and accountability in reading and mathematics would lead states and school districts to downgrade their emphasis on history, civics, and social studies in order to prove their capability in the subjects mandated by the federal government. The vice president of NCSS voiced the concern in *Education Week*: "You can't learn the lessons of history and civics as vocabulary words and reading lessons. We need to go beyond reading skills to the whole reason universal education was created to begin with, so we have an educated citizenry not just to ensure that the republic survives, but that it thrives."[8]

As 2002 wore on, funds for education became harder to squeeze out of the federal budget, and most states were faced with lower and lower revenues that made it increasingly harder for them to offer many kinds of services and curriculum activities, let alone promote civic education. In January 2003, the Center on Education Policy issued a useful commentary and summary of the first year of state and federal efforts to implement the No Child Left Behind Act:

> This far-reaching education law has two major purposes: to raise student achievement across the board and to eliminate the achievement gap between the students from different backgrounds. . . .
> [T]he main tasks required by the Act for 2002 involved building state-level systems for additional testing, greater accountability and data collection with only a few new requirements affecting some local schools. In the fall of 2003, however, this will change, as the force of this major challenge for American public education reaches every local school in the country.
> Our study found that the states are committed to the goals of the legislation and are trying hard to carry them out, but the prescriptive nature of the requirements is causing great concern. States are moving faster on the elements of the law where they have more experience, such as developing state tests, and slower on aspects where they need to create new procedures, such as approving nonprofit and for-profit groups to provide tutoring. We also found that the fiscal crisis in most states, coupled with the prospect of limited additional federal aid, could threaten the successful implementation of this very ambitious law . . . .
> The No Child Left Behind Act places greater demands on states and school districts than ever before. Some states must define the level of proficiency that all students are expected to reach and set a timetable for schools to bring all their students up to this level by school year 2013–14. States must also expand their testing programs, analyze and report test results in new ways, provide technical assistance to under-performing districts and schools, help teachers become better qualified, and much more. School districts must raise test scores in reading, math and science, close achievement gaps, design improvement strategies and interventions for under-performing schools, hire or develop better-qualified teachers and classroom aides, and create or expand public school choice programs, among other duties.[9]

I quote these paragraphs to emphasize the law's predictable state and district impact over the decade ahead. The effects promise a likely renegotiation of the compact that has shaped the formative evolution and interdependency of local, state, and federal education policy over the past two centuries. It may be that changes in this constitutional partnership are due, but historical investigations can help us anticipate and weigh our options. Specifically, the No Child Left Behind Act serves to remind us that we can use historical studies of moral and civic education to throw light on what the schools and teacher education institutions should be doing to strengthen education for democratic citizenship. We need to understand the possible consequences of (1) the Act's stress upon reading, math, and science, with little or no mention of the study of civics or government and (2) its provisions for faith-based initiatives that use public tax funds to support charitable activities carried out by religious institutions. What light does history throw upon the values and validity of a national system of American education that under-stresses civic knowledge, civic values, and civic participation, but encourages movements that could lead to federal funding of religious schools to compete with state-funded common public schools?

The Politics of Faith-Based Moral Education

Early in his first term, President Bush signed executive orders that "throw open the doors of government to religious and community groups as part of a broad effort to refashion the way government delivers social services."[10] He created a White House Office of Faith-Based and Community Activities as well as centers in five federal departments "to insure that they cooperate with religious and secular nonprofit institutions" in dealing with problems of the homeless, drug addiction, mental illness, imprisonment, and unemployment. In his announcement of these orders the President said:

> It is one of the great goals of my administration to invigorate the spirit of involvement and citizenship. We will encourage faith-based and community programs without changing their mission. We will help all in their work to change hearts while keeping a commitment to pluralism.... I approach this goal with some basic principles.... Government has important responsibilities for public health or public order or civil rights. And government will never be replaced by charities and community groups. Yet when we see social needs in America, my administration will look first to faith-based programs and community groups, which have proven their power to save and change lives. We will not fund the religious activities of any group, but when people of faith provide social services, we will not discriminate against them. As long as there are secular alternatives, faith-based charities should be able to compete for funding on an equal basis and in a manner that does not cause them to sacrifice their mission.[11]

I cannot describe here the details of what followed the announcement, but it was met with great criticism by civil rights groups and religious denominations as fraught with dangers to the separation of church and state under the First Amendment to the Constitution. ("Congress shall make no law respecting an establishment of religion, or prohibiting the free exercise thereof.") It was also met with concern by conservative religious leaders and groups that it might lead to government interference with their mission or message.

President Bush followed in many respects the pattern of President Reagan, who repeatedly appealed to religious faith as the wellspring of moral conduct for persons in their public and personal lives. In his campaign for re-election President Reagan put it this way, "The truth is, politics and morality are inseparable. And as morality's foundation is religion, religion and politics are necessarily related."[12] Indeed the 1980s redounded with debates, court cases, and controversies about the relations of politics, morality, and religion in education. The issues touched upon the role of organized prayer, Bible reading, creationism, and reciting the Ten Commandments in public schools, and tuition tax credits and vouchers to increase parental choice to send children to religious schools.

Similar debates have continued since then with the Supreme Court as well as the Bush administration leaning toward accommodating educational practices in public schools to religiously based moral outlooks. For example, on June 11, 2001 the Court decided by 6-3 that student Bible clubs should have the same access to school facilities' after school hours that are given to other community and school groups. The majority opinion by Justice Clarence Thomas ruled that such access was a matter of free speech rights and did not violate the First Amendment. In dissent, Justice David Souter wrote that "It is beyond question that Good News [the organizing club] intends to use the public school premises not for the mere discussion of a subject from a particular Christian point of view, but for an evangelical service of worship calling children to commit themselves in an act of Christian conversion."[13]

It has been widely noticed that President Bush himself has alluded often to Christianity. Jennifer Loven cited several examples in an Associated Press release in February 2003:

> President Bush ... has always peppered his speeches with exhortations to moral and civic duty. With war, tragedy and terrorism confronting him now, his allusions to spirituality and morality seem to be increasing.... "I welcome faith to help solve the nation's deepest problems," Bush told a convention of religious broadcasters last week. Referring to the Sept. 11 terrorist attacks, he said, "We carried our grief to the Lord Almighty in prayer." .... Bush praised Americans' "deep and diverse religious beliefs." But he also singled out a special place for Christianity, calling the gospel that the broadcasters share over the airwaves "words of truth." ... Earlier in his State of the Union address, he said, "The liberty we prize is not America's gift to the world, it is God's gift to humanity." ... Bush reflected on the challenges facing the nation as it prepares for possible war: "We Americans have faith in ourselves, but not in ourselves alone. We do not claim to know all the ways of providence, yet we can trust in them, placing our confidence in the loving God behind all of life and all of history. May he guide us now, and may God continue to bless the United States of America."[14]

President Bush's religious views seem to be reflected in his major U.S. Department of Education appointments. In April 2003, *Education Week* carried two stories to this effect. Sean Cavanaugh pointed out that Secretary Rod Paige had been the subject of much criticism for his statements published in the *Baptist Press* in which he said that he would prefer to send his own children to a Christian school in which the religious environment sets the value system rather than to a public school where "there are so many different kinds of values."[15] Paige later insisted that his personal views did not lessen his responsibility to maintain the separation of church and state. In "Doing the 'Right Thing' " Michelle R. Davis reported that Gene Hickok, who held the No. 3 position in the department and was the major point person in implementing the No Child Left Behind Act, was strongly in favor of vouchers, charter schools, and other forms of school choice during his tenure as education secretary in Pennsylvania.[16]

In general, pleas for teaching moral conduct range across the political and intellectual spectrum from conservative to centrist to liberal. At one extreme, activists of the Christian Coalition deplore the absence of traditional, religiously based morality in schools, demanding school-wide prayer, Bible reading, and the teaching of creationism in public schools as cures. Many centrists and liberals argue for a more generalized "character education" without explicit reference to religion. For example, President and Mrs. Clinton dwelt on themes dealing with moral imperatives, better instruction in civics and government, access of students to free religious expression in public schools, community service, and school uniforms to help develop a sense of community. Communitarians under the leadership of Amitai Etzioni have sponsored several White House Conferences on the general theme "Character Education for a Democratic, Civil Society." A bipartisan National Commission on Civic Renewal headed by William J. Bennett and former Senator Sam Nunn emphasized the need for greater participation by citizens in local community groups along with character education and service learning. Other proposals emphasizing character education have received an increasing amount of public and professional attention in recent years.[17] Their stress is often on the teaching of moral virtue based on religion rather than on specific civic virtues grounded in the values of democratic citizenship.

The Politics of Education for Civic Virtue

Virtue and character have also appeared in scholarly academic volumes ranging across a wide spectrum of political outlooks. Surveying recent scholarship to see what was being said about civic virtue, I found relatively little about the role public education should play in shaping the values of our common American citizenship.[18] But the literature contains a great deal about the moral education provided by "civil society," those voluntary associations praised by De Tocqueville that lie between government and the individual, stemming from religious, socio-economic, or charitable motivations. More rewarding is the research in political philosophy that appeared during the dozen years leading up to the Bicentennial of the Constitution and the Bill of Rights.[19] Much of this scholarship flowed into curriculum materials produced by the civic education movement of the 1970s and 1980s.[20] These various initiatives suggest that moral education for individual and public conduct could be released from a necessary basis in religious instruction in public schools by stressing "civic virtue," a term that the authors of the United States Constitution and Bill of Rights liked to use.

Education for civic virtue implies that a common core of civic knowledge and civic values is the one unifying "Unum" that must characterize all types of American schools and educational institutions for students from the earliest years through college. The morality of democratic citizenship is the common binding agent—not the morality of business, Hollywood, sectarian religions, partisan politics, ethnic, racial, or social class preferences, or even of philanthropy or charity, whether faith-based or not. Our common civic morality has substantive content. It teaches us to obey the law; shoulder responsibility for self, family, and community; practice respect and compassion for diverse others, whatever their backgrounds or affiliations; and follow the dictates of equal justice, honesty, and truth. Above all, it requires citizens to promote the public good, protect freedom and individual rights, and practice an enlarged and ennobling version of patriotism. The best vision of the institution that can do this job is still a public education system devoted to the civic, public policy business of democratic government. It offers the only long-term way in which to develop a citizenry that will make government and politics themselves more democratic than they are now.

Our troubled, complex times urge us to come to the aid of education for democratic citizenship and to do this by supporting rigorous civics teaching. One attempt to serve this purpose is set forth in *CIVITAS: A Framework for Civic Education*, a curriculum guide that informed much of the *National Standards for Civics and Government*.[21] Both documents were formulated by scholarly consensus regarding the core civic values and principles that should be taught in all American schools, public and private. They introduce exemplary, voluntary guidelines for the civic education conducted by states, local districts, teachers, and parents. They are quietly achieving their widely desired purposes without the divisive debates that erupted over the national standards for history and English.

CIVITAS warrants attention because it provides substantive background to answer the questions posed by the civics standards. Developed by scholars in political science, constitutional law, and education, *CIVITAS* reflects the influence of its National Review Council of civic leaders, a body chaired by the late Ernest Boyer, president of the Carnegie Foundation for the Advancement of Teaching. It also reflects the consensus of a 60-member Teachers Advisory Committee drawn from all 50 states. Every topic in *CIVITAS* presents a conceptual or philosophical perspective, a historical perspective, and a contemporary perspective. The three major topics proposed for study were based on a consensus of professional and citizen judgment: Civic Virtue, Civic Participation, and Civic Knowledge and Skills. *CIVITAS* revives the term "civic virtue" not only to call to mind the founding experience of the American Republic, but also to highlight the civic character needed by American citizens as they confront an increasingly complex, fractious, and interdependent world. This civic character includes such dispositions and commitments as civility, individual responsibility and self-discipline, civic-mindedness and open-mindedness, compromise and negotiation, respect for the rights of others, respect for the law, critical mindedness, patience and persistence, compassion, generosity, and loyalty. *CIVITAS* also discusses the more familiar principles and structures of American government usually dealt with in civics courses and textbooks, for example, popular sovereignty, the rule of law, separation of powers, checks and balances, separation of church and state, civilian control of the military, and federalism. Note that every one of these once dusty and dull topics in civics textbooks has become the subject of current bitter debates over the future role of government in American life.

The most distinctive aspect of *CIVITAS*, what makes it so different from most civics textbooks and curriculum frameworks, is its emphasis on inquiry into the fundamental civic values of American constitutional democracy, the very subjects calling for study and reasoned commitment by students: the public good; individual rights, including life, liberty (personal, political, and economic freedoms), and the pursuit of happiness; justice; equality (political, legal, social, and economic); diversity; truth; and patriotism.[22]

Schools alone cannot instill these necessary values of personal obligation and responsibility when other major social institutions concentrate on promoting their private interests. I hope that American educators will continue to develop interdisciplinary core courses to energize this study of constitutional government and citizenship as integral and cumulative ingredients of degree requirements in schools, liberal arts colleges, universities, and teacher education programs. At the very least, education for civic virtue should be a core requirement that runs throughout the P-12 school curriculum and the preservice preparation and the continuing professional development of teachers. All teachers must be enabled not only to teach an increasingly diverse student population but also to promote the cohesive values and principles underlying our common citizenship, no matter what their specialized fields of teaching may be.

So I reemphasize the urgency of agreeing upon national education standards in general, and especially on education for civic virtue. *CIVITAS* and the *National Standards for Civics and Government* together provide a common framework of civic education as a core study for all students in all U.S. schools whether they be compulsory-public, voluntary-public, charter-public, secular-private, religious-private, or whatever combination that the political process may produce in the states and the nation in coming years.

Teacher Education and Civic Virtue

Teacher education particularly must not shrink from the historic educational goal of civic virtue. The idea of civic virtue as a prime value of public education lost popular and professional support during the 1960s and 1970s, and thus was seldom heard in the teacher education programs of the 1980s. Perhaps the revival of the volunteering mood in service learning in the 1990s augurs a more hospitable climate for professional educators to deal with the values of civic virtue as objectives of study in schools and colleges. Indeed, the growth of the politics of mistrust of government has become so prevalent that the reenergizing of a sense of civic virtue in teacher education may be its most important agendum in the 2000s. We need more than ever not only a good public education but also a "public-good" education. We will not achieve either one, unless we create a public-good teacher education.

To this end, I suggest three propositions for professional educators and public policy-makers to consider:

1. We should work harder than ever to prepare citizens to preserve and improve constitutional democracy, which has been the most important stated purpose of P-12 education ever since there has been a United States of America. In contrast to President Bush, Thomas Jefferson said it most directly and succinctly in *his* first inaugural address: The principles of the U.S. Constitution "should be the creed of our political faith, the text of civic instruction." I urge readers to revisit it. He worked until his death to inject civic instruction about the Constitution into the curriculum of schools and colleges.

2. While education for democratic citizenship may be a purpose of all institutional schooling in the United States, it is peculiarly the prime function of *public* educational institutions that are designed to provide universal, free, compulsory, common schooling, equitable and accessible for all persons regardless of race,

ethnicity, religion, gender, sexual orientation, or social, physical, or economic condition.

3. Since the quality and the training of teachers are the most important elements in achieving educational goals in elementary and secondary schools, it is necessary that education for democracy should be the core of the studies that all prospective teachers undergo in their liberal arts and teacher education programs. These should be designed to provide the civic knowledge, civic values, and civic skills of citizenship in our constitutional democracy.

The problem is that these familiar propositions are too often not translated into specific content or practice, even by those who quote them and believe in them. And they tend to be ignored by those who are determined to pursue other educational practices more suited to their own private or group purposes, whether they be individual and personal development, economic or vocational competence, intellectual achievement, family values and parental choice, moral and character building, or other ethnic, racial, and cultural pluralisms. All of these civic and non-civic educational purposes and practices are subject to the prevailing political and constitutional agendas of influential groups in American society at any given time, and especially through the federal, state, and local agencies of government. In the political context of the themes of this book, I suggest three constitutional principles, defined and modified by the Supreme Court, as examples of what should be required areas of research in teacher education for P-12 schools:

1. In our constitutional democracy, parents are free to send their children to private and religious schools, but the state may mandate the teaching of the principles of democratic government and citizenship in all schools whether private, religious, or public. (*Oregon v. Society of Sisters*, 1925)

2. Education for citizenship in our constitutional democracy is best achieved by a state system of common public schools based on the separation of church and state as defined in the First and Fourteenth Amendments. (*Everson v. Board of Education*, 1947)

3. Civic learning in democracy must be available to all children and youth equally through a public educational system, for it cannot be fully achieved in schools that are segregated or separated by law on the basis of race, ethnicity, or religion. (*Brown v. Board of Education*, 1954)

My general point is that the study of court cases dealing with the role of education in our constitutional democracy, including their impact on schools and colleges, is a useful technique for teaching about the constitutional principles of separation of powers, checks and balances, separation of church and state, and federalism, topics usually dealt with in courses on civics and government, but often viewed by students as remote or simply boring. My more specific point is that as we look to the future, such civic learning may be still more important if new appointments to the Supreme Court tend to undervalue the common bonds that link our increasingly diverse people together. Whatever the faults of public schools, their main historical rationale has been their foundational contribution to civic education for all students. Nowadays such a rationale seems to be out of favor among the advocates of accountability and privatization. So, it becomes more necessary than ever that the civic learning involved in such "reforms" be evaluated in terms of its impact on the common good.

I end my chapter for this book dedicated to Ed McClellan with the hope that the book will do its share to inform and mobilize constituencies throughout the United States in such ways that civic knowledge, civic values, constitutional principles, and civic participation are balanced as core elements of civic learning in schools and in teacher education. Carefully and thoughtfully designed, these key dimensions of education can advance a responsible democratic citizenry, a healthy democratic government, and a vibrant democratic civil society. Readers in other countries where such aspirations are freshly energized will take notice of our efforts.

Author's Note

I have summarized the history and scholarship devoted to civic education through the 1980s in *The Revival of Civic Learning: A Rationale for Citizenship Education in American Schools* (Bloomington, IN: Phi Delta Kappa Educational Foundation, 1980); *The Morality of Democratic Citizenship: Goals for Civic Education in the Republic's Third Century* (Calabasas, CA: Center for Civic Education, 1988); and *The Civic Mission in Educational Reform: Perspectives for the Public and the Professions* (Stanford, CA: Hoover Institution Press, 1989).

The most recent of my publications upon which I have relied for parts of this chapter are articles in *CIVITAS: A Framework for Civic Education*, ed. Charles N. Quigley and Charles F. Bahmueller (Calabasas, CA: Center for Civic Education, 1991), especially "A Personal Preface," "Commentary on Civic Virtue," "Human Rights," "The Public Good," "Separation of Church and State," "Political Authority," and "The State as Educator." See also "The Politics of National Education Standards," in *Teaching and Learning in the New Millenium*, ed. Barbara D. Day (Bloomington, IN: Kappa Delta Pi, 1999), chap. 6 and "Education for Civitas: The Lessons Americans Must Learn," Working Paper in Education—ED-97-1, Hanna Collection on the Role of Education in Society (Hoover Institution, Stanford University, 1997) (also available on www.civiced.org).

Notes

1. *New York Times*, January 21, 2001: A1.
2. Ibid., A14–A15.
3. *The New Yorker*, July 2, 2001: 29.
4. Richard Rothstein, "Lessons," *New York Times*, January 16, 2002: B10.
5. *New York Times*, January 30, 2002: A22.
6. Ibid., June 29, 2002: A15.
7. Ibid., January 30, 2002: A22.
8. *Education Week*, February 20, 2002: 7.
9. Jack Jennings, et al., *From the Capital to the Classroom* (Washington, DC: Center on Education Policy, January 2003), iii–iv.
10. *New York Times*, January 30, 2001: A18.

11. Ibid.
12. Ibid., August 24, 1984: A1.
13. *Education Week*, June 20, 2001: 1.
14. Jennifer Loven, Associated Press, in *Star Ledger* (Newark, NJ), February 19, 2003: 1.
15. Sean Cavanaugh, "Paige Blasted for Praise of Christian Schools," *Education Week*, April 16, 2003: 21.
16. Michelle R. Davis, "Doing the 'Right Thing,' " *Education Week*, April 16, 2003: 24.
17. The most widely known book of this genre is William J. Bennett, ed., *The Book of Virtues: A Treasury of Great Moral Stories* (New York: Simon & Schuster, 1993). Republican William Bennett and former Democratic Senator Sam Nunn are co-chairs of the National Commission on Civic Renewal. See the Commission's website: www.puaf.umdedu/civicrenewal.
18. Mary Ann Glendon and David Blankenhorn, eds., *Seedbeds of Virtue: Sources of Competence, Character, and Citizenship in American Society* (Lanham, MD: Madison Books, 1995); Jean Befthke Elshtain, *Democracy on Trial* (New York: Basic Books, 1995); William A. Galston, *Liberal Purposes: Goods, Virtues, and Diversity in the Liberal State* (New York: Cambridge University Press, 1991); Don E. Eberly, ed., *The Content of America's Character: Recovering Civic Virtue* (Lanham, MD: Madison Books, 1995); Francis Fukuyama, *Trust: The Social Virtues and the Creation of Prosperity* (New York: The Free Press, 1995); and Stephen L. Carter, *The Culture of Disbelief: How American Law and Politics Trivialize Religious Devotion* (New York: Basic Books, 1993).
19. See, e.g., the eighteen quarterly issues of "This Constitution" published from the Summer of 1983 to the Spring of 1988 by Project '87, a joint effort of the American Historical Association and the American Political Science Association. James MacGregor Burns and Richard B. Morris were co-chairs, and Sheila Mann was Director and Executive Editor of the Project. It was the precursor in more recent years of such influential books as Amy Gutmann, *Democratic Education* (Princeton, NJ: Princeton University Press, 1987); Ralph L. Ketcham, *Individualism and Public Life: A Modern Dilemma* (New York: Basil Blackwell, 1987); Benjamin R. Barber, *An Aristocracy for Everyone: The Politics of Education and the Future of America* (New York: Ballentine Books, 1992); and Michael J. Sandel, *Democracy's Discontent: America in Search of a Public Philosophy* (Cambridge, MA: Harvard University Press, 1996).
20. See, e.g., the Center for Civic Education, the Constitutional Rights Foundation, the Special Committee on Youth Education for Citizenship of the American Bar Association, the Social Studies Development Center of Indiana University, and the Mershon Center of The Ohio State University.
21. Center for Civic Education, *National Standards for Civics and Government* (Washington, DC: U.S. Department of Education, Office of Educational Research and Improvement, ERIC, 1994); Charles N. Quigley and Charles F. Bahmueller, eds., *CIVITAS: A Framework for Civic Education* (Calabasas, CA: Center for Civic Education, 1991).
22. Ibid., 15–36.

This page intentionally left blank

Chapter 2

Can Civic and Moral Education Be Distinguished?

Barry L. Bull

Civic educators seem to be faced with an insoluble set of related problems. For example, they can teach students about the civic ideals of their particular nation as a set of empirical facts, what the people of this particular place at this particular time happen to believe about the political and social roles of government and the obligations of citizens to that government and to one another. Alternatively, to provide a moral foundation for civic education, they can teach students a particular comprehensive moral theory—Locke's liberalism, Mill's utilitarianism, or Kant's deontology, for example—from which principles of government, many of which coincide with the nation's civic ideals, can be deduced. The problem with the first approach is that the resulting civic ideals lack moral authority; they are only anthropological observations about the beliefs that we hold. The problem with the second is that, although the principles thus derived do make genuine normative claims upon students, they are based on controversial metaphysical premises that not all students can accept, especially in a nation of diverse cultures and religions. As a consequence, the second approach threatens to enmesh schools in deep and unresolved arguments about whether and how American civic ideals align with the beliefs of particular religious, cultural, and even ethnic groups within the society. In the teeth of this prospect, many civic educators in the public schools opt for the first approach, even though it leaves students without attractive normative justifications for the civic ideals that they are taught.

To be sure, various political and educational theorists have long sought solutions to this particular problem. One of the most familiar is to regard a nation's civic ideals as a kind of civic religion.[1] The values included in those ideals could thus be taught by catechism, as beliefs to be accepted rather than as assertions to be understood. Once accepted, the ideals can be given an internal justification, that is, an explanation of how they are consistent with and mutually reinforce one another. Indeed, these theorists often maintain that little else in the way of justification for normative political beliefs is possible. In schools, this position coincides with a third approach among civic educators today. It teaches civic ideals that have moral authority without seeming to raise the issue of their relationship to students' other moral commitments. But this approach has its problems as well. It asks students to develop a divided consciousness with regard to their moral commitments, with their civic morality widely separated from their various personal or cultural moralities. In maintaining such a divided consciousness, however, students have difficulty in attaining a real allegiance to the civic morality unless the nation also seeks to replace their personal moralities with the civic morality. For otherwise such a civic morality does not have the vividness and immediacy of the moralities supported by students' day-to-day contact with their families, religious institutions, and other intimate associations from which they may derive their personal moralities. Hitler, Lenin, and Stalin understood this well, but our commitments to diversity and liberty do not let us travel that path. Thus, this third strategy is for us a recipe for widespread civic apathy in which students' personal moral commitments far overshadow their civic commitments. As a result, the practices of civic educators today seem to have a common consequence. Those who practice the first approach provide students with knowledge about civic beliefs but do not provide those beliefs with a moral status. Those who practice the third approach provide civic beliefs that have a moral status, but they tend not to generate motivation for action based on students' civic morality. Both these approaches leave us with citizens whose attitudes and actions are effectively disengaged from our civic ideals, even though those citizens may profess a belief in them. And almost no one practices the second approach for the sensible reason that it is inconsistent with our civic ideals themselves, because it requires public institutions to advocate particular metaphysical assumptions in conflict with many of their citizens' fundamental commitments. This conflict would in turn leave students with an uncertain commitment to the moral foundations of our civic ideals and thus to the civic ideals themselves.

John Rawls's political philosophy may provide civic educators with an alternative response to these disturbing conclusions. At least that is the possibility that I will explore in this essay. In *A Theory of Justice*, Rawls lays out a complicated argument for a particular conception of justice, that is, his renowned Two Principles of Justice, the substance of which will not figure prominently in this essay.[2] However, as part of that argument, Rawls outlines a strategy called the method of reflective equilibrium for developing principles to govern a society, of which the particular argument in that book is an example. This strategy, rather than the specific application of it in *A Theory of Justice*, is the point of departure for this analysis. Indeed, his subsequent book, *Political Liberalism*, generalizes about and elaborates on this strategy of normative political reasoning.[3]

For Rawls, a politically liberal society is one in which citizens are free within reasonable limits to adopt for themselves the particular conceptions of the good that seem most appropriate to them as individuals and as members of cultures, communities, and other associations. In other words, they can determine the purposes and ways of living that seem to them to be most meaningful. For this reason, the members of a liberal society are likely to be in considerable disagreement over their most fundamental moral and intellectual commitments and in particular about the metaphysical premises that justify those commitments.

The civic ideals for this kind of society pose a special problem since one cannot rely on an existing consensus about the moral foundation of those ideals. After all, citizens of a liberal society may, by definition, have widely disparate commitments about that foundation, depending upon the particular conceptions of the good they find satisfactory. The difficulties and contradictions described at the beginning of this essay illustrate some of the apparent problems in rendering civic ideals consistent with this assumption about a liberal society: civic ideals, it seems, will have to be merely facts about what citizens of a liberal society happen to agree about politics at a particular time; otherwise, those ideals will make moral claims that compete with or displace citizens' existing moral commitments. Nevertheless, Rawls suggests, it may still be possible to create a *political* agreement about the principles that are to govern their larger association by seeking what he calls an "overlapping consensus."

Superficially, an overlapping consensus may appear to be simply the beliefs about government that citizens happen to hold in common. However, what keeps Rawls's overlapping consensus from being a simple catalogue of what citizens happen to agree about politically is the way in which it is established. In *A Theory of Justice*, Rawls appeals initially to citizens' intuitions of fairness and their settled convictions of justice. The former is what people in a particular society believe to be necessary conditions for a decision or a choice to be fair, such as, that those who make the decision should not have a personal stake in the result, or if they do that they should be capable of setting their personal interests aside in making the decision. The latter is the specific shared judgment that people reach about the justice or injustice of particular social practices, such as the currently widespread conviction of most Americans that slavery is wrong. Both intuitions of fairness and settled convictions of justice are examples of what people happen to believe. However, Rawls is not satisfied to derive principles of justice on the basis of those beliefs alone for the good reason that such beliefs almost certainly conflict with one another. Thus, for example, Americans' widely held commitment to equality of opportunity implies that a government should interfere in families' otherwise unobjectionable childrearing practices if they produce significantly different life outcomes for different children, especially different outcomes that cannot be corrected by extra-familial public institutions. However, such interference blatantly conflicts with the equally widely held belief that parents have a right to communicate their moral and social beliefs to their children as long as they do not abuse them in the process. According to Rawls, the very purpose of political thought is, by means of the process of reflective equilibrium, to resolve these conflicts by ascertaining and prioritizing principles that can generate such intuitions and convictions.

In doing so, the resulting principles do not necessarily simply leave the initial conflicting intuitions and convictions entirely or even substantially intact. The principles and the priorities among them that result from the process of reflective equilibrium almost certainly will adjust some beliefs to preserve citizens' most central commitments while avoiding some other logical implications of those convictions with which citizens find it most difficult to live. Responding to the example above, Rawls formulates a principle of liberty that does not imply parents' right to abuse their children, and he assigns to this restricted principle of liberty a priority above that of equal opportunity. Such principles, and not the raw intuitions themselves, represent for Rawls a genuine overlapping consensus in that they attempt to develop a special sort of consistency among our beliefs, that is, an equilibrium among our intuitions achieved by our careful reflection upon the applications of those intuitions that we hold to be inviolable and the applications that are less important to us. Indeed, noticing that some applications of our beliefs violate other important convictions is a good reason for us to modify or restrict our initial beliefs.

It is possible to infer a number of erroneous conclusions about this process of reflective equilibrium. First, it might seem that this process aims at a permanent and immutable state of belief. However, it is likely that any equilibrium that is achieved will be the occasion of new experiences and reflections that invite further modifications of our beliefs. After all, such an equilibrated configuration of beliefs becomes a new set of intuitions that initially direct action in ways that generate new social arrangements and, therefore, unfamiliar experiences that in turn help us discover contradictions in our beliefs that were previously obscure. Such experiences and our subsequent reflections upon them motivate further elaborations and modifications of belief toward new equilibria. Second, it might seem that this process is essentially solitary, involving each citizen in an inward-directed examination of the consistency and acceptability of his or her beliefs and their logical implications. There are, however, two reasons why this process is significantly public. One is that the new arrangements to which our equilibrated beliefs direct us have important public effects in that they naturally evoke responses from others, responses that help us understand their meaning and consequences. In adopting a restricted interpretation of a principle of liberty, for instance, I will come to regard some previously accepted arrangements as objectionable and others that were optional as now required. Further, this change in my expectations and actions is widely shared by others because it reflects an overlapping consensus. Therefore, the equilibrium produces a new social and ideological milieu in which even the thoughts and actions not directly implicated by the modified beliefs may have unanticipated consequences and interpretations. As noted, some of these results can become the motivation for continuing the process of modification and equilibration of belief. Third, and as a consequence, the process of reflective equilibrium might seem detached from individuals' most central moral commitments, operating entirely in an arena of political negotiation and compromise. However, this putative conclusion radically misrepresents the nature of the process. For the initial intuitions upon which the process is based are inevitably aligned with individuals' personal metaphysical commitments, that is, their own conceptions of the good. Thus, while those intuitions are shared with others, they are also deeply connected with the various nonpublic beliefs that a liberal society enables to flourish and that citizens have considerable freedom to adopt and modify. A change in those intuitions requires one to consider not only one's reactions to others' responses, actions, and experiences but also the consistency of those beliefs with one's own prior metaphysical commitments. This consideration, in turn, can be the occasion for a revision of one's conception of the good. My adopting a restricted principle of liberty can cause me to reconsider whether and how, for instance, my religious commitments are compatible with that modification in belief, which can further lead me, for example, to modify in appropriate ways the theology at the core of my conception of the good. Thus, the process of reflective equilibrium is continuous and can be simultaneously both inherently public and intensely personal.

What emerges, then, from Rawls's conception of the overlapping consensus is a distinctive view of liberal politics. On this view, politics involves significant intellectual and social activity that implicates and influences what citizens believe both about their relationships with other citizens and about themselves. As we have seen, what people believe about themselves and their relationships is modified by a simultaneous process of public and private reasoning. In this process, the political principles that emerge have a moral status because of their connection with what come to be publicly shared and mutually reasonable beliefs and because of their integration with individuals' various conceptions of the good. These principles are in essence civic ideals that are not simply facts about people's beliefs, nor are they merely a codification of a national civic creed that competes with or displaces citizens' metaphysical commitments. Because of the way that they are continuously developed and renewed, those ideals influence and are influenced by private commitments, but because they do not embrace any particular metaphysical foundations, they do not pose a direct challenge to such beliefs. In a real sense, citizens take up the task of seeking and constructing such foundations for themselves and in their own cultural and community associations, but any foundations that they develop do not become part of a society-wide public belief system. Of course, an emerging and evolving overlapping consensus certainly influences such private belief systems, but there is no reason to suppose that those systems converge into a single set of metaphysical commitments held by all citizens. Given citizens' initially divergent private beliefs and the commitment of a liberal society to freedom of conscience, in fact, such convergence is unlikely. Thus, an overlapping consensus is compatible both in principle and in fact with a wide diversity of private metaphysical structures of belief and justification. In this way, an overlapping consensus constitutes a set of evolving moral commitments about a nation's civic ideals that is nevertheless harmonious with a wide variation in citizens' private moralities.

The public education system of such a liberal society can be understood as, in part, a set of government institutions and practices that enable and promote the continual emergence of an overlapping consensus. From this perspective, civic education in public schools is the element of the public education system that undertakes and accomplishes this task for the young. This education is not adequately conceived as simply a vehicle for informing the young about adults' civic beliefs, for such information is at most only one element of what children need to learn in order to participate in the development of an overlapping consensus. Nor is such civic education adequately conceived as the enforcement on the young of an authoritative and determinate civic doctrine, for no such doctrine is characteristic of an overlapping consensus because its principles are subject to constant reconsideration and modification. Finally, an adequate civic education is certainly not instruction in a particular metaphysical system of belief, even one with specific civic content or purposes, for such instruction confuses public with private education. Of course, a fully adequate system of civic education almost certainly includes elements that address adults of various ages and in various public roles, but the primary function of the remainder of this essay will be to elaborate to the extent possible the school-based curriculum and instructional procedures appropriate to this conception of civic education.

Before considering the implications of this view for school curriculum and instruction, we are now able to confront the question posed in the title of this essay, that is, can civic and moral education be distinguished from one another? Civic education is certainly a kind of moral education in that it promotes and supports a public morality, that is, the agreements about the principles governing citizens' relationships with and obligations to one another that emerge from the process of reflective equilibrium outlined above. However, two observations about this answer are in order. First, civic education is not the only moral education that takes place in a liberal society. Obviously, there is also moral education guided by private metaphysical commitments and conducted by families, religious institutions, communities, and other associations. And, as we will see below, there is also another kind of moral education to which public schools can contribute, namely, an education for personal liberty. Second, the morality involved in civic education is concerned as much with citizens' commitment to the process of public and private reasoning from which an overlapping consensus emerges as it is with the substance of the principles that issue from it. Thus, a civic education that aims simply at children's knowledge and acceptance of the current version of citizens' agreements about principles is clearly insufficient in that it would not enable them to maintain awareness of and allegiance to the principles as they are modified by citizens' subsequent experience and reflection. Such an education would, indeed, be tantamount to an education in a particular civic doctrine. It could, moreover, mark the beginning of the collapse of an overlapping consensus in that the children so instructed would become citizens who are unable or unwilling to modify the consensus in reasonable ways that reflect their experience with the consequences of those principles. Such citizens would find that the principles were no longer capable of making adequate sense of some of their experience and would be driven to find that meaning based exclusively on their private moralities. In this way, the public consensus could gradually fragment into competing private commitments to and justifications for citizens' obligations to one another. Thus, a good deal is at stake in public schools' efforts at civic education, namely, the future public coherence of the society as a whole.

The aims of the curriculum for such a civic education are relatively straightforward. But in formulating those aims, we must place them in the context of the schools' full contribution to children's moral education. I have argued elsewhere that it is incumbent upon a liberal society to provide an education that makes it possible for each child to become his or her own person, an education for personal liberty.[4] Without going into details, such an education includes meaningful exposure to conceptions of the good beyond that of the family and immediate community, the child's coming to know about his or her own talents and proclivities, and instruction that enables the child to make reasonable judgments about available conceptions of the good in light of that knowledge.[5] In this way, public schools make a contribution to the developing private morality of children without determining the substance of that morality. Civic education must operate in conjunction with this education for liberty in developing children's private moralities.

Against this background, civic education's curriculum aims, first, to enable children to learn about the current state of the overlapping consensus—the civic principles of their society and how they derive from widely held intuitions about the relationships and obligations among citizens. Second, such a curriculum must enable children to learn about the meaning and consequences of those principles—how they have been interpreted in the society, the institutions and social practices in which they are instantiated, and the outcomes of those laws and practices, both intended and otherwise. Third, the curriculum must enable children to reflect on the relationship between, on the one hand, those principles and their consequences and, on the other, the overlapping consensus and their developing private moralities. If the curriculum succeeds in achieving these aims of helping children to understand the origin, meaning, consequences, and personal implications of the society's civic principles, children should emerge from the public school system with the ability to take part as adult citizens in the evolution of the overlapping consensus by means of a process of reflective equilibrium. However, not only must citizens have this ability, but they also must be inclined to make use of it. Finally, then, an adequate civic education curriculum must, in addition, enable children to see and appreciate the public purpose and personal meaning of what after all is an intellectually and morally demanding set of activities.

Many particular configurations of curricular content can enable public schools to achieve these aims of civic education, and the content appropriate to them may vary from one locality to the other, depending on the diverse initial socialization and circumstances of children. In other words, one cannot deduce a specific content or structure of the curriculum from these general philosophical considerations; they provide only a framework for constructing and evaluating particular proposals for the curriculum. Moreover, much of the school curriculum that has not traditionally been understood as part of civic education makes an indirect contribution to accomplishing these aims. Language instruction and logical training, for example, provide children with skills that facilitate the requisite learning. This section will, therefore, analyze only some general aspects of the school curriculum that are relevant to the specifically civic content appropriate to achieving these aims.

I have argued elsewhere that teaching children to understand and appreciate other cultures in their nation is an important element in education for personal liberty in that it enables children to consider for themselves conceptions of the good as alternatives to those available in their families and immediate communities.[6] Therefore, it expands their freedom to become their own persons rather than persons determined entirely by their immediate social environment. Such teaching simultaneously strengthens the entire system of personal liberty by helping children to appreciate others' cultures as real possibilities for their own lives, not just as alien curiosities to be benevolently or perhaps grudgingly tolerated. In addition, teaching about cultures also makes an important contribution to civic education for an overlapping consensus but for reasons at odds with those most frequently cited in the civic education literature, namely, to facilitate democratic deliberation by helping children to understand, anticipate, and negotiate the disagreements that they are likely to encounter in democratic societies.[7] Learning about other cultures in their society can also enable children to understand the commonalities as well as the divergences in belief among the members of those cultures. In this way, such teaching can provide children with knowledge of the current overlapping consensus about political principles and of the shared moral intuitions from which it derives. Thus, the content of an adequate civic education emphasizes whatever unity of belief that may exist across cultural differences rather than the differences themselves. Combined with instruction that emphasizes our diversity in order to foster and strengthen personal liberty, the content of the school curriculum, therefore, provides a robust conception of multiculturalism in the society, a conception that expresses both what unifies the nation's citizens and what divides them.

Undoubtedly, it is inherently valuable for children to learn about their own and other nations' histories, but the content of history also has a special relevance to civic education for an overlapping consensus. For it presents the opportunity to consider at a remove in time and place the relationships between nations' cultures, their civic ideals, and the results of the policies adopted to achieve those ideals. Especially when the nations under study are liberal societies, history can reveal the tensions among those three factors and the way in which the societies adapted their ideals and policies in light of those tensions. And when the nation under study is one's own, history reveals to children the mutable nature of the overlapping consensus and the reasons in the national experience for the changes that have taken place in the nation's civic aspirations and ideals. These lessons are crucial for children's gaining an accurate understanding of the nature of an overlapping consensus and for providing them with an appropriate perspective on the tentative status and justifiability of one's own nation's current political principles and policies. Without such a perspective, children might come to regard their nation's commitments to be either absolute or entirely culturally relative, neither of which would prepare them to take part seriously in the continuous reconstitution of the overlapping consensus. It is clear that learning about the changes that have taken place in a nation's civic ideals and their policy interpretations is an important corrective to the assumption that they are infallible. But also learning that those changes can be seen as rational, if sometimes mistaken, responses to experience also corrects the assumption that those ideals and policies are nothing but an expression of the majority's untutored cultural preferences. Either of these assumptions actively discourages children from taking the reformulation of a nation's overlapping consensus seriously, for on the first there is seemingly no need to do so, and on the second there is no point in expending one's energy on a matter that is immune from conscious influence.

As one possible example, the history curriculum in American schools might consider the social, economic, and religious controversies involved in the debate over slavery prior to and during the U.S. Civil War and the evolving public policies and policy proposals to which they led. Such a study of the evolving overlapping consensus during this time, the changing public policies in which it was instantiated, the social and economic consequences of those policies, and the various private and public reactions to those consequences can illustrate to children both the tentative nature of civic ideals and patterns of reasoning employed by citizens at the time to reconcile their private moralities, aspirations, and experiences with those of their fellow citizens.

Admittedly, this curriculum involves a particularly intellectualized view of history, for it entails the perspective that human reason and understanding play a significant role in the shaping of national ideals and the events that flow from them. And for that reason, it will not be easy for children to master. Nonetheless, it reveals just how profoundly intellectual the task of civic education for an overlapping consensus is.

This intellectual quality of the curriculum is equally on display in another crucial and related aspect of its content. For an overlapping consensus is the reasonable confluence of popular belief about abstract principles of government and the obligations of citizenship, not merely shared opinions or intuitions about what should be done in particular circumstances. For children to view the rights and duties of citizens as resulting from such principles, the civic education curriculum must also include a philosophical element, in its widest sense. The purpose of this element is to enable children to view their and others' actions as instances of the application of, to use Immanuel Kant's phrase, maxims of action.[8] Seeing one's actions as following such general rules involves and develops children's capacity to abstract from particular actions and to see patterns in them. It may also be one of humans' fundamental logical and moral capacities. Of course, in developing this capacity, one must avoid enforcing Kant's metaphysical doctrines about such maxims—such as, that the only genuinely moral maxims are universal and unconditional—because public education is not to indoctrinate children to accept controversial metaphysical positions. Nevertheless, it is possible to teach children this way of viewing human actions without any particular metaphysical accompaniment. In doing so, one enables children to analyze the actions of governments and their citizens as flowing from general principles, which they can then formulate, reflect on, and perhaps criticize, reinterpret, or reformulate on the basis of their and others' experience and their own private moralities. Indeed, these philosophical abilities can be developed in part in the context of the history curriculum as it has been conceived above. Children can be invited and encouraged to conceptualize, for example, the principles of government and their rationales that may have emerged from the commitments and circumstances of various social groups during the Civil War era. These abilities are crucial to children's eventual participation in the process of reflective equilibrium as I, following Rawls, have conceived it, for they make it possible to see actions, practices, and policies as serving principles.

This characterization of the content of the civic education curriculum as involving multicultural, historical, and philosophical elements is, no doubt, incomplete. But it demonstrates the kind of analysis necessary for formulating such a curriculum. However, there is one central element of civic education that the content I have outlined does not necessarily address, namely, children's motivation to involve themselves in the reflective process through which the overlapping consensus emerges. This aim, I believe, is less a matter of curricular content than of the instructional procedures through which that content is presented and learned.

Perhaps the key to such motivation is to enable children to explore the connection between the formulation of and adherence to civic principles, on the one hand, and their emerging private moralities, on the other. By this, I do not mean the consequences the principles have for the selfish interests of children, for private moralities, which are usually based in culture, are not inherently or even usually self-directed. Rather, what I do mean is what consequences these principles have for children's own self-defined interests, which are not necessarily interests in themselves. Nor do

I mean that such an exploration should focus only on the teleological outcomes of the principles, for children's emerging moralities can have deontological as well as teleological components. In short, this exploration involves the connection between the civic principles and what children are coming to believe is right and good.

To accomplish this exploration, it seems necessary to encourage children to assess from their own perspectives the principles that they are discovering in the overlapping consensus. In other words, the teaching about cultures, history, and principles must at some point make room for and facilitate children's reaching their own judgments about the nature and justification of the overlapping consensus. In part, this means that children must be encouraged to be active and independent in the search for the civic meaning of current governmental and social policies and practices. That is, they must be encouraged to formulate hypotheses about such matters, but they must also be encouraged to take seriously the hypotheses of others, including adults and other children. For what they are ultimately seeking is not their own private interpretations but an understanding of civic principles that can stand up to public scrutiny. But equally important, they must be encouraged to formulate their own judgments about the adequacy of these principles, judgments based in part on what is publicly known about the principles' consequences but also on what their emerging private moralities make of those consequences. What emerges from these observations is a portrait of a civic education classroom in which children are mutually engaged in the search for the formulation and meaning of their civic ideals and in which the judgments that children form about them are respected.

This analysis suggests that Rawls's conceptions of an overlapping consensus and of the process of reflective equilibrium from which that consensus emerges offer a solution to the problems of civic education with which this essay began. The aims, content, and instructional procedures of a civic education for an overlapping consensus do not require teachers to provide instruction in a metaphysical theory of public morality. While such an education takes note of what citizens happen to believe about the nature and significance of their civic ideals, it also enables children to make moral judgments about those ideals. Moreover, the judgments that children reach are not simply the application of an established and official civic doctrine but are the result of a thoughtful analysis of the public meaning of civic principles and of an assessment of those principles' capability of meeting the requirements of children's emerging private moralities. And because of that analysis and assessment, children have self- and public-referential reasons to engage honestly and actively with their society's civic ideals, to take seriously the rights and responsibilities of citizenship.

On this account, then, civic education contributes simultaneously to the construction of the self and to the construction of one's society, and it does so interactively, so that the emerging self is neither simply a matter of internalizing norms that are supplied from without, as a civic religion might imply, nor simply a matter of applying one's own conception of the good to the principles, policies, and institutions of society, as one's private morality might bid one to do. In this way, civic education can be a complex kind of moral education in which students learn from and teach themselves and others. And contrary to the claims of deliberative democrats[9] and communitarians,[10] the political liberalism that Rawls's ideas imply makes possible an attractive if demanding civic education that is much more public than they believe possible in a liberal society. Rather than an irresistibly privatizing civic morality, Rawls's conception of liberalism implies, as we have seen, an education for involvement in public dialogue about civic values that nevertheless does not require that the demands of private morality are ignored or eclipsed.

Notes

1. For example, Aristotle, *The Politics*, trans. T.A. Sinclair; rev. Trevor J. Saunders (New York: Penguin Books, 1981) and Amy Gutmann, *Democratic Education*, rev. ed. (Princeton, NJ: Princeton University Press, 1999).
2. John Rawls, *A Theory of Justice*, rev. ed. (Cambridge, MA: Harvard University Press, 1999).
3. John Rawls, *Political Liberalism* (New York: Columbia University Press, 1996).
4. Barry Bull, "A Political Theory for the Normative Assessment of School Reform in the U.S.," in T. Kvernbekk and B. Nordtug, eds., *The Many Faces of Philosophy of Education: Traditions, Problems and Challenges* (Oslo, Norway: University of Oslo Institute of Educational Research, 2002), 72–89.
5. Barry Bull, Royal Fruehling, and Virgie Chattergy, *The Ethics of Multicultural and Bilingual Education* (New York: Teachers College Press, 1992).
6. Barry Bull, "Standards-Based School Reform and Liberty: A Normative Assessment," in G. Jover and P. Villemor, eds., *Voices of Philosophy of Education* (Madrid, Spain: Universidad Complutense, 2004), 90–99.
7. Amy Gutmann and John Thompson, *Democracy and Disagreement* (Cambridge, MA: Belknap Press, 1996).
8. Immanuel Kant, *Foundations of the Metaphysics of Morals*, trans. L.W. Beck (New York: Macmillan, 1985).
9. Amy Gutmann, *Democratic Education*.
10. Robert N. Bellah, et al., *The Good Society* (New York: Alfred A. Knopf, 1991).

This page intentionally left blank

Chapter 3

Cato's Resolve and the Revolutionary Spirit: Political Education, Civic Action, and the Democratic-Republican Societies of the 1790s

Brian W. Dotts

In an address to friends and fellow citizens, published in the *National Gazette* in 1793, the German Republican Society of Philadelphia openly proclaimed one of its main principles: "The spirit of liberty, like every virtue of the mind, is to be kept alive only by constant action." One year later, at a civic festival in Philadelphia while commemorating the success of the French Revolution, the Democratic Society of Pennsylvania and its sister society, the German Republicans, raised their glasses and toasted: "Knowledge:—May every Citizen be so learned as to know his rights, and so brave as to assert them."[1] These societies and at least 40 similar associations emerged upon the American scene between 1793 and 1800 throughout the eastern seaboard, championing notions of citizenship, public education, political equality, and democracy. Action and knowledge formed the cornerstone of their democratic radicalism, a spirited ideology unleashed by the American Revolution and the Declaration of Independence.

This chapter explores the Democratic-Republican Societies' informal approaches to civic learning, their notions of education, and their interpretation of citizenship and civic virtue. Instead of focusing on the familiar disagreements between Federalists and Anti-Federalists or Jeffersonians, this chapter examines how the ordinary folk who were members of these societies engaged the revolutionary dialogue, a discourse of dissent emblematic of successive movements involving civil disobedience. How were these societies informed philosophically? What types of citizenship and civic education did they foster? How did their activities and philosophy contribute to ideas of morality and civic participation? What did they learn, and perhaps, teach others? How did the societies contribute to the enduring struggle to define republicanism and to reconstitute it within their own context?

Much like the earlier Leveller movement in England after Cromwell's defeat of King Charles, the Democratic-Republican Societies, many of whose members were soldiers during the American Revolution, contested traditional ideas of deference and social privilege, appropriating Enlightenment philosophy on their own terms. Resembling the Levellers, their members were drawn mainly from the less prosperous classes, including teachers, craftsmen, innkeepers, artisans, and mariners, but also included a few physicians, lawyers, and financiers.[2] Soon after Washington began his second term, the societies set out to redefine citizenship and civic virtue in entirely unconventional ways. They began negotiating and contesting the Constitution's meaning, which was left ambiguous by the founders' need to reach compromise among divergent factions. Members of the societies adopted a positive conception of citizenship believing that citizens' liberty was most effective when engaged in political action, and they struggled against the rhetoric of their contemporaries with the intention of creating a unique and radical brand of civic ideology, namely, the democratization of republican thought. They were, perhaps, more liberated from traditional preconceptions than were the Federalists, for their civic engagement represented more than an interest in mere knowledge and the science of politics; it reflected something deeper and more aesthetic, an *appetite*, if you will, for political association. Politics for them required more than mere voting; it necessitated a pursuit of truth and demanded a normative critique of social relationships and institutions.

The societies' democratic and egalitarian philosophy collided with Federalist desires to maintain a tradition of hierarchy, a collision that reveals unresolved views of citizenship and republicanism during the early years of the Republic. Furthermore, because elites knew their history and could draw upon a voluminous canon of political wisdom in verifying the fragility of republics, the societies' egalitarian views only heightened their anxieties, adding yet another strain to the tumultuous political environment during the late eighteenth century. As the country's focus turned inward after the struggle for independence, governing elites soon recognized, in many ways reluctantly, the potential consequences of their Whig ideology. Unlike elites who were conditioned to venerate the classical republican writers in order to maintain tradition and validate a social hierarchy, the societies' members, many of whom lacked formal education, appropriated the classical heritage in a radical way, sculpting and conforming it to their understanding of the "Age of Reason" while repudiating ideological impositions. Classical education was only one among many social distinctions that separated the leisure class from ordinary individuals and justified the former's legitimate right to govern the latter. Yet, the philosophy inherited from Radical Whigs and Dissenters across the Atlantic gave ordinary individuals a new sense of political efficacy as they employed it in defense against aristocratic aims, viewing it as the best sentinel of liberty. As Gordon Wood reminds us, the revolutionary period emerged, not as a result of oppressive class differences or as an attempt to cast off the shackles of a brutal tyrant; more accurately, it was a result of conscious reflection and judgment.[3]

Enlightened Interpretations of Republicanism

Just as elites questioned absolute monarchy, the Democratic-Republican Societies were suspicious of aristocratic rule. With a new sense of empowerment, government action that now failed to reflect the conscious demands and expectations of constituents was considered arbitrary and destructive of republican principles. The Republican Society of Philadelphia demanded of its politicians, "Go and do thou likewise," and in a letter signed "Cato," the Society in Newark described the system of representative government as a stringent contract between an "agent," the representative, and the "master," the constituent, whereby the latter has not only a right, but also a duty, to inquire about the former's public business.[4] And Abraham Bishop, a democrat in Connecticut, asserted that, not only does "the constitution [sic] of the United States . . . 'guarantee to every state in this Union a republican government,' which could never have been intended to [mean] a republican aristocracy," but also it expressly "acknowledg[es] a republican democracy. . . . 'We the people of the United States.' "[5] Unlike their counterparts whose "actual practice . . . more nearly adhered to the teachings of Burke," the societies were much more influenced by Radical Whigs and English Dissenters, including Milton, Sidney, Hampden, and Priestley. They were suspicious of institutions and concentrated power and rejected a trustee form of government; they viewed representatives as mere delegates who were expected to operate as agents of the people—a substitute for direct democracy.[6] "Power in the people," according to the Radical Whig James Burgh, "is like light in the sun, native, original, inherent, and unlimited by anything human. In governors," on the other hand, "it may be compared to the reflected light of the moon, for it is only borrowed, delegated, and limited by the intention of the people."[7] If the spirit of Renaissance republicanism rested on the principle of popular sovereignty and the duty to act in preventing the establishment of arbitrary government and ecclesiastical authority, it was not inconsistent to view civic virtue as a latent, yet potentially powerful trait in all citizens, despite one's station in life.

While many persons continued to regard democracy pejoratively, the democratization of republican thought had actually developed from a number of protracted influences, including more than 150 years of colonial home-rule, protestant individualism, Enlightenment impulses, and the English Radical Whig tradition.[8] The societies emphasized a democratization of political processes, including local participation in politics, popular means of checking government officials including delegate forms of representation, office rotation, frequent elections, strong state and federal jury systems, and constitutional conventions supporting generational sovereignty, all forms of political activity that forbear the stultifying effects of bureaucratic institutionalization and the concentration of power.[9] Indeed, all of these republican aims were to be achieved in a variety of ways, with particular emphasis given to publicly funded, secularized education, the role of which was considered central in developing a democratic and participatory politics. The new Enlightenment republicanism could just as easily be conceived as requiring the destruction of arbitrary rule by any means, political or social, and applicable to the property-less as well as to the propertied class. Likewise, members of the societies could look to the same authoritative classical and modern republican sources and employ them in defense of popular government and active citizenship.

The republican character was informed by, and always measured against, a large political literature, including the Roman analysis of classical Athens by the likes of Cicero, Sallust, Plutarch, and Livy, as well as the subsequent experiences of Italy's city-republics during that country's Renaissance, events separated by centuries of a Christian medieval framework that redefined governmental authority in terms of theology and divine right. Modern republicanism emerged as a radical critique of unlimited monarchy based on the conceptions of autonomy and popular sovereignty, which were developed further by Locke, Hume, and Bacon, but also by Harrington, Neville, Sidney, Trenchard and Gordon, Price, and Priestley. Both trajectories of thought, commonly known as *ancient* and *modern*, although in ways incompatible, would inform the revolutionary generation in their attempts to redefine the meaning of republicanism within their own context. Similarly, reactionaries and radicals of the revolutionary generation could all point to the Constitutional text in supporting their assorted and conflicting arguments.

Enlightenment ideas provided additional depth to late eighteenth-century republican thought. The various societies not only viewed republicanism through the refracted image of the Italian Renaissance as they looked back to ancient Rome for guidance, but also perceived it in the accompaniment of Enlightenment forces. With the dissemination of scientific knowledge and empiricist epistemology, people could now be judged by their actions and the use of their own intellectual and moral sense. Just as John Adams had reprimanded the British in 1774 for failing to heed the republican principles espoused by Aristotle, Livy, Cicero, Harrington, and Sidney, the societies too could pursue a similar agenda against aristocracy in their own country, for freedom was being defined in Lockean principles and grounded in one's capacity to reason.[10] Human beings could now take responsibility for changing the social and political environment by means of action enlightened by erudition. In Newtonian fashion, "a more perfect union" could only be realized by the new science of politics and the perfection of individuals toward the ideal citizen.[11] In addition to securing the rights of life, liberty, equality, and the pursuit of happiness, the Declaration supported the altering or abolishing of government whenever it "becomes destructive of these ends." Indeed, written with Jefferson's radical republican philosophy in mind, the Declaration inspired active citizenship in defining the more passive and nondescript Constitutional language. The value of citizenship and virtue took on novel and comprehensive meaning in this context.

Members of the Democratic-Republican Societies became keenly aware that social hierarchy and privilege were potentially as arbitrary as tyrannical rule or divine right, for the former also prevented a wide sharing of the formal benefits of citizenship and education. Although pressure groups representing mechanics and artisans emerged as early as 1772, in Pennsylvania, for example, through a newly formed and discriminating political consciousness ordinary workingmen no longer tolerated paternal authority in the political sphere. More readily, they sought ways to share in the benefits and obligations of citizenship and popular government.[12] It was Montesquieu who declared that "the more an aristocracy borders on democracy, the nearer it approaches perfection," and that "the growth of inequality would prove ominous to a republic."[13] A transformation took place between the presidencies of George Washington and Andrew Jackson whereby political parties took on new significance, from being seen "as destructive" in nature to being viewed "as valuable to the health of government."[14] Yet, during the late eighteenth century, a "loyal opposition" to those in power had not yet become acceptable; while the societies thought of themselves as checks against arbitrary rule, elites viewed them as inciting the passions of ordinary citizens and rupturing conventional mores. While elites maintained a paternal attitude and identified civic and moral virtue with deference and the community's dependence on well-educated men who knew best how to secure the public good, the societies contested this notion by advocating a spirit of communitarianism judiciously moderated by increased emphasis on individual agency.

The 1790s represents one of the first episodes of estrangement between commoners and elites as political invective was mutually exchanged. The competing parties began to polarize, each talking through the other in support of their arguments, and as the societies' increasingly promoted radical change, the schism crystallized causing elites to pull back from the revolutionary rhetoric and appeal to the reliance on tradition. Joel Barlow, a close compatriot of Jefferson's, explained the atmosphere of the age as two competing paradigms—the outdated model of feudal ideas analogous to Ptolemy's astronomy and Burke' traditionalism, the other and developing archetype he compared to modern ideas of Copernicus and Paine.[15] Indeed, neither group could prove the certainty of their arguments for moral virtue and civic citizenship beyond doubt; only practical experience could reveal the inevitable fate of the experiment. Yet, elites were unwilling to surrender to the undisciplined perils of the egalitarian undercurrent. Unlike Jefferson, many elites found minor comfort in the ideas expressed by Madison's *Federalist 10*, preferring uniformity and deference among the multitudes. Elites believed ordered liberty best represented republican ideas of virtue, and during the charged atmosphere, many began to search for ways to harness the excesses of political liberty as elites appeared to mistake change for decadence. They were heeding Plato's admonition against the passions and their acidic effects on the polis, resolving that a healthy political community demanded self-sacrifice, appreciation for one's rank, and respect for patrician rule. As Gordon Wood asserts, the efforts associated with the "destruction of aristocracy," which I find analogous to the societies' activities, epitomized "the real American Revolution." It is no wonder that the definitive characteristics of republicanism, with its diverse meanings and multiplicity of terms, would need elucidation as subjects began to see themselves as citizens. Political power was now being differentiated from paternal authority.[16]

Throughout the tumultuous period, the parties continued to educate and learn from each other about the meaning of republican virtue, illustrating what would become a protracted historic negotiation over the methods of civic education. For instance, the 1790s ushered in an incessant debate, more forcefully articulated in the antebellum period, wherein "schools would be assigned not only key roles in the diffusion of democratic culture," according to Katz, but also serve as a "site of mediation" amid "the contradictions between democratic ideals and the continuance of class and inequality."[17] Secular and political appeals began to transcend the traditional Puritan zeal for education, permeating the new justifications with Enlightenment rationalism. While the societies viewed education as a means of liberation, elites, who were not indifferent to the cause, generally identified it as a systemic means of regulating and homogenizing community values within a common Christian perspective.

Although their constitutions and resolutions mention religion intermittently, the societies' correspondence was virtually devoid of denominational references. As Link asserts, despite the fact that many of their members "were conservative in religion," they understood that religion was often used as a cloak in sustaining capricious political power. Tunis Wortman, a member of the New York Democratic Society wrote in 1800: "Ambition and tyranny have always been fond of assuming the masque of religion and making instruments of judges and divines."[18] It was John Adams who, in his more youthful radicalism, emphasized the inverse relationship between despotism and knowledge, insisting that it was the antiquated combination of canon law and feudal tenure that denied man's natural liberty and pursuit of knowledge.[19] The Norwalk Republican Society's constitution decried the fallacy of elevating persons above the principles of equality by bestowing on specific individuals the source of all authority. In acknowledging the new possibilities for generational reconstruction, the societies could sound the trumpet "to erect the Temple of LIBERTY on the ruins of *Palaces* and *Thrones*," a new catechism often appearing in their literature.[20] Whatever their religious influences may have been, the societies appear to have adopted the Radical Whig view of toleration, believing that the details of religious doctrine should remain a private matter, and instead, grounded their democratic arguments in terms of social contract and natural rights theories.

Their classical republican character can be understood from their support of the public interest and a citizen's positive duty to sustain a free polis; for members of the societies, integrity and virtue required a commitment to serve the common good above self-interest. An *Address* by democrats in New York proclaimed: "The character and worth of individuals ought ever to be estimated in proportion to the services they render to the community of which they are members. The active exertion of our talents, the industrious exercise of our abilities, is a debt we all owe to society from the first and most sacred principles of the social compact." Likewise, the Massachusetts Constitutional Society of Boston referred to "social," as opposed to individual, virtues in their constitution. They recognized a citizen's duty to act responsibly and passionately in maintaining a free government and protecting the common good above one's self-interest. The acquisition of knowledge rather than arbitrary social status was now viewed as the key in enabling persons to participate in ruling the republic: "It is incumbent upon each individual to use every exertion in acquiring a knowledge of the principles of government . . . and political institutions of their country, in the administration of which they may one day be called upon to take an active share," claimed the democrats in New York.[21] Virtue and patriotism were considered synonymous, and for citizens to appreciate and realize such moral goodness required the mass dissemination and exchange of political knowledge; information was the key to sustaining and protecting liberty and preventing imposition and domination. "Equal justice, virtue . . . and a general diffusion of knowledge, are . . . the principal pillars that must support the sacred temple of liberty," according to members of the Canaan Society, who, in an attempt to realize such radical reforms, went so far as to offer resolutions supporting alteration of the legal code, courts, and juries in order to subject them to greater popular oversight.[22] Knowledge would provide the defense against aristocratic ambitions, and the societies' addresses are replete with such warnings as "The eyes of the republican patriot, must ever be watchful." They, much like their elite counterparts, were skeptical of those who held political power, but instead of relying on inflexible institutions to curb man's ambition, they adopted more dynamic and straightforward approaches, finding it necessary to "act with *efficacy*," as a "great bulwark to protect themselves against the artful designs of men who are secretly endeavoring to destroy those fundamental principles of liberty and equality."[23]

The societies believed it necessary to include additional popular controls by engaging in political affairs vigorously, disseminating information, and exchanging ideas. The societies served as Socratic gadflies, questioning, critiquing, and refusing to accept a blind and passive obedience to authority. Theirs was an active citizenship infusing duty and obligation with the protection of natural rights and the acquisition of political information. Ideas of justice were no longer conceived as some predetermined set of directives imposed from above, but were now to be determined cooperatively with others in the pursuit of shared goals. They understood democracy to be more than a mere process. It was an experience that transcended politics and could be constructively exploited in multiple relationships, including for example, the pursuit of scientific inquiry, investigation, hypothesizing, experimenting, and reconstructing one's environment, all the while insisting that precedent yield to new insights and discoveries. Established systems tended to suppress novelty and difference. The societies viewed change optimistically, and they looked to the open plurality of ideas as a superior approach in the search for truth. Just as John Milton had claimed, "The State shall be my governors, but not my critics," the societies advocated free discussion: "The collision of opposite opinions produces the spark which lights the torch of truth."[24] And *Cato's Letters*, which were read throughout the colonies during the eighteenth century, quoted Tacitus extolling the virtues of free speech: "The rare good fortune of an age where one is allowed to feel what one wishes and to say what one feels."[25] Accordingly, the societies infused republicanism with a democratic commitment in securing for each individual the opportunity to engage in political discourse. Therefore, the societies entered into a campaign, a literary battle in many respects, to disseminate information throughout the states, hoping to inform citizens about the perceived pro-British and aristocratic policies of the Federalist administrations and the simultaneous betrayal of republican ideals. They were constructing a democratic-republican ideology out of the ruins of war and upon the principles of Radical Whiggism.

Of course such activities required a measure of leisure not commonly available to ordinary persons. The societies adopted the republican theme of independence and defended the right of all persons to own private property. As Robert Coram, an English-born schoolmaster, publisher of the *Delaware Gazette* and member of the New Castle Patriotic Society, noted in his diatribe against William Blackstone, "the unequal distribution of property was the parent of almost all the disorders of government." Coram confronted the issue of private property directly, arguing against any natural right to land. He believed history had proven that most governments were established by "conquest," which resulted in an "arbitrary" distribution of land.

Moreover, "the bulk of mankind," Coram argued, was "not only cheated" in the unequal distribution of land, but also considered "ineligible to offices in the government because they were not freeholders." Blackstone, he believed, was simply rationalizing the contemporary disparity in land holdings by justifying the arbitrary and capricious legal codes that had supported such a system. Coram suggested that while land can be used for private purposes its distribution should be made upon a roughly equal basis, reflecting the classical republican concern with political equality supported by agrarian laws. Coram did not call for redistribution, but he admonished Blackstone for declaring the current land holdings to be a natural outgrowth of society. In appropriate republican fashion, he argued that an equal division of land would be the most appropriate check "against the ambition of individuals" and viewed it as the most certain way to promote independence and political equality.

It was Locke before him who proposed limiting private property in order to prevent its accumulation from being used as an instrument of oppression. If one needed to maintain independence in order to participate in governing the polis, and independence required the moderate possession of property, Coram concluded that a broader division of property would affect greater political equality. Embracing the classical preference for agrarian laws, he pressed the classical republican argument of equal opportunity by claiming that the threat of force or a condition of dependence diminished one's liberty and led to tyranny. The only way to expose "Dr. Blackstone's sophistry," he argued, was to adopt "A SYSTEM OF EQUAL EDUCATION" so that everyone could recognize the same fallacies.[26] While the societies feared centralized systems they recognized the need for government regulation of social and economic policies to the extent necessary in protecting political equality. Agrarian laws and a broad-based education in republican principles would serve these purposes.

The societies' philosophy assigned unprecedented political power to ordinary citizens, but it was to be tempered by informed and enlightened judgment. In particular, the societies resisted and challenged the conservative interpretation of republicanism and advocated the active engagement of ordinary citizens, an episode of popular resistance often overlooked by historians of ideas. As Hannah Arendt remarked about the American Founding, "the Constitution had given all power to the citizens, without giving them the opportunity of being republicans and of acting as citizens," and indicating further, "that all power had been given to the people in their private capacity and that there was no space established for them in their capacity of being citizens," resulting in what she identifies as "the lost treasure of the revolutionary tradition."[27] By contrast, the Democratic-Republican Societies exhibited extraordinary exuberance, initiative, and dexterity in their crusade for democracy, and like Paine, they adopted a re-constructionist philosophy with regard to governing, believing that policies should adjust to changes in the general will.[28] Every generation, they held, must be free to pursue its own course of action, liberated from the constraints of tradition. Members of the societies resisted the authoritarian interpretation of the Constitution with the aim of conforming it to their understanding of the revolutionary spirit and the republican ideals codified in the Declaration of Independence. That is, they viewed the Constitution as furnishing the scaffolding upon which the Declaration's ideals could be realized. Therefore, they applied a much more popular and inclusive meaning to the Constitution, which supported their being *and* acting as citizens.

Revolutionary Civics

"The moral principle of revolutions is to instruct, not to destroy," explained Thomas Paine, who has been credited with inflaming the societies' fervor. In December 1778, referring to their educational provisions, Paine confirmed his aphorism, asserting that, "all the constitutions in America . . . are constructed . . . to make men as wise as possible so that . . . they may be rationally governed."[29] Likewise, the societies understood knowledge as power, and they were resolute in preventing an "EMPIRE OF DESPOTISM" from forming upon a pillar of "ABJECT IGNORANCE." Active learning was to take place through a number of methods including the study of the Constitution and the laws and proceedings of Congress, its debates and journals, general oversight of representatives, and through deliberation, speaking engagements, and writing campaigns.[30] Viewing it as a necessity in a republican government they sought support for public schooling, which was to serve all children including the indigent. Because they subscribed to Locke's epistemological view of human beings—that individuals are malleable and impressionable—the societies adopted the republican emphasis on education in shaping one's opportunities in life. Yet, the milieu of the early Republic reflected "a most glaring solecism," according to Coram: "The constitutions are *republican* and the laws of education are *monarchical*."[31] While American jurisprudence became increasingly differentiated from ecclesiastical authority and was associated with constitutional doctrines supported by republican principles, public education lost pace with the republican rhetoric and remained underdeveloped and ill suited to the revolutionary spirit, despite the widespread rhetoric of education serving a fundamental republican function.

While virtually everyone agreed upon the ends of education and the perfectibility of man, conflicts enveloped around who and how to educate, as illuminated by Benjamin Rush's ideas on fashioning "republican machines," Jefferson's goals to create a "natural aristocracy," and the radical political education advocated by the Democratic-Republican societies. Many of the efforts put forward at the time to create systems of education reflected less a desire to overcome ignorance than an attempt to instill respect for authority and law.[32] Although they were not opposed to the inculcation of such values, members of the societies identified this restricted curricula as a latent development in educational despotism. "May ignorance, bigotry and superstition be for ever banished from the earth, [and] may the crowns and scepters of tyrants be melted in the furnace of a perpetual reformation," was a toast given by the Democratic Society of the City of New York during its celebration of the recapture of Toulon. Robert Coram, Caesar Rodney, and their fellow democrats in the Newcastle Society adopted a resolution calling for the establishment of public schools in Delaware so that the "children of indigence and neglect . . . may be educated and enlightened among the children of opulence." Without public education, they asserted: "the bond of society becomes a rope of sand."[33] The democratic societies viewed education in a republic as the means through which each generation could eradicate archaic institutions and obsolete traditions while advancing political equality and scientific improvement. A connection between republican liberty and free inquiry had developed, and it is not surprising that the democratic societies included scientists and physicians like David Rittenhouse, George Logan, Benjamin Rush, and Samuel L. Mitchill.

Political institutions *and* schooling were expected to empower citizens and "aid in their quest to better society." As Coram explained, ". . . to make men happy, the first step is to make them independent. For if they are dependent, they can neither manage their private concerns properly, retain their own dignity, or [sic] vote impartially for their country: they can be but tools at best."[34] Coram was so firm in his commitment to public schooling that he sent his proposals directly to President Washington before the societies materialized. In an accompanying letter Coram exclaimed "I write it chiefly with a design of being useful to my country," and he expressed in the pamphlet his ideas on human nature and educational philosophy, including his proposal for the establishment of public schools throughout the United States, which were to be divided into districts according to population and paid by revenue collected from property taxes.[35] Like Noah Webster, with whom he agreed on little else, Coram pled for cultural independence by arguing that it was "high time to check that blind adherence to transatlantic policy, which has so generally prevailed," further complaining that schoolmasters were teaching anachronistic subjects no longer useful, antiquated "modes of faith, systems of manners, or foreign or dead languages."[36]

Although the Constitution lacked any mention of education, virtually everyone understood it as an essential ingredient of republican government. Only at an abstract level, however, could agreement be reached. Like Jefferson, the societies viewed education as a public matter, not in the New England conception of mixed financing and auxiliary charity schools, but a truly common enterprise intended to address a common concern. Education was to be supported solely by public revenues and deemed an entitlement to each citizen regardless of his or her social status. The societies believed individuals to be equal in their rights, but unlike Jefferson and other elites, they also believed individuals possessed equal capacities. The Revolution gave added recognition to the general public's empowerment and conferred a greater sense of political efficacy upon freemen.

Virtually all the societies published resolutions or constitutions insisting on the establishment of public schools. Their preferred curriculum was much more radical than what one would find in, say, the New England spellers or the popular nineteenth-century McGuffey readers. Citizenship required much more than the inculcation of honesty, hard work, thriftiness, and respect for law by "impressing [upon] every class of citizens . . . a true sense of their rights, duties, and obligation . . . and . . . a just knowledge of rational liberty," and political knowledge to prepare students to take part in public life. "The avenues of information," they claimed, must be open to all persons so that they may be better equipped "in their redress."[37]

"The venerable Dr. Priestley," as the Palmetto Society in Charleston referred to him, viewed the traditional approach to educating youth as oppressive and demeaning, an approach he associated with England's Anglican Church. He observed that, if "[students'] minds be cramped by systems, and thereby habituated to servitude, and disinclined to think for themselves in their early years, they will be prepared to oppose, instead of favoring, any great and noble efforts."[38] To the contrary, he viewed broad-based education as an instrument of progress: "It is the glory of human nature," he argued, "that the operations of reason, though variable, and by no means infallible, are capable of infinite improvement." Only by releasing human potential could individuals break free from oppressive "systems." The intellectual rigidity suffered under such methods degraded the dignity of individual nature by demanding only compliance. To be meaningful religious faith required a free conscience and virtue required individual liberty. The end of education, according to the Radical Whig Richard Price, "should be to teach how to think, rather than what to think."[39] Tunis Wortman went so far as to argue that, "the only measurable difference between a "Newton" and the "husbandman," is life circumstances and the degree of opportunity. "Without cultivation," he asserted, "Tully would not have been an orator; Newton could not have explored the laws of the universe, nor would Homer have stood unrivaled in the career of epic poetry."[40]

Echoing Rousseau, members of the societies believed that individuals would learn from nature and experience. The exercise of citizenship, guided by education aimed at instructing individuals on the importance of the common good or "general will," functions "as a moral imperative" intended to maintain political equality and justice. In other words, education is essential in apprehending the "general will," as individuals must understand their rights as well as their duties and obligations as citizens and maintain a sense of "reciprocity" congruent with the social contract.[41] Unlike Rousseau the societies endorsed the education of women as they were influenced by the work of Mary Wollstonecraft, the wife of the radical Englishman William Godwin. Women, "could add to the knowledge of the common fund," according to Benjamin Bache, publisher of the Philadelphia *Aurora* and member of the Pennsylvania Society.[42] While elites endeavored to narrow political involvement, the societies' egalitarian approach to civic education and political participation was highlighted in the continuing literary campaign carried on in the opposition press.

Newspapers as Education by Other Means

As education was defined by the societies as an experience in political participation, citizens were expected to learn in a variety of ways beyond those methods we typically associate with schooling. The educational philosophy of the societies, according to Walsh's analysis, was important for children, but was considered to be a "life-long" and "dialectical" process; a forum meant to sustain free inquiry and the clash of ideas imbued by the revolutionary spirit of equality and free speech.[43] As an alternative to perpetuating a dominant belief, the societies preferred to teach by means of democratic deliberation within and among their little republics. It was a form of teaching by example, and citizens were to digest information critically, reflect upon it, utilize it, and engage it among members of the community. Expectations included acquiring knowledge of politics and becoming active in political affairs, and while the societies sought information from many sources, newspapers served as their primary means of instruction. Since newspapers aided in the monitoring of public officials, Link has shown, they "found a democratic press indispensable for [their] educational purposes . . . and the strongest societies arose where a printer was at their beck and call."[44] Although subscription costs placed newspapers beyond the reach of some individuals, they could easily be recycled in coffee houses, taverns, and elsewhere.[45] Newspapers were the most effectual way to communicate the government's business, and according to Pasley, the federal government exempted newspapers from taxation so as to increase the means of informing citizens about public issues.[46] Moreover, viewing an opposition press as their most valuable device in countering Federalist actions, the societies' newspapers went far beyond reprinting government documents; they included essays on liberty and the events of the French Revolution, satirical poems, and diatribes against Federalist policies, including Jay's Treaty and the Alien and Sedition Acts, serving as a practical curriculum in American politics. Overall, the ability to publish ideas and commentary generated an extraordinary period of literary authorship and ideological ferment among the societies. The civic and moral learning that took place, therefore, occurred not in the schoolhouse, but within the tumultuous political arena, less formal and without rigid prescription.

Certainly, the Federalists considered the dissenting campaign as licentious, and they opposed the societies' efforts because their actions did not represent a deferential, orderly, and institutionally managed way of expressing popular opinion. Elites believed the personal character of ordinary citizens, that is, their moral rectitude, should have been emphasized over any active engagement in politics or public dissent. Elites considered popular legislative assemblies in the states to serve as appropriate venues of expressing popular opinion and to provide a comfortable distance between the governors and the governed. "The Federalist mind," according to Banner, "gained its sinister aspect because it was anti-republican."[47]

Nevertheless, members of the democratic societies were simply too extreme to be content with a trustee form of representation. They operated as an extra-parliamentary opposition outside the established political framework generating anxiety among elites over the disruption of the American experiment. Viewing civil disobedience as a natural function of a free society, Jefferson was continually surprised by what he believed to be Federalist overreactions to popular tumult. No "degree of power in the hands of government [will] prevent insurrections," he explained to Madison in a letter written earlier from Paris.[48] Undeniably, the Alien and Sedition Acts implemented during Adams's administration, and upon Hamilton's urging, were intended to stifle such stirrings.

While literacy rates were quite high during the period, especially among whites in the New England states, ordinary persons began to understand the value of education beyond the basics of reading and writing.[49] The societies viewed education not just in its utilitarian sense, but also valued it in developing independent judgment and reflection. The emerging capacity to normatively critique one's social, political, and religious environment increased one's ability to differentiate between social and natural phenomena more clearly, and knowledge could now be used to liberate individuals from socially ascribed roles.

Whether they were conscious of it or not, the Democratic-Republican Societies played a large role in preparing the ground for the eventual development of mass parties and may have been indirectly responsible for the ultimate expansion of the franchise.[50] After Jefferson's election in 1800, in which Democratic-Republicans garnered 66 seats in the House of Representatives compared to Federalists' 38 seats, members of the defeated party reluctantly adopted many of the political strategies used by the societies. While they remained paternalistic, their defeat at the polls caused Federalists to reorient their appeals to ordinary citizens.[51] The Democratic-Republican Societies were not only learning how to act as citizens, but also educating elites on how to organize an opposition party. An important example of their influence might be gleaned from the Whig Party's (primarily made up of former Federalists) advocacy of a common school system toward the end of the first quarter of the nineteenth century. Although their aims had more to do with political expediency and paternalism, the Whig Party made efforts to attract members of the Democratic Party after the election of Andrew Jackson in 1828.

Conclusion

Expressing the same concern as that of Arendt (above), Herbert Storing, asserts, "the Federalist solution not only failed to provide for the moral qualities that are necessary to the maintenance of republican government; it tended to undermine them."[52] Out of the revolutionary experience two distinct and opposing attitudes toward human nature materialized. One included an optimistic view of man's capacity to engage in politics and enlarge his moral agency by participating in political discourse in association with his compatriots. The Revolution established the veracity of Radical Whig ideas exemplifying man's ability to act upon his environment as a corrective power in remedying erroneous or antiquated institutions. The outcome gave added credibility to the virtues of self-rule, political equality, and the democratic methods necessary in maintaining a republican government, including citizen juries and militias, annual elections, rotation, localism, constitutional conventions, supported by education in the principles of active citizenship. What this group gained from the revolutionary experience was a greater sense of political efficacy and a better understanding of how the power of reason and judgment could inform concerted action. In Aristotelian terms, they recognized active political participation as essential in developing human character.

The other attitude was more pessimistic with regard to human nature precisely for analogous reasons. The revolutionary experience illustrated in tandem the potential dangers in democratizing republican thought and created a sense of alarm among elites. Their paternalism is illustrated in their belief that common folk should remain deferential and that they required the leadership of the gentry. They considered themselves superior judges of the moral character of others, and they sought ways to preserve their elevated standing in the community.

Whatever accounts for their demise by 1800, the Democratic-Republican Societies' withdrawal from the political arena reveals what may have been a lost opportunity in nurturing a strong civic obligation and revolutionary spirit among those most committed to the public good. The societies' educational philosophy served as an instrument of democratization with liberating potential, which explains the criticism that was directed at them. Members molded their conception of republicanism into a democratic and egalitarian catalyst for progressive change. Unlike many elites who considered inequality as natural, the societies adopted the view that individuals were conditioned to accept hierarchy, status, and social differences more willingly than viewing them as artificially contrived notions supported by legal codes and custom. The societies reasoned that individuals are roughly equal in intelligence, and therefore, equally capable in pursuing autonomous experiences and participating in civic activity. They viewed change and reconstruction as the norm, not the exception, and they came to recognize that democracy was linked to irregularity and plurality, not uniformity and static relations; to opposition, not deference; and to action, not passive acquiescence. They understood democracy as local in character so as to ensure the registering of diverse opinions, which was the only way to guarantee democracy's survival. It required closeness, not distance, in order for citizens to maintain a sense of inclusion and political efficacy. Not only did they consider democracy to be a practice that must adapt to new conditions and changing environments, but also a process without a prescribed outcome. The societies struggled to prevent the novelty and spontaneity of their politics from becoming institutionalized in the interests of administration. They too were part of the American experiment, developing a new civic ideology by contesting authoritarian conceptions of republicanism and contributing to the vortex of educational ideas being mediated during the early Republic.

Acknowledgments

The author thanks Donald Warren and Barry Bull for their insightful and editorial suggestions on earlier drafts of this essay. I thank them and Edward McClellan for stimulating my interest in the history and philosophy of education.

Notes

1. German Republican Society of Philadelphia, *Address*, April 11, 1793; The Democratic Society of Pennsylvania, *Manuscript Minutes*, May 1, 1794, in *Democratic-Republican Societies, 1790–1800: A Documentary Sourcebook of Constitutions, Declarations, Addresses, Resolutions, and Toasts*, ed. Philip S. Foner (Westport, CT: Greenwood Press, 1976), 53, 103.
2. Eugene P. Link, *Democratic-Republican Societies, 1790–1800* (New York: Columbia University Press, 1942), 13–15, 72.
3. Gordon S. Wood, *The Creation of the American Republic, 1776–1787* (Chapel Hill: The University of North Carolina Press, 1998), 4.
4. True Republican Society of Philadelphia, *Toasts*, May 7, 1800; Republican Society of the Town of Newark, "Cato" to the *New York Gazette*, March 12, 1794, in Foner, *Democratic-Republican Societies*, 111, 144.

5. Abraham Bishop, *Georgia Speculation Unveiled, Second Part Containing The Third and Fourth Numbers with a Conclusion, Addressed to the Northern Purchasers* (Hartford, CT: Hudson & Goodwin, 1798), 82–83.
6. Frank T. Carlton, *Economic Influences upon Educational Progress in the United States, 1820–1850* (New York: Teachers College Press, 1965), 7; Link, *Democratic-Republican Societies*, 102–103.
7. James Burgh, *Political Disquisitions: Or, An Enquiry into Public Errors, Defects, and Abuses*, 3 vols. (London, 1774 and 1775; reprint, New York: Da Capo Press, 1971), I: 3–4.
8. Bernard Bailyn, *The Ideological Origins of the American Revolution*, enlarged edn (Cambridge: The Belknap Press of Harvard University Press, 1992), chapter II.
9. For an intriguing discussion of how constitutions "repress democracy," see Sheldon S. Wolin, "Norm and Form: The Constitutionalizing of Democracy," in J. Peter Euben, John R. Wallach, and Josia Ober, eds., *Athenian Political Thought and the Reconstruction of American Democracy* (Ithaca, NY: Cornell University Press, 1995), 29–58.
10. John Adams, *Novanglus; or, A History of the Dispute with America, from Its Origin, in 1754, to the Present Time*, in *The Revolutionary Writings of John Adams*, selected and with a foreword by C. Bradley Thompson (Indianapolis: Liberty Fund, Inc., 2000), 147–284. John Locke, *Two Treatises of Government*, ed. Peter Laslett (Cambridge: Cambridge University Press, 1988), 309.
11. Lawrence A. Cremin, *American Education: The National Experience, 1783–1876* (New York: Harper & Row, 1980), 125. Allen Oscar Hansen, *Liberalism and American Education in the Eighteenth Century* (New York: Octagon Books, 1977), 4–5.
12. Regarding what is akin to contemporary interest groups during the early 1770s, see Gordon S. Wood, *The Radicalism of the American Revolution* (New York: Random House, 1993), 244–245.
13. Baron De Montesquieu, *The Spirit of the Laws*, trans. Thomas Nugent (New York: Hafner Press, 1949), ii: 15 and v: 5.
14. Cremin, *American Education*, 204.
15. Joel Barlow, *Advice to the Privileged Orders in the Several States of Europe: Resulting from the Necessity and Propriety of a General Revolution in the Principle of Government* (Ithaca, NY: Cornell University Press, 1956), 19–20.
16. Wood, *The Radicalism of the American Revolution*, 276.
17. Michael B. Katz, *Reconstructing American Education* (Cambridge: Harvard University Press, 1987), 16.
18. Link, *Democratic-Republican Societies*, 119.
19. John Adams, *A Dissertation on the Canon and Feudal Law*, in *The Revolutionary Writings of John Adams*, Thompson, 21–28.
20. Norwalk Republican Society, Connecticut, *Introduction to the Constitution*, April 4, 1798; The Democratic Society of Pennsylvania, Philadelphia, *Principles, Articles, and Regulations, Agreed upon, Drawn, and Adopted*, May 30, 1793, in Foner, *Democratic-Republican Societies*, 64, 254.
21. Democratic Society of the City of New York, *Address to the Republican Citizens of the United States*, May 28, 1794; The Massachusetts Constitutional Society, Boston, *Rules and Regulations and Declaration*, January 13, 1794; Democratic Society of the City of New York, *Address*, May 28, 1794, in Foner, *Democratic-Republican Societies*, 178–179, 257.
22. Democratic Society of Canaan, Columbia County, *Resolutions Adopted on the Need for Reform in Laws, Courts, and Juries*, July 10, 1794, in Foner, *Democratic-Republican Societies*, 240.

23. Republican Society of South Carolina, Charleston, *Manuscript Minutes*, August 1793; Massachusetts Constitutional Society, *Circular to All Republican Societies in the United States*, August 28, 1794, in Foner, *Democratic-Republican Societies*, 259, 382.
24. John Milton, *Areopagitica*, ed. George H. Sabine (New York: Appleton-Century-Crofts, Inc., 1951), 31. For an example of this phraseology, see The Patriotic Society of Newcastle County, Delaware, *Circular*, in Foner, *Democratic-Republican Societies*, 324.
25. John Trenchard and Thomas Gordon, *Cato's Letters, or Essays on Liberty, Civil and Religious, and Other Important Subjects*, ed. Ronald Hamowy (Indianapolis: Liberty Fund, Inc., 1995), No. 15: 113.
26. Robert Coram, *Political Inquiries: to Which is Added, A Plan for the General Establishment of Schools Throughout the United States* (Wilmington, DE: 1791), text-fiche, chapter II. For the similarities with Jefferson's land policy, see Richard Hofstadter, *The American Political Tradition & the Men Who Made It* (New York: Random House, 1974), 39. For Locke's ideas on property acquisition, see John Locke, *Two Treatises of Government*, 170, 292.
27. Hannah Arendt, *On Revolution* (New York: Penguin Books, Ltd., 1965), 253.
28. Thomas Paine, *Rights of Man* (New York: Penguin Books, 1984), 41.
29. Thomas Paine, *Dissertation on First Principles of Government* (Philadelphia, 1795), in Link, *Democratic-Republican Societies*, 156. Thomas Paine, *A Serious Address to the People of Pennsylvania on the Present Situation of their Affairs*, December 1778, in *The Complete Writings of Thomas Paine*, ed. Philip S. Foner (New York: The Citadel Press, 1945), 290. The state constitutions of Pennsylvania, North Carolina, and Vermont, ratified in 1776 and 1777, included educational language. See G. Alan Tarr, *Understanding State Constitutions* (Princeton, NJ: Princeton University Press, 1998), 62.
30. Democratic Society of the City of New York, *Address to "Fellow Freeman,"* January 26, 1795; The Democratic Society in the County of Addison, Vermont, *Constitution*, September 9, 1794, in Foner, *Democratic-Republican Societies*, 197, 277.
31. Coram, *Political Inquiries*, 78.
32. Benjamin Rush, "Of the Mode of Education Proper in a Republic," in Dagobert D. Runes, ed., *The Selected Writings of Benjamin Rush* (New York: The Philosophical Library, Inc., 1947), 92. Thomas Jefferson, "A Bill for the More General Diffusion of Knowledge," in Gordon C. Lee, ed., *Crusade Against Ignorance* (New York: Teachers College Press, 1961), 83–92. Peter S. Onuf, "State Politics and Republican Virtue: Religion, Education, and Morality in Early American Federalism," in Paul Finkelman and Stephen E. Gottlieb, eds., *Toward a Usable Past: Liberty Under State Constitutions* (Athens: The University of Georgia Press, 1991), 107.
33. Democratic Society of the City of New York, *Toasts Drunk at a Celebration of the Recapture of Toulon*, March 20, 1794; Patriotic Society of the County of Newcastle, Delaware, *Resolution Adopted on the Establishment of Public Schools*, August 30, 1794 and *Memorial to the Legislature on Schools*, December 23, 1794, in Foner, *Democratic-Republican Societies*, 168–169, 322–323.
34. Coram, *Political Inquiries*, 104.
35. Robert Coram to George Washington, March 5, 1791, *George Washington Papers at the Library of Congress, 1741–1799*: Series 4. General Correspondence. Image 377 of 1130; Coram, *Political Inquiries*, 99.
36. Jonathan Messerli, "The Columbian Complex: The Impulse to National Consolidation," *History of Education Quarterly* 7, no. 4 (1967): 421.
37. The Democratic Society of Pennsylvania, Philadelphia, *Resolutions Adopted on the Importance of Establishing Public Schools*, March 19, 1795, in Foner, *Democratic-Republican Societies*, 108–109.

38. The Palmetto Society of Charleston, *Toasts*, June 28, 1794, in Foner, *Democratic-Republican Societies*, 392. Joseph Priestley, *The Proper Objects of Education in the Present State of the World* (London: Printed for J. Johnson, St. Paul's Church Yard, 1791), 7.
39. Joseph Priestley, *An Essay on the First Principles of Government*, in Peter Miller, ed., *Political Writings* (Cambridge: Cambridge University Press, 1993), 45–46. Richard Price, *Observations on the Nature of Civil Liberty, and Observations on the Importance of the American Revolution*, in D.O. Thomas ed., *Political Writings* (Cambridge: Cambridge University Press, 1991), 23, 137.
40. Tunis Wortman, *A Treatise, Concerning Political Inquiry, and the Liberty of the Press* (New York: Printed by George Forman, No. 64, Water-Street, 1800; reprint, New York: Da Capo Press, 1970), 51–53.
41. Richard Dagger, *Civic Virtues: Rights, Citizenship, and Republican Liberalism* (New York: Oxford University Press, 1997), 83–87.
42. Benjamin Bache to M.H. Markoe, November 26, 1789, in Link, *Democratic-Republican Societies*, 171.
43. Julie M. Walsh, *The Intellectual Origins of Mass Parties and Mass Schools in the Jacksonian Period: Creating a Conformed Citizenry* (New York: Garland Publishing, Inc., 1998), 46, 52–55.
44. Link, *Democratic-Republican Societies*, 59.
45. Howard B. Rock, *Artisans of the New Republic: The Tradesmen of New York City in the Age of Jefferson* (New York: University Press, 1979), 37.
46. Jeffrey L. Pasley, *"The Tyranny of Printers" Newspaper Politics in the Early Republic* (Charlottesville: University of Virginia Press, 2001), 48–49.
47. Bailyn, *The Ideological Origins*, 79. James M. Banner, Jr., *To the Hartford Convention: The Federalists and the Origins of Party Politics in Massachusetts, 1789–1815* (New York: Alfred A. Knopf, 1970), 42.
48. Thomas Jefferson to James Madison, December 20, 1787, in *The Republic of Letters*, vol. 1, ed. James Morton Smith (New York: W. W. Norton & Company, 1995), 514.
49. Lawrence Cremin asserts that American literacy rates during the revolutionary period ranged from 70 to 100 percent if literacy is based on the signatures of wills, militia rolls, and voting rosters. However, Cremin provides a note of caution, arguing that, if one were to include white non-property holders, nonvoters, non-participants in the militia, as well as "Negro" and Indian non-property holders, American literacy rates would fall below 48 percent. See his *American Education: The Colonial Experience, 1607–1783* (New York: Harper & Row, 1970), 546.
50. William A. Robinson, *Jeffersonian Democracy in New England* (New Haven: Yale University Press, 1916), 10. It should be noted that Thomas Jefferson narrowly won the 1800–1801 presidential election after it was thrown into the House of Representatives, eventually carrying ten of the sixteen states on the 36th ballot, resulting in the proposal and ratification of the 12th Amendment to the U.S. Constitution. See Michael J. Dubin, *United States Presidential Elections, 1788–1860* (Jefferson, NC: McFarland & Company, Inc., 2002), 8–11.
51. Richard Hofstadter, *The Idea of a Party System: The Rise of Legitimate Opposition in the United States, 1780–1840* (Berkeley: University of California Press, 1969), 149. For election returns, see Michael J. Dubin, *United States Congressional Elections, 1788–1997* (Jefferson, NC: McFarland & Company, Inc., 1998), 22–26.
52. Herbert J. Storing, *What the Anti-Federalists were For* (Chicago: The University of Chicago Press, 1981), 73.

This page intentionally left blank

Chapter 4

Moral Educations on the Alaskan Frontier, 1794–1917

Milton Gaither

Canonical histories of moral education in the United States tend to follow a particular story line that goes something like this: Protestant foundations are laid in the colonial period that are gradually transformed and softened such that by the nineteenth century what was a father-dominated, church-centered education has turned into public schooling nurtured by the schoolmarm. Thus a mild Protestant morality is institutionalized in government schooling and used as the leading assimilative mechanism for immigrants, most especially for Roman Catholics. As the result of conflict between nonsectarian Protestantism and Roman Catholicism, the public schools gradually lose more and more of their explicit moral content until finally near absolute secularism becomes the only plausible option and a new ground for moral education is sought in the discipline of developmental psychology. With the failure of developmentalism, moral education becomes extremely problematic, with competing paradigms offering radically different prescriptions while schools themselves stumble along with an incoherent stew of virtue inculcation, self-esteem therapy, multiculturalism, utilitarian appeals to economic self-interest, or simple avoidance of the moral realm of experience entirely.[1]

There is much of value in the above story line. It's a good tale that fairly accurately accounts for much of what has happened in the public domain of moral instruction for children in the lower 48 states. The colonial history of much of North America is a Protestant history, and it was Protestantism that established the early institutions and sensibilities that played the lead role in the subsequent history of the United States. While in Europe Protestantism had to compete against long-established Christian customs, one of the most attractive elements of the New World for Protestants was the ostensibly virgin territory, the "wilderness." Absent a preexisting civilization, Protestants were free to create *ex nihilo* their own institutions and try to maintain them as newcomers arrived. Thus the post-Puritan history of moral education is one of Protestant efforts to maintain hegemony in the face of increasing diversification of the population.[2]

But in Alaska the story was different. In this chapter I would like to hold up the Alaskan experience as an alternative to the dominant narrative of the history of moral education in several senses. First, Alaska shows us a part of the United States that was colonized not by Protestants from Western Europe but by Orthodox Christians from Russia. Second, the purchase of Alaska by the United States created circumstances for a fascinating and unique case in the subsequent history of moral education, for the non-sectarian Protestantism that had always been dominant in the lower states was in Alaska a latecomer, meeting not an untamed wilderness but a long-established alternative model. Third, the Alaska example sheds new light on some important themes in the history of moral education and education more generally in terms of church/state relations, bilingual education, the education of indigenous Americans, and the clash between moral communities and the exigencies of modern life.

Russian Alaska and Orthodox Moral Education

Alaska was colonized by Russian *promyshlenniki* who began to trap and trade there in the decades after Vitus Bering's voyages that culminated in his discovery of the Aleutian islands in 1741. In 1784 the beginnings of a formal government was established on Kodiak Island under Grigor and Natalya Shelikof. Government of the lands and peoples of Alaska, originally a desultory affair with competing traders wrangling with one another and horribly mistreating the native populations, gave way to monopolistic control of the entire region by the Russian American Company. The Company, authorized by the Czar and concerned primarily with maintaining the lucrative trade in animal skins, governed the territory from 1799 until its sale to the United States in 1867.[3]

With the stabilization of governance came an effort by the Russian Orthodox Church to evangelize the native populations in Alaska. In 1794, 10 Orthodox monks arrived on Kodiak Island, assisted by two novices and ten Alaskan natives who had been trained in Russia. Under the Shelikofs, both very pious and generous (if patronizing) in character, a school had been established on Kodiak in 1784. The Shelikof school was from the beginning bilingual in nature, with a curriculum of basic language, history, agriculture, arithmetic, and religion delivered both in Russian and Kodiak. Monks Gideon and Herman continued this work into the nineteenth century, and by 1807 the school enjoyed an enrollment of around 100 students.[4]

Missionary efforts extended from Kodiak throughout the Alaskan interior. By 1824 settlements were sufficiently permanent for married clergy and their families to immigrate. That year a second wave of Russian clerics and evangelists arrived to strengthen an already thriving native Orthodox Church. Translation of Church services and the Scriptures into native languages, which had begun in a halting manner earlier, were now conducted more systematically. Schools were founded in growing numbers. By 1820 there were five Church schools in Alaska. By 1844 four hundred native children were educated in Church schools. By 1845 there was enough interest to begin a seminary in the town of New Archangel (Sitka). Crucial in this growth was the work and spirit of the leading Orthodox cleric in the region, Fr. John Veniaminov, who first came to Alaska in 1824 with his wife and three children. Veniaminov was by all accounts a man of astonishing and wide-ranging capacities, from woodworking to administration to scholarship. In his many years as priest and, upon the death of his wife, as bishop under the name Innocent, he kept copious notes, which he later published, on the geology, botany, anthropology, and meteorology of Alaska. He joined with Aleut leader Ivan Pan'kov in designing an Aleut alphabet and then translating the Scriptures and Orthodox services into the language. By 1840 he and many others had published several books in Aleut.[5]

But Veniaminov's major emphasis was on education. In 1845 he opened the New Archangel Seminary with 54 students, 23 of whom were native Alaskans. The curriculum included "six years of Alaska Native language: Aleut, Yupik and Tlingit" in addition to three years of medicine, instruction in Latin for understanding medical terminology, and other subjects from Theology to history to physics. Veniaminov, now as Bishop Innocent, continuously toured Alaska's vast borders, disbursing the graduates of his seminary to posts far and wide to spread native literacy and Orthodox Christianity. Correspondence from one of his priests, Father Gregory Golovin, suggests the impact of this venture. "There are" wrote Fr. Golovin in 1843, "249 Fox Islands' Aleuts who can read. Of this number, 172 were taught in clergy houses and 77 in the school. The present enrollment is 157." Over a dozen Alaskan natives in the nineteenth century published books in their native languages, and the best scholarly estimates place literacy at about 1/6 of the entire native population, with figures much higher in key population centers like Unalaska, which in 1852 was reported to have the following literacy rates, according to Lavrenty Salamatov, principal of the Unalaska school:

	Male	Female
Literate (able to read)	536	498
Illiterate adults	80	169
Illiterate children (too young to read)	65	67

By 1900 graduates of the seminary and other Orthodox leaders had established forty-four bilingual parochial schools throughout Alaska.[6]

Though the paper trail is incomplete, careful historical spadework has uncovered a remarkably successful educational venture by the Russian Orthodox Church, whose priests and monks battled not only the harsh climate and vast expanse of Alaska but also the brutal exploitation of the natives by the Church's own underwriters, the Russian American Company. Despite these setbacks, Orthodoxy was preached and accepted voluntarily by thousands of native Alaskans, leading to widespread literacy and the creation of an impressive tradition of intellectual production both in the Russian and native tongues. In 1861 New Archangel, the colonial capital, enjoyed, for a population of around 2,500, four lower schools, a college, a public library receiving shipments of new material four times a year from St. Petersburg, and two scientific institutes, one zoological and the other studying terrestrial magnetic phenomena. By 1860, 42 of the best graduates of Alaskan schools had traveled to St. Petersburg to pursue advanced studies in fields including navigation, commerce, carpentry, and medicine.[7]

There are many reasons for the success of the interaction between Orthodoxy and native Alaskan culture. On the Orthodox side, missionaries of the early and mid-nineteenth centuries favored non-coercive evangelistic techniques coupled with sensitivity to the cultures being proselytized. This had not always been the case in Russia, as the forced baptism of the *inorodtsy* (non-Russians) in lands conquered beginning with the 1522 conquest of the Kazan Khanate indicate. But the turn of the nineteenth century saw the revival of more historic patterns of Christian missionary activity as part of a larger revival of Patristic study. This return to the Church Fathers had tremendous impact on the American mission, for it restored to Russian Orthodox scholarship an emphasis on the natural and civil sciences, on personal ascetic discipline, and perhaps most significantly for moral education, on *tserkovnost*, defined variously as "churchness," "ecclesiality," or "community."[8]

Translation of the gospel message into the native language had been the hallmark of Church mission from the initial Pentecost experience, where the book of Acts describes each foreign tourist to Jerusalem miraculously hearing the Apostolic message "in his own language." While in the West Latin became the universal language of the Church, with all services being held in Latin from the early middle ages until Vatican II (1962–1965), in the Christian East the language of the Church had always been the language of the people. Thus when Cyril and Methodius brought Christianity to the Slavs in the ninth century, one of their most significant acts was to create a written form of the Slavic language (Cyrillic) and to translate the Scriptures, church services, and canonical laws into Slavonic. This same practice was continued throughout Orthodox lands, so it is not surprising that the Alaskan mission continued this tradition.[9]

Coupled with this emphasis on native language came an approach to native culture that strikes the contemporary mind as surprisingly enlightened given the ethnocentrism and cultural hubris of Europe and the United States in the nineteenth century. Here as elsewhere Russian Orthodoxy provides a historical example that belies the categories that so regularly appear in Western cultural analysis and history. We are accustomed to see sharp discontinuities in the history of the West between premodern and modern life. Many well-known formulae have emerged to articulate the rupture, from Sir Henry Maine's distinction between status and contract societies, to Ferdinand Tönnies's *Gemeinschaft und Gesellschaft*, to David Reisman's tradition vs. inner direction. The distinction has played a major role in educational historiography as well. It is one of the few common frames of reference for both progressives like Ellwood Cubberley and anti-progressives like Bernard Bailyn. The progressives took their cues from John Dewey, for whom the industrial revolution had transformed society such that the artificial school would now have to take the place of the natural premodern home. Bailyn's work as well is largely an account of how the American wilderness broke down the folkways of premodern Europe making necessary the rationalizing institution building of early America.[10]

But when one examines the Russians these categories fall apart. Russian missionaries saw no necessary connection between evangelization and civilization, between the spread of Christian faith and modern modes of economic life. The monks themselves were jarring (to Western sensibilities) hybrids of the most severe and sincere piety mixed with sophisticated intellectual acumen. One gets no sense reading through the curriculum recommendations and correspondence of Bishop Innocent Veniaminov that there is any contradiction between spreading the gospel and spreading smallpox vaccinations, nor between honoring tribal life built around seasonal hunting and fishing and instruction in physics. The same monks about whom stories are still told of miraculous healings, conversations with beasts, and the most severe bodily asceticism were also classifying flora and fauna and conducting electromagnetic experiments. This combination was very attractive to the Alaskan natives, whose Shaministic heritage caused them to be greatly impressed with charismatic holy men who possessed medicinal power. The curious blend of desert monasticism and modern medicine proved very appealing, especially as these holy men seemed to honor the culture they were trying to evangelize.[11]

The cultural sensitivity of Orthodox missionaries derived directly from their spirituality. Orthodox Christianity, unlike many forms of Protestantism, has never placed strong emphasis on a dramatic adult conversion. Salvation for Eastern Christianity has always been seen as a lifetime's work, a personal pilgrimage that begins at baptism and continues even after death, a process often called *theosis*. Thus there is no great need for the newly converted to immediately renounce her previous ways and become instantly transformed such as tends to be required of Protestant converts. Given this approach, an Orthodox monk could at one and the same time achieve the highest levels of personal sanctity and yet show remarkable leniency to novices just beginning to work out their salvation. In addition, Orthodox stress on asceticism in terms of fasting, prayer, and almsgiving has tended to promote a critical attitude toward the individual acquisition of wealth through commercialism. As Sergei Kan notes, in sharp contrast to Protestant missionary efforts, "most of the Orthodoxy clergymen laboring in Alaska . . . tended to encourage traditional subsistence activities and advocated measures that would protect the indigenous land base from commercial exploitation." Finally, sacramentalism seems to play a role in cultural tolerance. Membership in Protestant churches was determined largely by shared cultural background, but for the Orthodox and other liturgical churches, "one can be socially, linguistically, and ethnically different from other members . . . and still participate in the liturgical fullness of the church through receiving the sacraments."[12]

There is one last reason Alaskan natives were attracted to the communalism and ritualism of Orthodox Church life. Herein lies the heart of Orthodox moral education, of which its schools were only a piece. Vera Shevzov has described how nineteenth-century Orthodox thinkers employed the term *tserkovnost* to "articulate their vision of the communal dynamics underlying religious perspectives and rituals. . . . In general, believers used the term to refer to a collective religious experience and consciousness." *Tserkovnost* designated a conception of moral education not unlike that of some feminist and communitarian thinkers who argue that a child's moral vision is informed not so much by deliberate instruction as by participation in a shared moral culture. Shevzov explains how the notion of *tserkovnost*

> emphasized knowledge through experience more than through intellectual mastery. While those who used the term in the context of education and missionary work wrote of the importance of textual learning—the Bible, conciliar teachings, and so on—they also spoke of the importance of the non-discursive assimilation of those teachings.[13]

This shared moral culture was able to work its way seamlessly into the habitual patterns of life already experienced by Alaskan natives. Shamans gave way gradually (and with periodic conflict) to priests. Nuptial and burial traditions like the potlatch became incorporated into Orthodox services and feast days. Social stratification lived on in the Orthodox Brotherhoods; Clan Mothers became Godmothers. In these and many other ways Orthodox Christianity was preached by missionaries and experienced by natives less as a replacement of indigenous culture than as its fulfillment. Conversion to Orthodoxy tended to be a tribal event that did not really upset the communal structure of tribal life, for Orthodoxy itself was communal in ways congruent with what natives were accustomed to.[14]

When we turn to the natives themselves we find that Orthodox Christianity was often attractive for reasons quite other than those cherished by missionaries. Andrei Znamenski, in a fascinating comparative study of three tribal groups in Siberia and Alaska, one accepting Orthodoxy, one rejecting, and one reacting more ambiguously, describes how and why the various tribes responded as they did. Shamanism, which all of these groups shared, tended toward syncretism, "concerned with a constant search for spiritual power in order to maintain the natural harmony of the world. Under certain circumstances in this framework all types of useful experiences with neighboring tribes or the Europeans could be added as potentially helpful medicine." Moreover, this syncretistic outlook was wedded in the case of the Athapaskan Dena'ina, the group that embraced Orthodoxy, with a longstanding tradition of cultural adaptability, "Traditional Athapaskan culture must be thought of as essentially accommodating culture, and accommodation, in turn, greatly facilitated survival in a demanding environment."[15]

Thus when the Russian American Company invaded native habitats and disturbed the balance of hunting and fishing with their mass commercial enterprises, spreading novel diseases against which the Shamans were powerless, the arrival of Orthodox missionaries with their gentle ways and smallpox vaccinations seemed to many tribes just the solution to the new dilemmas. The primary role of the Shaman was that of healer, "not only a simple curing of ailments but as a general restoration of cultural, economic, and political balance." While in some cases local shamans clashed with monks and priests as rivals, in others the Shamans were actually responsible for the conversion of the tribe as they recognized in Orthodoxy the means of restoring balance. Legends of prophecies given to the shamans concerning the coming of Christianity still circulate among several Alaskan groups.[16]

Interestingly, many Alaskan tribes, including the Dean'ina studied by Znamenski and the Tlingit studied by other ethnohistorians, did not embrace Orthodoxy completely until after enduring a decade or more of governance by the United States. Therefore, it seems that that in addition to being attracted to the holiness of the monks, the sensuality of liturgical ceremonies, and the tangible rewards of medicine and literacy, natives especially "used the Russian church as an instrument for survival to cope with the Euroamerican society that was being established in their territories."[17]

Not all tribes were equally receptive to the Orthodox message. Znamenski offers two reasons why some tribes embraced Orthodoxy and others did not. First, pastoral tribes tended to be less receptive than hunting and fishing societies, for "in pastoral societies the more abstract and differentiated gods maintained a fixed cosmic order, unlike the gods in the hunting societies, which were open to innovations." The second reason pertains to the historical particularities of each situation. Some tribes felt a need for something to cope with the uncertainties of their situation, while others seemed more secure in maintaining their established ways. That a great number of Alaskan tribes accepted Orthodox Christianity whereas tribes with very similar belief systems in Siberia did not is at least partly due to the added strain of governance by the United States after 1867. It is to this U.S. era that we now turn.[18]

Protestant Moral Education in American Alaska

In terms of the moral education offered by the Orthodox Church, 1867 is something of a non-event. David Nordlander has argued that since terms of sale had required that all of the lands held by the Orthodox Church remain Church property even after the American takeover, the period before and after 1867 should be treated as a unit. The Russian Orthodox Church continued to fund the Alaskan mission until the Communist revolution of 1917. At the time of sale the Orthodox Church ran 17 schools and 4 orphanages. Bishop Innocent Veniaminov, excited about the possibility of an American Orthodox Church, welcomed the sale and suggested that oversight of churches and schools be transferred to San Francisco, that a new English-speaking bishop be appointed, and that church services and schools begin to be conducted in English. As the Alaskans had adapted to the Russian situation, so they were willing and able to adapt to the new American situation. By 1887, despite the withdrawal of most of the Russian population from Alaska, there were 43 schools, most founded and run by Creole or native clergy, and most offering English. That number continued to grow into the early 1900s. Indeed, for several decades after the sale the Orthodox Church was annually spending more on schooling than the United States, much to the horror of American officials, one of whom in 1887 used this fact to convince the Federal government to increase appropriations.[19]

The horrified official in question was Sheldon Jackson, Presbyterian minister, missionary, longtime activist and government agent for the territory of Alaska. Jackson is one of the more colorful figures in Alaskan history, and critical opinion about his influence and legacy has ranged widely. Some historians have portrayed Jackson as the Horace Mann of the Alaskan frontier, working tirelessly to establish public education for all Alaskans, though this interpretation has waned in recent years. Other writers have pointed out the failures of his regime and have drawn attention to the more unseemly attributes of Jackson's educational philosophy and policies. In this writer's view, Jackson should be neither celebrated nor scapegoated, for in truth he was only one actor in a drama that was being played out throughout the American west as the Indian wars drew to a close and the United States sought some way to govern its native populations.[20]

When Alaska was purchased by the United States in 1867 it was placed under military rule for ten years. By all accounts this was the worst period in Alaskan history, as lawless military authorities simply did as they pleased, looting homes and churches, flagrantly breaking laws, and perpetuating a culture of rampant alcoholism as they accomplished their mission of maximizing profits from the trade in seal fur. In 1877 due to uninterrupted protest, Congress withdrew the military, and for seven years there was no government save local vigilantism. Into this situation Sheldon Jackson and other Protestant missionaries entered, seeking to establish in Alaska the same civilization that was being spread throughout the Pacific Northwest. Jackson lobbied hard and won from Congress the so-called organic act, which established Alaska as a civil and judicial district complete with governor, court system, and sundry well-paying offices at the service of the fur industry, a generous campaign financier. Of the overall appropriations, $25,000 were dedicated to the education of all Alaskan children "without reference to race," to be overseen by the Secretary of the Interior. Jackson himself was named general agent of the fund by the Secretary and quickly went about building a school system.[21]

The appropriation, though it increased modestly over the next several years, was manifestly inadequate to the task at hand, so Jackson and other Americanizers developed very creative mechanisms for financing English language schooling. Jackson established local agents, who in most cases were Protestant missionaries, paying their salaries from the federal funds and underwriting schools run by missionaries as "contract" schools. There had been a handful of Protestant mission schools opened before 1884. Jackson himself had started one in 1878 at Fort Wrangell. It was "simple common sense" to Jackson to combine the limited resources of the various religious groups with the limited federal dollars to maximize the impact of "representatives of the civilization of the States." Mission contract schools were given on average about $130 per pupil per annum by Jackson for the industrial education of Alaskan children in English. For nine years the Federal government funded a total of 15 religious boarding schools at a total amount of $135,404.73. In sum 5,410 native children were educated in this fashion. In most cases, the various denominations sponsoring the contract schools more than matched funds. Here is a breakdown of the appropriations by denomination for the school year 1891–1892:

Denomination	Govt. Grant($)	Denominational Grant($)
Episcopalian	2,480	1,187.61
Independent	1,500	5,000
Moravian	2,000	6,613.37
Presbyterian	15,000	31,724.65
Methodist	1,000	1,953.33
Catholic	3,000	10,300
Congregational	2,000	4,107.65
Swedish Evangelical	1,000	7,325
Total	28,980	68,211.61*

* Sheldon Jackson, *Report on Education in Alaska*, 34. Lester D. Henderson, "The Development of Education in Alaska, 1867–1931" (Ph.D. Diss., Stanford Junior University, 1935), 122, 124, 125.

Some of Jackson's contemporaries, especially white Alaskans resentful that any of the meager appropriations for schooling were going to Alaskan natives, criticized this scheme as unconstitutional, and perhaps it was. But, as Stephen Haycox has noted, Jackson's approach here was no different than that taken by the Bureau of Indian Affairs when dealing with other native Americans. Post Civil-War Indian policy was at heart a religious one, carried out largely by Protestant church groups and religious leaders who dominated government positions in these areas due to Congress' barring of military personnel from superintending over Indian affairs. By 1883 on the mainland, mission societies "maintained twenty-two boarding schools and sixteen day schools with government aid." And this aid continued into the 1890s. To most white Protestants, "the employment of missionaries as public school teachers seemed quite natural, because it seemed quite natural to them to view . . . evangelical Protestant Christianity as one of the distinguishing characteristics of the civilized life."[22]

So Jackson's policy of synchronizing religious and government funds for missionary boarding schools was not a uniquely Alaskan phenomenon. But just who was included and how funds were meted out was unique. First, it is remarkable that Jackson, a Presbyterian of the late nineteenth century, was willing to underwrite schools run by the Roman Catholic Church. At the very time that nativism was redounding in force, leading to anti-parochial school legislation in several states, the Federal government was underwriting five Catholic boarding schools for Alaskan natives. Second, as many Orthodox churchmen pointed out repeatedly, Jackson's annual reports and federal appropriations completely ignored the work of the Orthodox Church. This is all the more striking given his support of Roman Catholicism.[23]

Jackson's policy was, for his day, generously non-sectarian (though Presbyterian appropriations were always the largest by far). In the mid-1880s he assembled representatives of the various denominations interested in proselytizing in Alaska, and together the group carved out non-overlapping jurisdictions: the Methodists in Unalaska, the Baptists in Kodiak, the Catholics in the mid and lower Yukon, the Presbyterians in the Southeast and Northern Arctic coast, etc. Many of these sites, especially those given to the less liturgical Protestant groups, were inhabited not by pre-contact native tribes but by largely literate Orthodox Christians living in communities with many of the amenities American missionaries would appreciate. The American groups promised not to steal from each other, but they would all steal together from the Orthodox.[24]

Stealing is not too strong a word to use. From the beginning the Protestant missionaries establishing schools in Orthodox regions met such resistance from native populations that they had to resort to coercive methods to obtain native children, ranging from English-only legislation and compulsory school laws to outright theft of children. At first many native groups were excited about the possibility of learning the "white man's ways" from the Americans, but as the educational philosophy of the missionaries was carried out upon their children, native groups grew increasingly alarmed. The conception of moral education of the Americans was quite different than that of the Russians who had established a presence earlier, and even though most of the Russians were now gone, many native communities during the 1880s and 1890s turned to the Orthodox Church as a means of resisting the erasure of their language and culture by forced civilization.

Indian boarding schools run by Protestant mission societies with government aid were in the 1880s and 1890s the great hope of white Americans for the assimilation and civilizing of native populations throughout U.S. territories. Established for the "sole purpose of severing the child's cultural and psychological connection to his native heritage," writes David Wallace Adams, "this unique institution figured prominently in the federal government's desire to find a solution to the 'Indian problem,' a method of saving Indians by destroying them." Back of this agenda was a conception of civilization that permeated American society in the nineteenth century. Born of the congress of Evangelical millennialism with Enlightenment rationalism and social Darwinism, the concept of civilization held that societies could be ranked in ascending order from the savage through the barbarous, the semi-civilized, and the civilized. Though it had taken Western Europe several centuries to attain its present state, it was hoped that through modern education backward groups would be able to advance at least to the point where they could assist and not hinder civilized life. And there were no more backward groups in the eyes of late nineteenth-century Protestant America than the native populations of Alaska. Here is James Weir, for example, arguing in *The American Naturalist* against female suffrage:

> I see, in the establishment of equal rights, the first step toward that abyss of immoral horrors so repugnant to our cultivated ethical tastes—the matriarchate. Sunk as low as this, civilized man will sink still lower—to the communal *kachims* of the Aleutian Islanders.[25]

Jackson and his missionaries sought through the contract schools to pass civilization on to native Alaskans. Several curricular positions followed from this commitment. First and foremost natives must learn English. Presbyterian missionary S. Hall Young, reflecting back on his adventures among Alaskan natives in the 1870s and 1880s, explains why:

> One strong stand, so far as I know I was the first to take, was the determination to do no translating into . . . any of the native dialects. I realized . . . that the task of making an English-speaking race of these Natives was much easier than the task of making a civilized and Christian language out of the Native languages. We should let the old tongues with their superstitions and sin die—the sooner the better—and replace these languages with that of Christian civilization, and compel the Natives in our schools to speak English and English only.[26]

English-only was the policy of the U.S. Government from its missionary teachers to its highest levels of national leadership. Jackson's views on the matter are recorded in an 1888 issue of the Sitka periodical *The North Star*:

> The Board of Home Missions has informed us that government contracts for educating Indian pupils provide for the ordinary branches of an English education to be taught, and that no books in any Indian language shall be used, or instruction given in that language to Indian pupils. The letter states that this rule will be strictly enforced in all government Indian schools. The Commissioner of Indian Affairs urges, and very forcibly too, that instruction in the vernacular is not only of no use to them but is detrimental to their speedy education and civilization.

And here is Commissioner of Education William Torrey Harris, in a personal letter written to encourage Alaskan missionary Julia Ward Howe in 1901, "We have no higher calling in the world than to be missionaries of our idea to those people who have not yet reached the Anglo-Saxon frame of mind."[27]

Throughout the 1870s and 1880s Jackson's local agents complained repeatedly of a lack of interest in English schools and a desire for instruction in Russian and native tongues. Parents frequently expressed concern that English instruction would weaken their children's commitment to the Orthodox Church. He responded by criminalizing the use of any language other than English, first in schools, and eventually in any context whatsoever. Such laws were challenged by native leaders, especially churchmen, and an uneven battle ensued. In 1891 Charles Foster, the secretary of the Treasury, wrote to Seal Islands special agent Major W.H. Williams, "Russian is not to be taught in the schools and the church officers must be restrained from interfering with the children in acquiring a knowledge of English." First compulsory attendance laws were passed, stipulating attendance of English-only schools, with fines and imprisonment the penalty for failure to comply. Historian Hubert Howe Bancroft, writing in 1886 about a native Alaskan population of whom "excepting perhaps the Chinese, there is no living nation in which the moral idea is so utterly dormant," relates the following story regarding the effects of compulsory schooling:

> In February 1881 Capt. Glass established a rule making attendance at the day school compulsory. Forcing the natives to cleanse, drain, whitewash, and number the dwellings in their village, he took an accurate census of the inmates. He then caused a tin label to be tied round the neck of each child, on which were two numbers, one of the house where he lived, and the other of the child. If a pupil was found on the streets during school hours, the numbers on his tag were reported to the teacher by a native policeman, appointed for the purpose; and unless his absence was satisfactorily explained, the parent, or chief Indian of that house, was fined. In a few weeks the attendance ran up to 250.[28]

Yet despite 20 years of such strategies, Major W.H. Williams complained in the early 1890s that American teachers "have not succeeded in teaching a pupil to read or write a sentence in the English language." Teachers' views in a report authored by Stanford University President David Starr Jordan in 1898 include the following:

> *July 31, 1887*—Native children are stupidly dull . . . [The parents] would not send a child to school if not compelled by the treasury agent to do so.
>
> *1890*—It seems incredible but it is true that young men and women who have been to school here for several years do not know how to speak or read a sentence of the English language . . . There has been one day each week devoted to the Russian school, which, in my opinion, has a bad effect upon the children in their attempt to master the English tongue, and I, therefore, respectfully suggest that the practice of teaching Russian to the school children be abolished.[29]

Such suggestions were taken to heart, and beginning in 1910 when the Department of Labor assumed responsibility of native schools from the local agents a more rigorous enforcement of the English-only policy was instituted. Orthodox Church schools and orphanages, some of which had been in operation for 75 years or more, were forcibly closed by the Federal government. Despite the fact that all of the 23 new Orthodox parish schools that had opened between 1890 and 1904 included English instruction in their curriculum, a systematic purge of Orthodox education was undertaken by the Alaskan authorities. The result was that, despite continued resistance from natives, over the next several decades all but two of Alaska's 21 native languages were killed off, and the two remaining survived only meagerly. Russian was treated no more kindly. In 1886 Jackson received a request from Father Vladmir Donskoy, priest of the Russian Orthodox church in Sitka and author of a book in Tlingit:

> Sir:
> In behalf of the Russian speaking residents of Sitka, I respectfully request your permission to occupy one hour each school day in teaching the Russian language in the public school. My and their only desire is that Russian children while learning the English shall not be permitted to lose all knowledge of their mother language. I ask and shall expect no compensation, and will most cheerfully take into my Russian class American children who may desire to be taught how to speak the Russian.

The request was denied. Schools were closed, fines meted out to recalcitrants, and children forcibly removed to boarding schools, sometimes quite distant. In 1903, for example, there were 81 Alaskan native children enrolled at the Indian school in Carlisle, PA.[30]

The Orthodox did not give up without a fight. Archimandrite Anatoli, writing in the 1899 *American Orthodox Messenger*, fumed that "the substance of the entire educational scheme in Alaska may be reduced to a propaganda carried on among the Orthodox natives by the different Protestant denominations, the government schools being used as tools in this campaign work." Anatoli noted that on Kodiak Island there were hundreds of Orthodox children in schools and orphanages yet the only government salaried position was for a teacher in the lone Baptist home with 28 children in attendance. Despite such tactics Anatoli was convinced that the Protestants would have little success because Alaskans were "repulsed by the 'civilizing' methods practiced by the missionaries." The following year Hieromonk Antonius petitioned the American government to cease its destructive policies and defended *tserkovnost* against what he dubbed the "crushing egotism and coarse materialism" of American society:

> The school can bring living fruit only if supported, in word and in deed, by the community.... It is not enough to build schoolhouses, to fill them with aids to learning, to place them in charge of patented teachers. We must ourselves live the moral and spiritual life which we wish to inculcate into the learners of our school.[31]

But such words were powerless against overwhelming American consensus backed up by police power. Petitions to the Alaskan and federal authorities, such as that of the Aleuts in 1916 to be permitted to speak their language and to reopen the church school that had been forcibly closed in 1912, fell on deaf ears. William Amarok and Michael Oleksa's detailed account of these conflicts concludes:

> Eventually, the increasing number of federally funded monolingual schools and the decreasing of financial support from Europe for the Aleut schools ended this uneven struggle. The Russian Revolution and civil war suddenly and completely cut off all funds for the remaining Aleut schools. In a few scattered communities, elders and teachers continued to teach children the four R's for another thirty or forty years. But ultimately, Sheldon Jackson's assimilationist policies completely dominated Alaskan education.[32]

Monolingualism was not the only curricular policy emerging from the civilization mandate, nor was contract schooling the only creative mechanism for funding native assimilation. When Congress, worried about constitutionality, stopped funding mission contract schools in 1894, Jackson turned to another potential source of revenue. Beginning in the late 1890s Jackson imported from Siberia reindeer and herdsmen, hiring educational officials to teach native Alaskans how to herd. The goals of this program were commensurate with the civilizing mandate, as Commissioner William Torrey Harris explained in his annual report of 1896. For Harris the reindeer were "the schoolbooks and apparatus necessary for the education of the western and northern natives." Herding would break these tribes of their nomadic hunting and fishing economy, "they must take the long step from nomadic fishermen and hunters to dwellers in villages with permanent employments that will support them and also render them useful to the white population." But not only would herding advance them up the chain of civilization and make them of economic use to white people, it would also teach them key principles of Christian civilization like individualism and acquisitiveness, or as Harris put it, "the education of these natives in thrift." Only the most "trustworthy natives—those ambitious enough to learn the civilization of the white man, those ambitious to hold and increase property" would be given a herd to manage.[33]

Again, this aim was consistent with Indian policy throughout the Pacific territories. It was recognized by many that tribalism itself was holding back natives from appreciating the essence of American life. Hence the General Allotment Act of 1887, commonly known as the Dawes Act, that began the process of subdividing reservations into individual plots in an effort to make natives into yeoman farmers like the European peasantry displacing them in the region. Superintendent of Indian Schools John Oberly endorsed the policy in 1888, noting that the Indian must be weaned from "the degrading communism of the tribal-reservation system" until he is filled "with the exalting egotism of American civilization, so that he will say 'I' instead of 'We' and 'This is mine' instead of 'This is ours.'" Merrill Gates, president of the Lake Mohonk Conference, concurred:

> We need *to awaken in him wants*. In his dull savagery he must be touched by the wings of the divine angel of discontent.... Discontent with the tepee and the starving rations of the Indian camp in winter is needed to get the Indian out of the blanket and into trousers,— and trousers with a pocket in them, and with a pocket that *aches to be filled with dollars!*[34]

The problem with the reindeer idea was that it seemed to make more dollars for Presbyterian mission activities than for native herdsmen. The allotment of reindeer was too small to sustain a livelihood, and most government agents knew little about herding. The mismanagement involved in what today might be called "Reindeergate" cost Jackson his job in 1906. His successor, Harlan Updegraaf, improved the administrative infrastructure of the educational system but did not veer from the vision established by his predecessor. "The education of the natives of Alaska," wrote Updegraaf in his 1909 annual report, "is conceived as meaning their advancement in civilization." Under Updegraaf and his successor W.T. Loop, Jackson's local agents were replaced by more centralized leadership in the Department of Labor, leading to a more rigorous suppression of non-English education and strict enforcement of compulsory school laws. In 1913 the legislature's compulsory school law required native children to attend only Bureau schools. Failure to do so would result in a fine of $5 to $20 and imprisonment failing payment.[35]

The year 1917 serves as a fitting end to this chapter for two reasons. On one hand, as has been mentioned, it was the date of the Russian Revolution, whereupon the Russian Orthodox Church was thrown into chaos and its funding for mission activity in Alaska and everywhere else completely cut off. After that date, whatever education in Orthodox Christianity and in native and Russian languages Alaskans received would have to come from within the community alone. 1917 was also a key date in the history of American educational policy in Alaska. Despite the 1884 organic act's original intent to create schools that would serve "regardless of race," over the ensuing decades, especially after the 1905 Nelson Act, a segregated, dual-system of public education had developed in Alaska. Natives were trained in federally funded industrial schools while whites and "children of mixed blood who lead a civilized life" were educated in public schools financed territorially, largely through the sale of liquor and trade licenses. But in 1918 Alaska was scheduled to go "bone dry" under Prohibition. In 1917, anticipating a funding crisis for the white schools, a full-scale reworking of the Alaskan education law was undertaken. The result, the Uniform School Act of 1917, systematized and bureaucratized the dual system of segregated schooling that had been developing over the preceding four decades. Funding for white schools now would come from property tax as well as what territory funds remained after the demise of liquor licensing, while the Federal Bureau of Education would oversee the training of natives. And so the American policy of segregated yet assimilationist schooling for native Alaskans in an English-only, anti-Orthodox, anti-tribal morality of individual acquisitiveness and servant trades was finalized. Its tragic results are with us still.[36]

Notes

1. For good histories written in this tradition see B. Edward McClellan, *Moral Education in America: Schools and the Shaping of Character from Colonial Times to the Present* (New York: Teachers College, 1999); James Davison Hunter, *The Death of Character: Moral Education in an Age without Good or Evil* (New York: Basic Books, 2000), 31–78; James W. Fraser,

Between Church and State: Religion and Public Education in a Multicultural America (New York: St. Martin's Griffin, 1999); Douglas McKnight, *Schooling, the Puritan Imperative, and the Molding of an American National Identity: Education's "Errand into the Wilderness"* (Mahwah, NJ: Erlbaum, 2003).

2. Of course the Protestant conception of virgin territory was a fiction. That the native populations of North America were viewed as having no civilization or religion speaks more to the anthropological obtuseness of European Protestants than to the native situation. On the ironies of New England attitudes toward the land and its native populations see Alden T. Vaughan, ed., *New England Encounters: Indians and Euroamericans ca. 1600–1850* (Boston: Northeastern University Press, 1999); William Cronon, *Changes in the Land: Indians, Colonists, and the Ecology of New England* (New York: Hill and Wang, 1983).

3. For a full account of this history, see S. Frederick Starr, *Russia's American Colony* (Durham, NC: Duke University Press, 1987); Hector Chevigny, *Russian America: The Great Alaskan Venture, 1741–1867* (New York: Viking, 1965); Hubert Howe Bancroft, *History of Alaska, 1730–1885* (Darien, CN: Hafner Publishing Co., 1970).

4. Bishop Gregory (Afonsky), *A History of the Orthodox Church in Alaska, 1794–1917* (Kodiak: St. Herman's Theological Seminary, 1977), 31–32. Richard A. Pierce, ed., *The Russian Orthodox Religious Mission in America, 1794–1837* (Kingston, ON: Limestone Press, 1978), 62–63, 146, 158, 162, 168, 171.

5. Afonsky, *History of the Orthodox Church*, 68–69. Paul D. Garrett, *St. Innocent, Apostle to America* (Crestwood, NY: St. Vladimir's Seminary Press, 1979). Lydia T. Black, "Ivan Pan'kov: Architect of Aleut Literacy," in Stephen W. Haycox and Mary Childers Mangusso, eds., *An Alaska Anthology: Interpreting the Past* (Seattle: University of Washington Press, 1996), 43–65.

6. Richard L. Dauenhauer, *Conflicting Visions in Alaskan Education* (Juneau, AL: Tlingit Readers, Inc., 1997), 7. Golovin cited in Jerome Lincoln Starr, "The Cultural and Educational Development of Aborigines and Settlers in Russian America, 1784–1867" (Ph.D. diss., New York University, 1961), 364. Michael Oleksa and Richard Dauenhauer, "Education in Russian America" in Gary W. Stein, ed., *Education in Alaska's Past* (Anchorage: Alaska Historical Society, 1983), 58–59. For literacy rates and native authors, see Richard L. Dauenhauer, "Spiritual Epiphany of Aleut" in *Orthodox Alaska* 8 (1979): 13–42. Figures for Unalaska literacy in Starr, "Cultural and Educational Development," 365.

7. Hector Chevigny, *Russian America: The Great Alaskan Venture, 1741–1867* (New York: Viking, 1965), 247. P. Tikhmenov, *Notes on the History of Education in Russian-American Colonies from Origin of the Russian-American Company and its Activity to the Present Time, 1861*, trans. Dimitri Krenov (Seattle: Works Progress Administration, 1937), 10.

8. On forced conversions, see Paul W. Werth, "Orthodoxy as Ascription (and Beyond): Religious Identity on the Edges of the Orthodox Community, 1740–1917," in Valerie A. Kivelson and Robert H. Greene, eds., *Orthodox Russia: Belief and Practice Under the Tsars* (University Park: Pennsylvania State University Press, 2003), 239–251. On the Patristic revival, see Sophie Deicha, "Patristics in Russia, the 19th Century," *Greek Orthodox Theological Review*, 44, 4 (Spring 1999): 575–585. On *tserkovnost* see Vera Shevzov, "Letting the People into Church: Reflections on Orthodoxy and Community in Late Imperial Russia," in Kivelson and Greene, *Orthodox Russia*, 59–80.

9. Acts 2:6. On language in the Orthodox Church, see Anthony-Emil N. Tachiaos, *Cyril and Methodius of Thessalonica: The Acculturation of the Slavs* (Crestwood, NY: St. Vladimir's Seminary Press, 2001).

10. John Dewey, *School and Society* (Chicago: University of Chicago Press, 1899); Ellwood Patterson Cubberley, *Public Education in the United States* (New York: Houghton

Mifflin, 1919), 332–364; Bernard Bailyn, *Education in the Forming of American Society* (Chapel Hill: University of North Carolina Press, 1960), 14–49.

11. On the monks, see John H. Erickson, *Orthodox Christians in America* (New York: Oxford University Press, 1999) and Andrei A. Znamenski, *Shamanism and Christianity: Native Encounters with Russian Orthodox Missions in Siberia and Alaska, 1829–1917* (Westport, CT: Greenwood Press, 1999), 47–63.

12. On salvation, see Kallistos Ware, *The Orthodox Way* (Crestwood, NY: St. Vladimir's Seminary Press, 1979). Sergei Kan, *Memory Eternal: Tlingit Culture and Russian Orthodox Christianity, 1794–1994* (Seattle: University of Washington Press, 1999), xix; Dauenhauer, *Conflicting Visions*, 12.

13. Vera Shevzov, "Letting the People into Church," 66, 68. Founding texts in recent feminist and communitarian moral thinking include Carol Gilligan, *In a Different Voice: Psychological Theory and Women's Development* (Cambridge, MA: Harvard University Press, 1982) and Robert N. Bellah, et al., *Habits of the Heart: Individualism and Commitment in American Life* (New York: Harper & Row, 1985). For an account of these and other thinkers working with the tensions between community and individualism, see Wilfred McClay, *The Masterless: Self and Society in Modern America* (Chapel Hill: University of North Carolina Press, 1994), 281–295.

14. On these and other cultural parallels, see Znamenski, *Shamanism and Christianity* and Kan, *Memory Eternal*.

15. Znamenski, *Shamanism and Christianity*, 3–4. James Van Stone, *Athapaskan Adaptations: Hunters and Fishermen of the Subarctic Forests* (Chicago: Aldine Publishing Company, 1974), 125, cited in Znamenski, *Shamanism and Christianity*, 17.

16. Znamenski, *Shamanism and Christianity*, 30–31.

17. Ibid., 106.

18. Ibid., 117.

19. David Nordlander, "Veniaminov and the Expansion of Orthodoxy in Russian America," *Pacific Historical Review* 64, 1 (1995): 19–36. Michael Oleksa, *Alaskan Missionary Spirituality* (New York: Paulist Press, 1987), 251. Constance J. Tarasar and John H. Erickson, eds., *Orthodox America 1794–1976: Development of the Orthodox Church in America* (Syosset, NY: Orthodox Church in America, 1975), 112.

20. For a recent celebratory view, see Nathaniel H. Cole, *A General History of Public School Finance in Alaska, Operating and Capital Costs* (Alaska: Alaska Department of Education, 1985). A wide range of views is presented in the essays collected in Gary Stein, ed., *Education in Alaska's Past* (Anchorage: Alaska Historical Society, 1983). Jackson's own views on Alaskan natives and education can be read in his *Report on Education in Alaska With Maps and Illustrations* (Washington: Government Printing Office, 1886). His report admits the high levels of literacy and educational accomplishment among many Alaskan groups even as it calls for compulsory English education to replace it. See pp. 11–23, 30–33.

21. On the early history of U.S. Alaska, see Ted C. Hinckley, *The Americanization of Alaska, 1867–1897* (Palo Alto, CA: Pacific Books, 1972). Sheldon Jackson, *Report on Education in Alaska*, 42.

22. Stephen W. Haycox, "Sheldon Jackson and the Constitutionality of the Contract School System: A Chapter in the History of Federal Indian Policy," in Gary Stein, ed., *Education in Alaska's Past* (Anchorage: Alaska Historical Society, 1983), 28, 29, 30, 31.

23. On nativism and education during the 1880s and 1890s, see Lloyd P. Jorgenson, *The State and the Non-Public School, 1825–1925* (Columbia: University of Missouri Press, 1987), 146–204.

24. Michael Oleksa and Richard Dauenhauer, "Education in Russian America" in Gary Stein, ed., *Education in Alaska's Past* (Anchorage: Alaska Historical Society, 1983), 62.
25. David Wallace Adams, *Education for Extinction: American Indians and the Boarding School Experience, 1875–1928* (Lawrence, KS: University Press of Kansas, 1995), x–xi. On the concept of civilization see Milton Gaither, *American Educational History Revisited: A Critique of Progress* (New York: Teachers College Press, 2003), 58–77, and Adams, *Education for Extinction*, 12–21. James Weir, Jr., "The Effect of Female Suffrage on Posterity," *The American Naturalist* 29 (1895): 825.
26. Quoted in Michael Krauss, *Alaska Native Languages: Past, Present, and Future* (Fairbanks, AK: University of Alaska, 1972), 23.
27. Jackson cited in Dauenhauer, *Conflicting Visions*, 14. Harris cited in Glenn Smith, "Education for the Natives of Alaska: The Work of the United States Bureau of Education, 1884–1931," *Journal of the West* 6, 3 (1967): 442.
28. Foster cited in Henderson, "Development of Education in Alaska," 67. Herbert Howe Bancroft, *History of Alaska, 1730–1885* (San Francisco: A.L. Bancroft and Co., 1886), 726–727.
29. Williams cited in Henderson, "Development of Education in Alaska," 67. Jordan cited in Dauenhauer, *Conflicting Visions*, 18.
30. Michael Oleksa, *Orthodox Alaska: A Theology of Mission* (Crestwood, NY: St. Vladimir's Seminary Press, 1992), 171–184. Dauenhauer, *Conflicting Visions*, pp. 38–39; Henderson, "Development of Education in Alaska," 105.
31. Cited in Michael Oleksa, ed., *Alaskan Missionary Spirituality*, 254, 256, 257–258, 261, 262. For a full account of native responses to Americanization, see Michael Oleksa, "Native Alaskan Resistance to Assimilation: The Legacy of Saints Cyril and Methodius," *Sourozh* 47 (Fall 1992): 4–18.
32. Barbara Torrey, *Slaves of the Harvest* (St. Paul Island, AL: Tanadgusix Corporation, 1978), 113. William Allen Amarok and Rev. Michael J. Oleksa, "The Suppression of the Aleuts: The Conflict in Alaskan Education, 1876–1916," *St. Vladimir's Theological Quarterly* 28, 2 (1984): 111–112.
33. Harris cited in Henderson, "The Development of Education in Alaska," 263, 262.
34. Oberly and Gates cited in David Wallace Adams, *Education for Extinction*, 23.
35. Updegraaf cited in Henderson, "Development of Education in Alaska," 115.
36. Henderson, "Development of Education in Alaska," 148. For more recent history of Alaskan natives see, Oleksa, *Orthodox Alaska*, 187–205; Dorothy Miriam Jones, *A Century of Servitude: Pribilof Aleuts under U.S. Rule* (Lanham, MD: University Press of America, 1980); David H. Getches, *Law and Alaska Native Education: The Influence of Federal and State Legislation upon Education of Rural Alaskan Natives* (Fairbanks: Center for Northern Educational Research, 1977); Judith Kleinfeld, *Alaskan Native Education: Issues in the Nineties* (Anchorage: Institute of Social and Economic Research, 1992); Diane Beth Hirshberg, "Northern Exploring: A Case Study of Non-Native Alaskan Policymakers' Social Constructions of Alaskan Natives as Target Populations" (Ph.D. Diss., University of California, Los Angeles, 2001).

This page intentionally left blank

Chapter 5

Social Capital and the Common Schools

John L. Rury

Over the past several decades much has been written about the development of the common school and its contributions to education in the nineteenth-century United States. As many historians have noted, the central purposes of the common school were essentially moral: imparting civic virtues, building character, and preserving basic social values. In his path-breaking work on the history of moral education, B. Edward McClellan observed that "(Americans) expected schools . . . to extend and reinforce the moral education of the home as they taught children elementary skills of literacy and numeracy." In fact, McClellan argued that the common schools came to play an increasingly important role in moral education with the passage of time.[1]

While there has emerged a broad consensus among historians on the moral purposes of the common school, there is considerably less agreement as to how these critical functions were undertaken or accomplished. This is especially striking in light of the common school's many achievements, and its status as one of the celebrated institutions of its time. McClellan, like many others, has noted the moralistic tone and content of the period's curricular materials, including the famous McGuffey series of readers. But most of these schools functioned in a social context that also helped to define their purposes, and contributed a great deal to their success. As Wayne Fuller, the principal historian of the country school, has observed, the students in these schools "owed much to their school-district community for their interest in education and success in life."[2] This essay considers the role of this social context in shaping the development of common schools as an institutional form, and giving definition to their role in moral education.

In 1988, James Coleman published an article in the *American Journal of Sociology* introducing the concept of social capital and outlining its relevance to education. This marked the start of a rapid integration of this theoretical construct into social theory and research on education and a wide variety of additional topics. Most of the historical writing about common schools, of course, occurred well before the appearance of Coleman's seminal article. There arises, consequently, the question of just how this new element of social science theory and research may be related to the historical question of the common school. More pertinent to the purposes of this volume is the matter of how social capital might be relevant to comprehending the moral contributions of common schools in the nineteenth century. Drawing upon Coleman and other social scientists, this essay will explore these questions at some length, examining historical evidence in light of relatively recent developments in sociology and other social sciences, and identifying possibly fruitful lines of research for the future.

Social Capital, Past and Present

Perhaps the most fundamental feature of social capital is that it resides in relationships. According to Coleman, social capital is rooted in the bonds that people have with one another, and in the relations between other types of social actors, such as institutions or other corporate entities. The basic premise is that certain types of relationships—or specific qualities of relationships—are endowed with properties that make them productive. Hence the term "capital," which suggests that such relations, or aspects of them, represent a tangible resource for individuals or for groups of people as they strive to succeed in various contexts. "Like other forms of capital," Coleman wrote, "social capital is productive, making possible the achievement of certain ends that in its absence would not be possible." For society, social capital can be a vital source of social, institutional and economic advancement, as it enhances the productive capacities of individuals and groups. As Coleman suggested, social capital can be essential to realizing the benefits of human capital, permitting the transfer of skills and knowledge necessary for intergenerational transmission of various productive capacities and modalities. Put more simply, social capital, in a variety of forms and qualities, is essential to success in the very broad process of education.

From an empirical standpoint, however, social capital represents a very difficult problem. It is not easy to identify; in fact it is downright elusive. Coleman argued that social capital "inheres in the structure of relations between actors and among actors" and thus is indeterminate in quality and "not completely fungible but may be specific to certain activities." In other words, "a given form of social capital that is valuable for facilitating certain actions may be useless or even harmful for others."[3] This makes it both an intriguing and troublesome concept for research purposes. With respect to the common school, consequently, it is necessary to begin by imagining the sorts of relationships that might have represented social capital, and identifying the ways that it may have contributed to the institution's moral purposes.

There was a good deal more to Coleman's argument, however, that has proven helpful to other researchers interested in education. He suggested, for instance, that social capital depends on the "trustworthiness of the social environment" and "the extent of obligations" that actors—of various kinds—have to one another. He cited the importance of "information channels" in the definition of relationships that help to facilitate action—and one might also speculate that such information-oriented relationships help in the transmission or production of human capital. He also argued that social norms and sanctions that are widely observed can comprise a vital form of social capital. In this regard, he specifically noted that "norms in a community that support and provide effective rewards for high achievement in school greatly facilitate the schools' task." Finally, Coleman also specified the importance of "closure" in relationships, or the definition of interlocking relationships that are necessary for the enforcement of norms and social sanctions, suggesting that such networks of relationships make norms of behavior effective. They help to broaden the purview of social capital, investing individual relationships with greater power. Specifically, Coleman postulated that a high degree of closure in relationships can help enforce social norms, and add to the "trustworthiness of social structures that allow the proliferation of obligations and expectations."[4]

Coleman's definition of social capital was quickly embraced among sociologists, and eventually found expression in the work of educational researchers, although not as much as might be expected, especially given his interest in schooling when introducing the concept. It also drew the attention of other social scientists, particularly political scientists and economists. Social capital became famously associated with the writings of Robert Putnam, the Harvard political scientist who argued that Americans are losing touch with one another and the rich tradition of associationalism that has marked the country's history.[5] Putnam's work has generated a flurry of studies focusing on national "stocks" of social capital and ways that it affected political behavior, but some researchers also followed Coleman's lead in exploring ways that the concept may be useful in understanding education. Most of the latter studies looked for evidence of social capital as a factor promoting school success, especially in immigrant communities, among certain types of students and their families, or in particular social settings. Some research was quantitative, assigning variables to represent the influence of social capital in light of Coleman's suggestions. Proxy factors, such as family size or membership in organizations, were taken as evidence of the strength of relationships, and in various analyses produced inconsistent results when linked to school achievement.[6] As noted earlier, since social capital is impossible to observe directly, it has proven very difficult to measure obliquely. While it is possible to imagine its importance, it is another matter to demonstrate it thoroughly.

Historians have been considerably slower in exploring the utility of social capital as an explanatory factor in educational development. While it has received more attention from political and social historians, in two noteworthy instances it has been considered in connection with schools, both appearing in a special issue of the *Journal of Interdisciplinary History*. In one, Reed Ueda examined the experiences of immigrant children in secondary schools and settlement house youth groups, institutions that self-consciously sought to foster associational bonds in their clientele.[7] In the other, economists Claudia Goldin and Lawrence Katz examined the rise of high schools in the first half of the twentieth century, arguing that social capital was a critical factor in boosting secondary enrollments in the nation's agricultural heartland. Much of the evidence that Goldin and Katz presented is quantitative, and like other researchers, they relied upon proxy variables to capture the effects of social capital. In this case, factors such as social and cultural homogeneity, economic wealth, and demographic stability were deemed conditions contributing to the formation of social capital in support of secondary school expansion. "Smaller towns and villages in the United States were the locus of (this) activity," Goldin and Katz observed, "high school attendance there was the greatest. We suspect that these small towns and villages were reservoirs of social capital that helped to fuel the high school movement."[8] In other words, relationships that spanned these communities contributed to the development of a broad consensus of opinion about the importance of secondary schooling, and helped to persuade young men and women to attend them in large numbers. This is an argument with important implications for the history of education, some of which will be explored herein.

The still budding literature on social capital as a factor in social development, in that case, provides a few clues about where to begin in considering the role of the common school in fostering moral education and academic achievement. One is the importance of certain conditions that appear to have been basic requirements for the formation of social capital across communities. If Goldin and Katz were correct, the absence of cultural diversity and economic disparity allowed greater communication within a community, and facilitated the transmission of relevant values across generations. Evidence of associational activity, sharing resources and upholding norms, also can be considered a sign of social capital that may have contributed to public support of education. These and other indicators can illuminate patterns of association in the past, and help to formulate a research agenda for further investigation of these questions.

Historical Circumstances of the Common Schools

To begin an examination of these issues, it is necessary to consider what is known about the social context of the early common schools. Across much of the northern tier of states, the schools that existed in the nineteenth-century countryside had changed relatively little since colonial times. These were profoundly local institutions, created by small communities of farm families. Most were isolated, small in size, conducted for relatively short periods of time, and taught by itinerant masters with little formal training. They also had become quite ubiquitous by the third decade of the century. By and large, the typical rural district school served an area of two to four square miles, accessible by walking, and populated by some twenty to fifty families. Thus by the early nineteenth century they literally dotted the countryside, serving millions of children in small, intimate settings bound by an immediate community. Levels of enrollment, attendance at any type of school for any part of the year, were already quite high in the opening decades of the century, over seventy percent for children aged 9 to 13. On the whole, Americans clearly valued this form of formal education, as only Germany had higher enrollments in 1830, and by 1880 the United States led the world.[9]

It is not unreasonable to ask why rural Americans sent their children to school in such high numbers. The answers historians have provided are related to civic education and to religious values. As Lawrence Cremin observed of the schools, "they provided youngsters with an opportunity to become literate in an increasingly standard American English," along with critical moral purposes: "a common belief system combining undenominational Protestantism and nonpartisan patriotism."[10] Preparing future citizens for the responsibilities of voting and holding office, and thinking about the important issues facing state, nation, and local community, were understandable preoccupations of educational reformers. But there was considerable unevenness in regional attendance levels, a pattern suggesting that political socialization was not universally valued. The more salient purpose seems to have been religious beliefs, or perhaps theological traditions, grounded in local customs. Historians have noted a clear and persistent association between enrollment levels and religious orientation. So-called Yankee Protestants, emanating from New England and the Mid-Atlantic States, displayed the strongest attachment to the common school. Theirs was a tradition that emphasized personal reading of the Bible, and the perpetuation of a literate culture focused on a range of additional texts. They also lived in a rapidly commercializing world, where the assessment of documents and the ability to calculate were vitally important. Thus it is possible to speculate that a combination of cultural (religious) and functional (economic) influences probably contributed to the growth of school attendance in most settings.[11]

Given this, potential connections to social capital are not hard to imagine. As Goldin and Katz noted in discussing secondary schools, small, tightly knit communities were logical repositories of social capital. This certainly seems to have been true of the rural communities that established the district schools of the early nineteenth century. These were places without much inequality. As Hamlin Garland recalled of his "typical" rural boyhood, "our neighbors all lived in the same restricted fashion as ourselves, in barren little houses of wood or stone, owning few books, reading only weekly papers." Social status was defined by deeds and character: "it was a pure democracy, wherein my father was a leader and my mother beloved by all who knew her . . . and in all of the social affairs of the township we fully shared."[12] The latter point was especially significant, as many observers remarked upon the long-standing relationships that often animated these communities. In his detailed account of "everyday life" in this period, Jack Larkin has suggested that "the villages and neighborhoods of the northeastern countryside had intricate social webs," consisting of women socializing on a regular basis and men lending one another assistance in times of need. Indeed, Larkin noted that "neighborhoods were often roughly defined by the boundaries of rural school districts," often the only institution that a particular collection of families shared in a given district. As Wayne Fuller put it, "the Midwestern school community was like an extended family," one that provided "a sense of security and encouragement." Within these rather well-defined and intimate communities, it was not uncommon for residents to see one another regularly, Larkin observed, as they "visited and traded with their neighbors weekly if not daily." Of course, they also saw each other at church, and at civic celebrations such as the Fourth of July. Larkin tells of women visiting the sick or infirm and men congregating at the country stores during the slow winter months, occasions when stories were told and politics debated.[13]

Of course, life in the nineteenth-century countryside was hardly a series of social events; it also entailed untold hours of arduous labor, much of it in isolation. But work also was another opportunity for sharing, probably even more than purely social gatherings, especially around such critical moments as harvest and planting. These tasks often were not as difficult as they were tiresome, and enjoining the aid of family, friends and other community members became a well-established rite in many places. "Neighbors were notified rather than invited," one contemporary observed, "for it was an affair of mutual assistance." Corn husking was a popular occasion for such cooperation, along with friendly competition, but rural residents also came together for clearing trees, de-stoning fields, and raising barns, houses or other structures. The same spirit extended to other tasks, including the founding of public institutions. "Cooperative effort was necessary in early enterprises of a quasi-public sort such as building of schools," Merle Curti wrote in his influential study of Trempealeau County, Wisconsin, "but mutual helpfulness also operated in purely private relationships." Indeed, Paul Theobald has noted that the schools themselves were affected by the exigencies of rural life. "A cloudy day threatening to rain on several acres of hay" could result in children being pressed into service, reflecting a widely held understanding of shared obligations. While a general spirit of courtesy and teamwork animated these sentiments, and few participants counted the favors granted, over time this process helped to define a web of mutual responsibility and trust that cemented the bonds of local communities.[14]

All of this appears to have been very much in line with Coleman's definition of social capital; indeed, it might be considered an axiomatic case. Coleman grounded his ideas in a theory of rational action, wherein individuals or groups informally exchange favors, leading some to accumulate a stock of commitments that could be considered a form of wealth. This was social capital in perhaps its most tangible form, but it also resided in the networks of association that underlay such obligations, patterns of communication, and shared responsibility that facilitated action. In his study of rural schooling in the Midwest, Theobald has argued that it was the most long-standing members of local districts who were likely to become involved in school affairs, drawing upon their knowledge of the community and commitment to core values. This observation is consistent with Coleman's finding that adult participation in informal networks often resulted in interlocking relationships that served to reinforce essential values and mores, norms of behavior that governed a given community, especially with respect to education.[15] This sort of moral environment was yet another manifestation of social capital, a stock of behavioral expectations that guided the development of a group, neighborhood or district, but especially its most impressionable residents, children, and youth. Of course, it also is possible to idealize the social environment of early district schools. Contemporaries were quick to note that the reality of schooling in many towns was a far cry from ideal. Even the most idyllic of places had their share of petty conflicts and grievances.[16] But the overall atmosphere of many small towns appears to have been well suited to the development of relations of mutual assistance and shared values.

Coleman hypothesized that the extent of parental relationships outside of a school context would define the density and potency of this type of social capital. The associational traditions and mores of the rural United States, particularly in the Northeast and upper Midwest, would seem to represent an especially fertile ground for its development. As Curti noted, "the helpfulness brought out on successive frontiers from the beginning of American history has influenced the American character," as original values were passed from one generation to the next.[17] For the youth of these communities, these maxims must have been difficult to ignore, much less escape. The continual sharing of resources, exchanging opinion and judgement, and providing mutual amusement no doubt created a field of activity that comprised a powerful vehicle of moral training. Such was the immediate social context of many of the nation's common schools through much of the nineteenth century, and the setting in which their educational objectives were undertaken.

Given the physical conditions of most common schooling, the role of its community setting must have been very important indeed. As most districts were quite small, the actual school buildings were famously diminutive and often suffered from a good deal of neglect. The schools were un-graded, which meant that everyone was instructed together, and as Larkin has noted, "the custom of reciting aloud often made their interiors a constant buzz of discordant voices."[18] These schools may have helped to impart basic literacy and calculation skills, but they built on a foundation established by Protestant family values. Reading and writing were abilities highly prized in most devout Protestant households, simply because they were considered essential to piety and to basic communication. Consequently, historians agree that most rural children probably were introduced to reading at home and in church before they were asked to read anything in school. Fuller wrote that former students "recalled the times their mothers or fathers had read to them such literature as was in the house, and how their mothers, who had never heard of 'reading readiness,' taught them their ABC's and even to make out words, so that more than one of them knew how to read when they first entered school." This was an early expression of expectations at work in the history of American education, especially in the North, a behavioral norm reinforced by the local community. It can be considered an indication of social capital at work in support of elementary academic achievement, but it also contributed to moral education. In a similar fashion, schools also conveyed basic mathematical and computational principles, along with a smattering of history, geography, and "moral philosophy," depending on the teacher's knowledge and interests. The moral lessons conveyed in such lessons were woven into the fabric of instruction, through the readers of the day, but also through the expressions, words, and actions of the teacher. As Carl Kaestle has noted, "far more emphasis was placed on character, discipline, virtue and good habits than on literacy, arithmetic skills, analytical ability, or knowledge of the world." This included the all-important question of comportment, as children were disciplined for bad behavior, praised for obedience and conformity, and were required to be respectful of others. These too were moral lessons, often those with the greatest impact.[19]

The role of the teacher was critical to the moral purposes of common schooling, but success also hinged decisively on the attitudes of parents. The cooperation and attentiveness of children often depended heavily on parental support for the school, a point widely observed by reformers of the day. A veteran common school teacher, Hiram Orcutt, noted that discord between parents and teachers imperiled the educational process. "The influence of such opposition," he wrote, "is always destructive of good order, and tends to foster a spirit of rebellion in the school." Success depended critically upon cooperation between school and household, with both emphasizing the importance of students behaving properly. Orcutt advised that education occurred best when "the children imbibed the same spirit at home, and brought it to the school-room." The chief instructional technique of the day was recitation, requiring students to repeat portions of text that they had memorized while reading either at school or home. It was a form of training that called for an unusually high degree of orderly behavior. There was scarcely any advanced instruction, as most teachers knew little beyond the "three Rs," and not much continuity since teachers seldom remained longer than a year or two. On top of this, a heavy emphasis on discipline prevailed, with rules often enforced by harsh physical punishments, measures that certainly required at least tacit parental approval. There also were contests and games, such as spelling bees or multiplication tournaments that helped to break up the monotony, and storytelling occasionally made for memorable lessons. But classroom management was vital to the entire enterprise. As Orcutt noted, the role of parents in securing this end was substantial: "while (the teacher) reveals to them his views and plans for the management and instruction of his school, they should give assurances of their willingness and determination to aid him in carrying out his measures."[20]

In short, without a great deal of parental support for the goals and objectives of such schools it is unlikely that children would have undertaken such a tedious and disagreeable road to learning. Carl Kaestle noted that when parents withdrew their support of a teacher in one rural district, attendance fell to just nine students. Such incidents, while relatively rare, demonstrated the critical connections between home and school during this era, and even between households. Benjamin Justice has described the relative infrequency in which religious conflict disrupted the district schools in late nineteenth-century New York. In rural communities he noted "a strong undertone of compromise beneath the waves of rhetoric and reform over religious education" at the national level. Common interests in the welfare of the children and community advancement helped to overcome occasional sectarian squabbles. Parental commitment to the schools, after all, was often reinforced by the attitudes and values of other adults in the immediate community, who saw the children regularly in the course of day-to-day activities. Thus it is probably accurate to say that the achievements of nineteenth-century rural schools were significantly dependent on the degree or amount of social capital extant in a given community, available to students, and upheld by their families and neighbors. Such sentiments were reinforced by community events staged around the schools. "To see their parents and other members of the community crowded into the little schoolroom on a Friday afternoon or evening. as they recited the pieces they had learned, or sang songs, or spelled down their class," Wayne Fuller wrote, "assured them of their parents' and the community's approval of their schoolwork and helped kindle their own interest in learning."[21] The schools succeeded when the importance of learning basic lessons was widely agreed upon, and the necessity of mastering them was impressed on children by a dense web of relationships.

It is possible to hypothesize, in that case, that the apparent success of the common school, its popularity and strong reputation for proper moral education, were largely due to the circumstances of its social setting. In particular, it seems likely that the dynamic and inter-dependant quality of life in many rural communities contributed to the formation of stocks of social capital that served to support both the moral goals of these institutions and their limited academic purposes. Conversely, in areas where social capital was less developed, where the bonds of mutual obligation and support were less in evidence, it would follow that the character of the common schools would be different. The crucial difference was the degree of parental and community support for the underlying purposes and day-to-day operation of the institution.

Social Capital and Common Schools: North–South Differences

Much of the foregoing, of course, is little more than informed speculation, and it raises the critical question of evidence: how does one go about testing the proposition that social capital of the sort described above contributed to the moral and academic purposes of the common school? What kind of evidence will help to identify the role of social capital in moral education in these contexts? Fortunately, answers to these questions are not hard to imagine, and in a few instances it is possible to point to research that can begin to address them.

A good place to start is simple geography. Schooling in the nineteenth century, as now, was an extremely place-bound enterprise. For social capital to develop and function in support of schooling, families had to communicate, engage in a certain threshold of common activities, and share resources in a manner that engendered trust and mutual respect. This would call for relatively high population density and commercial activity, or economic interdependency. It may have also required a degree of equity in wealth and status, to facilitate communication and the sharing of information and other resources. These are factors that Goldin and Katz posited as important to social capital formation in the twentieth century, and it is not unreasonable to surmise that they were important during the ante-bellum period.

One of the most striking patterns in the development of American education is the dramatic regional variation that characterized enrollment patterns until the twentieth century. These differences were notable in the common school era, when the census first showed that inter-regional differences were especially pronounced. While attendance rates were high in Northern states in 1850, ranging from two thirds of the children aged 5 to 19 to more than ninety percent, they rarely exceeded a quarter in the South. The contrasts are especially striking when states in the nation's upper and lower tiers are compared. While nearly nine out of ten potential students were enrolled in Vermont, New Hampshire, and Maine, less than three in ten white children attended in South Carolina, Georgia, Alabama, and Mississippi. These startling differences, moreover, existed in states that were similar in many respects. All were predominantly rural and agricultural in 1850, with relatively low levels of urbanization and industrial development. They were chiefly Protestant, albeit with different denominational profiles, and still within the political mainstream, at least in 1850.

Even so, they exhibited quite different patterns of educational development. None were centers of educational reform, although several—both North and South—had active reform groups that advocated greater state support for schooling.[22]

General patterns of regional educational development in this period are well known. The usual explanations have to do with the lack of a tradition of popular education in the South, insufficient population density to make schools a success there, and the opposition of conservative Southern leaders to the very idea of public schooling. With respect to the latter point, there also is the critical question of slavery, and the concerns of White elites at the prospect of slaves learning to read and write, especially following the Nat Turner rebellion in 1831. The rationale for high enrollments in the rural North, as noted above, has been linked to Protestant and republican concerns for literacy and moral education, and the absence of competing diversions for young people in small country communities. These explanations are reasonable, but still beg the question of how children in one context were induced to attend school while their counterparts in another setting were not.[23]

As suggested above, two features of northern farm communities stand out with respect to the formation of social capital: their relatively narrow range of inequality, and their interdependent quality of life. This was an environment unusually well suited to the formation of the sort of social capital that would lead children to follow their parents' wishes and attend school in large numbers. The population density argument may have a bearing on this, apart from the simple matter of accessibility to schooling. In the northern tier of states, population compactness could be considerable, even in places with relatively low levels of urbanization such as Vermont or New Hampshire. In these states the density had reached some 33 persons per square mile by 1850, greater than any of the other states under consideration. The average size of farms was small in these settings, and communities were tightly knit. Proximity during the nineteenth century was an aid to communication and the sharing of resources. It is little wonder, in that case, that school attendance rates were above 85 percent. These states represented a fertile field for the development of social capital in support of schooling. Nearby Maine exhibited a somewhat lower density at 18 persons per square mile, but most of its population was concentrated in the southern half of the state, and lived in communities not unlike those in neighboring states. It featured an attendance rate in excess of ninety percent. This is prima facie evidence of the power of social capital to affect the reach of common schooling.[24]

In the South, on the other hand, population densities were much lower, at least for the White population. In Georgia, Alabama, and Mississippi there were fewer than 10 whites per square mile on average, and in South Carolina the figure was only 12. These states were dominated by the cotton economy, at the core of which stood the region's large plantation owners and their thousands of slaves. Communities in these areas often were marked by considerable inequality in wealth and status, with correspondingly weaker traditions of interdependency and mutual support. Indeed, stretching from South Carolina west to Mississippi was the infamous "black belt," a region where "King Cotton" prevailed and the planters reigned supreme. Southern agriculture, in that case, was quite different from its Northern counterpart. Dominated in many areas by a single cash crop and the wealthy elite who farmed it, this social and economic system was hardly well suited to the formation of bonds of trust and collective responsibility. Even if some adults valued schooling in such a context, and happened to live in smaller, tightly knit communities, it was still a challenge to marshal the resources to maintain schools like those in the North. Without a broad consensus on the importance of schooling, it would have been a considerably greater task to persuade their children to continue attending school, especially the older ones.[25]

A recently published study of two counties in 1850 and 1860, one in northern Virginia and the other in lower Pennsylvania, provides yet more evidence on these points. Written by William Thomas III and Edward Ayers, it compares two areas of roughly equal size, just two hundred miles apart. As Thomas and Ayers note, these counties "shared similar geographic locations, soil, climate, crops, white ethnicity, and religious denominations," and yet one "was built around slavery" and the other was not. The result was a host of differing "social arrangements," including schooling. While Augusta County, Virginia counted just 23 schools for its population of about 20,000 in 1850, Franklin County, Pennsylvania had 177 for nearly 40,000 residents. This meant that there was a school for about 40 families in the latter, a figure similar to most northern communities, and more than 100 families per school in the other. The population was less concentrated in the Virginia county, and with the exception of churches (which numbered about the same per capita) there were fewer places for people to congregate, such as stores, taverns, and other commercial establishments. These were characteristics that undoubtedly distinguished many places on either side of the Mason-Dixon Line.[26]

Perhaps most telling, however, was the degree of inequality in the two regions, and the role of slavery in the South, even outside of the "Black Belt." While the median household wealth in the Virginia county was 38 percent higher than its Pennsylvania counterpart, the mean was 64 percent greater, indicating the overall distribution of wealth was considerably wider. Farms were larger even in this part of the South: on average there were 1.6 farms per square mile, while the figure was 3.2 for Franklin County, Pennsylvania. This undoubtedly made the task of establishing networks of mutual commitment and trust more complicated and difficult. In addition to this, there was the all-important question of slavery. Even in Northern Virginia, slave labor was ubiquitous, touching on almost all areas of economic life. As a consequence, the widespread use of slave labor in the South rendered the traditions of shared exertion that were so common in Northern communities superfluous. There were fewer reasons for White people to come together, and even less cause for them to assist one-another directly. Coleman's reasoning would lead one to expect a lower stock of social capital in such settings, fewer shared values, and a lower commitment to the sacrifices necessary to support a public institution such as the schools.[27]

This suggests that experiences in these different types of communities, linked with political traditions and clear preferences regarding public education, may have had an important bearing on the development of common schooling. When debates occurred over public education in Southern states, it usually was the cotton districts that most opposed them, but there also were a few counties that supported them. Where schools existed and even flourished in the South, it was most often in areas dominated by small farmers, animated by experiences not dissimilar to those reported in the North. For the region as a whole, however, the cotton-growers' mentality carried the day partly because support for schooling among other social strata was quite limited. Moral education, in the view of many Southerners, was not the function of the school. Where there was little shared experience and trust born of mutual obligations there could be few common values, and a consensus on the content and importance of moral education was inherently problematic.

In many Northern farm communities just the opposite was true. Shared customs, and the experience of exchanging information, resources, and exertion helped to establish the trust and understanding necessary to build and support institutions, and to make moral education a priority. This appears to have been true even in the newly settled states in the old Northwest, which were dominated by migrants from New England and other northern states. The traditions of sharing, cooperation, and mutual support that these people had acquired from experience, perhaps reinforced by frontier conditions, may have become sources of social capital. This could help explain the higher degree of school enrollment even in these relatively sparsely settled states.

Social Capital and the Common School Curriculum: Moral Community

All of this points to the possible importance of local networks of association in the development of common schooling, and by extension moral education. If, as Coleman suggested, social norms and behavioral expectations are upheld by dense, interlocking relationships, bound together by reciprocal obligation and trust, one would expect moral education to be more evident in places with these characteristics. This raises a question for research: is there evidence that communities with these characteristics were more likely to value moral education than others? This is largely a matter of curriculum, a question of what children were being taught, and an area that has received relatively little attention from historians. Fortunately, there is a small body of research that has marshaled evidence on these matters, and it turns out that these data also reveal patterns pointing to the influence of social capital.

Perhaps the most pertinent of these studies was conducted by the sociologist Charles Bidwell and published in 1966. Titled "The Moral Significance of the Common School," it examined the correlates of common school instruction in moral education in Massachusetts and New York in the 1830s and 1840s. Bidwell amassed a very unusual dataset, using townships and city wards as the units of analysis. He was particularly interested in the extent to which these locales represented "a moral community," or places where "a system of moral sentiments is widely shared." To describe this system of shared beliefs, Bidwell used the term "moral integration," reflecting the "shared sentiments" that bound a community together. He believed that the degree of such cohesion could be tied to religious interests, especially in towns with histories of revivals, home missions, or the Sunday school agitation. Bidwell hypothesized that these places would be more likely to exhibit strong religious influences in the common schools, a direct measure of the type of moral education being practiced. As a gauge of this, he used state school reports from 1837 to 1840 to determine whether the Bible was used in opening school exercises, along with an accounting of other texts. The latter were coded for religious content, and Bidwell performed a similar analysis for texts listed in the early 1840s. He also amassed a host of additional variables on these places, including demographic, economic, and cultural (mainly ethnic and religious) characteristics. He then proceeded to statistically determine patterns of association between these factors, focusing on the correlates of religious materials in the common school curriculum.[28]

Bidwell wrote long before the concept of social capital came into currency, but it turned out that his analysis was well suited to exploring the characteristics of towns that might have been associated with it. He was interested in inter-denominational conflict and evidence of moral education, but of course these questions may have been related to social capital as well. The statistical measures Bidwell employed uncovered telltale patterns of behavior. While there was considerable variation in his indicators of moral education, the correspondence between a town's moral or religious environment and the use of religious materials in the schools was highest in the smaller Massachusetts communities. Towns that exhibited noteworthy religious activity were more likely to feature religious texts if they were smaller and more tightly knit, and less stratified and not economically developed. This was the clearest evidence that Bidwell could identify regarding the influence of a "moral community" on the common schools. His discussion of the matter is telling:

> Apparently the effects of a township's moral integration on patterns of school control and moral education were contingent on certain of the town's structural attributes. These effects were strong when the town was neither socially nor economically differentiated. One might argue that this relationship, in point of fact, resulted from some variable other than moral integration that was active under conditions of low social and economic differentiation.[29]

Of course, Bidwell had no way of utilizing the concept of social capital to help account for these findings. In this respect his reference to an unknown variable that operated in relatively undifferentiated communities is quite consistent with current conceptions about the influence of social capital. His subsequent explanations of patterns in the data seem to bear this out.

> A more likely explanation is that under conditions of structural complexity, indicated by large size, stratification, and economic development, the force of moral integration was blunted. In these towns the elements of social action lost their common meaning, and responded variously to the more diverse beliefs and interests of the population and to alternative pressures from groups and organizations within the community. But in the structurally simpler towns, the effects of moral integration remained pervasive. In these towns, given the centrality of moral sentiments to social structure and action, variations in moral integration were directly reflected in the common school curriculum and the composition of local school committees.[30]

This discussion of the effects of social and economic differentiation on the development and expression of social norms was very much in keeping with the subsequent ideas of Coleman, Putnam, and others who have written about social capital. Bidwell suggested that smaller communities were able to achieve greater cohesion around questions of moral thinking and conduct, and that these ideas found expression in the local schools. This is powerful if somewhat circumstantial evidence of the importance of social capital in the development of moral education in these settings. Bidwell also found evidence of class conflict in larger towns, with moral education reflecting the interests of the most politically potent strata: the middle class. But the story was different in smaller places. The development of a strong consensus regarding norms of behavior and the ideas that govern them is necessarily a function of the degree of communication and trust in a given community.

While Bidwell's evidence on this was hardly conclusive, it certainly is suggestive. Other scholars have noted similar trends. In their comprehensive analysis of ante-bellum Massachusetts education, Kaestle and Vinovskis found that primary school enrollments were highest in the small, less differentiated towns, especially those dominated by agriculture and with few immigrants. While they did not explore curricular issues, the attendance patterns that they discovered were consistent with Bidwell's findings. Enrollments were lower in the larger, more differentiated towns and cities, especially those with recent immigrants and greater inequality in wealth and social status.[31] This also is consistent with the regional trends observed previously, and the description of the historical circumstances of rural schools. It was states with a greater proportion of these communities that exhibited the highest levels of participation in the common schools. In certain respects, this too is a reflection of moral integration, at least insofar as there was a community-wide consensus on the importance of formal education. In smaller, undifferentiated communities of the sort that existed in Massachusetts, schooling was a highly valued activity for the young. Even if there were questions about the quality of the schools in many such districts, and the level of interest in reform measures, there was a broad consensus about the importance of education.

Conclusion: Toward a Research Agenda on Social Capital and Moral Education

While the evidence described above may be important, it is hardly a comprehensive exploration of social capital as a factor in explaining the development of common schools in general and moral education in particular. In his 1988 article outlining the concept, Coleman offered a number of suggestions for examining the links between social capital and education that seem quite as pertinent to historians as to other social scientists. He did not dwell on the examination of community characteristics, but instead recommended considering the types of relationships that exist within groups or communities that are related to schooling. He suggested that researchers examine family resources that may have a bearing on relationships that could contribute to success in education. Coleman also recommended examination of the relationships of teachers to students, yet another dimension of social capital with a direct effect on school achievement. Finally, there is also the relations between students, some of which are supportive of schools and their goals, and others that may not be.[32]

In developing a research agenda for exploring the role of social capital in the development of common schooling and moral education, it seems that each of these areas represents a potentially fruitful line of inquiry. Historians have performed limited analysis of the effects of family size on school enrollment, for instance, but this is a question that bears additional consideration, especially for children living in the countryside. If indeed the family was such a critical element of education in this period, did variation in the number of children in a household have a bearing on how much formal education they received? With respect to the topic of interest in this volume, did it affect moral education as well?[33]

There is also the matter of relationships outside of families that may have affected schooling and education, bonds that extended across groups or communities. Levels of associational activity, membership in religious institutions and fraternal organizations are just a few of the possible indicators of adults forming relationships outside of the school setting, representing the sort of closure that Coleman hypothesized to be associated with school participation. Informal activities no doubt were important as well, although they are notoriously difficult to document in a systematic fashion. There are teacher and student characteristics that also may have been linked to social capital. In the common school setting, for instance, did having a cohort of boys at roughly the same ages pose a challenge to teachers? Would it be possible to consider the effect of age groups on attendance, or even the tenure of male or female teachers across districts in a given area? This too could reflect the power of relationships, a particular kind of social capital, with somewhat different implications for the educational enterprise.[34]

Altogether, in that case, social capital would appear to be a highly generative concept for the history of education, and for the question of moral education in particular. As Coleman argued, social capital is especially pertinent to the formation of social norms and behavioral expectations with a group or community, and in this regard it is a markedly appropriate concept for the study of values in education, and the transmission of moral standards from one generation to another. Considering this relatively new element of social theory has the potential to considerably enrich our understanding of the forces that contributed to the growth of American education during a critical period of its development.

Acknowledgments

I would like to acknowledge the research assistance provided by Sylvia Martinez in preparing this chapter. Helpful comments were also provided by Charles Bidwell, Carl Kaestle, David Tyack, and Donald Warren.

Notes

1. B. Edward McClellan, *Moral Education in America: Schools and the Shaping of Character from Colonial Times to the Present* (New York: Teachers College Press, 1999), 21. For the most influential recent treatment of the common school, see Carl F. Kaestle, *Pillars of the Republic: Common Schools and American society, 1780–1860* (New York: Hill & Wang, 1983), chapters 2–6.
2. Wayne E. Fuller, *The Old Country School: The Story of Rural Education in the Middle West* (Chicago: University of Chicago Press, 1982), 6; McClellan, *Moral Education in America*, 25.
3. James S. Coleman, "Social Capital in the Creation of Human Capital," *American Journal of Sociology* 94 (Spring 1988): 98.
4. Ibid., 100–108.
5. Robert D. Putnam, *Bowling Alone: The Collapse and Revival of American Community* (New York: Simon & Schuster, 2001), passim.
6. For an overview of recent research, see Nan Lin, "Inequality in Social Capital," *Contemporary Sociology* 29, 6 (November 2000): 785–795. Also see Alejandro Portes, "Social Capital: Its Origins and Applications in Modern Sociology," in J. Hagan and K. S. Cook, eds., *Annual Review of Sociology* (Palo Alto, CA: Annual Reviews, 1998), 1–24.
7. Reed Ueda, "Second-Generation Civic America: Education, Citizenship, and The Children of Immigrants," *Journal of Interdisciplinary History* 29, 4 (1999): 661–681; reprinted in Robert I. Rotberg, ed., *Patterns of Social Capital: Stability and Change in Historical Perspective* (New York: Cambridge University Press), 273–294.
8. Claudia Goldin and Lawrence Katz, "Human Capital and Social Capital: The Rise of Secondary Schooling in America, 1910–1940," *Journal of Interdisciplinary History* 29, 4 (1999): 683–723; reprinted in Rotberg, ed., *Patterns of Social Capital*.
9. Maris A. Vinovskis, "Trends in Massachusetts education, 1826–1860," *History of Education Quarterly 12*, 4 (1980): 501–529. Jack Larkin, *The Reshaping of Everyday Life, 1790–1840* (New York: Harper & Row, 1988), 259.
10. Lawrence A. Cremin. *American Education: The National Experience, 1783–1876* (New York: Harper & Row, 1980), 181.
11. Kaestle, *Pillars of the Republic*, chapter 3. In a revealing analysis, John Meyer, David Tyack, and two colleagues found that educational expansion in this period could not be explained by urbanization and industrialization, and that it proceeded most rapidly in rural areas. They argued that religious factors and political movements seemed to explain much of the state level variation in enrollment. This analysis, of course, also preceded Coleman's discussion of social capital as a factor in determining enrollment levels. See John W. Meyer, David Tyack, Joane Nagel, and Audri Gordon, "Public Education as Nation-Building in America: Enrollments and Bureaucratization in the American States, 1870–1930," *American Journal of Sociology* 85, 3 (November 1979): 591–613. Paul Theobald has pointed to similar factors in his study of rural schools in the Midwest, especially the importance of religious homogeneity and political harmony in local communities. Theobald also highlighted the influence of property owners in making decisions about the schools. See his book, *Call School: Rural Education in the Midwest to 1918* (Carbondale: Southern Illinois University Press, 1995), chapters 1 and 3.
12. Quoted in Fuller, *The Old Country School*, chapter 1.
13. Ibid., 7; Larkin, *Reshaping of Everyday Life*, chapter 7.
14. Merle Curti, *The Making of an American Community; A Case Study of Democracy in a Frontier County* (Stanford, CA: Stanford University Press, 1959), 117–118; Larkin, *Reshaping of Everyday Life*, 266; Theobald, *Call School*, 119.

15. Theobald, *Call School*, chapter 3; Coleman, "Social Capital in the Creation of Human Capital," 105–109.
16. See, for instance, the discussion of Boxford, Massachusetts in Carl F. Kaestle and Maris A. Vinovskis, *Education and Social Change in Nineteenth Century Massachusetts* (New York: Cambridge University Press, 1980), chapter 6. Theobald also notes the issue of transience in many rural communities, especially in the Midwest, which also could undermine the development of social capital. See Theobald, *Call School*, chapter 2.
17. Curti, *The Making of an American Community*, 139.
18. Kaestle, *Pillars of the Republic*, chapter 2; Larkin, *Reshaping of Everyday Life*, 35.
19. Fuller, *The Old Country School*, 4; William. J Gilmore-Lehne, *Reading Becomes a Necessity of Life: Material and Cultural Life in Rural New England, 1780–1835* (Knoxville: University of Tennessee Press, 1989), chapters 1 and 2; Kaestle, *Pillars of the Republic*, 100.
20. Hiram Orcutt, *Gleanings from School-Life Experience* (Boston: Rutland, 1859), 135–137. On teaching conditions and accommodations in the schools, see Barbara Finkelstein, *Governing the Young: Teacher Behavior in Popular Primary Schools in Nineteenth-Century United States* (New York: Falmer Press, 1989), passim; Andrew Gulliford, *America's Country Schools*, 2nd ed. (Washington, DC: Preservation Press, 1989), passim; Kaestle, *Pillars of the Republic*, chapter 2.
21. Carl F. Kaestle, "Social Change, Discipline and the Common School in Early Nineteenth Century America," *Journal of Interdisciplinary History* 19, 1 (Summer 1978): 12; Benjamin Justice, *The War that Wasn't: Religious Conflict and Compromise in the Common Schools of New York State, 1865–1900* (Albany: State University of New York Press, 2005), 140; Fuller, *The Old Country School*, 4. On broad public support for knowledge and learning in this period, see Richard D. Brown, *The Strength of a People: The Idea of an Informed Citizenry in America, 1650–1870* (Chapel Hill: University of North Carolina Press, 1996), passim.
22. For state-level enrollment rates, see John K. Folger and Charles B. Nam, *Education of the American Population* (Washington, DC: Bureau of the Census, 1967). On regional differences in enrollments, see Albert Fishlow, "Level of Nineteenth Century Investment in Education," *Journal of Economic History* 26 (1966): 418–436, and Lee Soltow and Edward Stevens, *The Rise of Literacy and the Common School in the United States: A Socioeconomic Analysis to 1870* (Chicago: University of Chicago Press, 1981), passim.
23. Kaestle, *Pillars of the Republic*, chapter 8.
24. These figures are taken from the 1850 U.S. Census. For a discussion of population dynamics in this period, see Michael Haines and Richard Steckle, *A Population History of North America* (New York: Cambridge University Press, 2000), passim.
25. For a discussion of southern education during this period, see Kaestle, *Pillars of the Republic*, 192–215. The best recent discussion of North-South differences in education and social development can be found in Joel Perlmann and Robert A. Margo, *Women's Work? American Schoolteachers, 1650–1920* (Chicago: University of Chicago Press, 2001), chapter 2. For consideration of these factors in a later period, see Robert A. Margo, *Race and Schooling in the South, 1880–1950: An Economic History* (Chicago: University of Chicago Press, 1994), chapter 2.
26. William G. Thomas III and Edward L. Ayers, "An Overview: The Differences Slavery Made: A Close Analysis of Two American Communities," *The American Historical Review* 108, 5 (December 2003): 1299–1307. As the published version of this study is only a summary of evidence and arguments developed in a more extensive web-based discussion, see http://www.vcdh.virginia.edu/AHR/ for additional information. On differences between Pennsylvania and Virginia at this time, also see John D. Majewski, *A House Dividing: Economic Development in Pennsylvania and Virginia Before the Civil War* (Cambridge: Cambridge University Press, 2000), especially the Introduction and chapters 1–3.

27. These figures are taken from data presented in the web-based version of Thomas and Ayers, "The Differences Slavery Made," particularly tables related to education and community development.
28. Charles E. Bidwell, "The Moral Significance of the Common School," *History of Education Quarterly* 6, 3 (Autumn 1966): 50–91.
29. Ibid., 75.
30. Ibid., 76–77.
31. Carl F. Kaestle and Maris A. Vinovskis, *Education and Social Change in Nineteenth Century Massachusetts*, chapters 5 and 6.
32. Coleman, "Social Capital in the Creation of Human Capital," 116–120.
33. See, for instance, Kaestle and Vinovskis, *Education and Social Change in Nineteenth Century Massachusetts*, chapter 4, for discussion of a "work/consumption index" that included family size as a consideration. Family size also was considered in examining school enrollment in a later period, along with birth order, in John L. Rury, *Education and Women's Work: Female Schooling and the Division of Labor in Urban America, 1870–1930* (Albany: State University of New York Press, 1991), 54–60. Neither of these studies, however, was concerned with the possible influence of social capital or related concepts.
34. On associational activity of this sort, see the following chapters in Rotberg, *Patterns of Social Capital*: Gerald Gamm and Robert Putnam, "The Growth of Voluntary Associations in America, 1840–1940," 173–220; Mary P. Ryan, "Civil Society as Democratic Practice: North American Cities During the Nineteenth Century," 221–246; and Elisabeth S. Clemens, "Securing Political Returns to Social Capital: Women's Associations in the United States, 1880s to 1920s," 247–272. A classic study of these issues remains useful: Alice Felt Tyler, *Freedom's Ferment: Phases of American Social History from the Colonial Period to the Outbreak of the Civil War* (Minneapolis: University of Minnesota Press, 1944) especially part three, which addresses education and other reform issues during the antebellum period. On gender issues in the rural common schools, see David Tyack and Elisabeth Hansot, *Learning Together: A History of Coeducation in American Schools* (New Haven, CT: Yale University Press, 1990), chapter 3.

Chapter 6

Between Hogs and Horse-Trots: Searching for Civic Learning in 1850s Indiana

Glenn Lauzon

In the early 1850s, the scattered efforts of agricultural reformers throughout the northern United States coalesced into a movement for civic reform.[1] In the twenty-first century, it may seem strange to classify agricultural improvement as civic education. At the nineteenth century's midpoint, when the vast majority of the citizenry lived on farms or in rural places, Thomas Jefferson's postulate in his *Notes on the State of Virginia* resonated strongly: farmers' virtue and proportion in the populace would be a "good-enough barometer" of the nation's civic health.[2] For many, agriculture remained the wellspring of virtue and prosperity and the farmer continued to be the ideal citizen. Yet, the America of Jefferson's imagination was moving away from its agricultural roots. The market revolution, with its small-scale manufactories, was supplanting the home economy; subsistence farming was giving way to commercial farming. Territorial expansion, rapid growth, and technological progress were inspiring new thoughts about what the United States could be as a society. As leading Americans refashioned their civic visions, the farmer was not immune from rethinking. He remained central to reformers who envisioned a new farmer for a steadily improving society.

Thomas Jefferson had praised the husbandman for his independence and self-reliance. Secure in his ownership of land, he provided for his family by the fruit of his labor. Neither dependent upon foreign markets nor in debt to urban moneylenders (as was Jefferson), the farmer was free, beholden only to God and Nature. Antebellum reformers (many of whom, like Jefferson, were gentlemen farmers) redefined Jefferson's farmer-citizen. By becoming part of the locally based, market-oriented society and taking advantage of advances in technology and cultivation practices farmers would fulfill an updated Jeffersonian vision. What farmers accepted or rejected of that vision, and how reformers adapted their educational strategies to farmers' responses, may provide some insight into the dynamics of civic learning. That, at least, is the intent of this attempt to capture the initial moments of agricultural uplift in the Indiana of the 1850s. Decidedly rural and committed to various notions of what the Jeffersonian heritage prescribed, Indiana may be ideal for examining the reformulation of a civic vision for rural America in the middle decades of the nineteenth century.

The Role of Agricultural Improvement in a Civic Vision for Indiana

The United States of the 1850s was a nation on the move. As commerce and growth rippled through the settled life of the east, booming river cities and inland towns with their small-scale industries held out promises of opportunities undreamed of on the farm. State-sponsored internal improvements in turnpikes, canals, railroads—many completed finally after decades of frustration—opened the continent's interior to settlement. In the 1850s alone, the United States sold nearly 50 million acres; over 100 million acres (nearly four times Indiana's acreage) of new farmland was put under cultivation. As thousands streamed westward or into the cities, the spirit of optimism and opportunity-seeking propelling them onward sparked anxiety-pangs among stay-putters who hoped to build civilization in the places migrants left behind.[3]

Much has been made of the frontier's "pull." In the nineteenth century, reformers focused more on a "push": eastern soils' exhaustion from wasting cultivation. Successive planting of wheat (or cotton in the South) for decades depleted the soil's natural fertility; declining crop yields drove people west. The remedy? Scientific agriculture. By growing and rotating multiple crops, raising livestock and manuring, and using new implement technologies the soil could be continually renewed. What was good for the soil would be good for the wallet. Growing fruits and vegetables for nearby townsfolk, raising hay and grains for their horses, and dairying offered moneymaking prospects unknown to past generations of farmers. Scientific and commercial, agriculture provided a chance for opportunity-seeking at home. To take it, the farmer would have to take up self-education in farming. Northeastern farmers living near cities, rivers, and railroads were making the change. But for Hoosier farmers, it was a new kind of farming, one that required far more work and agricultural knowledge than raising a small surplus of corn.

When he extolled the farmer's virtues, Thomas Jefferson surely did not have in mind his Appalachian hillbilly neighbors who barely scratched the soil when they tilled and let their hogs roam wild.[4] These men claimed the Jeffersonian mantle in Indiana. As they interpreted it, at least, they had taken his vision of a decentralized rural society to heart. As part of the Old Northwest, in legal terms, Indiana was an "old" state, but it had frontier-like conditions. Its northern tier was a thinly populated land of marshy plains; much of the state was heavily forested; and, it was occupied mainly by upland southerners who had done little to erect the trappings of civilization. Stamped by the first Northeastern migrants as a land of malaria and bogs, southerners and hogs, Indiana held little appeal for the migrants of the 1850s. Seemingly, it did not appeal to its own sons and daughters; already, large numbers were moving on to Illinois, Iowa, and Missouri. The reform-minded had made limited headway in improving the state.[5]

Agricultural improvement, agriculturally derived manufacturing, and railroad building were the three prongs of progress in the Indiana of the 1850s. Improved agriculture would supply raw materials and foodstuffs for town-dwelling laborers; small towns dotting the landscape would provide steady demand for a wide range of agricultural products; and, railroad lines would bind town and country together. Mutually dependent for growth and interlocking in their results, these three prongs of progress composed a formula for bringing "the loom and the anvil into close proximity with the plow," for transforming the "howling wilderness" into a flourishing rural civilization. Measured against this aim, Indiana was not even half-finished. It lacked the most crucial ingredient—an educated yeomanry—and was just developing manufacturing capabilities. Reformers hoped to produce both. The pioneering era was over; it was time to expel "scratch-and-scatter" from Indiana's soils. A rational system of agriculture would take its place.[6]

At the outset, S.B. Gookins informed his fellow reformers what their cause was up against: the hog-dollar. With cities like Chicago, St. Louis, and Cincinnati on the rise, pork-packing had emerged as a major industry. Inclined to raise corn and hogs, Hoosier farmers grew more. Corn fattened hogs in the fall. Herded to river cities, hogs fetched $10–12 apiece. The ease with which the hog could be "speedily converted into money" was the great obstacle. This "one idea of hog" swept farmers into "an uncertain and precarious business," more akin to gambling and land speculation than to "an intelligent system of farming."[7] While profitable, corn and hogs were injurious to the soil. The combination did little to foster well-rounded local economies, as it connected farmers to markets in distant cities more so than to nearby towns. Hoosier farmers had to learn that farming, properly understood, involved more than corn and hogs.

Four days after a new state constitution was adopted, Indiana's General Assembly enacted new agricultural legislation. Explicit in the plan was a lesson learned from the growth of eastern cities: "Association is the origin and impulse of all progress." The opportunity to learn by exchanging ideas was the city's decided advantage over the country, but no longer. At monthly agricultural society meetings farmers could share innovations and results. New seeds being disseminated by the United States Patent Office could be tested for suitability to Indiana's soils. By culling ideas from farm journals and comparing practical experiences, each farmer could benefit from costly mistakes and missteps made by others.[8]

The plan provided for more, however, than the mutual improvement of gentleman farmers. Men like Henry Ellsworth, of Tippecanoe County and formerly the US Commissioner of Patents, were already improving their agriculture; they needed little incentive to carry on. Agricultural societies were intended to amplify their efforts and to persuade the mass of Indiana's farmers to improve themselves. In a state where approximately 20 percent of the adult population was classified as illiterate by US census-takers, reformers hoped to shake off indifference to "book-farming."[9] If little else, they hoped to convince farmers to adopt improved implements, livestock, and seed, and to apply the proverb, "whatever is worth doing at all is worth doing right," to their farming. To encourage self-improvement, premium awards would be given to farmers who demonstrated their efforts in "the improvement of soils, tillage, crops, manures, improvements, stock, articles of domestic industry," and any other desirable productions. Liberal premiums for cattle, horses, and sheep—anything but hogs—would induce the farmer to change his unreasonable behavior. Public competitions at annual agricultural fairs would encourage innovation through friendly rivalry, while showing farmers what could be accomplished and how it could be done.[10]

At the fair the farmer might be introduced to crops imported from exotic locales throughout the world or to improved breeds of cattle from northern Europe. The all-purpose Morgan horse and the fine-wooled Merino sheep might be on display. He might see for the first time McCormick's reaper, Gatling's wheat drill, or John Deere's steel plow. From competitors he could hear the merits of different styles of drainage, planting, cultivating, and harvesting, and be instructed in how best to perform improved methods. Inspired by direct contact, and given the chance to learn through observation, hands-on experience, and informal conversation, the farmer could learn the greatest lessons of the new era: manual labor, when combined with educated intelligence, produced results that mattered. Every man could make "two blades of grass grow where only one grew before" and bring forth hidden wealth from the soils of his farm. Those who plodded mindlessly "in the beaten tracks of their fathers" could not prosper. They would have to "learn to think constantly of their pursuits, and the means of improving them" if they hoped "to reap their best reward."[11]

By putting practical results on display, fairs would furnish the incentive to self-education; agricultural societies, aided by the growing agricultural press, would provide the thoroughgoing instruction necessary. As he learned a rational system of diversified farming, the Hoosier farmer would learn a new vision of rural citizenship, a vision that brought him into more continuous contact with urban life but preserved his independence by sheltering him from the vicissitudes of a single-crop market. Entwining him in the fabric of civilization, agricultural improvement would yield the best of all possible worlds: the refinements of the city and a life in the country.

Implementing the Vision: Institutionalization and Transformation

With their vision in place, agricultural reformers launched their campaign to uplift the Hoosier farmer. Within two years (1851–1853) they organized agricultural societies in 45 counties and hosted at least 20 fairs. The farmers' response was overwhelming. But not in the manner reformers had hoped. Of Indiana's 92 counties, 47 showed few signs of agricultural awakening; counties that formed agricultural societies found little popular enthusiasm. The Ohio and Switzerland district agricultural society met "a strong tide of opposition" from "superstitious enemies" opposed to book-farming. In Tippecanoe County "considerable labor and vexation" had a negligible impact on the "time-honored prejudices" of local farmers. Given the absence of interest in his agricultural society, John Barbour thought, the scrub cattle and "scrub farmers" of Fayette County would be removed only "by emigration or death."[12]

Why were farmers not interested in agricultural societies? Rural traditionalism and mistrust of innovation played its part in Indiana, as it did elsewhere. This was the preferred explanation of reformers. But, what is often overlooked is the extent to which agricultural societies were a part of a broader civic agenda. Most leading reformers fell into three categories. They were gentleman farmers (often retirees from other professions), town-dwellers who had businesses connected with agriculture and owned large estates, and people with a general interest in reform. Unlike most farmers, reformers tended to be well educated and involved in other improvement campaigns such as temperance, abolition, and the common school movement. The call to uplift agriculture carried more than the promise of farm profits. It was advocacy for a new way of life, and that way of life was, literally, foreign to the typical Hoosier farmer. Wittingly or not, talk of poor farming, scrub stock, and soil depletion smacked of regional chauvinism, since many reformers were recent migrants from the northeast. Coming from new arrivals whose livelihood didn't depend on the soil, such talk, no doubt, pushed many away. Envisioned as a "system of plain, practical *conversational* series" of meetings, the associations offered an improvement fare that was beyond the comprehension and inclination of most farmers.[13]

Like the societies, early fairs were mismatched to their intended audience. For a ten-cent fee anyone could attend, but the competitions reflected men of substance. Imported livestock and farm machinery dominated the grounds. Priced at $125 or more, McCormick's famous reaper was beyond the average farmer's means; "fancy" cattle cost even more. Unsurprisingly, the charge of favoritism toward "a few wealthy exhibitors" was leveled at judges. What dirt farmer would want to place his shaggy nag against a Kentucky thoroughbred? Or his long-legged "alligator breed" hog ("whose well developed representative can look over and root under a medium sized log at the same instant") alongside a finely shaped Berkshire? Could he hope to stand against gentlemen farmers who employed several hands in the "best cultivated or most improved farms" category? Would he want to compete at all, given the rewards offered?[14]

"First place" winners received silverware, in the form of pitchers, goblets, and bowls; second and third placers found themselves lucky recipients of an agricultural report, a learned treatise, or a subscription to the newly established *Indiana Farmer* journal. Reformers hoped supplying reading materials would encourage farmers "to investigate, read, think, examine and improve by their own observations and experiments." Displaying a rare talent for understatement (among fair boosters), J. P. Brady soberly reported that "quite a discrepancy exists between the amount of premiums offered, and those awarded" at his society's agricultural fair. Most competitors, reformers discovered, preferred one dollar in cash to agricultural books.[15]

Despite the mismatches, the first fairs brought some encouraging signs of progress. Any doubt about the fair's ability to arouse the public mind "would speedily be removed" declared C. L. Murray, "if they could hear the general inquiry prevailing in all corners" of Elkhart county. In southern Indiana farmers were "beginning to see the folly of destroying their lands by cultivating corn and raising hogs." Doubting the "wise saws of their fathers," in Decatur County, "the most obstinate conservatists [sic] and *stand-stillers*" were casting aside "antiquated agricultural implements" and "worthless breeds of stock." For so long "the rusty chain of agricultural *ignorance*" had bound down the farmer; it was "giving way, to the gradual *friction* from the silver chain of science."[16]

Inspired by public enthusiasm for fairs, agricultural societies moved to secure their future. Early fairs were on privately owned land, or, occasionally, in the courthouse and public square. Borrowing grounds consumed considerable labor and money. Rail-fences and pens for livestock had to be erected, and stands built for exhibits and food-selling; at the end of the fair, all of it had to be torn down. Members of agricultural societies sought to avoid repeating this year after year. Flush with cash from successful fairs, some made leasing agreements with local landowners. Others less well-endowed appealed to the "kindly and liberal spirit" of local citizens. By 1855, agricultural societies had demonstrated their public utility sufficiently to gain the right to own 20 acres.[17] So empowered, they could acquire central locations and suitable facilities; equipped on a permanent basis they could infect more people with the spirit of agricultural improvement.

As fairs grew, membership rolls grew. The expanded rolls were illusory; of this, reformers were painfully aware. Warren County could boast of having 300 members, but "a great many of them" showed "little interest" beyond paying the membership fee. The Marshall County society's regular work was "generally performed by ten or twelve persons"; the rest were content to attend the fair, "bringing with them some article which owes its superiority to the wealth and generosity of Dame Nature." A one-dollar annual fee entitled a man to join an agricultural society. It also entitled his family to unrestricted fair admission; and, memberships were seldom renewed at times other than the fair. In theory, the fair was supposed to serve as the entry point into the agricultural societies' more-formal educational activities; in reality, few practical farmers accepted the invitation. In counties across the state, reformers could only hope it would not be long "before the Society will find relief in this serious particular."[18]

As few working members were gained, growing fair-going crowds increased the workload of active members. With greater numbers of competitions to manage, prizes to award, and organizational details to attend to, the labor fell to "the very few" who stood "the blunt of all calumny," receiving "but little credit for their efforts." The public's willingness to receive the fair's benefits without contributing to its success took its toll. No fair was held in Huntington County in 1856 or 1857 "in consequence of the great apathy with which the great mass of the community regarded the efforts of the society." Within three years, Knox County's leading farmers appeared "to have lost their first love." They were becoming "lukewarm in their attachments, if not totally indifferent" to their duties. Experience made the lesson clear: an agricultural society "cannot flourish without the aid of professional men."[19] Hosting a successful fair required more time, labor, and money than most counties' full-time farmers were willing to supply; increasingly, they looked to townsmen to make up the difference.

If agricultural societies' members weren't losing their "first love" for improvement, their passion for spreading its spirit through agricultural societies was waning. In 1851, Shelby County launched its campaign by purchasing 25 scientific-agricultural books and subscribing to 12 different farm journals; the subscriptions were dropped three years later. In 1852, the Franklin County society could "scarcely see how a society can discharge the duty it owes to community without holding frequent meetings." They found a way in 1855. With "some doubts as to its propriety," they revised their constitution to hold meetings four times annually. Monthly meetings, although "interesting and profitable," failed to awaken much interest and proved to be "a heavy tax" upon members who hosted them. In 1858 the Jasper County society reorganized as a joint-stock company. Three years later, the General Assembly authorized others to follow.[20] If ever an agricultural society combining features of the scientific society and the lyceum had a chance to flourish in Indiana, that day was past. They were agricultural societies in name, but functioned, more or less, as fair-hosting societies.

As agricultural societies transmuted, agricultural fairs were capturing public attention; as privately sponsored educational programs, however, they were struggling financially. One might expect admission and entry fees to cover costs. Fair-revenues covered only one-third to one-half; the remainder was subsidized through membership fees and contributions solicited from citizens. Even the Washington and Orange district society, host of Indiana's largest local fair in 1856 (with over 10,000 visitors), required $750 in subscriptions to have sufficient funds for its next fair. Most were less fortunate. At the close of 1856 only seven societies had more than $150 in the treasury; seven were in debt; the rest were on the margin of subsistence. Only ten owned their fairgrounds. The fair was failing. The State Fair could not survive without constant aid from the citizens of Indianapolis and the General Assembly: was it reasonable to expect that a rural county fair could?[21] For the fair to continue as a purveyor of agricultural knowledge, it would have to pay its own way.

Tired of using personal funds to subsidize fairs, some agricultural societies opened the gates to the traveling shows, hucksters, and curiosities with which the county fair has become identified. Desperate for pecuniary life, Boone County departed from the legitimate objects of the fair in 1859. "Whatever may have been the experience of others," the introduction of hucksters "was a decided success" in Boone County. The treasury balance increased from $11 to $299. Huckster stands had even less connection to farming than the ladies' equestrian contest that was the "animating feature" of the 1857 Miami County fair, but the license fees they paid helped. Huckster stands enhanced the fair's earning power, but probably did little to boost attendance; at the least, their inclusion did not boost attendance enough to offset premium list expenses. For that purpose, fair organizers latched onto an innovation that some agricultural societies were finding to be an irresistible crowd-pleaser: the horse race.[22]

Some early fairs in Indiana may have had some unsanctioned horse racing, but showing horses had always been a part of the fair. Displayed in the same show ring as cattle, horses were judged for overall quality. When they stepped into the time ring, other horse-qualities were forgotten. Only speed mattered. The trial of speed—whether saddle, pacing, or trotting—sparked greater interest than even the rowdiest political campaign. On the first day of the 1859 Warrick County fair about 1,000 people attended; next day, the Princeton Brass Band and livestock competitions brought in around 4,000; the third day "was emphatically the *day of the Fair*." More than 5,000 people showed up for the trotting. An unparalleled success, an extra day was added, courtesy of citizens who agreed to sponsor more time trials. The same year, LaPorte County introduced horse racing to equally impressive results. Poor weather notwithstanding, on the day appointed more people came to the fair than ever before assembled at one place in the county. Lack of a good high fence, however, prevented LaPorte's agricultural society from fully capitalizing on their new-found popularity: "about as many witnessed it from the outside of the enclosure as within" by standing in their wagons. Getting the farmer to the fairgrounds accomplished, agricultural societies set out to get him inside. Time rings were built (along with high board fences) and "speed" was made an official part of the program.[23]

In response, the State Board of Agriculture condemned offering premiums on "speed alone" as "impolitic, immoral and unwise" and "against the best interests" of agricultural improvement. Some thought agricultural fairs were "in danger of being perverted from their proper design"; others were confident "a little innocent amusement" might be "combined advantageously with the more serious business of the occasion." It was inevitable, insisted A. J. Boone, "the populace in all ages and in all countries have and will have their public amusements and contests." Why not use that to advantage? With premium competitions, exhibits, and addresses furnishing the "serious business," and horse-trots, sideshows, and other features drawing the crowds, the fair could serve as both "a school of instruction and a source of amusement" for the rural community. A few societies resolutely committed themselves to the "legitimate objects and aims" of agricultural improvement, and refused to give in to the "morbid desire for popularity and excitement" behind crowd-pleasing and money-making innovations. They were fighting a losing battle against the popularization of the agricultural fair.[24]

A. J. Boone realized something that those who opposed the fair's non-agricultural features no longer recognized as a part of the educational process: to fulfill its outreach mission, the fair had to incorporate the priorities of its constituency. By the late 1850s the agricultural fair served the town (usually the county seat) as much as, if not more than, the countryside. How important fairs had become to towns became apparent when towns began competing for the privilege of hosting them. For several years, the Switzerland and Ohio District Fair alternated between the two county seats (Vevay and Rising Sun) until the promise of permanent facilities on a larger site brought it to the aptly named town of Enterprise. At its first fair, in Lawrenceburg, Dearborn County's agricultural society had all it could do to attract a respectable showing. By 1859, the citizens of Aurora launched "an independent opposition fair," with a bigger premium list, hoping to attract Dearborn County's farmers to their town. Struggling to survive and improve their facilities, agricultural societies found friends nearby who were willing to aid them. Hosting a successful fair doubled or tripled a town's population during fair-week, and provided an opportunity to sell "big ticket" items to farmers. Merchants and manufacturers were quick to recognize the advantages of supporting agricultural improvement.[25]

Beyond the advantages of fair-hosting, non-agricultural attractions *were* legitimate features of the county fair: it was no longer strictly an agricultural fair. Facing farmers' apathy, agricultural societies had greatly expanded their premium lists beyond livestock and agricultural products.²⁶ An ever-growing number of competitions broadened the base of public participation. By the mid-1850s, women could display their talents in table articles, needlework, butter- and cheese-making, and fine arts. The model farmer could display his orchard products, vegetables, and livestock; the mechanic his cabinetry, wagons, and tools; and the merchant his ready-made clothing and household wares. Starting as a livestock show, in just a few years, the county fair encompassed virtually the entire domain of American life. With its panoramic display of the nineteenth century's wonders, it had the power to stir the rural imagination, to close the distance between isolated farmsteads and the scattered outposts of an emerging industrial civilization.

As the spirits of local boosterism and material prosperity merged with the spirit of agricultural uplift, a new lesson was learned about the fair as an educator. With thousands attending and only dozens competing, it was clear that the fair's greatest impact was more so upon those who came to see the exhibits than on those who did the exhibiting. If the fair's educative power lay in exposing local residents to the exhibits, only the biggest fairs, with the largest premium lists, and the very best livestock, manufactures, and displays would do. With that, agricultural societies began introducing what turned out to be their last innovation before the outbreak of civil war. Premium competitions were declared "open to the world."²⁷

After the Civil War, as fairs continued to evolve with their communities, prominent competitions became dominated by "professional" exhibitors. Traveling from county to county, these professionals were livestock breeders, implement dealers, and representatives of urban centers' commercial establishments. Inducing farmers to improve remained vital to the fair. But, the educational style had changed. Generating "home-grown" improvement through friendly rivalry and emulation within the local community had been largely supplanted by introducing innovations and exemplary models of performance from "outside." Fairs, as serious agriculturists complained constantly, had degenerated from their original mission. For all the accuracy of their grumblings, the county fair had achieved a permanent place alongside Election Day and July Fourth as a premier civic education event for the rural community.

Assessing Agricultural and Civic Learning

As county fairs were the only educational institutions devoted to agricultural improvement in Indiana, in 1857, Ignatius Brown, Secretary of the State Board of Agriculture, thought it was time to take careful appraisal of their influence. It was plainly evident that "great changes" had "taken place within the last ten years in agriculture." How much of the change should be attributed to fairs? No one could deny that fairs "excited a spirit of emulation," or that fairs commanded public attention "when other agencies might have failed." But was it credible to maintain that an event "so transient and local" as a fair held only a few days each year could "produce such broad and lasting" changes in Hoosier farmers' habits? The extravagant claims of fair-boosters aside, Ignatius Brown thought it was not.²⁸

Far more influential, the spread of the railroad within Indiana was teaching farmers how to improve their farming, and giving them reasons to do so. In 1851 "general carelessness" in wheat cultivation prevailed in Monroe County; looking to the New Albany Railroad's completion, Lewis Bollman predicted "carelessness will soon vanish." Until rail was pushed through Shelby County, the burden of transporting crops 75 miles overland to Madison had been "so heavy a tax as to almost amount to a prohibition of their production." With one line complete and another nearly so, the "principal hindrance" to improvement had been removed. Knox County's farmers once seemed to have forgotten "that there is in the English language the word 'improvement.'" Now, they were "applying it to everything connected with agriculture."[29]

From less than 200 miles of track in 1849, Indiana's railroads were extended to over 2160 miles by 1860. With state and local government barred from aiding private investments by the 1851 state constitution, nearly all construction was privately financed, and much of the capital came from subscriptions by Indiana residents.[30] A powerful stimulus, the railroad's effects reached many previously isolated farmers of Indiana. It made it easier to transport bulky grain crops and livestock long distances and to receive higher prices for them. It supplied the means to improve in the form of imported livestock and farm implements. Most importantly, it gave incentives to improve in the form of consumer goods and modern conveniences. Between 1850 and 1860, as the state's population and nearly every sector of the economy grew rapidly, home-made manufactures declined almost 40 percent. With each ready-made shirt, labor-saving farm implement, and household item purchased, the Hoosier farmer found reason to improve his crop cultivation, livestock quality, and farm management. Given the railroad's impact, Ignatius Brown concluded, "some agency more powerful, permanent and constant in its effects than any number of fairs" compelled farmers "to make rapid improvements in their animals and products, and they must have made them though no societies had existed and no fairs had been held."[31]

Some Hoosier farmers were abandoning reliance on the corn-and-hog-combination; of that there was little doubt. Between 1850 and 1860 Indiana's total population and town-dwelling proportion increased slightly more than one-third. Increasingly connected to towns through webs of commerce strung by the railroads, farmers responded to new opportunities. The total value of Indiana's market garden vegetables increased 650 percent; orchard products' value almost tripled. Rye and barley increased 748 and 486 percent. To cultivate more acres more often, farmers tripled the number of asses and mules they had on hand to pull farm machinery.[32] Despite their smaller proportion in the population, farmers were growing a greater variety of crops, and more of them, to meet expanding town demand. Contrary to reformers' initial expectations, however, these changes bore only an oblique relation to scientific agriculture. Indiana's farmers were willing to adopt innovations and new crops; this did not, of necessity, require an alteration in how they conceived of themselves and their work.

High staple crop prices, cheap land values, and improved animal-powered machinery encouraged many farmers to continue farming extensively (i.e., tilling large acreage with little soil renewal) rather than intensively. By 1860, despite a decade-long campaign to turn farmers' attention away from staple crop production, wheat cultivation doubled, corn remained king, and Hoosier hogs still outnumbered Hoosier people by a 2.3 to 1 ratio. For most farmers, the new practices were additive, not transformative. In large measure they farmed—and, in all likelihood, thought of farming's role in society—as they always had. With one eye on the world market (via Chicago and other pork-and-grain cities) and the other on a nearby town, the Hoosier farmer was learning to farm differently. But the fair did not, and never could, supply the education necessary to transform him into a scientific farmer. And, the fair itself was increasingly becoming a flashpoint for contention between town and country—between respectable full-time farmers and fair-sponsoring merchants and professional men—over its program's priorities and moral concerns raised by the gambling, drinking, and debauchery that followed horse-racing, huckster stands, and sideshows (and crowds) into the fair.

Faced with the countervailing pulls of market forces on farmers' behavior and the fair's deficiencies, Ignatius Brown rendered his judgment upon the fair's utility as an educator: "The day has probably gone by, if it ever existed—when the mere dispensing of premiums could effect lasting improvements" in agriculture. A fair was good for introducing possibilities only. Which crops, livestock, machinery, and methods farmers adopted, and how they fit them to existing practice was beyond reformers' control. If the State Board of Agriculture hoped to "extend and perpetuate" what influence it exercised on Indiana's agriculture, some combination of agricultural colleges, model farms, and specifically targeted premiums for experiments in conjunction with county fairs would have to be erected.[33] Focused efforts—carried out by institutions capable of exerting a constant influence on the minds of those exposed to them, and targeting the leading edge of farmers and agriculturists rather than broadcasting among ordinary farmers—were preferred. Farmers would take advantage of such efforts (or not) once self-interest or changes in the conditions of life compelled them. This was the lesson taught by the railroad and nearly a decade's worth of educational outreach frustration.

In one respect, Ignatius Brown offered a minority viewpoint. Few men in the 1850s placed much stock in the overblown claims of public necessity made by practical colleges' advocates. As Secretary of the State Board of Agriculture, however, Ignatius Brown was in a position to survey the landscape of agricultural improvement, to draw broad conclusions from isolated local experiences, and to gauge the sentiments of local leaders. As such, his learning is suggestive of learning that may have taken place among agricultural reformers as they discovered, and attempted to bridge through trial and error experimentation, profound differences in educational and civic expectations between themselves and the common farmers they sought to engage in the educational process.

One thing all "serious" agricultural reformers were certain of by the decade's end: the agricultural improvement institutions that came of age in Indiana were not quite what had been imagined in 1851. When they launched their campaign to educate the Hoosier farmer, reformers pinned their hopes on the agricultural society. Continued indifference to the work of agricultural societies made clear just how far apart reformers' and common farmers' views were. Formal lectures, books, journals, and crop-experiment discussions were not elements of the farmer's self-conception. Reformers' initial assumption behind the fair's role—that proving the superiority of scientific agriculture's profit-making potential was the main obstacle to reform—proved erroneous. The more they relied on the fair, the more it absorbed its character from the surrounding community. Evolving rapidly into an institution that was one part agricultural education, and three parts entertainment, marketplace, and social gathering, the fair became an institution *of* the rural community (town and country) more so than *for* it. Eventually (although with reluctance and reservations), agricultural reformers learned a new public role for themselves. With leading townsmen, they became the sponsors of a civic event rather than the self-designated "instructors" of farmers. The event derived its claim to public utility from its original mission of agricultural education, but in the post-Civil War decades it would function as a nexus of civic learning in a variety of unexpected ways.

What of the civic learning of farmers who were not active "voices" in agricultural improvement? Of them, far less can be inferred, for the documentary record is almost nonexistent. Surely, their learning—whether through fairs, farm journals, observation, conversation, or hard experience—was more sharply conditioned by the market than gentlemen farmers' learning. But, a sizable contingent of farmers did learn something significant from the would-be educators of the 1850s. When the agricultural boom came to a sudden halt after the Civil War, Hoosier farmers, along with farmers across the United States, discovered fully the implications of the changing nature of rural citizenship. In response they launched their own agricultural education campaign through the Grange. In its educational–social gatherings—its monthly meetings, suppers, picnics, and "strictly agricultural" fairs—farm families sought to teach each other about scientific agriculture, farm economy, and the political economy of town and country relations; through its economic cooperatives they sought to extend self-help into the economic domain; and, through its political campaigns and lobbying they sought to teach town-dwellers about the impact modernization was having on farm life. Within a generation Hoosier farmers had learned that farming encompassed much more than growing corn and raising hogs.

Postscript: Reflections on the Civic Education of History[34]

At this point, a sensible historian who has been mentored by Ed McClellan would call a halt, and, out of courtesy, leave implication-drawing to the reader's imagination. The civic educator's inclinations, stereotypically, run in the opposite direction. I propose a compromise that seeks to straddle the historian's reserve and the civic educator's bluntness: a brief reflection on the civic education of history and a few questions that occurred to a civic educator trying to piece together the dynamics of civic learning at work in agricultural improvement.

The concerns lurking between-the-lines in Indiana's agricultural improvement campaign—worries about the moral shortcomings of individualism, indifference to identified problems of community, and disregard for the long-term consequences of individual behavior—are all too familiar. These things may be, as is often asserted, defining traits of the American character; or, they may be, as Alexis de Tocqueville speculated, inevitable products of democracy's strange admixture of free will and authority. Whatever else they might be, they are the closest things to constants that can be found in civic education.

Responding to expressions of these traits, generations of educators have imagined what a civically healthy or "good" community might be. Designing policies and institutions to move people toward a peculiar conception of well-being, they often have viewed themselves (in their fashion) as fulfilling promises implicit in the American Founding. Their mission, it seems, is to preserve aspects of a shared heritage while, at the same time, tailoring that heritage to suit their perceptions of altered conditions and their anticipations of the future. It is, by definition, a selective effort at redefinition. Awed by necessity's imperatives, civic educators, at times, seem unaware of how they have departed from popular perceptions of heritage and present conditions. At times, they seem acutely aware of this departure, but oblivious to the circumstances and patterns of thought that prevent others from joining them. If much civic education corresponds, more or less, to this characterization, what sort of questions might aid us in uncovering and reconstructing the dynamics of civic learning?

From what ingredients, past and present, remembered and perceived, are civic educators' visions of citizenship formed? What efforts do they make, as self-appointed guardians of the public, to ground themselves in the past, while experiencing the present and peering into an unknowable future? Why do reformers adopt certain strategies to teach others (who hold different notions) their civic vision? In the meeting grounds of educational and persuasive efforts, what happens to produce actual civic learning, for reformers and those they seek to reform? As they come into contact with deliberate attempts to remake the American character, how do citizens learn what American society (or "community") is and should be, and the "proper" role in it (articulated or otherwise) for people like themselves?

Admittedly, this is an incomplete list of "big" questions. Comprehensive responses to them may lie beyond the historian's grasp. Civic educators may be incapable of refraining from mutually identifying with past generations of civic educators to engage in the self-scrutiny necessary to pursue such questions very far. But, might these sorts of questions point us, as scholars, toward filling in the dark space that lies between civic education and civic learning?

To study civic education, in years past, historians and civic educators relied largely on the intentions of reformers as stated in policy documents, curriculums, articulated philosophies, mission statements, and so on. These abound; as "easy targets" of inquiry they remain heavily utilized. But, as idealizations and aspirations, they reveal a partial and distorted view, and we have become sensitive enough to the fullness of historical context to recognize how easily proclaimed intentions can be misconstrued. To gauge civic learning, we know too little of what happens after intentions have been formulated and plans set into motion; engaging in education has a way of "turning back" upon those who seek to educate. We know even less about the "targets" of civic reform: direct evidences of their hopes and worries, life experiences, awareness of the larger society, and the impact of educational efforts upon them are rare in the documentary record. How can we overcome this situation so peculiar to civic education: too much data that lead us astray and too little of the data most necessary for taking stock of how people experience curricula and pedagogies promoted to advance civic imperatives?

Two generations ago—goaded by the methodological and substantive critiques issued by Bernard Bailyn and the members of the Committee on the Role of Education in American History, "radical" revisionists, and "new" social history advocates—educational historians began to search for civic learning. Few of them called it "civic learning," although most, if not all, were alert to its civic implications. Following their leads, this case study has attempted to infer civic learning from changes made to a set of institutions devoted to agricultural education. It may not be a worthy model for application to other topics. Exploring agricultural improvement, however, has caused me to wonder: how much of "the civic" will we find in places we do not customarily associate with civic education? In examining these other places, what might we learn about civic learning that our preconceptions encourage us to overlook?

Notes

1. The most thorough treatment of early agricultural improvement is Donald Marti, *To Improve the Soil and the Mind: Agricultural Societies, Journals, and Schools in the Northeastern States, 1791–1865* (Ann Arbor, MI: University Microfilms International, 1979).
2. *Thomas Jefferson: Writings* (New York: Literary Classics of the United States, 1984), 290–291.
3. Jeremy Atack and Fred Bateman, *To Their Own Soil: Agriculture in the Antebellum North* (Ames: Iowa State University Press, 1987), 6.
4. Roger G. Kennedy, *Mr. Jefferson's Lost Cause* (Oxford: Oxford University Press, 2003), 58.
5. Richard Lyle Power, "Wet Lands and the Hoosier Stereotype," *The Mississippi Valley Historical Review* 22, 1 (June 1935): 33–48. The 1850s mark the turning point for Indiana's in-migration; the out-migration rate for the decade was −4 percent. Richard K. Vedder and Lowell E. Gallaway, "Migration and the Old Northwest," in David C. Klingaman and Richard K. Vedder, eds. *Essays in Nineteenth Century Economic History: The Old Northwest* (Athens: Ohio University Press, 1975), 160–161.
6. These are recurring themes in agricultural addresses. As an example, see Joseph A. Wright, "President's Report," *Indiana State Board of Agriculture Annual Report* (1852): 5–12. Hereafter, these reports will be designated as *SBAR*.
7. S.B. Gookins, Address to the Vigo County Fair, *SBAR* (1852): 304–305. In the 1850s, Indiana's town-dwelling proportion increased from 4.5 to 8.6 percent; John D. Barnhart and Donald F. Carmony, *Indiana: From Frontier to Industrial Commonwealth*, vol. 2 (New York: Lewis Historical Publishing Company, 1954), 14–16. On a per capita basis, corn and hog production held steady at 53 bushels and 2.3 hogs. With a smaller proportion of farmers, this represents an increase in production per farmer; see U.S. Census for raw data.
8. B.F. Morris, Address to the Ohio and Switzerland District Fair, *SBAR* (1852): 205.
9. John D. Barnhart and Donald F. Carmony, *Indiana*, vol. 2, 112–121.
10. "An Act for the encouragement of Agriculture" (February 14, 1851), 35th session, *Indiana Laws*: 6–8. How biased against the hog were the premiums? At the State Fair of 1852 some prize-values for livestock were: for cattle ($202 and 10 silver cups, each probably worth $25) horses and mules ($164 and 6 silver cups), and sheep ($138). Hog premiums were $20 and 2 silver cups. See *SBAR* (1852): 31–35.

11. T.H. Bringhurst, Address to the Cass County Fair, *SBAR* (1852): 85; J.W. Gordon, Address to the Hendricks County Fair, *SBAR* (1853): 125–126.
12. Joseph A. Wright, "Annual Message to the General Assembly," *SBAR* (1852): 1; Arthur Humphrey, Ohio and Switzerland County District Report, *SBAR* (1853): 168; Tippecanoe County Report, *SBAR* (1851): 189; John M. Barbour, Fayette County Report, *SBAR* (1853): 85.
13. A general characterization of agricultural reformers is provided in Clarence H. Danhof, *Change in Agriculture: The Northern United States, 1820–1870* (Cambridge: Harvard University Press, 1969), 64; David Blanke, *Sowing the American Dream* (Athens: Ohio University Press, 2000), 16–17; J. Morgan, Decatur County Report, *SBAR* (1852): 103.
14. *SBAR* (1856): 99; Bartholomew County Report, *SBAR* (1851): 120; Daniel T. Smith, Wells County Report, *SBAR* (1859): 182. Early fairs also required entry fees from competitors.
15. Joseph A. Wright, "President's Report," *SBAR* (1852): 6–7; J.P. Brady, Franklin County Report, *SBAR* (1852): 113. By 1857 only ten societies reported awarding books or journals; *SBAR* (1857): 713–714.
16. C.L. Murray, Elkhart County Report, *SBAR* (1852): 108; Nathan Kimball, Washington and Orange District Report, *SBAR* (1853): 214; J. Morgan, Decatur County Report, *SBAR* (1852): 104; William Keaton, Johnson County Report, *SBAR* (1852): 155.
17. Hancock County Report, *SBAR* (1854–1855): 48; "An Act authorizing county agricultural societies to purchase and hold real estate" (February 7, 1855), 38th Session, *Indiana Laws*: 49.
18. G.W. Crawford, La Porte County Report, *SBAR* (1854–1855): 84; G.D. Wagner, Warren County Report, *SBAR* (1854–1855): 164; Mark Cummings, Marshall County Report, *SBAR* (1859): 77; H.E. Woodruff, Porter County Report, *SBAR* (1853): 174–175.
19. Ignatius Brown, *SBAR* (1857): 4; John B. Elliott, Posey County Report, *SBAR* (1859): 101; Huntington County Report, *SBAR* (1857): 132; A.B. McKee, Knox County Report, *SBAR* (1854–1855): 77; H.E. Woodruff, Porter County Society, *SBAR* (1853): 174–175.
20. Shelby County Report, *SBAR* (1851): 179 and (1854–1855): 134; Franklin County Report, *SBAR* (1852): 113 and (1854–1855): 34. Counties Hendricks, Knox, Madison, and Greene also discontinued monthly meetings the same year; others followed. "An Act to amend . . . An act authorizing county agricultural societies . . ." (March 9, 1861), 41st Session, *Indiana Laws*: 2–3.
21. Calculations are based on counties with full data sets in the tables in *SBAR* (1857): 712–714; for financial status, see *SBAR* (1856): 158–159. Besides an annual legislative subsidy ($1–2,000), the State Board solicited voluntary contributions totaling over $25,000 between 1852 and 1869; *SBAR* (1869): 375–376.
22. A.J. Boone, Boone County Report, *SBAR* (1859): 5; Miami County Report, *SBAR* (1857): 143–144. Returns on licensing varied, ranging from 2 to 43 percent. Calculations are based on tables in *SBAR* (1857): 712–714.
23. W.G. Ralston, Warrick County Report, *SBAR* (1858–1859): 291–292; John Sutherland, LaPorte County Report, SBAR (1858–1859): 177.
24. Proceedings, *SBAR* (1858–1859): xii–xiii; J.C. Helm, Delaware County Report, *SBAR* (1858–1859): 72; Miami County Report, *SBAR* (1857): 143–144; A.J. Boone, Boone County Report, *SBAR* (1858–1859): 10; Washington County Report, *SBAR* (1857): 163–164.
25. Switzerland and Ohio District Report, *SBAR* (1859): 117; Dearborn County Report, *SBAR* (1859): 24–28; Franklin County Report, *SBAR* (1857): 126–127; Porter County Report, *SBAR* (1857): 149–150.

26. For comparison: in 1853, for the 20 societies reporting such data, the mean premium list value was $107.50; in 1857, for 36 societies reporting, $316.82. See *SBAR* for specified years.
27. Fayette County declared its competitions "open to the world" in 1855; *SBAR* (1854–1855): 26. At its next meeting, the State Board did likewise, recommending counties do the same; SBAR (1856): 8–9. Most counties appear to have taken a few years to follow suit.
28. Ignatius Brown, "Secretary's Report," *SBAR* (1857): 95–109.
29. Lewis Bollman, Monroe County Report, *SBAR* (1851): 122–123; David Whitcomb, Shelby County Report, *SBAR* (1851): 181; Nathaniel Usher, Knox County Report, *SBAR* (1854–1855): 79.
30. Barnhart and Carmony, *Indiana*, vol. 2, 35–36, 256–257.
31. Ignatius Brown, "Secretary's Report," *SBAR* (1857): 98–100.
32. Changes in production are computed using 1850 and 1860 U.S. Census data.
33. Ignatius Brown, "Secretary's Report," *SBAR* (1857): 98–100, 16.
34. My thinking on the historian's quest for learning has been profoundly influenced by Richard Storr, "The Role of Education in American History: A Memorandum . . ." *Harvard Educational Review* 46, 3 (1976): 331–354, and "The Education of History: Some Impressions," *Harvard Educational Review* 31, 2 (1961): 124–135.

Chapter 7

Widening the Circle: African American Perspectives on Moral and Civic Learning

Paulette Patterson Dilworth

We have failed. They are worse citizens today and more dangerous to the State than they were 30 years ago. Education has had no more effect on them morally and intellectually than it has physically. God made them [N]egroes and we cannot by education make them white folks. We are on the wrong track. We must turn back.

—*Allen Daniel Candler, Governor of Georgia, 1901*

We must, whatever else we do, insist on those studies which by the consensus of educators are calculated to train our people to think, which will give them the power of appreciation and make them righteous.

—*Anna Julia Cooper, 1930*

As these comments illustrate, in the early twentieth century black and white perspectives on the kind of education that would be beneficial to African Americans were loaded with controversy. At the center of the debate was the issue of just what content and practice should shape moral and civic learning for African Americans, who at that time were denied full constitutional and natural human rights. Few other cases show the tension between myth and reality or prove to be as stark as the African American pursuit of racial justice through education. Georgia Governor Allen Candler expressed a sentiment that was at that time reflective of southern whites' thinking about what should be the proper aim of education for blacks. Coming some 30 years later, Anna Julia Cooper's comments suggested that the controversy had not been resolved in the North or the South. The distance between the ideal and actual educational practices focusing on the African American experience is key to understanding the unfulfilled promise of democracy in the United States.[1]

More than 60 years ago, Gunner Myrdal identified what he called "the American dilemma." Myrdal observed that the United States was a society that proclaimed the ideals of liberty, justice, and equality. Simultaneously, white people in the United States tended to accept, condone, and sometimes exhibit attitudes and behaviors toward African Americans that were antithetical to such ideals.[2] Yet, the ideals were made explicit in the nation's founding documents, including the Declaration of Independence, the U.S. Constitution, and the Bill of Rights. From the beginning, however, the commitment to a republic of laws and moral reasoning was constrained and contradicted by the expectation of the nation's founders that the citizens participating in our democratic experiment would be white and male. This then was the American dilemma posed by Myrdal. It has affected moral and civic education in unique ways. Since those early times, diverse groups of people and African Americans in particular have attempted to alter that inheritance. Many of the social and political tensions that have shaped moral and civic learning in the past persist in the twenty-first century, albeit in new forms.

Indeed, fostering moral and civic consciousness among citizens has been an enduring educational concern in the United States. Educators and scholars continue debates about what knowledge and skills should be advanced in the learning process. Yet, today's challenges are not easily understood or addressed in the absence of broader historical insights. Since the inception of public education in the United States, the ideals of moral and civic education have been inextricably linked with the American definition of a republican government. In the late nineteenth century and the early decades of the twentieth century, a number of African American educators and scholars like Anna Julia Cooper, Mary McCloud Bethune, Nannie Helen Burroughs, Lucy Kraft Laney, W.E.B. DuBois, Booker T. Washington, and Carter G. Woodson began to express a vision of African American education that emphasized resistance and the need for a black perspective on moral and civic learning.[3] These individuals acted with rhetorical force, speaking and writing to a national audience that did not recognize their full rights of equality as citizens. Although there was variation in their points of view and in the specific social, political, and economic issues addressed, they shared a common and unyielding concern about the nature of African American racial justice. They were generally motivated by the moral imperative to respond to and render null the deeply held white views about black inferiority.[4]

Despite the presence of unequal power relations between white and black Americans, until recently, there has been very little systematic inquiry into the development of core moral and civic values specific to African American cultural traditions and the contradictions emerging from their socially marginalized position in society.[5] Janie Ward maintains that the African American differences in moral perspectives have rarely been examined in any serious manner in mainstream moral education scholarship.[6] Similarly, Walker and Snarey point out that "race matters in moral formation" and that new understandings are needed to better explain the role of race in the contemporary discourse on moral development and moral education. Likewise, social science scholars have called attention to the lack of a critical race perspective in civic learning.[7] Consequently, mainstream historical and contemporary discussions about moral and civic education provide only a partial explanation of the ways in which African Americans and other diverse groups of people come to understand what it means to become and be a moral citizen.

In this essay, I synthesize a varied collection of scholarly literature written by and about nineteenth- and twentieth-century African American scholars and activists focusing on moral and civic learning. Particular attention is paid to understanding how African Americans ascribed meaning to moral and civic learning for racial justice. The essay seeks to widen the historical landscape of moral education by examining the parallel experiences and thinking of African Americans and the contradictory themes they sought to address. According to Christian ethicist Katie Cannon, throughout African American history, blacks have developed different ethical values in response to perilous social, economic, and political circumstances.[8] Given the complexities of those conditions, what actions and thoughts shaped African American perspectives on civic and moral learning? What role did the black church play in fostering African American moral and civic learning? How did the social and political conditions in which they lived shape differences in thinking among African American men and women about civic and moral learning? As will be shown in the sections to follow, in developing and articulating ethical and civic values, African Americans were most concerned with challenging the moral peril that framed unjust civic, economic, political, and social structures that denied them their full humanity and equal citizenship rights. In the essay I combine and synthesize published literature written by and about African Americans to extend the moral and civic learning dialogue. Interdisciplinary in nature, this literature tends to reflect a range of perspectives by African American scholars and writers. Collectively, their voices help to create a portrait that represents more clearly the diversity of views among African Americans.

Early Roots of African American Moral and Civic Learning

In *Moral Education in America*, Edward McClellan writes that "the vast array of European peoples who settled the American colonies brought with them both an extraordinary commitment to moral education and a rich variety of approaches to the task."[9] At the same time, it is intriguing to note that many of these immigrants and their descendents would eventually sanction African slavery as a viable economic enterprise in the newly formed nation.[10] In part, the moral rationale offered to justify the slave trade was to "civilize and Christianize" the Africans. For a brief period, missionary efforts to teach slaves about Christianity were allowed because some slaveholders believed that Biblical teaching would make slaves more content and efficient workers and accepting of their plight.[11] As noted below, not all owners accepted the justification. In any case it rested uneasily in a moral paradox, and many of those in bondage recognized the irony of using the Bible to justify slavery. Although slaves were taught to obey, respect, and fear their masters, eventually some would come to understand that even the selected Biblical teachings about slavery were inconsistent with their inhumane treatment on southern plantations and especially with fundamental Christian beliefs.[12]

Apparently, owners expected slaves to comply willingly with teachings from scriptures, but they were not prepared to live by the same religious principles. Slaves could see the contradiction but, at the same time, many did not allow the dissonance to interfere with their receiving spiritual teachings that would support their eventual moral and civic agency to act privately and publicly to resist oppression. African American history is replete with examples from the lives of activists like Harriet Tubman, Frederick Douglass, Sojourner Truth, and the thousands of former slaves who enlisted in the Union Army to fight for their freedom.[13] Once slave owners recognized the potential liberating force of biblical instruction, they acted to restrict missionary teaching among the slaves. Historian Henry Louis Gates, Jr., has explored and documented this relationship between literacy and freedom in the slave narrative. Gates chronicles the source of this connection in detail. Drawing from such European philosophers as Kant, Hume, and Hegel, he illustrates how illiteracy was used as the basis for arguing that slaves were subhuman. In this western philosophical tradition a consensus could be summarized: A person's capacity for reason exercised through literacy became the ultimate means of separating him or her from animals. Gates points out that slaves like Frederick Douglass believed that learning to read and write was the most important way to prove they were human. Gates rightly concludes that for slaves, literacy was not essentially a skill, rather, it "was a commodity they were forced to trade for their humanity."[14]

Indeed, most slave owners were hesitant to introduce Christianity to their slaves, believing that such teaching would eventually lead them to ideas about freedom and equality. In the South, slave owners moved to control literacy among blacks by placing limits on slave preachers and slave worship services. Philosophy and religion scholar James Cone maintains that members of pre-Civil War black churches began to recognize Christianity as a gospel of liberation, and for that reason, they refused to accept an interpretation of Christianity that did not focus on civic freedom.[15] Indeed, the idea is intriguing that even during slavery African Americans recognized Christianity as a belief system that nurtured and promoted a message of deliverance. To some degree, this act of resistance represented the beginning of an organized civil rights movement for African American racial justice. Slaves integrated what they knew of their native African religions with what their masters, literate blacks, and white missionaries taught them about Christianity. From these lessons, they forged their own form of Christianity, devising a moral creed of hope and liberation.

After the southern states outlawed basic literacy for black people, slaves turned to clandestine activities to learn to read and write. African American historian Heather Williams notes that black people would engage in bartering boxing lessons for reading and writing lessons, eavesdropping on white classrooms and private tutorials, and holding secret schools in large pits in the woods. In her analysis of how "ordinary African Americans in the South" provided education for themselves, Williams uses the individual stories of slaves and freedmen to illustrate how they acted with moral and civic courage to learn to read and write. Williams's account also shows that during Reconstruction, after it was no longer illegal to teach blacks to read and write,

African Americans built their own schools or set up schools in churches. African Americans who already knew how to read and write became the first teachers. When they exhausted their skills, they wrote letters to missionaries in the North asking them to come teach African Americans in the South.[16]

To summarize, during and after slavery African Americans viewed literacy as necessary to their moral and civic struggle for racial justice in the United States. They understood the potential of literacy to be a powerful weapon in their quest for civil rights. Foremost, to the enslaved it was important that they learn to evaluate texts such as the Bible critically, as a way to resist white indoctrination and Christian hypocrisy. Although whites in the South actively discouraged a culture of learning among African Americans by making it illegal to teach them to read and write, literacy would eventually become an important mission of the black church. Ultimately, this was the institution that accepted the challenge of teaching African Americans to value literacy as a moral and civic imperative.

The Role of the Black Church in Moral and Civic Learning

Scholars of African American education, history, religion, and activism have illustrated that historically the black church has been an important agent of social control and civic organization among African Americans.[17] Several white religious organizations and churches contributed to meeting the educational needs of ex-slaves. Between 1846 and 1867, sixty-five white societies were supporting the education of African Americans. Between 1862 and 1874, sixteen of these donated approximately $4 million to support the education of African Americans.[18] These organizations also assisted with recruiting teachers and providing school supplies. Still, the black church provided one of the earliest and most acknowledged means for African Americans to initiate their own systems of moral support and social control within their own communities. Yet, despite the historical significance of the black church as a unique and powerful social institution within the African American community,[19] its potential influence for promoting moral and civic behavior among black Americans has been largely disregarded in mainstream historical and contemporary scholarship on moral and civic learning.[20]

Black church historians agree that in the United States the role of the black church in civic and social reform cannot be overstated.[21] Over the past 30 years, scholars have noted that the communal influence of the black church made it one of the most important institutions in the African American community.[22] Primarily, it promoted black self-expression and creativity amid perilous social and political movements. As a religious agent, the black church provided a refuge from the daily oppression slaves faced, and after Emancipation, the church played a significant role in promoting civic and moral learning as a critical path to racial uplift. It became a site for developing black leadership skills that were grounded in fostering moral courage and civic responsibility.

As DuBois noted in *The Souls of Black Folk*, the black church, especially after Emancipation, represented in the "peculiar circumstances of the black man's environment as the one expression of his higher life."[23] Like DuBois, contemporary black church historians maintain that the public function of the church as a social and religious institution must be considered more broadly because black churches were not solely confined to traditional roles.[24] DuBois observed:

> Various organizations meet here,—the church proper, the Sunday-school, two or three insurance societies, women's societies, secret societies, and mass meetings of various kinds. Entertainments, suppers and lectures are held beside the five or six regular weekly religious services . . . . This social, intellectual, and economic centre is a religious centre of great power.[25]

In his scholarship on the black church, E. Franklin Frazier supported DuBois's observation by noting the expansive role of the church in African American communities. Frazier noted that the churches' activities covered economic, educational, social, and political issues. In Frazier's view, the church provided African Americans with the agency to develop moral courage and the language of resistance they needed to challenge white oppression and discrimination. Frazier observed that black churches continuously negotiated their charge to serve the religious needs of its members and to respond to the social and political realities shaping the conditions of black life in the United States. Historically, during times of crisis in the African American community, black people turned to the church for direction, support, and leadership. In general, the black church responded by moving beyond its religious mission to embrace broader needs of the African American community, particularly in the years following the Civil War, when African Americans' efforts to push for a national response to their plight moved forward with urgency.[26]

In the North and South, African American educators, scholars, and social activists continued pressing for equal educational opportunity for black people. African American education historians have documented how black women and men engaged in vigorous public debates about the educational needs of their community.[27] Education for liberation and racial uplift was another primary concern of black churches. As noted above, after the Civil War, churches took up the task of formally educating many of the newly freed slaves. During these years, black churches established a large number of elementary schools, high schools, and colleges. In many instances, church halls were used as temporary classrooms. The commitment to education by black churches responded to long-standing needs and also to signs of achievement. The literacy rate among their people was rising significantly.[28]

Education for Moral and Civic Learning

By the middle of the nineteenth century there were 4.5 million blacks in the United States. The earliest education provided to them was by northern missionaries who hoped to convert them to Christianity. At the same time, white southerners opposed the education of blacks because they saw it as a threat to the continuation of slavery. In spite of individual efforts, the education of blacks remained low and sporadic until Lincoln issued the Emancipation Proclamation in 1863. The literacy rate that was around 5 percent in the 1860s rose to 40 percent in 1890 and by 1910 it was at 70 percent.[29] The American Missionary Association (AMA) opened schools in several areas and later assisted in the opening of several historically black colleges. Most notably, those institutions included Fisk University, Talladega College, and Hampton Institute. In short, the educational picture was improving.

In time, controversy erupted between Booker T. Washington and W. E. B. DuBois over the issue of what educational policy would be most beneficial to African Americans. Washington argued for industrial or vocational education as the major focus while DuBois advocated a liberal classical education. DuBois believed that preparing a "talented tenth" would provide the intellectual leadership and education needed by the masses of black people. While the debate centered on education, the two held different socio-political philosophies. Washington's accommodationist philosophy, in combination with his emphasis on industrial training, appealed to northern industrial capitalists who sought not only to produce more efficient black workers but also to restore acceptable relationships with southern whites. In contrast, DuBois's more radical call for full equality and his emphasis on struggle created tension between blacks and whites. At the center of the Washington/DuBois debate was the Hampton Model of education that James Anderson characterizes as one of the "great ironies of Afro-American history." Anderson writes that "the ex-slaves' conception of universal schooling and social progress was conceived and nurtured by a Yankee, Samuel Chapman Armstrong, and a former slave, Booker T. Washington."[30] The Hampton curriculum focused on teaching students "what" to think as opposed to teaching them "how" to think. Essentially the Hampton curriculum was devoid of intellectual criticism and thought, and laid the foundation for teaching students to understand and accept a second-class citizenship status.[31]

A number of African American educators and intellectuals were eager to respond to the Hampton model of educational practices reflecting the values and interests defined by white men. The Hampton curriculum was the educational precedent of Washington's accommodationist strategies found in the curriculum at Tuskegee Institute. In part, Washington spoke about the need for a union of "head, heart, and hand" as integral to developing the whole black person. In the early twentieth century, it was becoming apparent that a spirit of enterprise prevailed among large numbers of blacks. Washington's goal was to find the appropriate means to transmit this spirit to greater numbers of African Americans. He appealed to black identity, and to the individual's responsibility to contribute to racial uplift. Washington's view of racial uplift was blacks supporting and helping each other as a necessary part of their efforts. Self-help began with individual willingness to commit to the discipline of work, no matter how modest or lowly the labor. Washington associated moral virtues to his "bootstraps" philosophy of self-help. The defining expression born in this period pressed African Americans to live their lives so that each would be a "credit to the race."

Historically, discrimination and inequality have always characterized the education of blacks in the South. Education historians have demonstrated this by analyzing discrepancies in the allocation of federal, state, and local funds for teachers' salaries, schoolbooks, supplies, and buildings.[32] In North Carolina, considered one of the more "enlightened" states, during 1924–1925 about $6.7 million was spent on new buildings for rural white children while only $444,000 was spent for black children. Blacks in the North did not fare much better after public schools were sanctioned for African Americans. Inadequate facilities and scarce resources were typical in segregated black schools.[33] Inequity and discrimination faced those few students who attended integrated schools.

Washington believed there was moral value in economic enterprise and work. Elizabeth Wright described how his message of economic development was valued by a great many blacks of the time.[34] For example, in 1899, William Pettiford headed the black-owned Alabama Penny Loan & Savings in Birmingham, Alabama. He was determined to establish the bank as a place for economic education for Birmingham's African American community. Pittiford's goal was to educate everyday people in the principles and economy of saving, stressing the importance of "sacrificing today to build for tomorrow." Pettiford launched a campaign to attract new bank patrons and found that approximately 90 percent of his new customers had never owned bank accounts. He also viewed it as his moral duty to educate African Americans about "the wise use of money." He set about educating bank patrons about finance and investment, while "providing loans and other services." Pettiford maintained that by encouraging blacks to save and make wise investments, "it has been possible to stimulate a wholesome desire among our people to become property owners and substantial citizens." Penny Savings became well known for granting loans for home building and business development. The bank was praised also for the role it played in keeping the money of blacks "constantly in circulation in our immediate community." Washington called the operation of Penny Loan & Savings the best example of "how closely the moral and spiritual interests of our people are interwoven with their material and economical welfare." He praised Pettiford as "far-seeing enough to attempt to develop this wealth that is latent in the Negro people." Washington believed that using financial clout to combat racism was just as moral as more public displays of resistance.[35]

According to Wright's account, Washington also praised Harlem Realtor Philip Payton, who gained national attention when he and other black realtors bought two apartment buildings in order to prevent the eviction of black tenants by white landlords. A newspaper editorial cited Payton's actions as an "unexpected and novel method of resisting race prejudice." Payton's sense of moral responsibility provided an example of the ideas that Washington aimed to teach. Washington believed that by acquiring wealth as Payton had done, African Americans would gain economic capital to confront discrimination and oppression.[36]

Education scholar Derrick Aldridge points out that while DuBois pressed for more education that was intellectually rigorous and classical in nature, he did understand the need for industrial and vocational education. In *The Souls of Black Folk* he wrote:

> I insist that the question of the future is how best to keep these millions from brooding over the wrongs of the past and the differences of the present, so that all their energies

may be bent toward cheerful striving and cooperation with their white neighbors toward a larger, juster, and fuller future. That one wise method of doing this lies in the closer knitting of the Negro to the great industrial possibilities of the South is a great truth. And this the common schools and the manual training and the trade schools are working to accomplish. But these alone are not enough.[37]

Clearly, DuBois did not dismiss entirely the benefits of industrial education for African Americans. Through a critical analysis of DuBois's educational philosophy, Aldridge clarifies the ways in which DuBois's and Washington's "goals for racial uplift through economic means and hard work were similar."[38] DuBois acknowledged that African Americans must take responsibility for addressing the moral tension relating to their educational needs by taking charge of their own fate. Again, he wrote:

> The foundation of knowledge in this race, as in others, must be sunk deep in the college and university if we would build a solid, permanent structure. Internal problems of social advance must inevitably come, problems of work and wages, of families and homes, of morals and the true valuing of the things of life; and all these and other inevitable problems of civilization the Negro must meet and solve largely for himself.[39]

Carter G. Woodson expressed disapproval of the Hampton Model in his classic work, *The Mis-Education of the Negro*.[40] As a historian, Woodson emerged to offer his perspective on the debate about what kind of educational aims would best respond to the needs of African Americans. Primarily, Woodson believed that the education blacks received after Emancipation helped them to develop a negative racial identity. He advocated moral and civic learning that would help blacks and whites to confront what he characterized as the "mis-education" about African American life.

As these debates unfolded, Washington developed a counter-argument in defense of his philosophy of education. He explained his belief this way: "Industrial training will be more potent for the good of the race, when its relation to the other phases of essential education is more clearly understood." He concluded that "education to fulfill its mission for any people anywhere should be symmetrical and sensible."

The difference between the perspectives of DuBois and Washington was that of expediency versus tolerance; civic protest versus self-help; overt activism versus the persistence of personal and moral development in the home; seeking redress of rights in the courts of America for better jobs, schools, and educational opportunities versus seeking knowledge to create their own jobs, schools, and educational opportunities. Yet, moral and civic learning was the educational imperative that was important to the racial uplift of the African American community. The fact that African Americans claimed education as a civil right challenged the moral fabric of U.S. democratic practices.

This synthesis of the major issues and debates shaping African American perspectives about moral and civic learning is dominated mostly by male voices. However, African American women were not silent in public and private discussion about the necessity of moral and civic learning for racial justice.

Womanist Perspectives and Moral and Civil Learning

Enslaved and free black women in the United States developed their own politics of resistance that positioned them uniquely at the intersection of race, class, and gender. Consequently, there is a need to clarify and understand the thinking of African American women on the issue of moral and civic learning. As mentioned in the introduction. African American women mounted their own efforts for racial justice. In her discussion of African American women in the Baptist Church in the late nineteenth century, Higgenbotham observed that the black church provided a discursive space where African American women criticized both Jim Crow and women's subordination in the black community. They developed and used their own networks to launch reform campaigns focusing on causes like inequality of educational opportunity, fighting poverty, anti-lynching, and racial uplift.[41]

Anna Julia Cooper believed strongly that education was the key to social equality for women and that access to higher education was critical to women to become a distinct political and social force. In *A Voice from the South*, Cooper writes that "the fundamental agency under God in the regeneration, the re-training of the race, as well as the ground work and starting point of its progress upward, must be the black woman."[42] As Cooper saw it, "Only the Black Woman can say when and where I enter, in the quiet, undisputed dignity of my womanhood, without violence and without suing or special patronage, then and there the whole Negro race enters with me." Cooper's vision of the black woman and her involvement in racial uplift revealed, in part, the influence of nineteenth-century bourgeois ideals of "true womanhood," which assumed that women represented the moral center of a society. At the same time, Cooper argued consistently for the unique position of black women in a male-dominated, racist society, contending that they brought to bear on contemporary problems an invaluable perspective forged in the crucible of multiple and intersecting oppressions. The full development of their talents—especially through formal education, Cooper reasoned—would be invaluable not just to women or blacks generally but to the nation as a whole. It also followed that no one could or should speak for black women. Cooper believed that it was critical that the black woman's voice be raised on her own behalf. By the mid-1890s, Cooper had come to be recognized as an important member of the black intelligentsia. She was active in the Bethel Literary and Historical Association in Washington, D.C., and she received an invitation to join the American Negro Academy, the previously male-only organization of such leading black thinkers as DuBois and Francis Grimke.

African American feminist scholar Patricia Hill Collins identified three themes that are instructive for understanding the black woman's political activism: racial solidarity; structural analyses of black economic disadvantage; and the centrality of moral and ethical principles to black political struggles.[43] Collins maintains that this choice of political agendas came at a cost to black women, namely, the sacrifice of their interests as women, and the sacrifice of their interests as individuals. Collins maintains that because of present historical conditions of social and geographical mobility among U.S. blacks that generate new "politics of containment," traditional models of black women's activism may not be adequate within the current context. Collins explores the notion of public and private, noting that historically, to be able to move into the white-dominated public sphere signified political and social freedom. As slaves, blacks existed as private property, not public citizens. As a result of these historical conditions, activism was centered on the ability of black women to participate in the public sphere.

The over-arching lesson from the African American woman's perspective is that black women were subjected to conflicting moral concerns. In addition to advocating changes in social, economic, and education policies, black women were striving to be "good women and good workers." For example, Cooper's distinguished record as a scholar and teacher did not protect her from scandal. In 1904 she was the subject of gossip in what became known as the M Street School Controversy. Cooper was criticized for allegedly condoning smoking and drinking by her students and morally questionable behavior by her teachers, and she was the focus of rumors linking her romantically with a member of the school's faculty whom she raised as a foster child. Despite the support of many local blacks, Cooper was fired from the M Street School in 1906. After teaching in Missouri, she returned in 1910 to the school, known as Paul Laurence Dunbar High School after 1916, where she worked until her retirement in 1930.

Cannon notes that black women live out a moral wisdom that is different from that of black men because of the uniqueness of black women's vulnerability and exploitation. This moral wisdom does not liberate black women from the confusing demands of institutionalized race and gender discrimination, but rather it exposes an ethical assumption that is hostile to the ongoing survival of black womanhood. The moral guidance of black women captures the ethical qualities of what is real and what is of value to women in the African American community. The resulting narratives bear witness to their wisdom in the face of "the insidious effects of racism, sexism and economic exploitation on members of their communities."[44] Because of their loyalty to black community culture—especially traditions and social mores— the work of black women serves as a repository for folk-knowledge preserving the past and ushering in the future of black community life. "I have found," writes Cannon, "that this tradition is the nexus between the real, lived texture of Black life and the cultural values implicitly passed on and received from one generation to the next."

Conclusions

As we have seen, African American perspectives on moral and civic learning have been defined by contradictions both in theory and among actual historical figures. In a continuous whole, nineteenth- and early twentieth-century educators and scholars accomplished their mission of challenging the process by which blacks were divested of moral and civic status through slavery and white Christian ideologies. African American men and women acting with moral and civic agency relied on accommodationist and resistance strategies in their pursuit of racial justice.

This focus on the African American perspective on moral and civic learning reveals a vibrant network of blacks who insisted upon the value, first, of literacy as critical to their fight for civil rights. The role of this network in legitimating education as a moral and civil right has a politically potent feature in the African American community. In the United States moral and civic learning have been heavily influenced by historically defined political and social contexts. Yet, education scholars and researchers rarely acknowledge the context and distinctive nature of moral and civic learning and its implications for African Americans. I have attempted to illustrate how locating discussions of moral and civic learning in a wider context can reveal insights that have been obscured absent considerations of racial and gender issues. In this inquiry, the most important dilemma was the question of what kind of moral and civic learning processes emerged as the dominant ones from among the ambivalent traditional tendencies and possibilities in the United States Today, when one asks the question of what it means to be an American citizen, the response must somehow take into account both democracy and diversity in the United States. Accounts of U.S. history show that every generation has been challenged by diverse ethnic and racial groups to expand the meaning of democracy and citizenship. In 1903, at the dawn of the twentieth century, W.E.B DuBois observed that "the problem of the twentieth century is the problem of the color line." At the dawn of the twenty-first century the crisis of race remains an enduring and unresolved "American dilemma."

For African Americans during the early twentieth century, the socialization process was rooted in a political ideology of *accommodation*. The accommodationist philosophy was institutionalized in the form of an industrial education curriculum. Accommodationist thought dictated that African Americans accept the social order as it existed. That the educational philosophy and scholarship of an African American provided the perspective to frame the educational agenda for subjugated members of society is significant. However, with regard to citizenship education what is more revealing is how some African American educators and scholars used their thinking and writing to resist the indoctrination and hegemony of whites.

In recent years, political science scholars have focused on exploring ideology as a meaningful way of understanding African American political behavior and thinking.[45] Michael Dawson noted that political ideologies ingrained in African American cultural and intellectual traditions have worked to challenge the premises of conventional American political thinking and actions. More importantly, this body of work shows that these understandings are tied to a history of African American intellectual tradition that can inform contemporary tactical thinking about education for democratic citizenship.[46] A careful reading of this work reveals that an African American counter-public has always operated beyond the reach of powerful whites, and that the work being done in that counter-public is distinct from the hegemonic work of the elite discourse. To fully understand the complex dimensions of moral and civic learning and its significance to African Americans and other disenfranchised groups, we must give more attention to this counter-public. More important, contemporary moral and civic education should focus not only on the rights and responsibilities of citizens but also on the meanings and conflicting interpretations that have shaped its history and practice in the United States.

Implications for Practice

African American perspectives on moral and civic learning can contribute to improving education in these areas. The lessons learned from looking back at the ways in which African Americans embraced moral and civic learning in the past can support efforts to improve practice in the present. The growth of an educated person is much more than achievement of academic and technical skills. The act of learning involves awareness and growth culminating in moral and civic maturity. Therefore, a wholly educated individual should be able to analyze and critique traditional moral principles and customs. A fully educated person should be able to evaluate the adequacy of moral and civic systems by raising questions about the suitability for theory and practice and assemble those concepts, principles, and judgments using consistent moral criticism. Clearly, public education should not take on the role of indoctrination or imposing particular moral values or ideas on students. At the same time, moral and civic education should not be content with cynical questioning of all moral concepts and traditions. Rather, the civically enlightened and responsible citizen equipped with moral reasoning is able to apply the following:

- recognize and study a wide range of moral and civic concepts, standards, and assumptions;
- discuss and deliberate about moral issues openly; develop a respect for and acceptance of ambiguities and disagreements;
- and form reasoned moral judgments responsibly, while examining the different judgments of others.

Notes

1. See James D. Anderson, *The Education of Blacks in the South, 1860–1935* (Chapel Hill: University of North Carolina Press, 1988). The quote from Allen Candler was originally cited in Leon F. Litwack, "The White Man's Fear of the Educated Negro: How the Negro Was Fitted for His Natural and Logical Calling," *The Journal of Blacks in Higher Education* 20 (1998):104. For Anna Julia Cooper's quote see Charles Lemert and Esme Bhan, *The Voice of Anna Julia Cooper: Including a Voice from the South* (Lanham, MD: Rowan & Littlefield, 1998), 251. In this essay, *African American* and *black* are used interchangeably as I recognize each as a legitimate and accurate name for persons of African ancestry in the United States.
2. Gunner Myrdal with the assistance of R. Sterner and R. Rose, *An American Dilemma: The Negro Problem and Modern Democracy* (New York: Harper & Row, 1944).
3. Paulette P. Dilworth, "Competing Conceptions of Citizenship Education: Carter G. Woodson and Thomas Jesse Jones," *International Journal of Social Education* 18, 1 (2004): 1–15.
4. Derrick P. Aldridge, "Conceptualizing a DuBoisian Philosophy of Education: Toward a Model for African-American Education," *Educational Theory* 49, 3 (1999): 359–380.
5. See, e.g., Vanessa Siddle Walker and John R. Snarey, eds., *Race-ing Moral Formation* (New York: Teachers College Press, 2004).
6. Ibid., Janie Ward, "Forward," xi.

7. See e.g., Gloria Ladson-Billings, ed., *Critical Race Theory Perspectives on Social Studies: The Profession, Policies, and Curriculum* (Greenwich, CT: Information Age Publishing, 2003), 1.
8. Katie G. Cannon, *Black Womanist Ethics* (Atlanta, GA: Scholars Press, 1988).
9. B. Edward McClellan, *Moral Education in America: Schools and the Shaping of Character from Colonial Times to the Present* (New York: Teachers College Press, 1999), 1.
10. John Hope Franklin, *From Slavery to Freedom: A History of Negro Americans*, 4th edn. (New York: Alfred A. Knopf, 1974).
11. Janet Duitsman Cornelius, *Slave Missions and the Black Church in the Antebellum South* (Columbia: University of South Carolina Press, 1999); John Hope Franklin, *From Slavery to Freedom*, 57.
12. William H. Swatos, Jr., ed., *Encyclopedia of Religion and Society* (Walnut Creek, CA: AltaMira Press, 1998).
13. John Hope Franklin, *From Slavery to Freedom*.
14. Henry L. Gates, Jr. and Charles T. Davis, eds., *The Slave's Narrative* (New York: Oxford University Press, 1985), xi–xxxiv.
15. James H. Cone, *A Black Theology of Liberation* (New York: Orbis Press, 1990).
16. Heather Williams, *Self-Taught: African American Education in Slavery and Freedom* (Chapel Hill: University of North Carolina Press, 2005).
17. For more detailed accounts of the historical significance of the African American church, see W.E.B. DuBois, "Some Efforts of the American Negroes for Their Own Betterment," in E. Franklin Frazier, ed., *The Negro Church in America* (New York: Schocken Books, 1963); C. Eric Lincoln, *The Black Experience in Religion* (New York: Anchor Books, 1974); C. Eric Lincoln and L.H. Mamiya, *The Black Church in the African American Experience* (Durham, NC: Duke University Press, 1990); P.J. Paris, *The Social Teaching of the Black Churches* (Philadelphia, PA: Fortress Press, 1985); and J.R. Washington, Jr., *Black Religion: The Negro and Christianity in the United States* (Boston: Beacon, 1964).
18. James D. Anderson, *The Education of Blacks in the South*.
19. Andrew Billingsley, "The Social Relevance of the Contemporary Black Church," *National Journal of Sociology* 3, 8 (1994): 1–24.
20. E. Franklin Frazier, *The Negro Church in America*.
21. See, e.g., C. Eric Lincoln and L. H. Mamiya, *The Black Church in the African American Experience*.
22. Ibid.; Andrew Billingsley, "The Social Relevance of the Contemporary Black Church," *National Journal of Sociology* 3, 8 (1994): 1–24.
23. W.E.B. DuBois, *The Souls of Black Folk* (New York: Signet Classic, 1995), 212.
24. See, e.g., C. Eric Lincoln and L.H. Mamiya, *The Black Church in the African American Experience*.
25. W.E.B. DuBois, *The Souls of Black Folk*, 214.
26. E. Franklin Frazier, *The Negro Church in America*.
27. James D. Anderson, *The Education of Blacks in the South*; William H. Watkins, *The White Architects of Black Education: Ideology and Power in America, 1865–1954* (New York: Teachers College Press, 2001).
28. Tom Snyder, ed., *120 Years of American Education: A Statistical Portrait* (Washington, DC: National Center for Education Statistics), 1993.
29. Ibid.
30. James D. Anderson, *The Education of Blacks in the South*.
31. William H. Watkins, *The White Architects of Black Education*.
32. James D. Anderson, *The Education of Blacks in the South*; Vanessa Siddle Walker, *Their Highest Potential: An African American School Community in the Segregated South* (Chapel Hill: University of North Carolina Press, 1996).

33. Ibid.
34. Elizabeth Wright, "Booker T. Washington," *American Enterprise Magazine*, September/October 1995: 57–59.
35. Ibid.
36. Ibid.
37. W.E.B. DuBois, *The Souls of Black Folk*, 214.
38. Derrick P. Aldridge, "Conceptualizing a DuBoisian Philosophy of Education."
39. W.E.B. DuBois, *The Souls of Black Folk*, 214.
40. Carter G. Woodson, *The Mis-Education of the Negro* (Trenton, NJ: Africa World Press, 1990 [1933]).
41. Evelyn B. Higgenbotham, *Righteous Discontent: The Women's Movement in the Black Baptist Church, 1880–1920* (Cambridge, MA: Harvard University Press, 1993).
42. Charles Lemert and Esme Bhan, *The Voice of Anna Julia Cooper*.
43. Patricia Hill Collins, *Black Feminist Thought: Knowledge, Consciousness, and the Politics of Empowerment* (Boston: Unwin Hyman, 1990), 221–238.
44. Katie Geneva Cannon, *Katie's Canon: Womanism and the Soul of the Black Community* (New York: Continuum International Publishing Group, 1996).
45. Michael C. Dawson, *Black Visions: The Roots of Contemporary African-American Political Ideologies* (Chicago: University of Chicago Press, 2001).
46. Melissa Harris-Lacewell, *Barbershops, Bibles, and B.E.T.: Everyday Black Talk and the Development of Black Political Thought* (Princeton, NJ: Princeton University Press, 2004).

This page intentionally left blank

Chapter 8

Land, Law, and Education: The Troubled History of Indian Citizenship, 1871–1924

David Wallace Adams

In the introduction to his monumental *Civic Ideals*, Roger M. Smith identifies three traditions that have at various times determined the requirements for U.S. citizenship. The first two—liberalism and republicanism—were mainly an outgrowth of the Age of Enlightenment, and as Smith points out, were both overlapping and distinctive in their basic tenets. Whereas liberalism embraced individual rights, government by consent, and free market capitalism, republicanism stressed the guiding principles of republican self-government, civic virtue, and the common good. Among the ideas that both traditions shared, at least on the face of it, was that all groups were fit candidates for citizenship. Not so in the instance of the third tradition, which Smith characterizes as "inegalitarian ascriptive." In this instance, hierarchical notions of race, culture, gender, and religion constituted essential determinants in assessing whether a given population merited full citizenship status. Smith goes on to point out that while the liberal, republican, and inegalitarian traditions are "in some respects logically inconsistent, ... most American political actors have nonetheless advanced outlooks combining elements of all three."[1]

One factor contributing to both the intermingling and tension between the three traditions was the extent to which the perceived characteristics of a particular ethnocultural group were perceived as being alterable—that is, amenable to acculturative influences, including education. This essay explores this theme in Smith's analysis as a framework for understanding the story of Native American citizenship over a span of time in which Indians went from being "wards" of the government to that of citizens. Specifically, the following discussion addresses three themes in this transition: the shifting definitions of the group's political and legal status; the connection between Indian citizenship and ethno-cultural change; and finally, the role of schools, including the place of civic education, in facilitating the group's changing status.

As the history of Indian citizenship is inextricably intertwined with shifting conceptions of Indian sovereignty, the discussion necessarily begins in the early nineteenth century when the extent to which Indian societies possessed the attributes of sovereign nations emerged as a pressing constitutional issue. With white settlers moving into the western territories, and with much of this movement taking place in violation of Indian treaties, the issue could not long be postponed. The status of "Indian nations" was the paramount issue confronting Chief Justice John Marshall in the Cherokee cases in the 1830s. In *Cherokee Nation v. Georgia* the issue before the Court was whether Georgia possessed the constitutional authority to extend its jurisdiction over Cherokee lands, based in part on the state's assertion that the Cherokee were not in the true sense a sovereign nation. The Cherokee, on the other hand, argued that the state's action was in violation of Cherokee sovereignty, which was equivalent to that of a foreign state. Had not the United States and the Cherokee entered into treaty agreements as equals? After reviewing the history of Cherokee–federal relations, Marshall declared that Georgia was wrong to entirely dismiss Cherokee claims: "The acts of our government plainly recognize the Cherokee Nation as a State, and the Courts are bound by those acts." Still, Marshall was unwilling to concede that the Cherokee—and by extension other Indian societies—were full-fledged nation states. They were, rather, "domestic dependent nations." Hence, the Cherokee's constitutional argument for resisting Georgia's aggression was rejected. As devastating as Marshall's ruling was, the following year the Cherokee won a victory when the high court in *Worcester v. Georgia* ruled that the Indians' quasi-state status invalidated Georgia's presumed jurisdiction over Cherokee affairs. Under the U.S. Constitution the power to make treaties and conduct Indian policy was the province of the U.S. Government, not that of any state. Unstated, but always understood at this juncture, was that Indians were members of their respective societies, not citizens of the United States. For those Indians willing to sever their political and cultural associations with their tribal societies the door of citizenship was theoretically open to them.[2]

Meanwhile, as whites continued to push ever westward, power relations between Indians and whites were being dramatically altered. For Indians, the white invasion seemed unrelenting. And it came in many forms—lethal diseases, waves of Conestoga wagons, army posts, gold-crazed miners, buffalo hunters, the great smoking "iron horse," and finally, land offices. By 1890, the once powerful Sioux, Cheyenne, and Apache were subjugated, colonized, and reduced to a desperate struggle for survival behind the walls of the reservation. As tribal census counts dipped lower and lower, some wondered if Indians might become extinct altogether. During this period the image of the Indian as the "vanishing American" was increasingly viewed as more than an artistic convention. All these developments convinced policy makers that Marshall's earlier description of Indian societies being that of "domestic dependent nations" was now all but irrelevant. Indeed, the idea of Indian sovereignty hit rock bottom in 1871 when Congress declared the end of treaty-making. Indians were now simply "wards" of the nation.[3]

It was in the wake of these developments that discussions of Indian citizenship, and ultimately civic education, took place. With Indians defeated and colonized, policy makers, spurred on by several reform organizations—notably the Board of Indian Commissioners, the Indian Rights Association, and the annual gathering of reformers at Lake Mohonk, New York—set upon a bold new course to fully incorporate Native Americans into the body politic, with the granting of citizenship being one of the principal aims. As Thomas J. Morgan, Commissioner of Indian Affairs, asserted in 1889: "The logic of events demands the absorption of the Indians into our national life, not as Indians but as American citizens." Note the condition—"not as Indians." As reformers saw matters, the Indian's *Indianness* was patently incompatible with citizenship. For citizenship presumed that one thing that most Indians did not possess, and that one thing was "civilization." Indians in their native state were, in effect, "savages," throwbacks to an earlier stage in social evolution when primitive societies were governed by tribalism, paganism, communalism, and brutish passions of the wild. As such, they were all but devoid of those ideas and institutions associated with civilized societies—individualism, the nuclear family, capitalism, republicanism, and Christianity.[4]

Viewing the so-called "Indian Question" through the various and sometimes conflicting perspectives of Christian humanitarianism, social evolution, the idea of progress, and social Darwinism, reformers viewed rapidly changing conditions on the western frontier with alarm. As reformer Henry Pancoast observed in 1883: "The rush of western settlement grows more and more; an enormous army pours continually into our eastern seaports to spread itself over the West. How can we keep these still places in the midst of the current, a bit of stone age in the crush and fever of American enterprise?" Clearly, this was impossible. Hence: "We must either butcher them or civilize them, and what we do we must do quickly." In 1886 Secretary of Interior, Lucius Q. Lamar, essentially concurred, declaring that the "only alternative now presented to the American Indian race is speedy entrance into the pale of American civilization, or absolute extinction." In laying out the alternatives facing Indians, there was never any doubt as to what the object of government policies should be. As Philip Garrett remarked before the Lake Mohonk Conference, the Indian should be made to "lay aside his picturesque blanket and moccasin, and, clad in the panoply of American citizenship, seek his chances of fortune or loss in the stern battle of life with the Aryan races." In short, the Sioux, the Cheyenne, and the Navajo must be absorbed into American life, and time was of the essence.[5]

The extent to which reformers framed the discussion of Indian citizenship within the larger context of "civilization" cannot be overstated. As Carl Shurz, Secretary of the Interior, declared in 1881, full citizenship for the Indians "must be regarded as the terminal, not the initial, point of their development. The first necessity, therefore, is not at once to give it to them, but to fit them for it." The idea of "fitting" Indians for citizenship was a central point in Henry Pancoast's pamphlet *The Indian before the Law*:

> In justice to the Indian and to ourselves, I certainly think we should insist on one thing. There must be at least an approximate fitness in the individual Indian for the duties of citizenship before he is made a citizen. There must be some education, some elevation of the Indian toward our standard of right and morality, before we can with any justice punish him under laws which he had no part in making, and of which he is now blindly

ignorant. This education should be general and immediate: every effort should be made to fit the individual Indian to take his place as soon as possible as an American citizen.[6]

When reformers turned their attention to the question of how best to accomplish the necessary changes in Indian lifeways, they placed their faith in three broad areas of policy: law, land, and education. Extending the jurisdiction of law and courts over Indian life was seen as one of the principal means of weakening the reservation Indian's connection to traditional tribal authority. In 1885, Congress took a major step in this direction when it extended the jurisdiction of federal law over seven major crimes that strictly involved Indians: murder, manslaughter, rape, assault with intent to kill, arson, burglary, and larceny. To go further than this, policy makers were hesitant. Imposing the entire legal structure on Indians in the beginning stages of their assimilation was simply impractical. As Commissioner of Indian Affairs, Ezra Hyat, warned Congress in 1878: "Indians of full age are infants in law; and in fact they need a long tutelage before launching them into the world to manage their own affairs." Like citizenship itself, extending the white man's laws over Indian life would be meaningless until deeper transformations were accomplished.[7]

Turning Indians into self-reliant property owners constituted a second policy aim. In this regard, reformers were all but unanimous in their belief that the communalism of the Indian reservation—aggravated by tribal kinship structures and traditions of ritualized gift-giving—was a central impediment to the granting of citizenship. In such an environment the treasured American values of self-reliance, possessive individualism, and republican liberty could never take root. As Merrill Gates observed at Lake Mohonk in 1885: "The tribal organization, with its tenure of land in common, with its constant divisions of goods and rations per capita without regard to service rendered, cuts the nerve of all that manful effort that political economy teaches us proceeds from the desire for wealth. True ideas of property with all the civilizing influences that such ideas excite are formed only as the tribal relation is outgrown." Under the reservation system, Commissioner of Indian Affairs, John Oberly, told a gathering of reformers, "the laziest man owns as much as the most industrious man, and neither can say of all the acres occupied by the tribe, 'This is mine'." What Gates and Oberly wanted was to divide reservations into separate landholdings, each family receiving title to an allotment of acreage for self-sufficiency. With euphoric optimism, reformers saw land allotment as a major step forward in preparing the Indian for citizenship.[8]

In 1887, Congress passed the Dawes General Allotment Act, named after one of the law's principal proponents, U.S. Senator Henry Dawes of Massachusetts. The new legislation authorized the President to survey those reservations with good agricultural or grazing potential and to allot 160 acres to the head of each family, with smaller allotments going to single persons and orphans. Title to the allotment would be held in trust by the government for twenty-five years, after which it would be remitted to the owner. Significantly, citizenship was granted immediately to all Indians receiving allotments. As for "surplus land" (that land left over after all the Indians had been provided for), this acreage would be sold off to homesteaders. All funds garnered from the selling of surplus land would be set aside for the tribe's further economic and cultural advancement.[9]

While reformers hailed the Dawes Act as a major step forward on the pathway to Indian citizenship, some soon began to question whether new allottees, simply by virtue of their new condition, were really prepared for citizenship at a moment's notice. The stroke of a pen, it was argued, could hardly transform former bison hunters into self-reliant plowers of the earth capable of negotiating either the technical language of territorial and state laws or the economic obligations incurred by contracts and ledger books. In 1906, the Commissioner of Indian Affairs, Francis Leupp, was moved to report: "Experience has demonstrated that citizenship has been a disadvantage to many Indians. They are not fitted for its duties or able to take advantage of its benefits." It was this idea that prompted Congress in the same year to pass the Burke Act, which stipulated that in the future allottees would be granted citizenship at the end, not the beginning, of the trust period. The law also authorized the President, on the one hand, to extend the trust status for those allottees judged incapable of managing their affairs, and on the other, to reduce the period for those deemed "competent."[10]

Competency was now deemed the criterion for granting allottees fee patents and citizenship. In 1915, Secretary of Interior, Franklin Lane, went so far as to appoint a "competency commission," whose express purpose was to move from reservation to reservation, and, with the assistance of the agency superintendent, assess the "qualifications of each Indian who applied for severance of tribal relations, or who, in its judgment, has arrived at the degree of business competency that he should assume the duties of citizenship." By 1916, three separate roving commissions were conducting a scripted ceremony—the so-called "Last Arrow Ceremony"—in which Indians deemed competent were ritualistically inducted into citizenship.[11]

Secretary Lane's description of one such ceremony is more than a little revealing. Imagine the scene. On some unnamed reservation in the West a crowd of Indians, former warriors and bison hunters, gather to hear a representative of the "Great Father" usher them into their new status as citizens. Several public officials are gathered behind a large table on which are placed several items, including a flag. Another large flag has been staked in the ground and is fluttering over the whole proceedings. A large hand plow also sits on the ritual ground. The ceremony begins when the Secretary of Interior steps before the first Indian candidate. The Indian has a new name, Joseph T. Cook. The Secretary asks Cook his old Indian name. The Indian responds with "Tunkansapa." The Secretary hands Tunkansapa a bow and arrow and instructs him to shoot the arrow into the sky. Tunkansapa draws the bowstring and unleashes the arrow. The Secretary now declares: "Tunkansapa, you have shot your last arrow. That means you are no longer to live the life of an Indian. You are from this day forward to live the life of the white man. But you may keep the arrow. It will be a symbol of your noble race and of the pride you may feel that you come from the first Americans." Addressing Tunkansapa by his new name—Joseph T. cook—the Secretary instructs him to place his hands on the plow standing before them, and explains: "This act means that you have chosen to live the life of the white man. The white man lives by work. From the earth we must all get our living, and the earth will not yield unless man pours upon it the sweat of his brow." And so the ritual unfolds. Next the Secretary presents Cook with a small purse and explains: "It will always say to you that the money you gain must be wisely kept. The wise man saves his money, so that when the sun does not smile and the grass does not grow he will not starve." Cook is now presented with a flag: "This is the only flag you will ever have. It is the flag of free men, the flag of a hundred million free men and women, of whom you are now one." Repeating after the Secretary, Cook now promises to give "my hands, my head, and my heart to the doing of all that will make me a true American citizen." The ceremony concludes with the Secretary pinning on Cook's chest a small button decorated with the national colors and an American eagle. "Wear this band always," Cook is instructed, "and may the eagle that is on it never see you do aught of which the flag will not be proud." And so at a considerable price, the Indian Tunkansapa, now Joseph T. Cook, enters the realm of American citizenship. One can find no better evidence than the "Last Arrow Ceremony" to illustrate policy makers' assumption that the Indian's acquisition of citizenship required the complete abandonment of ancestral traditions.[12]

In the end, the cultural transformation required for citizenship called for education, the third component of reformers' campaign.[13] Indeed, Lyman Abbott announced at Lake Mohonk in 1888 that of the three principal means of incorporating Indians into the body politic—law, land, and education—the last was "by far the most important." Nothing could be clearer: "Put an ignorant and imbruted savage on land of his own, and he remains a pauper, if he does not become a vagrant and a thief. Open to him the courts of justice, and make him amenable to the laws of the land, and give him neither knowledge nor a moral education, and he will come before those courts only as a criminal." And Congress agreed. Between 1877 and 1900, it increased appropriations for Indian education from $20,000 to $2,936,080. During the same period, the number of Indian schools jumped from 150 to 307, most of the expansion accounted for by the growth of reservation and off-reservation boarding schools. Meanwhile, during the same period the number Indian students enrolled in schools exploded from a mere 3,598 to 21,568.[14] Through an "army of Christian school-teachers," reformers fully believed, Indian youth would be won over to the ways of civilization. "That is the army that is going to win the victory," Merrill Gates declared at Lake Mohonk. "We are going to conquer barbarism, but we are going to do it by getting at the barbarism one by one . . . We are going to conquer the Indians by a standing army of school teachers, armed with ideas, winning victories by industrial training, and by the gospel of love and gospel of work."[15]

The challenge facing educators was a daunting one. As John Oberly explained at Lake Mohonk, the Indian student "is a prickly thorn that must be made to bear soft roses; he is a twig bent out of the perpendicular, and he must be straightened so that the tree will stand erect, inclining in no way; he is a vessel of bronze that must be made bright by constant rubbing." Oberly never doubted that teachers, armed with missionary and patriotic zeal, were up to the challenge. But the task of civilizing savages would not be an easy one. As one of Carlisle Indian School's teachers would write in a poem titled "To a Teacher at Carlisle":

Your task is hard, my FRIEND, day after day
To tread the same severe, unvaried way,
Through minds whose wild soil never knew the plow
Of learning, or of cultured sense, till now.[16]

Indian schools focused on four educational aims. First, educators should instruct students in the Three Rs. Without an elementary understanding of the knowledge and skills necessary to conduct business with the white man, they would be lost. In this regard educators were expected to place particular emphasis on teaching English. As Commissioner of Indian Affairs, J.D.C. Atkins, explained in 1887, in the Indians' future role as citizens, "the rising generation will be expected and required . . . to transact business with English-speaking people. When they take upon themselves the responsibilities and privileges of citizenship their vernacular will be of no advantage. Only through the medium of the English tongue can they acquire a knowledge of the Constitution of the country and their rights and duties thereunder." Moreover, in the process of learning English, students would encounter simple lessons in geography and history, wherein they would come to the realization that the tribal world of their childhood was hardly the center of the universe. What educators hoped to accomplish in this regard was a response in students similar to that of Charles Eastman's when he experienced his first geography lesson. As Eastman would later recall, "when the teacher placed before us a globe, and said that our world was like that—that upon such a thing our forefathers had roamed and hunted for untold ages, as it whirled and danced around the sun in space—I felt that my foothold was deserting me." Creating such psychological dislocation, created for teachers the opportunity to enlarge students' cultural and political identities.[17]

Second, teachers were expected to wage an unrelenting campaign on behalf of self-reliant individualism. As we have seen, in the minds of reformers, the tribal connection was a major barrier to Indian progress. Just as land allotment was designed to destroy tribalism by introducing the concept of private property, so schools were expected to inculcate those skills and values necessary for survival in a competitive agricultural economy. The economic aims of Indian education were reflected in two areas of the school program. First, half the school day was devoted to industrial training where boys learned the arts of farming, stock raising, and wagon repair, while girls learned those of sewing, cooking, and poultry raising. The second area of the curriculum was devoted to inculcating in Indian youth the spirit of possessive individualism. As Merrill Gates proclaimed at Lake Mohonk in 1896, one of the foremost aims of Indian education should be to take the dull child out of savagery and to "awaken in him wants." In pursuance of this end the Indian boy must be stripped of his blanket and then gotten into trousers. Moreover, these trousers should possess a "pocket to be filled with dollars." Thus, it was an ordinary occurrence for students at Haskell Institute to open their newspaper and encounter a poem about "The Boy Who Succeeds."

> There is always a way to rise, my boy,
>   Always a way to advance;
> Yet the road that leads to Mount Success
>   Does not pass by the way of chance,
> But goes through the stations of Work and Strive,
>   Through the Valley of Persevere;
> And the man that succeeds, while others fail,
>   Must be willing to pay most dear.[18]

Third, Indian schools should do everything possible to reshape students' religious and moral beliefs. Besides the fact that Indian religious traditions were perceived as being hopelessly pagan and barbaric, reformers saw the Indian's conversion to Christianity as being inextricably connected to the reconstruction of Indian youths' political and economic selves. Reformers wondered: How could the Indian's future success as an independent farmer be divorced from such Christian virtues as moral rectitude, personal responsibility, and painful perseverance? As William T. Harris explained at Lake Mohonk, Christianity was not merely a religion, but an "ideal of life penetrating the whole social structure." It was in this same frame of mind that Senator Dawes, also speaking at Lake Mohonk, made the point that Christians not only made better farmers, they made better citizens. "He must be taught how to work, how to take care of himself, and then he must have the elevating influence of the Christian religion to inspire, and make him feel that to do this makes a man of him, and that he has to obey the laws of the land, and the laws that govern him in his relation to his fellow man and his Creator. In this way you will have done some good by making him a citizen of the United States residing upon a homestead." Thus, preaching, praying, Bible reading, and hymn singing were all seen as important elements of the school program.[19]

The fourth aim of education was citizenship training. This crucial area of the school program was pitched at two levels. On one level the goal was to instruct Indian youth in the rights, privileges, and obligations of citizenship. Thus, Commissioner of Indian Affairs, Thomas J. Morgan, directed Indian service teachers in 1889 to emphasize the basic provisions of the U.S. Constitution, the importance of voting and elections, and the concept of trial by jury. While most of this instruction would take place in the classroom in the form of textbook readings and "familiar talks," citizenship themes were also the topic of weekend assemblies. In February 1890, for instance, students at Carlisle were treated to a lecture on citizenship by the school's assistant superintendent, Alfred Standing. According to the *Indian Helper*, "Mr. Standing spoke well and understandingly last Saturday night on the benefits and protection of citizenship. He explained Habeas Corpus, protection by jury, the benefits of a warrant, cited the incident of an American in Cuba being saved by the flag, and explained the Magna Charta, and had an attentive audience all through." In off-reservation schools, debating societies were seen as a particularly effective strategy for teaching civic participation. In October 1906, for instance, Haskell students debated such topics as "Resolved: that the reins of Cuba should not be held by the United States in the present disturbance," and on a less weighty level, "Resolved: that football should be abolished as a school or college game."[20]

A second objective of citizenship education—and an especially tricky one given the history of Indian–white relations—was that of awakening in students a deep and abiding love of the country that had conquered them. Toward this end, Commissioner Morgan advised: "They should be taught to look upon America as their home and upon the United States Government as their friend and benefactor. They should be made familiar with the lives of great and good men and women in American history, and be taught to feel pride in all their great achievements." Because older Indian youths had seen first hand the death and destruction that had accompanied the white invasion of Indian lands, Morgan knew full well that inspiring patriotism in students was no easy task. The best course to be adopted, Morgan suggested, was to explain that the Indians' present lowly state was an unfortunate consequence of both the "wrongs of their ancestors" and white "injustice." Moreover, "if their unhappy history is alluded to it should be to contrast it with the better future that is within their grasp." A beneficent government was now offering them the opportunity to escape a savage past, to lift them to a higher level of civilization, and to walk through the door of citizenship.[21]

Building patriotism was to be accomplished in several ways. While textbooks carried a good deal of the burden, policy makers recognized them as insufficient by themselves. Requiring students to sing patriotic songs and to recite patriotic selections as a part of their reading exercises would surely help. Moreover, Morgan announced that "the 'Stars and Stripes' should be a familiar object, and students should be taught to reverence the flag as a symbol of their nation's power and protection." Combining flag exercises with elaborate drill and marching routines was yet another means of implanting bone-deep patriotic sentiments. And on those special occasions, when a major public figure paid the school a visit, such as when President William McKinley visited Phoenix Indian School in 1901, fluttering flags, band music, and split-time military maneuvers could create an irresistible atmosphere for winning students' political loyalty. As the school newspaper, *The Native American*, described the scene,

> the scholars marched quickly in ranks to a position immediately in front of the grand stand, forming a solid square. In a very short space of time, probably two or three minutes, they were all assembled. Each pupil knew his place and occupied it. The movement was executed like clockwork, unmarred by a single mistake or bungle. There they stood for an instant, 700 pairs of eyes gazing sharply and intently at the "great father." The bugles sounded. Seven hundred pupils saluted the occupants of the reviewing stand. Again the bugles sounded. Then 700 voices rang out in repeating the following sentiment: "I give my head and my hand and my heart to my country; one country, one language, and one flag."[22]

Observing national holidays was another means used to reconstruct Indian students' political identities. If the main objective of Columbus Day, Washington's Birthday, Memorial Day, and Independence Day, was to forge a deeper emotional connection between students, the nation, and its founders, a secondary objective was to further undermine students' former cultural identities. At the Carlisle's Independence Day celebration in 1890, Pratt used the occasion to give the broadest meaning possible to the holiday. "There must be a declaration of independence on the part of every man if he would be a man," Pratt declared. "I don't care what race he springs from. He must not be tied even to his father's family, or to his people. He must be an independent man and stand out for himself. No one stands in the way of the Indian but the Indian himself." The true message of Independence Day for Indians, Pratt asserted, was self-reliant individualism. The communalism fostered by the tribal association was no substitute for "the advantages of being an independent citizen in this great America." Pratt ended his remarks with this observation: "There is no end to the Indian problem as long as the Indians hang together, separate and apart from the rest of us. They must become individuals, scatter and seek broad opportunities."[23]

But the Indian Office announced in 1890 that the existing national holidays were insufficient. Indians must be made to see more clearly the intimate connection between citizenship, on the one hand, and the abandonment of tribalism on the other. Thus, school officials were instructed to design activities for a special holiday to be celebrated at Indian schools. The new February 8th celebration was being created to commemorate passage of the Dawes Act in 1887. "Franchise Day," or "Indian Citizenship Day," as it was more commonly known, was designed to convince students that the price of losing tribal lands was worth the prize of citizenship. The new holiday also served as an opportunity to celebrate the Indians' rise up the ladder of civilization as well as the school's role in facilitating the process. All these themes played themselves out in classroom exercises, school newspapers, and special student assemblies. Whenever possible, school officials highlighted students' declarations of support for the aims of the Dawes Act. On one occasion, for instance, a student was moved to proclaim in the school newspaper:

> This is a day but little understood by many of us, which gives us the opportunity to reclaim ourselves from an obscure life of barbarism, to climb the ladder of civilization. We rejoice that at last we are emerging from unknown ages of darkness on this great continent, and are beginning to cooperate in the work which God has intended for all men to do. The cloud which once shadowed our atmosphere is now clearing away, and every day skies are growing brighter. We hope the day is not far distant, when we shall have demonstrated to the people of the United States, that we have become self-supporting citizens, and capable of commanding the esteem of our fellow men.

Another trumpeted:

> Now we are citizens
> We give him applause:
> So three cheers, my friends,
> For Senator Dawes![24]

A particularly tricky aspect of the holiday's message was to convince students that the provision of the Dawes Act that called for selling off "surplus" lands was worth the price of gaining citizenship. Again, showcasing model students in school assemblies was deemed to be a promising strategy for winning over suspicious minds. As one Carlisle student explained, the incoming settlers were putting the Indian allottee "in direct contact with the better element of the white race." These new settlers were teaching "by example what civilized life is." Another student gave poetic expression to the idea that the prize to be gained was well worth the cost.

> But welcome our ruin, if now by our losses,
> We gain thousandfold in a better estate.
> A man may be chief in the empire of reason.
> Education, not land, makes a citizen great.

Meanwhile, the students at Haskell Institute were singing:

> Uncle Sammy feeds us turkey
> And he sends us books to read.
> He has been our friend in trouble,
> Oh, he is a friend indeed.
> Now if Congress will allot us,
> With our quarter section farm,
> A good girl apiece to tend it,
> We will take it like a charm.

One can only imagine how many students—including the school's female students—took such sentiments to heart.[25]

After 1900 one can detect a more nuanced position on the connection between patriotic citizenship and race pride. While never fully developed, policy makers began flirting with the proposition that loyalty to the nation need not obviate a vague honoring of one's ancestral past. (One can detect this in the "Last Arrow Ceremony.") Speaking at Carlisle's commencement ceremonies in 1909, Commissioner of Indian Affairs Francis Leupp declared: "When you young people go out into the world I trust you will never forget or regret that you are Indians." Leupp went on to explain that "pride of race is one of the saving graces," and then reminded his audience of a historical fact: "Don't overlook for a minute that you were the first Americans, and that we, of what is now the dominant race, were your guests a good while before we became your guardians." To be sure, Leupp's advocacy of race pride was hardly a denunciation of the underpinning doctrines by which the nation had justified its subjugation of Indian populations. In the end, Leupp seemed to be saying that Indians should at once be proud of their heritage but understand that the near extinction of their cultural ways was inevitable. Meanwhile, they should be thankful that their federal guardian was looking out for their welfare. "Do not let your patriotism lie idle until there is a war in which you can enlist as soldiers or nurses, but begin at once among your own people to cultivate true confidence in the Government. That Government is, after all, the best friend you have now."[26] A few years later, Indians would have the opportunity to demonstrate the full measure of their patriotism.

World War I sparked the next phase in educators' campaign to foster patriotism. An essential context for understanding this chapter in Indian civic education is the fact that Native Americans gave widespread support to the war effort. "Probably it may seem strange to see an Apache in a sailor's uniform," observed Phoenix Indian School's the *Native American*, "but it merely shows that he has become an American and has passed the tribal stage." Estimates on the number of Indians in uniform during the war vary, but a reasonable estimate is 12,500, roughly divided between draftees and enlistments. As only citizens were eligible for the draft, and because by 1917 over a third of Indians had still not achieved citizenship status, a good number of enlistees were clearly not citizens. The motivations for enlisting were complicated and numerous. Surely, racial pride, warrior traditions, the search for adventure, and the desperate economic conditions in Indian communities were all contributing factors. Also, many older students apparently saw soldiering as a logical extension of the pervasive military regimen of boarding school life. One recruit from Chilocco Indian School wrote home: "The instruction I received in military discipline certainly was help to me on my enlistment. I had no trouble in mastering the execution of different commands and, glad to say, have never appeared with the awkward squad."[27]

But not to be discounted either was the force and legacy of years of being schooled in patriotic discourse. The fact that the larger off-reservation schools served as virtual recruiting stations for Indian enlistments suggests that the long-term campaign on behalf of patriotic citizenship was bearing fruit. Indeed, one historian estimates that 90 percent of Indian students entering the armed services did so as voluntary enlistments. In April 1918, Haskell's *Indian Leader* reported that 200 of its former students were in uniform. Earlier in the year, Richard Pratt, now retired from Carlisle, boasted that 165 former Carlisle students were a part of the then 5,000 enlistees that were scattered throughout the army and navy, "some in active service in France and our war vessels in submarine zones." For Pratt this was incontrovertible proof of the Indians' fitness for full-fledged citizenship. Meanwhile, the Indian schools had proven to be the "bone and sinew" of Indian recruitment.[28]

One reason that the large boarding schools were such a fruitful source of recruits was that school officials were doing everything in their power to whip up enthusiasm for the war, and judged by essays written by students at Haskell Institute, with considerable effect. In May 1917 the *Indian Leader* reported that a Miss Neff's sixth and seventh grade pupils were "writing some patriotic and thoughtful compositions of late." One example: "Our country had done much for us. It has protected us from the day of our birth and will continue to do so as long as life shall last. Why can't we in such a time as this do what we can for our country?" A year later, Haskell, in conjunction with the local chapter of the Daughters of the American Revolution, sponsored an essay contest on the topic "For What Are We Fighting." One student offered: "We declared war on her [Germany] to protect our people, our rights, and our name. But the uppermost reason is to make other people free." To say the least, given the history of Indian–white relations, such pronouncements are truly remarkable. But these pale in comparison to this prize-winning response: "Less than 50 years ago, the bloodthirsty Sioux were scalping and mutilating the dead bodies of Custer's men, but today we find the sons and grandsons of those Indians standing in the trenches, facing the cannons, bombs, and poison gas, offering their lives as a sacrifice, that justice, mercy, humanity, and freedom shall not perish from the earth."[29]

If the citizens of Lawrence, Kansas, and the Office of Indian Affairs found such views reassuring, they could be no less impressed by Haskell's prominent role in the city's liberty loan parade in April 1918. As Lawrence's *Journal World* described the scene:

> Probably the best show of the parade was that put on by the Haskell boys and girls. The girls marched in step and kept almost as good formation as the boys whose military work was excellent. The school also showed several floats and special features that were a credit to their designers. At the head of their division was carried a service flag bearing 200 stars and an explanatory banner saying that there are 5000 Indians in the military service and 200 of them from Haskell. At the rear of their column marched a group of young bucks in full costume, bearing a sign "Show us the Kaiser," and a litter on which a dummy of the gentleman was supposed to repose.

One after another the patriotic floats and displays rolled on: Haskell bakers in white suits carrying a banner "We Bake Our War Bread Brown"; a group of agricultural students marching with their rakes, hoes, and pitchforks; a flag-draped float of Haskell girls doing Red Cross work. Here indeed were true citizens of the land. Meanwhile, students at Haskell and other institutions were purchasing liberty bonds. As the *Indian Leader* advertised: "Every liberty bond you buy goes toward a return ticket for our boys in France."[30]

Again, if the reasons for Indians' support for the war effort went beyond patriotic zeal, the simple fact that so many alumni willingly joined the armed services reinforced growing sentiment among policy makers that educators had gone a long way toward fitting Indians for citizenship. On April 17, 1917, the Commissioner of Indian Affairs issued a declaration that any Indian student twenty-one years of age or over who had completed the full course of instruction and had demonstrated competency was now eligible to receive full control of any money and land to which he was entitled, "after which he will no longer be a ward of the Government." Still, by 1919 more than 125,000 Native Americans were without citizenship. But this was soon to change. The same year Congress passed legislation conferring citizenship on veterans of World War I. Indians' general support for the war also weighed heavily in law makers' passage of the Curtis Act of 1924. All Indians were now deemed citizens of the United States.[31]

In tracing the history of Indian citizenship two general observations are in order. First, the Curtis Act did not put an end to the question of the Indians' legal status. In the area of voting rights, for instance, thousands of Indians were denied the ballot by various state statutes that set a variety of qualifications aimed at denying Indians the franchise. Any number of criteria—that Indians be civilized, that they be taxpayers, that they not live on a reservation—were used as a pretext for disqualifying potential voters. Then too, Indians' historically complicated relationship with the federal government continued to undergo periodic reassessment in a series of Supreme Court decisions, culminating in the legal doctrine that Indian citizenship did not obviate the government's historic role as guardian over important aspects of Indian life. Indeed, in *United States v. Nice* (1916) the Court ruled: "Citizenship is not incompatible with tribal existence or continued guardianship, and so may be conferred without completely emancipating the Indians or placing them beyond the reach of congressional regulation adopted for their protection." The Curtis Act did nothing to alter this principle. In a sense, Indians, while citizens, were still wards of the government—or at least partially so.[32]

Second, the story of Indian citizenship and its relation to federal educational policy lends support to Ronald Smith's thesis that hierarchical theories of race and ethnicity, as well as the negative ascriptive associations that flowed from these demarcations, constitute a major counter theme to both the republican and liberal traditions at the heart of American civic ideals. In that connection, the story of Indian citizenship illustrates, on the one hand, the faith of policy makers in their ability to erase through education the ethno-cultural barriers to citizenship, and on the other hand, the failure to accomplish this end in the face of prevailing legal doctrines, cultural attitudes, and political forces that held to more constricted visions of Indian citizenship—even as Indians paid the ultimate price for their patriotism on the battlefields of Europe. It would be a long time before policy makers would come to see that conceptions such as Indian identity, Indian self-determination, and patriotic citizenship need not be contradictory phenomena. Until that occurred, Native Americans' encounter with citizenship and civic education would continue to be a troubled one.

Notes

1. Roger M. Smith, *Civic Ideals: Conflicting Visions of Citizenship in U.S. History* (New Haven, CT: Yale University Press, 1997), 1–4, 507–508. On the other hand, Gary Gerstle sees two traditions of citizenship running through U.S. history: "civic nationalism" and "racial nationalism." See Gerstle, *American Crucible: Race and Nation in the Twentieth Century*, (Princeton, NJ: Princeton University Press, 2001).
2. For the two Cherokee cases, see Vine Deloria, Jr. and Clifford M. Lytle, *American Indians, American Justice* (Austin: University of Texas Press, 1983), 25–33; Francis Paul Prucha, *American Indian Treaties: The History of a Political Anomaly* (Berkeley: University of California Press, 1994), 165–168. For general treatments of Native Americans' constitutional status over time, including issues related to sovereignty, see Frank Pommersheim, *Braid of Feathers: American Indian Law and Contemporary Tribal Life* (Berkeley: University of California Press, 1995); and Charles F. Wilkinson, *Native Societies in a Modern Constitutional Democracy* (New Haven, CT: Yale University Press, 1987).
3. Robert M. Utley, *The Indian Frontier of the American West, 1846–1890* (Albuquerque: University of New Mexico Press, 1984); Ralph K. Andrist, *The Long Death: The Last Days of the Plains Indians* (New York: MacMillan, 1964); and Robert A. Trennert, Jr., *Alternative to Extinction: Federal Indian Policy and the Beginnings of the Reservation System* (Philadelphia: Temple University Press, 1975); and Prucha, *American Indian Treaties*, chapter 12.
4. The story of reform organizations and their outlook is told in Frances Paul Prucha, *The Great Father: The United States Government and the American Indians*, vol. 2 (Lincoln: University of Nebraska Press, 1984), chapter 25; William T. Hagan, *The Indian Rights Association: The Herbert Welsh Years, 1882–1904* (Tucson: University of Arizona Press, 1985); Helen M. Bannan, "The Idea of Civilization and American Indian Policy Reformers in the 1880s," *Journal of American Culture* I (Winter 1978): 787–799; and Alexandra Harmon, "When Is an Indian Not an Indian? The 'Friends of the Indian' and the Problems of Indian Identity," *Journal of Ethnic Studies* 18 (Summer 1990): 95–123. Morgan's comments are reprinted in Frances Paul Prucha, ed., *Americanizing the American Indians: Writings by the "Friends of the Indian," 1880–1900* (Cambridge: Harvard University Press, 1973), 75.
5. Henry S. Pancoast, *Impressions of the Sioux Tribes in 1882, with Some First Principles in the Indian Question* (Philadelphia: Franklin Printing House, 1883), 6–7; *Annual Report of the Secretary of the Interior, 1886, Executive House Document*, 49th Cong., 2nd sess., serial 2467, p. 4; and *Proceedings of the Lake Mohonk Conference of Friends of the Indian* (hereafter cited as *LMC*), 1886, reprinted in Prucha, *Americanizing the American Indians*, 65.
6. Carl Schurz, "Present Aspects of the Indian Problem," *North American Review* 133 (July 1881), reprinted in Prucha, *Americanizing the American Indians*, 16; and Pancoast, *The Indian Before the Law* (Philadelphia: Indian Rights Association, 1884), reprinted in Prucha, *Americanizing the American Indians*, 165.

7. Prucha, *The Great Father*, vol. 2, 679; and *Annual Report of the Commissioner of Indian Affairs* (hereafter cited as ARCIA), 1878, *House Executive Document*, 45th Cong., 3rd. sess., serial 1850, p. 444.
8. Merrill E. Gates, "Land and Law as Agents in Educating Indians," *Annual Report of the Board of Indian Commissioners, 1885*, reprinted in Prucha, *Americanizing the American Indians*, 50–51; and *ARCIA*, 1888, *House Executive Document*, 50th Cong., 2nd sess., serial 2637, p. 89. Important treatments of land allotment include Janet A. McDonnell, *The Dispossession of the American Indian, 1887–1934* (Bloomington: Indiana University Press, 1991); and D.S. Otis, *The Dawes Act and the Allotment of Indian Lands*, ed. Francis Paul Prucha (Norman: University of Oklahoma Press, 1973).
9. It should be noted that one of the principal consequences of the Dawes Act was the devastating loss of Indian land. Whereas Indians held some 138 million acres in 1887, by 1934 the number was reduced to 48 million. See Prucha, *The Great Father*, vol. 2, 896. The Dawes Act is reprinted in Otis, *The Dawes Act and the Allotment of Indian Lands*, 177–184.
10. Leupp is quoted in Prucha, *The Great Father*, vol. 2, 875. For changes in allotment policy see Otis, *The Dawes Act and the Allotment of Indian Lands*, chapter 8; McDonnell, *The Dispossession of the American Indian*, chapter 2; and Prucha, *The Great Father*, vol. 2, 872–879.
11. Lane is quoted in Prucha, *The Great Father*, vol. 2, 879–885.
12. The ceremony is reprinted in Louis J. Pfaller, *James McLoughlin: The Man with an Indian Heart* (New York: Vantage Press, 1978), 335–336. Also see Russel Lawrence Barsh, "An American Heart of Darkness: The 1913 Expedition for American Indian Citizenship," *Great Plains Quarterly* 13 (Spring 1993): 91–115.
13. For discussions of Indian education during this period, in addition to Prucha, *The Great Father*, vol. 2, chapter 27, see David Wallace Adams, *Education for Extinction: American Indians and the Boarding School Experience, 1875–1928* (Lawrence: University Press of Kansas, 1995); Adams, "Fundamental Considerations: The Deep Meaning of Native American Schooling, 1880–1900," *Harvard Educational Review* 58 (February 1988): 1–28; Michael Coleman, *American Indian Children at School* (Jackson: University of Mississippi Press, 1993); K. Tsianina Lomawaima, *They Called It PrairieLight: The Story of Chilocco Indian School* (Lincoln: University of Nebraska Press, 1994); Clyde Ellis, *To Change Them Forever: Indian Education at the Rainy Mountain Boarding School, 1893–1920* (Norman: University of Oklahoma Press, 1996); and Robert A. Trennert, *The Phoenix Indian School: Forced Assimilation in Arizona, 1891–1935* (Norman: University of Oklahoma Press, 1988).
14. Adams, *Education for Extinction*, 26–27, 58.
15. For Abbott's and Gates's remarks, see *LMC*, 1888, p. 11; and *LMC*, 1891, in *ARCIA*, 1891, *House Executive Document*, 52nd Cong., 1st. sess., serial 2934. p. 1 144.
16. *Indian Helper*, April 25, 1890: 1.
17. For an overview of curriculum in federal Indian boarding schools see Adams, *Education for Extinction*, chapter 5. Atkins's views on language are in *ARCIA*, 1887, *House Executive Document*, 50th Cong., 1st. sess., serial 2542, p. 19. Particularly insightful on the question of language instruction is Ruth Spack, *America's Tongue: American Indian Education and the Ownership of English, 1860–1900* (Lincoln: University of Nebraska Press, 2002).
18. *LMC*, 1896, 11–12; and *Indian Leader*, May 2, 1902: 4. Eastman is quoted in Adams, *Education for Extinction*, 143.
19. Harris is quoted in Adams, *Education for Extinction*, 23; and *LMC*, 1896, reprinted in Prucha, *Americanizing the American Indians*, 108.
20. *ARCIA*, 1889, *House Executive Document*, 51st Cong., 1st sess., serial 2725, p. 102; "Instructions to Indian Agents in Regard to Inculcation of Patriotism in Indian Schools,"

House *Executive Document*, 51st Cong., 2nd sess., serial 2841, p. 167; *Indian Helper*, February 21, 1890: 3; and *Indian Leader*, October 26, 1906: 3.
21. *ARCIA*, 1889, 233.
22. "Instructions to Indian Agents in Regard to Inculcation of Patriotism in Indian Schools," 167. The account of McKinley's visit is reprinted in *ARCIA*, 1901, *House Document*, 57th Cong., 1st sess., serial 4290, p. 524.
23. "Instructions to Indian Agents in Regard to Inculcation of Patriotism in Indian Schools," 167; and *Indian Helper*, July 11, 1890: 2.
24. "Instructions to Indian Agents in Regard to Inculcation of Patriotism in Indian Schools," 167; *Talks and Thoughts*, February 1892:1; and Cora Folsom, "Memories of Old Hampton," Cora Folsom Papers, Hampton Archives, Hampton University.
25. *Red Man*, March 1890: 5; and *Indian Helper*, February 21, 1890: 4. It should be noted that almost all discussions of preparing Indians for citizenship focused on males. The reason for this was simple enough: during most of the period that this essay covers, white women were themselves denied many of the rights of citizenship, including the franchise. Thus, when reformers addressed the future status of Indian women it was almost always in the context of "civilization," not citizenship rights. Convinced that the status of women in Indian societies was for the most part that of slave-like "drudge" (a perception that modern scholarship has challenged), reformers believed that white civilization would necessarily lift Indian women to a higher level of existence. Educators presumed that Indian women's destiny was to be helpmates to their farmer-husbands and civilized mothers of the next generation of Indian children. The best discussion of Indian female education during this era remains Robert F. Trennert's, "Educating Indian Girls at Nonreservation Boarding Schools, 1878–1920," *Western Historical Quarterly* 13 (July 1982): 271–290.
26. *Red Man*, May 1, 1909, reprinted in *Red Man*, 4 (New York: Johnson Reprint Corp., 1971): 5–6.
27. The *Native American* is quoted in Russel Lawrence Barsh, "American Indians in the Great War," *Ethnohistory* 38 (Summer 1991): 276; also Thomas A. Britten, *American Indians in World War I: At War and at Home* (Albuquerque: University of New Mexico Press, 1997), 52, 59–67, 71–72, 84; and Barsh, "American Indians in the Great War,":278–280.
28. Britten, *American Indians in World War I*, 67; *Indian Leader*, April 26, 1918: 16; and Richard H. Pratt, *Evening Bulletin* (Philadelphia), reprinted in *Native American*, 23 (February 1918): 50.
29. *Indian Leader*, May 18, 1917: 1; April 26, 1918: 20; and 7, 14 June 1918: 20.
30. *Indian Leader*, April 12, 1918: 3. For the extent and reasons for purchasing liberty bonds see Britten, *American Indians in World War I*, 135–136.
31. *ARCIA*, 1917, *Annual Report of the Department of Interior*, 1917, Administrative Reports, 2, 3–4; Britten, *American Indians in World War I*, 176–181; and Gary C. Stein, "The Indian Citizenship Act of 1924," *New Mexico Historical Review* 47 (July 1972): 257–274.
32. Particularly good on this subject is Hoxie, *A Final Promise*, chapter 7. The quotation is cited in Michael T. Smith, "The History of Indian Citizenship," *Great Plains Journal* 10 (Fall 1970): 33.

Chapter 9

"Let Virtue Be Thy Guide, and Truth Thy Beacon-Light": Moral and Civic Transformation in Indianapolis's Public Schools

Paul J. Ramsey

In 1866, two school officials visited the elementary school in Indianapolis's sixth ward and noted approvingly of the students' presentation of the Psalms and the Lord's Prayer. The daily Bible readings and recitations, the observers commented, "cannot fail to exert a high moral influence in the schools." While the moral mission of Indianapolis Public Schools (IPS) was central and overt in the 1860s, there were slight changes in the schools by the middle of the decade that hinted at a radical transformation. These barely perceptible shifts—such as Miss Nebraska Cropsey's promotion of the new "object lesson" method—signaled a sharper turn was forthcoming. The change on the horizon in Indianapolis was the emergence of a modern industrial and consumer society, a new society that was subtly transforming the rigid Protestant moralisms—what Charles Peirce once suggested were a form of "moral terrorism"—of the first three quarters of the nineteenth century. The "modern" America that was to emerge in the late-nineteenth and early-twentieth centuries challenged the moral "certitude" of the antebellum era by worshipping at the feet of new, more "progressive" gods: the gods of science, business, and efficiency.[1]

By the last quarter of the nineteenth century, the new secular gods began to penetrate IPS, and this growing interest in science, industry, and efficiency changed the nature of moral and civic education in the schools. In the 1880s, the old-time moral and religious training mission of IPS—long at its heart and soul—was on the wane, allowing Austin H. Brown, president of the Board of School Commissioners, to articulate new, "modern" moral and civic purposes. The schools, Brown stated, would "give the boys and girls of our city that education which will best fit them for useful citizenship." By the twentieth century, the tenor of the IPS educational mission changed dramatically from that of the 1860s. In 1909, Superintendent Calvin N. Kendall reported that one of the district's central aims was to prepare students for "modern life."[2]

The evolution of IPS's moral and civic mission was far from unique; it was part of a larger pattern of transformation that occurred throughout the United States. B. Edward McClellan outlines this change in some detail. He argues that for much of the nineteenth century, American schools attempted to give students an explicit set of values, which if "rigidly adhered to could provide a reliable guide to behavior and protect against the temptations of the day." By the century's end, the impact of industrialization, urbanization, consumerism, and the "new" immigration was beginning to be seen in America's schools. McClellan notes that the "modern society placed a premium on specialization, technical expertise, and the ability to interact smoothly in an impersonal, rule-governed corporate structure"; the schools, therefore, increasingly promoted the types of skills necessary for students of diverse cultures, in urban and rural communities alike, to navigate their way through this new bureaucratic environment. The change noted in McClellan's analysis is essentially what David Riesman has described as a transition from an "inner-directed" to an "other-directed" society, a shift from a culture in which morality "*is implanted early in life by elders and directed toward . . . inescapably destined goals*" to one in which values are adopted from "*contemporaries*[, who] *are the source of direction for the individual.*"[3]

The switch from rigid, "inner-directed" values to a set of skills and dispositions that allowed for the sort of "ethical flexibility" and "other-directedness" necessary for modern living was not always a smooth transition; the changing nature of moral education in America's schools was often contested, particularly by those who hoped to retain some aspects of the older value system and by those who explicitly called for religious training in the schools.[4] While some religious sects understandably opposed many facets of the emerging modern, "progressive" forms of character training that were making their way into America's schools, some ethnic groups—for a variety of reasons—did as well.

The chapter explores the shift from an "inner-directed" moral and civic education to one of "other-directedness" in Indianapolis, a city that had a large and politically powerful ethnic community. It argues that the small, but influential leadership of the city's German community helped pave the way for IPS's transformation to modernity. Rather than the religiously based moral education of the 1860s, the liberal Germans of the city pushed for a broader form of moral and civic education, an education that increasingly prepared students for modern living by helping them *search* for meaning in their own lives. This new type of moral learning was perhaps best captured by the lines of a poem written by one of IPS's supervisors of German instruction, Robert Nix: "Let virtue be thy guide, [a]nd truth thy beacon-light."[5] As the new skills and dispositions came to hold a place in the IPS curriculum, the modernization movement intersected with new patterns of American nativism. Within a growing anti-foreign atmosphere, knowledge of the English language came to be seen not only as a skill to help ease students' entry into the business world, but also as the only legitimate language for modern America. The leaders of Indianapolis's German community had to redefine the purpose and defend the value of their linguistic and cultural maintenance programs in the city's public schools. Although once among the most "progressive" citizens in the city, the elite Germans came to be viewed as a bulwark against IPS's complete transformation to the developing notion of modernity.

"A Peaceable City"

After the Civil War, Indianapolis—the capital of the state that artist Franklin Booth would later describe as uniquely "different—inquisitive, speculative, [and] constructive"—was a city on the rise and ready to realize its potential. Between 1860 and 1870 the city's population increased over 150 percent. By 1880, Indianapolis had around 75,000 residents, and a generation later the population had grown to nearly 250,000. Indiana's capital did not attract as many of the "new" immigrants (eastern and southern Europeans) as did other American cities, particularly New York and Chicago. Rather, Indianapolis's foreign population consisted primarily of the "older" immigrant groups, such as the Irish and, especially, the Germans. Although German immigration began to slow at the close of the nineteenth century, Indianapolis still had numerous foreign-born Germans among its residents; over 6,000 German foreigners lived in the Hoosier capital in 1880. A decade later, first- and second-generation Germans made up a quarter of the city's population, and perhaps more than a third of the residents could boast German heritage.[6]

The dramatic increase in Indianapolis's population naturally led to a growth in the city's common schools. Public schooling began in the Indiana capital in 1853, and by the late 1870s, the city had 25 schools. Three decades later, IPS operated over 60 district schools—a combination of both elementary and grammar grades—and two high schools; this increased access to public education did not escape the notice of Indianapolis's German community. The Germans of the city were particularly interested in schooling because they hoped to teach their *Muttersprache* to the generations of Germans born outside of the fatherland. German-language instruction was essential because, to use historian George Theodore Probst's words, it was an attempt "to preserve what the Germans considered, correctly or not, to be a superior cultural environment." The need to teach German became more acute after the Civil War when English, rather than the mother tongue, was becoming the language of choice for many of the city's second- and third-generation German immigrants. Theodore Stempfel, a leading German-American in Indianapolis, noted that at "events of the German societies, conversing in English ... became dominant" after the war.[7]

With growing concern over the generations born in the United States, the Germans sought to maintain their culture through a variety of means, and Indianapolis proved to be an excellent environment in which to attempt cultural and linguistic preservation. Midwestern Germans tended "not to look upon themselves as guests in a well-established commonwealth, but as co-founders and partners in a newly-founded enterprise." In addition to being a developing "enterprise," Indianapolis was also, as Stempfel put it, "a peaceable city," where Know-Nothingism "had a hard time taking hold." Facilitated by the favorable local context, German immigrants were able to set up a variety of institutions that helped preserve the culture and language of their fatherland, such as German churches and German-language newspapers. There were also more than 50 secular German clubs in Indianapolis by the turn of the century, including the well-known Indianapolis Turnverein.[8]

Formal schooling was another means of promoting the Germans' "superior" culture in America. In the 1850s, many German families in Indianapolis were leery of the public schools because, as Stempfel testified, they "were still in a deplorable state." A variety of private schools emerged with the purpose of maintaining the linguistic and cultural heritage of German-Americans. But private schools, such as the German-English Independent School, "exceeded the financial resources of many German families," underscoring the need for a more accessible means of preserving *Kultur*. By the mid-1860s, IPS began to experiment with German-language instruction in the heavily German ninth-ward elementary school. The Germans, however, wanted the position of German instruction in the schools to be legally secure, perhaps in order to have a safety net against any sort of anti-foreign sentiment. They began to petition the state legislature for an amendment to the existing public school law to include German-language instruction. In 1869, John R. Coffroth, a state representative from Huntington, Indiana, introduced the legislation. Indianapolis's German-language newspapers, especially the *Telegraph*, advocated for the school law, noting that many parents who send their children to private schools could hardly afford paying a public school tax on top of private school tuition. The German bill easily passed; only three senators opposed the legislation. The amended school law stated that "it shall be the duty of the School Trustee or Trustees . . . to procure efficient teachers and introduce the German language" into a public school if the parents of at least twenty-five students make such a request.[9]

After Indiana's German school law passed, IPS began the process of working out the details of its German program. The school board created a standing committee that oversaw German, music, and drawing and employed Theodore Dingeldey of the German-English Independent School to coordinate the program. Most pressing, IPS had to decide how much time should be devoted to the foreign language, in which grade instruction should begin, and whether or not German-speaking children and English-speaking children would be educated together. Although there was some variation over the years, the negotiated arrangement was that German would be an elective subject; instruction would begin in the second grade and would continue through the high-school years. For most students, German lessons would last about 30 minutes a day, but in 1882 the supervisor of German consolidated all of the sixth, seventh, and eighth-grade German students into a select few schools that offered a bilingual German-English curriculum. Lasting into the 1890s, these "German annexes" were eventually located in the city's high schools and taught half of the school subjects in German, including geography and American history. By 1875, IPS also decided that the German-speaking and English-speaking students—if, presumably, they lived in mixed districts or attended one of the German annexes—would study the language together.[10]

As IPS worked out the logistics of foreign-language study, the German program began to grow rapidly. In the early years, German was offered in two district schools, with only four teachers employed. By 1879, the program offered German in a dozen district schools, employed 12 teachers, and enrolled over 2,400 students. Much of the rapid growth in the 1880s and 1890s was in the number of schools offering the language; the number of students in the program increased only steadily. At the turn of the twentieth century, more pupils elected to continue with their German studies in the grammar grades, which dramatically increased the number of students in the German Department. In 1895, there were only 821 grammar-level students taking German, but there were over 2,400 by 1901. By 1909, the enlarged German Department employed 42 educators who conducted over 400 classes in German, and some 6,000 students studied the language at 38 district schools.[11]

Although many German-Americans in Indianapolis supported IPS's German-language program, the Germans, as well as all ethnic groups, were not a monolithic lot. European immigrants sometimes divided themselves along Old-World provincial lines, as well as by social class, which occasionally intersected with regionalism. Perhaps more importantly, Germans were also fragmented by ideology. Those that came to America after the European revolutions of 1848, the so-called "Forty-eighters," were oftentimes highly educated rationalists and atheists—"freethinkers"—while the Germans who arrived after 1871 tended to have a less liberal and worldly outlook. Ideological factionalism in the German-American community was also apparent by the vast philosophical separation between "*Kirchendeutsche*" and "*Vereinsdeutsche*," the church Germans and club Germans, respectively. Indianapolis's "liberal German population" consisted of club Germans, but they too experienced fragmentation due to "[s]ocial and political differences" and "private quarrels."[12]

While the more conservative *Kirchendeutsche* tended to promote their vision of culture through a system of parochial schools and churches, German liberals typically used private secular schools and public schools in a similar way. The liberal Forty-eighters were often forward-looking humanitarians who thought of Germany as a " 'Kulturnation,' [that is,] a cultural ideal rather than as a political construct." These Germans began many of the gymnastic societies in the United States, not surprising since the "Turners" were among the leaders of the 1848 revolutions in Europe. The Turner clubs in America, the *Turnvereine*, typically had a leftist political flavor in addition to their focus on physical fitness. Because the Turners hoped to "educate men physically, ethically, intellectually, and culturally" by being "a force for progress in culture and freedom and good citizenship," they often had alliances with the schools, both public and private, to promote that vision in America. For many Forty-eighters, preserving the German language and culture was not a conservative endeavor; rather, like many of their views, cultural preservation was "progressive," because the intellectual culture of their beloved "Kulturnation" was more liberal than what they found in the United States.[13]

In Indianapolis, the membership of the Turner, Freethinker, and German-English School societies overlapped considerably, and members of these German clubs were prominent in IPS's German program. For example, in addition to being the first supervisor of German for IPS, Dingeldey of the German-English Independent School was an officer of Indianapolis's Freethinker Society. Charles Emmerich, Dingeldey's successor as supervisor of German and fellow freethinker, taught language arts and pedagogy at the North American Gymnastics Normal College when it temporarily moved from Milwaukee to Indianapolis from 1889 to 1891. Educated in

Prussia, Emmerich was also a member of the German-American Teachers' Association. Like Emmerich, Clemens Vonnegut—great grandfather of the novelist Kurt Vonnegut, Jr.—was born in Germany and was a leading freethinker in the city. In addition to his help in founding the German-English Independent School, Vonnegut served as a member of IPS's Board of School Commissioners for 27 years and, from that position, became one of the most powerful supporters of cultural and linguistic maintenance in the city. Emmerich and Vonnegut were part of the generation of Germans that believed in the ideals of the Forty-eighters, but as they became older and less involved in the IPS German Department they made sure that the younger leaders also shared many of their principles and interests. After Emmerich left the German program, Robert Nix, from the liberal, Forty-eighter-inspired town of New Ulm, Minnesota, was selected to serve as supervisor of German. Before coming to the Hoosier capital, Nix had studied at the universities of Berlin and Leipzig and had been an educator in his hometown's German-English public schools. In Indianapolis—like Emmerich and Vonnegut before him—Nix was an active member of the city's Turner societies.[14]

Preparation for "Modern Living"

Because the German Department consisted of liberal freethinkers, its values had the potential of undermining the "inner-directed" moral mission of the remainder of the IPS curriculum. Until the 1880s, IPS advanced what H. L. Mencken once termed "neo-Puritanism"; the schools promoted simple, unambiguous virtues through the recitation of prayers and through the school board's careful selection of "moral" textbooks and teachers. The books elementary teachers were required to use consisted of moral tales and fables that provided students with a guide for proper behavior. Marcius Willson's readers, which were used in the 1860s, were designed "to teach important MORAL LESSONS; and especially to enforce, by example, the principles of *right* and *duty*." In order to meet those goals, Willson's *Fourth Reader* contained numerous stories and poems that showed students how to be thrifty, honest, and industrious. Jacob Abbott's books promoted these virtues as well, along with those of obedience, fidelity, kindness, purity, and forgiveness. By 1883, IPS's "list of books for home reading for [elementary-level] children" showed some signs of secularization, but the rigid moral tone continued in many of the books. Abbott's *History of Julius Caesar* had the dual purpose of providing accurate historical information and helping students "to draw . . . moral lessons from the events described." IPS's textbooks, as well as most others during much of the nineteenth century, underscored the notion that "virtue is superior to knowledge."[15]

Although potential for conflict between the German Department and the remainder of IPS was ever present, the school leaders were able to find some common ground. While praying—an important moral activity of the schools—seemed somewhat ridiculous to the freethinking Germans, they conceded that if prayer was simply "a colloquy with one's own mind," such a ritual could be quite beneficial and therefore tolerable for students. The values the German elites put forth in the schools sometimes paralleled those of IPS's Protestant curriculum. Like the moral textbooks, Germans spoke of the importance of kindness, honesty, obedience, and industry. For both the Protestant school leaders and the freethinkers, one of the central aims of education was to develop students' moral "conscious[ness]" so that they could recognize right from wrong. The content found in IPS's textbooks, which were carefully chosen by the school board, frequently intersected with the interests of the German liberals. (German board members often sat on the textbook-selection committee, presumably to ensure that their values received treatment in the curriculum.) John Ridpath's American histories—part of the IPS curriculum from 1877 to 1883—were known for their critical treatment of the European explorers' abuses in the New World and the cruelty of the Puritan witch hunts; these criticisms were very much in line with the Forty-eighters' humanitarian ideals. The IPS texts also paralleled the Germans' praise of the fatherland. In general, nineteenth-century textbooks portrayed Germany as progressive and modern, while its countrymen were heralded as virtuous, intelligent, and hard working. Charlotte Yonge's *Young Folks' History of Germany*, one of IPS's recommended books for young readers, suggested that the leaders of the European revolutions in the 1840s were freedom-loving citizens attempting to change the repressive governments of the German and Austrian nobility.[16]

Although the German freethinkers and the other IPS school leaders found some commonalities in their beliefs, the underlying value systems that guided both groups diverged significantly. The leaders of the IPS German program were fiercely antireligious, characterizing Christianity as an "absurd" superstition. While many "blueskin" schoolmen received their "inner-directed" morality from biblical truths, the freethinkers' value system was derived from "reason, observation of nature, history and experience"; as the lines from Nix's poem suggested, virtue came from the search for truth. The elite Germans in Indianapolis found moral wisdom in German literature. Johann Wolfgang von Goethe, Heinrich Heine, and Friedrich Schiller were more than mere literary figures; their works were often used as models for virtue. Schiller was the "champion of freedom," and Heine's work was quite popular among the Forty-eighters. In his *Proposed Guide for Instruction in Morals*, Vonnegut frequently quoted German literary giants in order to demonstrate moral lessons. Because German literature had such a virtuous power, students in the IPS German program, after learning the essentials of the language, were expected to read these classic and contemporary German works. The German teachers were also expected to have an intimate familiarity with this value-laden literature. During the 1901–1902 school year, Supervisor Nix, an expert on Goethe's work, conducted 35 professional development seminars for his teachers, 18 of which were dedicated to *Faust*. In May, the German teachers had to write essays on the play in order to renew their teaching positions in the German Department.[17]

Despite some areas of common interest, the German freethinkers were not entirely satisfied with the direction of IPS's moral and civic training endeavors. As Louis Menand notes in *The Metaphysical Club*, the antebellum era was marked by moral "certitude"; the alternative would be a society at "sixes and sevens," as Americans once colloquially described confusion and chaos. After the devastation of the Civil War, good and evil, for some, seemed much more ambiguous and dependent upon context. The German freethinkers understood the contextual nature of morality, and they sought to broaden the moral and civic mission of Indianapolis's public schools to include an "other-directed" form of character education. Such an education would help students ease into their roles in the modern urban society that was quickly emerging in Indianapolis. Vonnegut, Emmerich, and the other members of the city's German intelligentsia looked to science and literature to help articulate their notions of modern morality. In Goethe's *Faust*, German freethinkers found not an articulation of the simple and rigid moral rules that characterized the IPS curriculum of the 1860s and 1870s, but a thoughtful discussion of the complex intertwining of good and evil. Unlike in the IPS textbooks, the right and wrong courses of action were not easily identified in Goethe's work; this relativity meshed well with the Germans' stance on such moral issues as temperance. (Straying from "Adam's ale" and occasionally indulging in alcohol was not inherently wrong, as Victorian teetotalers suggested; rather, one simply needed to moderate one's consumption and avoid becoming a "soaker.") What the leaders of the German program were attempting to do was to broaden the notion of moral training beyond a set of controls for private behavior (although those were important) to include also a public morality that sought to make students active thinkers and humanitarians. Like other progressives, the freethinkers "did not simply accept modernity; they believed that the new order offered hope of an unprecedented period of social and moral progress if only Americans would abandon the tyranny of tradition . . . through the application of science and reason to the complex problems of the day."[18]

The elite Germans in the city were among the strongest advocates pushing for the schools to incorporate the skills that were perceived as necessary for life in an industrial society. While the development of a moral "consciousness" and a set of virtues were important to the freethinkers, the cultivation of the intellect was a primary concern. Intelligence helped students become more virtuous and promoted the skills needed for success in the modern world. Not only did the German leaders promote the virtuousness of intelligence among their charges, they also lived by the creed. Nix, for instance, was a brilliant scholar who cultivated his own mental powers by learning numerous languages, translating classic literature, writing poetry, and studying philosophy. (William T. Harris—a leading Hegelian philosopher, superintendent of St. Louis schools from 1869 to 1880, and future U.S. commissioner of education—thought Nix was among the foremost Aristotelian philosophers in the United States and consequently published some of his essays.) The elite Germans' focus on the intellect helped transition IPS away from the inner-directed, Bible-based form of moral training that was the hallmark of the educational mission during the decades immediately following the Civil War. By emphasizing science and scholarship, the Germans of Indianapolis were challenging the "neo-Puritanism" that was present in modern America.[19]

The Germans also tried to bring the Indianapolis schools in line with modern thought by promoting students' health and providing them with training for expertise. Because of their connection with the Turner societies, the German intelligentsia in Indianapolis believed that one of the ultimate moral "duties is to promote our good health." The leaders of the German program brought physical education into the IPS curriculum; the supervisory position was typically held by Germans active in the Turner societies. The German leaders also pushed for the inclusion of vocational and manual training in the city's public schools, a campaign that was quite successful. For many Germans, vocational education was a progressive and modern addition to the traditional school curriculum. In the 1890s, Emmerich left his position as supervisor of German in order to become the principal of the newly opened Industrial Training School. (In 1916, the school was renamed Emmerich Manual High School.) By the turn of the twentieth century, manual training played a central role in the city's elementary schools as well; students learned skills such as sewing, drawing, and cooking.[20]

When Superintendent Kendall outlined the new mission of the city's public schools in 1909, he noted that the most pressing aim of public education was to provide students with the skills and knowledge needed to succeed in industrial America, such as reading, writing, health, mechanical arts, and a sampling of specialized information found in the content areas. Kendall stated that "manual training is a poor substitute for the old, all-around training which rural life at one time gave. It is useless, however, to lament changes in social conditions. We are training boys and girls who must live in twentieth century conditions." The old-time moral mission had lost its centrality in the curriculum. The superintendent mentioned moral training only briefly as the final goal of the schools, as though it were an afterthought.[21]

Besides manual training, knowledge of the English language came to be seen as one of the most essential skills necessary to live in twentieth-century America. As with the other progressive changes, the German leadership supported the emphasis on English as well; their teachers were required to be "proficient in English." Although the Germans were among the most active supporters of modernizing the curriculum, the school-board members—many of whom were non-German—and the superintendents had the final say over the new course of study, and the teaching of English quickly became the most valued activity of IPS under their leadership. The IPS superintendent noted that English was much more important for "modern living" than a knowledge of mathematics.[22] As the focus on modern skills in the curriculum became more pronounced, it intersected with an American nativist movement, which gave the emphasis on English even more urgency and ultimately threatened the position of German instruction in the curriculum.

"A Polyglot Boardinghouse"

While perennially cropping up on American soil, nativism again began to flourish in the United States during the late 1880s and early 1890s, which led to a growing concern about German-language instruction in schools around the country. The nativism that emerged in that late-nineteenth century partly reflected some Americans' growing uneasiness with new patterns of immigration, which largely came from southern and eastern Europe. The Poles, Italians, and Russian Jews were the primary targets, but with a nativist mood sweeping over the United States, all non-native Americans were marked for persecution. After a bitter political campaign in 1887, the German-American community in St. Louis was unable to defend the study of the German language in the city's public schools. Two years later, the Bennett and Edwards Acts emerged in Wisconsin and Illinois, respectively. While these legislative manifestations of nativism primarily targeted German parochial schools, they attempted to mandate the supremacy of the English language. Educators in Indiana watched the events in their neighboring states rather carefully. By the late 1880s, nativism was making headway in the "peaceable city" as well, and it had its sights set on the German-language programs in the public schools. In an 1888 editorial, the *Indiana School Journal* reported that if the German-language issue were to "be settled by a popular vote, as in St. Louis," the German language would "probably go out of all Indiana cities except as a high-school study." But a popular vote could not decide the question in Indianapolis because, unlike in St. Louis, German instruction in the elementary schools was guaranteed by state law.[23]

It was within this regional context that the attack on Indianapolis's German-language program occurred. In 1886, the opposition to German in the public elementary schools began, but the opposition was, at least officially, driven by financial concerns. Throughout the late 1880s, Indianapolis's German-American community successfully countered the attacks. At a May 1890 school-board meeting, Theodore P. Haughey suddenly moved to have German-language instruction removed from grades two through five, leaving German study in only the high schools and the upper levels of the district schools. Although Vonnegut, A.R. Baker, E.L. Williams, and J.W. Loeper opposed the resolution, they did not have enough votes to stop it. The German supporters on the board were quick to point out that their opponents "waited until one of our men was in Europe, and another sick." The German-language press protested, as did the German community in general. Advocates took the case to court and won in July, and by 1891 the Indiana Supreme Court had reconfirmed the legality of German in the public schools of the state.[24] As it turned out, the writing of German-language instruction into the state's school law proved to be an effective means of protection during times of nativism.

When the news of the removal of the German language from Indianapolis's public schools reached Baltimore, one of its local German-American newspapers called the action "*ein Kulturkampf*," and perhaps that was not an exaggeration of what was occurring in Indiana's capital. At the May 1890 school-board meeting that temporarily ended the German program, board members opposed to German instruction made comments that hinted at their nativist sympathies. John Galvin stated that he had heard of a recent German-American Teachers' Association meeting where it had been uttered that "[i]f the Americans can not amalgamate the Germans, we Germans will amalgamate them"; since its formation in the early 1870s, the association had always been a predictable and easy target for nativists because of its opposition to religious exercises in the public schools. Emmerich was present at the meeting that Galvin spoke of and denied that such a statement was ever made. He noted that "[t]he German-American teachers meet once a year . . . for mutual improvement in their profession," not for planning to Germanize America. But in this era of nativism, many of Indianapolis's citizens were suddenly leery of anything foreign. The *Indianapolis News*, drawing on reports from Ohio, made note of "the uselessness of a foreign language in the public schools where the American citizen is being made," while the *Indianapolis Journal* suggested that "the teaching of German" was "anti-American."[25]

Unlike the nativists, the German intelligentsia in Indianapolis had a broader, more inclusive notion of "American." For Germans in the United States, "Americanization" did not necessarily mean "Anglification," and the teaching of the German language did not seem unpatriotic because "Americanism," for many German-Americans, "represented a metalinguistic concept." Being American did not merely entail speaking English. For the German leadership in Indianapolis, being a good citizen meant working for "the improvement of the condition of his country." It also connoted respecting one's fellow citizens and obeying the laws of the nation, which suggested another reason why the Germans were so adamant about having German instruction written into state law. "American" was therefore a more nuanced concept for the German elites than it was for the nativists, who sometimes resorted to breaking laws to enforce their narrower vision of the good American.[26]

Nativism and avid patriotism made the English instruction of the public schools all the more pressing, and, in such a charged atmosphere, the German program came to be seen as subversive because it undermined the mission of the American schools. In 1887, the *Indiana School Journal* reported on the conservative *Indianapolis Journal* view "that every teacher in Indianapolis was opposed to the teaching of German in the lower grades of the schools." Although this was surely an exaggeration, perhaps there was some truth to the report since some American teachers clearly did not support German in the public schools. In Ohio, John B. Peaslee, although later an advocate of German instruction, stated that he "begrudged the German teacher his time" when he first began as an educator in Cincinnati's public schools. The *Indianapolis News*, more moderate than the *Journal*, also called for English-only public schools. These sentiments impacted the thinking of Indianapolis's schoolmen. In 1892, the superintendent of IPS noted that one of the central aims of the city's public schools was to "give culture," but in the late nineteenth century, it became increasingly clear that what was meant was "American" culture, which often translated into the study of the English language, as well as American and English literature. In 1909, Superintendent Kendall made similar comments in his annual report regarding the cultural purpose of the schools. It was in this atmosphere of anti-immigrant feeling that Karl Knortz, a supervisor of German in Evansville, Indiana, openly proposed the need for "discreet [German] teachers" in order to preserve the fatherland's culture in America.[27]

With English and a narrowly defined notion of citizenship being emphasized in the schools, discretion seemed advisable, and the study of German in the elementary grades had to be defended in a more cautious manner. Although a supporter of cultural maintenance, the supervisor of German had to make the case for German instruction in a less threatening way. In 1909, Supervisor Nix justified the elementary study of German by drawing on contemporary science, particularly the findings of the Modern Language Association. He wrote that German was important in the elementary years because "[i]n childhood the organs of speech are still in a plastic condition"; therefore, the childhood years formed a critical period for language acquisition, and, as Nix stated, any "later period of youth is distinctly a bad time to begin." Other teachers of German in the United States made similar arguments about the importance of German in the early grades, but they began to justify the study of German by emphasizing its usefulness in the modern world as well. Although English "should be the first aim of our national education," wrote M. D. Learned in the *German American Annals*, German should also be taught because "[i]n the nineteenth century the language of international culture has shifted from French to German . . . [;] the German people have risen to the foremost place in modern intellectual life in all the fields of science and letters." German was therefore a pragmatic modern language; it would help students achieve specialized expertise in the sciences, but it would also improve the "prosperity of our great nation" by providing students with the necessary skill for international business.[28]

The new rationale for elementary German study seemed to work. The German program was secure in the IPS curriculum for the time being and continued to grow in the early part of the twentieth century. By 1916, there were nearly 7,500 pupils studying German in the city's elementary schools. The German program was [apparently attractive enough to some students that they themselves became teachers] at IPS; a majority of the German elementary teachers in the early years of the twentieth century had graduated from the city's bilingual program. In spite of its popularity, German was increasingly marginalized from the "modern" mission of Indianapolis's public schools. In the first decade of the twentieth century, Superintendent Kendall justified the study of the "content subjects" by explaining their importance for "good citizenship." Additionally, some subjects, such as history and music, were also important because they "furnish resources in life," but German went unjustified; it was simply there from "the laws of the state."[29] The German program, once thought of as a progressive innovation by the city's ethnic elite, had become a bulwark in the struggle for a "modern" curriculum, a curriculum that had been partially energized by nativist sentiments.

Although the German program survived the nativism of the 1880s and 1890s, it did not endure surging patriotism that swept across the country during and immediately following World War I. During the war, Hoosiers such as James Woodburn of Indiana University were calling for a *"united nation*—with *one* people, . . . *one* allegiance, and, let us not be afraid to say, *one* language." "Let us strive," Professor Woodburn added, "to save America from being a polyglot nation—a conglomeration of tongues and nationalities, like a 'polyglot boardinghouse,' as Mr. Roosevelt has put it." Rather than appealing to nativism, other educators felt the time was right to halt the teaching of German in public schools because it did not fit with the curricular focus on the skills and dispositions most necessary for modern living; students simply did not need German to function efficiently in modern America. Fanatical Americanism prevailed, however. Indiana State Senator Franklin McCray and Lieutenant Governor Edgar D. Bush drafted legislation that ended German-language instruction in all of Indiana's public and private elementary schools in 1919. Although the anti-German school laws were eventually undermined by the United States Supreme Court in the 1920s, German-language instruction in Indianapolis's public elementary schools never recovered.[30]

Conclusions

The rigid moral mission of IPS lessened as the city made its transformation into a modern urban center. The simple moral lessons characteristic of the decades immediately following the Civil War were supplanted by an emphasis on the skills and dispositions needed for modern living. Although German freethinkers and more conventional school leaders managed to coexist rather peacefully in the 1860s and 1870s, the German leaders felt somewhat restrained by the rigid set of moral truths put forth in the IPS curriculum. They thought that students needed more than an "inner-directed" sense of morality in order to cope with the newly emerging conditions of modern America. German leaders became some of the strongest supporters of curricular change, a type of change, as Nix's poetry suggested, that saw the search for truth as its own form of virtue. As IPS began to incorporate the focus on modern skills into its curriculum, increasing nativism denigrated anything deemed as foreign, making the focus on the English language all the more pressing. As the German program came under attack for being un-American, or at the very least, un-modern, the German leaders had to articulate a justification for the study of German in the elementary grades that fit with the new mood of the nation. It was rationalized as a skill that would help students succeed in the emerging global economy, and in order to teach that skill scientifically and efficiently, it had to be done in the early years of childhood. Although German in the elementary schools of Indianapolis was safe for a time, the nativism of World War I destroyed the "polyglot boardinghouse" that the Germans had painstakingly built and maintained for so many years.

This transformation of moral and civic education in Indianapolis during the decades surrounding the turn of the twentieth century demonstrates the importance of the local context for a fuller understanding of curricular and social change. When historians maneuver solely at the national level, the nuances of transformations and how those changes impacted people are sometimes lost. The story of IPS's use of a more modern form of character education parallels the national trend, but that is only the end of the tale. The cast of characters, their goals, and ideologies are part of the story as well. At the local level, a multitude of forces come together to allow for the educational and intellectual trends to be implemented. For instance, regardless of the national industrial interests lobbying for vocational education in the public schools, in Indianapolis manual training partially emerged because of the liberal German leaders' desire to have more "progressive" and modern schools.[31] A close examination of local communities and their members also reveals that it was not only nationally known intellectuals such as Oliver Wendell Holmes, Jr., William James, Charles Peirce, and John Dewey who were questioning the moral "certitude" of the nineteenth century, as Menand's *Metaphysical Club* suggests. Rather, local school leaders in Indianapolis had similar doubts about the old-time morality and put into practice curricular ideas that helped usher in a new ethical code, one that surely influenced the generations of children who would come of age in modern America.

Notes

1. *Annual Report of the Public Schools of the City of Indianapolis, for the School Year Ending Sept. 1, 1866* (Indianapolis: Douglass and Conner, 1867), 20–21, 37, 48–49, 89; William J. Reese, "Education," in David J. Bodenhamer and Robert Barrows, eds., *The Encyclopedia of Indianapolis* (Bloomington: Indiana University Press, 1994), 76; Charles Peirce, "The Fixation of Belief," in David A. Hollinger and Charles Capper, eds., *The American Intellectual Tradition: A Sourcebook*, vol. 2, 4th edn. (New York: Oxford University Press, 2001), 14; Oliver Wendell Holmes, Jr., "Natural Law," *The American Intellectual Tradition*, 138–139; Julie A. Reuben, *The Making of the Modern University: Intellectual Transformation and the Marginalization of Morality* (Chicago: University of Chicago Press, 1996), 133–174; Morton Keller, *Regulating a New Society: Public Policy and Social Change in America, 1900–1933* (Cambridge: Harvard University Press, 1994), 4–6, 44–66.
2. *Twenty-Second Annual Report of the Public Schools of the City of Indianapolis, for the School Year Ending June 30, 1883* (Indianapolis: Sentinel Co., 1883), 4, 7; Indianapolis Public Schools, *Annual Report of the Secretary, Business Director, Superintendent of Schools and the Librarian, 1908–1909* (n.p. [1909?]), 35–39.
3. B. Edward McClellan, *Moral Education in America: Schools and the Shaping of Character from Colonial Times to the Present* (New York: Teachers College Press, 1999), 26–27, 46–47; David Riesman, in collaboration with Reuel Denney and Nathan Glazer, *The Lonely Crowd: A Study of the Changing American Character* (New Haven, CT: Yale University Press, 1950), 15, 22.
4. McClellan, *Moral Education*, 48–62; Lloyd P. Jorgenson, *The State and the Non-Public School, 1825–1925* (Columbia: University of Missouri Press, 1987), 69–108.
5. Robert Nix, *Poems* (Spokane, WA: Else M. Nix, 1930), 16.
6. Theodore Dreiser, *A Hoosier Holiday* (1916; reprint, with an introduction by Douglas Brinkley, Bloomington: Indiana University Press, 1998), 432; James J. Divita, "Demography and Ethnicity," *The Encyclopedia of Indianapolis*, 53–55; U.S. Bureau of the Census, *Population 1910: Reports by States with Statistics for Counties, Cities and Other Civil Divisions, Alabama—Montana*, vol. 2 of *Thirteenth Census of the United States Taken in the Year 1910* (Washington, DC: Government Printing Office, 1913), 518, 543; George Theodore Probst, *The Germans in Indianapolis, 1840–1918*, revised and illustrated edn. (Indianapolis: German-American Center and Indiana German Heritage Society, Inc., 1989), 82, 90–91; Giles R. Hoyt, "Germans," in Robert M. Taylor, Jr. and Connie A. McBirney, eds., *Peopling Indiana: The Ethnic Experience* (Indianapolis: Indiana Historical Society, 1996), 150–151.
7. *Annual Report, 1909*, 24–26; Reese, "Education," 73–78; Probst, *The Germans*, 55, 76; Hoyt, "Germans," in *Peopling Indiana*, 164; Frederick Gale, *A Biographical Study of the Persons for Whom Indianapolis Schools Are Named* (Indianapolis Public Schools, 1965), s.v. "Clemens Vonnegut"; Theodore Stempfel, *Fifty Years of Unrelenting German Aspirations in Indianapolis* (1898; German/English edition, ed. Giles R. Hoyt, Claudia Grossmann, Elfrieda Lang, and Eberhard Reichmann, Indianapolis: German-American Center and Indiana German Heritage Society, Inc., 1991), 28.
8. Heinz Kloss, "German-American Language Maintenance Efforts," in Joshua A. Fishman, ed., *Language Loyalty in the United States: The Maintenance and Perpetuation of Non-English Mother Tongues by American Ethnic and Religious Groups* (London: Mouton and Co., 1966), 226; John Bodnar, *The Transplanted: A History of Immigrants in Urban America* (Bloomington: Indiana University Press, 1985), 172; Probst, *The Germans*, 80–140; Hoyt,

"Germans," in *Peopling Indiana*, 161, 164; Stempfel, *Fifty Years*, 21, 45–79; James P. Ziegler, *The German-language Press in Indiana: A Bibliography* (Indianapolis: Max Kade German-American Center and Indiana German Heritage Society, Inc., 1994), 15–19.

9. Kloss, "German-American Language Maintenance Efforts," 225; Frances H. Ellis, "Historical Account of German Instruction in the Public Schools of Indianapolis, 1869–1919," *Indiana Magazine of History* 50, no. 2 (1954): 123–136; Probst, *The Germans*, 70; Stempfel, *Fifty Years*, 19, 28–30; La Vern J. Rippley, *The German Americans* (Boston: Twayne Publishers, 1976), 122; *Annual Report, 1866*, 89; Frank L. Jones, Superintendent of Public Instruction, *The School Law of Indiana with Annotations, and the State Constitution* (Indianapolis: Wm. B. Burford, 1901), 204.

10. Ellis, "German Instruction: I," 137; Frances H. Ellis, "German Instruction in the Public Schools of Indianapolis, 1869–1919: II," *Indiana Magazine of History* 50, no. 3 (1954): 252–264; William A. Fritsch, *German Settlers and German Settlements in Indiana* (Evansville: n.p., 1915), 45; *Manual of the Public Schools of the City of Indianapolis, 1884–85* (Indianapolis: Carlon & Hollenbeck, 1884), 66; *Manual, of the Public Schools of the City of Indianapolis, with Rules and Regulations of the Board of School Commissioners, the Public Schools, and the Public Library, 1889–90* (Indianapolis: Sentinel Printing Co., 1889), 53; *Annual Report, 1883*, 27–32; Indianapolis Public Schools, *Annual Report of the Secretary, Business Director, Superintendent of Schools, and the Librarian* (n.p., 1902), 87; *Annual Report, 1909*, 151–154.

11. Ellis, "German Instruction: I," 137; Indianapolis Public Schools, *Eighteenth Annual Report of the Public Schools of the City of Indianapolis for the School Year Ending June 30, 1879* (Indianapolis: Douglass and Carlon, 1879), 73–74; *Manual of the Public Schools of the City of Indianapolis: Rules and Regulations of the Board of School Commissioners and Public Library, 1878–79* (Indianapolis: Wm. B. Burford, 1878), 38–55; *Manual of the Public Schools of the City of Indianapolis: Rules and Regulations of the Board of School Commissioners of the Public Schools and the Public Library, 1881–82* (Indianapolis: Wm. B. Burford, 1881), 129–147; *Manual, 1889*, 56–57, 142–164; *Annual Report, 1883*, 27–28; *Twenty-Seventh Annual Report of the Public Schools of the City of Indianapolis for the School Year Ending June 30, 1888* (Indianapolis: Sentinel Printing Co., 1888), 45; *Annual Report, 1902*, 87–89; *Annual Report, 1909*, 151.

12. Stempfel, *Fifty Years*, 27, 66; Bodnar, *The Transplanted*, 117–120; Hoyt, "Germans," in *Peopling Indiana*, 162; Carl Wittke, *Refugees of Revolution: The German Forty-Eighters in America* (Philadelphia: University of Pennsylvania Press, 1952), 122–129; Probst, *The Germans*, 89–90; Kloss, "German-American Language Maintenance Efforts," 224, 229.

13. Kloss, "German-American Language Maintenance Efforts," 225, 231–232; Rippley, *The German Americans*, 123, 180–181; Fritsch, *German Settlers*, 59–61; M.D. Learned, "German in the Public Schools," *German American Annals* 2 (1913): 100–106; Wittke, *Refugees of Revolution*, v–vi, 123–129, 152, 300–308; L. Viereck, "German Instruction in American Schools," *Report of the Commissioner of Education for the Year 1900–1901*, vol. 1 (Washington, DC: Government Printing Office, 1902), 577–580; "Brief History of the Normal College N.A.G.U.," *The Gymnast* 1 (1913): 9; Hoyt, "Germans," in *Peopling Indiana*, 147, 169; Clemens Vonnegut, *A Proposed Guide for Instruction in Morals for the Standpoint of a Freethinker: For Adult Persons Offered by a Dilettante* (1900; reprint, n.p., 1987), 11, 30–31; Probst, *The Germans*, 15, 143.

14. Stempfel, *Fifty Years*, 29–30, 40–41, 63–64; Fritsch, *German Settlers*, 45, 52–53; *Annual Report, 1879*, 129; Probst, *The Germans*, 70–71, 80, 101, 137, 140; Hoyt, "Germans," in *Peopling Indiana*, 165; Ellis, "German Instruction: I," 119; Ellis, "German Instruction: II," 252, 256–257; Ellis, "German Instruction in the Public Schools of Indianapolis, 1869–1919: III," *Indiana Magazine of History* 50, no. 4 (1954): 357–358; "Brief History

of the Normal College," 9; "Board of Trustees," *The Gymnast* 1 (1913): 13; "Faculty," *The Gymnast* 1 (1913): 13–14; "Verzeichnis der gewonnenen Mitarbeiter," *Pädagogische Monatshefte* 1 (Dezember 1899): 6; Gale, s.v. "Clemens Vonnegut"; Charles Titus, "Emmerich, Charles Emil," *The Encyclopedia of Indianapolis*, 542–543; Robert M. Taylor, "Freethought," *The Encyclopedia of Indianapolis*, 602–603; Giles R. Hoyt, "German-English School Society," *The Encyclopedia of Indianapolis*, 615; Giles R. Hoyt, "Germans," *The Encyclopedia of Indianapolis*, 618–621; William L. Selm, "Vonnegut, Clemens, Sr.," *The Encyclopedia of Indianapolis*, 1388–1389; Nix, *Poems*, iv–vi.

15. H.L. Mencken, "Puritanism as a Literary Force," *The American Intellectual Tradition*, 195; *Annual Report, 1866*, 21, 48–49, 70–75, 84–87; McClellan, *Moral Education*, 25–27; Marcius Willson, *The Fourth Reader of the United States Series* (New York: Harper and Brothers, 1872), iii, 21–22, 30–31, 117–118; *Annual Report, 1883*, 10–11; Jacob Abbott, *A Primer of Ethics*, ed. Benjamin B. Comegys (Boston: Ginn and Company, 1891), 1–31, 58, 102–113; Jacob Abbott, *History of Julius Caesar* (New York: Harper and Brothers, 1877), vii–viii; Ruth Miller Elson, *Guardians of Tradition: American Schoolbooks of the Nineteenth Century* (Lincoln: University of Nebraska Press, 1964), 226.

16. Vonnegut, *A Proposed Guide*, 4–27; Abbott, *A Primer of Ethics*, 82–88; John A. Nietz, *Old Textbooks: Spelling, Grammar, Reading, Arithmetic, Geography, American History, Civil Government, Physiology, Penmanship, Art, Music—As Taught in the Common Schools from Colonial Days to 1900* (University of Pittsburgh Press, 1961), 245–248; *Annual Report, 1883*, 5, 10–11, 40–41; Elson, *Guardians of Tradition*, 143–145; Charlotte M. Yonge, *Young Folks' History of Germany* (Boston: D. Lothrop and Company, 1878), 456–458.

17. Vonnegut, *A Proposed Guide*, 6–11, 13, 21–23, 31; Nix, *Poems*, 16; *Annual Report, 1902*, 90–91; *Annual Report, 1909*, 154–157; Indianapolis Public Schools, *Annual Report: Business Director, Superintendent of Schools and Librarian* (n.p., 1916), 132–133; Wittke, *Refugees of Revolution*, 311–313; Ellis, "German Instruction: III," 357. "Blueskins" were rigid Protestants, often Presbyterians; see John Russell Bartlett, *Dictionary of Americanisms: A Glossary of Words and Phrases, Usually Regarded as Peculiar to the United States* (1848; reprint, with a foreword by Richard Lederer, Hoboken, NJ: John Wiley & Sons, Inc., 2003), 39.

18. Bartlett, *Dictionary of Americanisms*, 2, 304, 319; Louis Menand, *The Metaphysical Club* (New York: Farrar, Straus and Giroux, 2001), ix–69; McClellan, *Moral Education*, 55–58; Vonnegut, *A Proposed Guide*, 8–31; Walter Kaufmann, ed. and trans., *Goethe's Faust* (New York: Anchor Books, 1990), 21–26, 155–173, 273–291, 325–335, 359–387; Wittke, *Refugees of Revolution*, 139.

19. Mencken, "Puritanism," 195; Vonnegut, *A Proposed Guide*, 8–13, 29; Nix, *Poems*, iii–ix; McClellan, *Moral Education*, 25–27, 46–47, 55–61.

20. Vonnegut, *A Proposed Guide*, 12; Hoyt, "Germans," *The Encyclopedia of Indianapolis*, 620; Titus, "Emmerich," 542–543; *Indianapolis Turnverein: Seventy-fifth Anniversary, 1851–1926* (n.p., 1926), 17–20; *Annual Report, 1909*, 35–52.

21. *Annual Report, 1909*, 35–52.

22. *Manual, 1889*, 53; *Annual Report, 1909*, 38–39; Learned, "German in the Public Schools," 101.

23. Oscar Handlin, "Education and the European Immigrant, 1820–1920," in Bernard J. Weiss, ed., *American Education and the European Immigrant, 1840–1940* (Urbana: University of Illinois Press, 1982), 9–12; John Higham, *Strangers in the Land: Patterns of American Nativism, 1860–1925* (New Brunswick: Rutgers University Press, 1955), 36–105; Selwyn K. Troen, *The Public and the Schools: Shaping the St. Louis System, 1830–1920* (Columbia: University of Missouri Press, 1975), 60–62, 68–78; Board of Education of the City of St. Louis, *Official Report*, vol. 3, 1878–1880 (St. Louis: Board of

Education of the City of St. Louis, n.d.), 47; Rippley, *The German Americans*, 120–121; Kloss, "German-American Language Maintenance Efforts," 226, 236; Heinz Kloss, *The American Bilingual Tradition* (McHenry, IL: Center for Applied Linguistics and Delta Systems, 1998), 83–86; "The Bennett Law," *Indiana School Journal* 35, no. 12 (1890): 665–666; "The Indianapolis Journal vs. the Public Schools," *Indiana School Journal* 32, no. 5 (1887): 303–305; "Editorial," *Indiana School Journal* 33, no. 4 (1888): 218.

24. "German in the Schools," *Indianapolis News*, May 3, 1890, evening edn, 1; *Manual, 1889*, 5; Ellis, "German Instruction: II," 262–276; "The German Teaching Decision," *Indianapolis News*, July 18, 1890, 2.

25. C.E. Emmerich, "No Such Sentiment Uttered," *Indianapolis News*, May 3, 1890, evening edn., 1; "German in the Public Schools," *Indianapolis News*, May 28, 1890, 4; "The Indianapolis Journal vs. the Public Schools," 303; Wittke, *Refugees of Revolution*, 308–309; Ellis, "German Instruction: II," 272.

26. Kloss, "German-American Language Maintenance Efforts," 229; Vonnegut, *A Proposed Guide*, 30–31; Frederick C. Luebke, *Germans in the New World: Essays in the History of Immigration* (Urbana: University of Illinois Press, 1990), 36–42; Eric Foner, *Who Owns History?: Rethinking the Past in a Changing World* (New York: Hill & Wang, 2002), 160–163.

27. "The Indianapolis Journal vs. the Public Schools," 304; John B. Peaslee, *Thoughts and Experiences in and out of School* (Cincinnati: Curts and Jennings, 1900), 203; "German in the Public Schools," 4; *Annual Report, 1892*, 43; *Annual Report, 1909*, 35, 38–39; Viereck, "German Instruction," 646.

28. *Annual Report, 1909*, 154; Learned, "German in the Public Schools," 101–106.

29. *Annual Report, 1902*, 40–43, 90–91; *Annual Report, 1909*, 39–40; *Annual Report, 1916*, 130–131.

30. L.N. Hines, ed., *Proceedings and Papers of the Indiana State Teachers' Association, October 31, and November 1, 2, 3, 1917, Indianapolis* (n.p., n.d.), 350; *Meyer v. Nebraska*, 262 US 390 (1923); *Pierce v. Society of Sisters*, 268 US 510 (1925); Kenneth B. O'Brien, Jr., "Education, Americanization and the Supreme Court: The 1920's," *American Quarterly* 13, no. 2 (1961): 161–171; Paul J. Ramsey, "The War against German-American Culture: The Removal of German-Language Instruction from the Indianapolis Schools, 1917–1919," *Indiana Magazine of History* 98, no. 4 (2002): 294–300; "Potent Reasons Why German Should Not Be Taught in the Public Schools," *Indiana Instructor* 2, no. 3 (1917): 3–4.

31. For a detailed look at how industrialists were able to successfully advocate for vocational education, see Herbert M. Kliebard, *Schooled to Work: Vocationalism and the American Curriculum, 1876–1946* (New York: Teachers College Press, 1999).

This page intentionally left blank

Chapter 10

Berkeley Women Economists, Public Policy, and Civic Sensibility

Mary Ann Dzuback

Yielding to no one in her demand for thoroughness, precision, and objectivity in investigation, she has never cultivated . . . pleasure gardens for the favored few, walled off from the man on the street . . . She has done yeoman service in the common fields of daily life, trying to wring from the stubborn soil harvests of knowledge that the housewife and workingman can use.[1]

The production of knowledge was a critical component of progressive reform in the early part of the twentieth century in the United States. For many social scientists, it was also a conscious manifestation of their moral and civic commitment to ensuring that democratic institutions became responsive to all citizens, from the poorest to those of the comfortable middle class, in the face of corporate expansion and monopoly of labor and production and political officials more concerned with their own gains than with the daily problems of the citizenry. Women social scientists resolved the question of how to connect research to policy and to their moral and civic commitments in various ways between 1890 and 1940. Some remained closely involved with settlement houses, while others became researchers in such government-sponsored agencies as the Women's Bureau and the Children's Bureau, and still others conducted research for municipal charitable agencies, or with philanthropic organizations, including the Russell Sage Foundation. Many were reluctant to submit to the pressure to divorce scholarship from civic commitments, principally commitments to research addressing social and economic problems, and focusing on women and families. They based their research on the kinds of concerns explored in the social survey movement of the 1880s and 1890s. Such concerns were largely eclipsed as social science research became increasingly male-dominated, professional, and university-based just as "objectivity" and "science" took precedence over other ideals in professional social science research after the turn of the century. This trend was particularly evident in economics, where, as Nancy Folbre and others argue, these ideals were "defined in highly gendered terms" among economists who questioned "not only the possibility, but also the desirability of female objectivity."[2]

This chapter examines why and how women economics scholars at Berkeley continued to connect their research to real problems in which they were deeply interested, and to see that research as legitimately possessing ethical dimensions. A central factor in the why aspect of their work rests on their conceptions of the purposes of social science research and how deeply embedded those purposes were in the understanding that social science should improve lives, communities, and the conduct of political, social, and economic institutions. Male scholars also believed in these goals, but women at Berkeley and elsewhere held these commitments well into the 1930s even as it became harder to do so and remain professional scholars in academic economics. Further, the Berkeley women, and some of their male colleagues, did not see their deep interest as an impediment to doing first-rate research. Women scholars at a number of institutions maintained this commitment—among them Susan Kingsbury at Bryn Mawr College, Sophonisba Breckinridge and Edith Abbott at the University of Chicago's School of Social Service Administration, and Amy Hewes at Mount Holyoke College. But the case of women scholars at the University of California at Berkeley illustrates particularly well how this commitment survived in a striving research university in which the criteria for valuing social science research shifted significantly between 1900 and 1940.

As B. Edward McClellan suggests, such shifting criteria contributed to decreasing emphases on moral education in the formal curricula of colleges and universities. But, I argue here, by looking at the research of particular women social scientists, one can find instances of embedded ethical and civic commitments in how research problems were selected and framed, and how research findings were taught and otherwise disseminated. I focus on the Berkeley women for two reasons. First, unlike the others, the University of California at Berkeley was a public institution. But like other progressive universities in the early twentieth century, Berkeley shaped its culture to encourage teaching and research that met state and other public needs, even as the claims of "objectivity" and "science" increasingly attracted researchers' allegiance. Its public character provided openings for justifying research and policy involvement in ways that may have been more difficult in private institutions. Second, where most women academic economists worked at women's colleges or in departments and schools of social work or home economics, the Berkeley case offers the unusual instance of women's participation in an economics department in a rising research university.[3]

Women economists at Berkeley developed a program of research and teaching that sustained policy reform commitments within the economics department. They did this even as the discipline increasingly went the way of academic social science—less reform-oriented over these decades, and more focused on developing theory and quantitatively based methodologies that were divorced from ethical concerns about poverty, industrial capitalism, labor, and employment by the middle 1930s. This phenomenon started having an impact on discussions about the Berkeley economics department's direction by the late 1930s. These latter emphases on the discipline distanced faculty research from both the social context of economic activity and state policymaking that specifically addressed underserved populations, including women. But the process was slowed in Berkeley's unusually liberal economics department by shared concern for the uses of social and economic knowledge among the women and some of their male colleagues, particularly those focused on labor and immigration. They believed that a central duty of social science scholars was to try to understand and address, through their research, social and economic issues that shaped real people's lives. Theirs was a civic concern for laborers, the poor, the unemployed, children, women, and the living conditions of middle-class families and citizens of California and elsewhere, who faced uncertain economic and social change. And they held that the state had an important role in redressing disadvantage created by industrial capitalism, gross inequities in the distribution of wealth, and unfair labor practices. As Dorothy Ross suggests "the new institutionalists [such as the economists in the 1910s and 1920s at Berkeley] were self-consciously left of the neoclassical mainstream."[4]

The women principally responsible for sustaining the policy orientation in the department were Jessica Peixotto, Barbara Nachtrieb Armstrong, and Emily Huntington. Peixotto remained in the department from 1904 until her retirement in 1935. Armstrong worked in the department from 1914 to 1919 as an assistant (during which time she also completed law school and practiced law), and 1919 to 1928 as a doctoral student in economics, and then instructor and assistant professor of law and economics. In 1928, she moved full-time to the law school, but continued work in economics and participated in committee and other projects related to the activities of the economics department. Huntington was an undergraduate at Berkeley who returned in 1928 after completing her doctorate at Harvard/Radcliffe, and remained until her retirement in 1961. They were joined by a number of women doctoral students and by women researchers who contributed to the social work program and to the department's research projects.[5]

These women formed effective strategies to secure space and support for their research commitments in the department and to maintain them despite increasing pressure in the late 1920s to transform the department's composition and research agenda. First, they claimed an area of economic research that was not well developed in the department and then developed it. Moreover, they supported each other within the institution and fully involved themselves in departmental activities. Second, they developed the department's clinical program in social work, which was somewhat related to their work. The program enabled them to offer course work based on their research and to hire other women to work in clinical as well as research, service, and teaching capacities. This increased the presence of colleagues dedicated to work in social economy, established an institutional justification for their own teaching and scholarship, and provided trained social workers for the state. Third, they received and sustained external as well as internal funding for their research. In addition, they disseminated their research to the relevant local, state, and federal government departments and offices. Aside from the clinical program, their strategies did not differ much from their male colleagues' in academia who were expanding on social science knowledge, developing new courses and programs, and using their research to contribute to policy making. But their case is unusual in that they were women doing this work within the male domain of the research university, in a period when most women scholars either were employed by colleges that lacked many of the resources of universities, including funding, graduate students, and ready connections to the state or were located in municipal, state, and federal agencies. And it was unusual in that they focused on what had been considered the private, and therefore less important, domain of economic activity, including the household, and on women in the work force.[6]

Social Economy, Social Research, and Policy Reform

Jessica Peixotto, with her colleague Lucy Stebbins, created the social economy program in economics at Berkeley. She was the second woman to earn a Ph.D., the first in political economy (1900), and the first appointed to a regular faculty position at the University of California. These distinctions were grounded in a strong and determined personality. Raised in San Francisco, Peixotto was the only daughter and oldest among five children in the Raphael and Myrtilla Peixotto family. The Peixottos were Portuguese-American Jews with businesses in the South who lived in New York where Jessica was born, until the end of the Civil War, and then migrated to California seeking a livelier economy to grow the family's wealth. Peixotto's father was actively involved in civic affairs and philanthropy in the city. He was also the family patriarch and held restrictive views of women's roles, so much so that he opposed Peixotto's continuing formal education after her graduation from Girls' High School. He believe that her proper place as the only daughter in this prominent San Francisco merchant family was at home, studying on her own or with tutors, and serving in a voluntary capacity in city clubs and social institutions, focusing on skills appropriate for housewives of the Peixottos's social class. She learned to make her own clothing, studied music and languages, and volunteered in a settlement house, where she interacted with some of San Francisco's most prominent women, including Phoebe Apperson Hearst. But this activity was not enough to feed her intellectual needs and social concerns. She persuaded her father to allow her to enroll at the University of California and finished the Ph.B. in 1894, at the age of 30. She immediately started doctoral work in political economy, working with Bernard Moses, whose training in the German historical school shaped her own research in French socialism. In 1896, she went to France to study. Initially she spent a few weeks taking a rest cure and "daily douches" (showers) to recover from neurasthenia, a common illness among middle-class women who had broader aspirations than housewifery and motherhood and were frustrated at their lack of work opportunities. Observing the French, she noted that young, middle-class French women were "mere puppets being prepared... for the matrimonial market." In the end, though, she thought "the position of women, mental, rather than anything else, makes your heart ache."[7] Such observations are telling in light of her later interest in creating and protecting places for women in the academy.

After research and study at the Sorbonne, she finished her doctorate in 1900. Her dissertation *The French Revolution and Modern Socialism*, was published in 1901. In

1904, Benjamin Ide Wheeler, president of the university, asked her about her postdoctoral plans, and then suggested that she begin lecturing at the university. Perhaps reflecting on her own disinterest in marriage and hoping for a larger, more public opportunity, she accepted.[8]

Her appointment to the faculty was remarkable. Before the turn of the century, the university paid little attention to women students on campus—no dormitories, athletic teams, or facilities for social and cultural activities existed for women, despite the fact that they made up nearly forty percent of the undergraduate student body. But Phoebe Apperson Hearst, the first woman regent of the University of California, insisted on making a place for women at Berkeley. She pressured the administration to hire women faculty and administrators and contributed funds for a women's gymnasium and other facilities and activities.[9]

In 1904 Wheeler appointed Peixotto as lecturer in the economics department and in 1906 he appointed Lucy Sprague, whose brother-in-law Adolph Miller chaired economics, as dean of women. Where Sprague had a powerful influence on the daily lives of students, building on Hearst's efforts to provide spheres of activity for women, Peixotto focused on locating a place for women's intellectual work in the social sciences at Berkeley. Their influence was complementary as well as mutually reinforcing; one major concern Sprague explored was professional roles for women beyond teaching, the occupation most female Berkeley graduates chose.[10]

Given Berkeley's historical resistance to women's institutional access and power, one might ask why Wheeler invited Peixotto to join the faculty, particularly as Adolph Miller thought women's place was in the home. That Hearst knew Peixotto from their civic work San Francisco, and that she had a close friendship and advising relationship with Wheeler, likely contributed to his willingness to consider Peixotto. But Peixotto herself was an appealing candidate. With dark hair and blue eyes, she was an attractive, even elegant, woman of diminutive stature. She also was tenacious and determined. As the eldest of five children and the only female, she was accustomed to proving herself. Her work with Moses demonstrated her intellectual capabilities. Further, Wheeler did not have to contend with conflicting perceptions of married women's domestic roles when he asked Miller to find "a place for her," because, at forty, Peixotto remained unmarried. Her family's prominence in the city vouched for her respectability. Facile with languages and sophisticated in her cultural tastes, she fit well with the close-knit, but cosmopolitan social and intellectual climate of Berkeley in the early years of the century. In the end, she was so valued by the department, and successful with her teaching and research, that the university made a long-term commitment by promoting her to assistant professor of sociology in 1907, associate professor of social economy in 1912, and professor of social economy in 1918, the first woman full professor at the university.[11]

This appointment in social economy carried with it certain nineteenth-century assumptions. The term had been coined by John Stuart Mill to characterize an area of study broader than political economy, according to Nancy Folbre, that would include not only wealth, but also ethical concerns. In the United States, the American Sociological Association's Franklin Sanborn designated it as the feminine branch of political economy concerned with "particulars" rather than generalizations. Berkeley was one of the few universities offering such study after the turn of the century; the program was developed under Peixotto's instigation and guidance.[12]

When Lucy Sprague left the university in 1912, Lucy Stebbins, another San Francisco native was appointed Dean of Women. Stebbins's father was pastor of the First Unitarian Church and had been involved in establishing the university's predecessor, the College of California. Stebbins studied at Berkeley for a time and finished her B.A. at Radcliffe. She had worked in a variety of social service agencies before returning to the university in 1910. She also held a position in the economics department, teaching a course in charities beginning in 1911, and was eventually promoted to a professorship in 1923, a position she held, with the deanship, until her retirement in 1941. Although Stebbins never developed into a scholar like Peixotto, her presence in the department and university suggested possibilities for women and offered Peixotto a female colleague who supported the program in social economy.[13]

The two, together with Sprague in the early years, helped to found the Department of Home Economics in the wake of the establishment of the American Home Economics Association (AHEA, 1908) and in the context of President Wheeler's desire to broaden educational options for women students that would better fit them for their primary role within households and families. Peixotto and Stebbins had a different motivation—to train women in sciences, where they were underrepresented at Berkeley, in accord with the larger goals of the leaders in the AHEA, which focused on domestic science. At Berkeley, this meant that students were expected to study "architecture, chemistry, drawing, economics, engineering, hygiene, physiology, political science, and textiles," based in theory and specific methodologies, and prepare to become reformers and professionals "outside the home." Peixotto, Sprague, and Stebbins also saw home economics as a way, in addition to the social economy program in economics, to introduce students to civic issues, such as public health, nutrition, and adequate housing. They hoped that the university would support a graduate department in the field, one that would not segregate women from men students and that would offer study based on a firm foundation in the liberal arts, sciences, and social sciences. When it opened in 1916, though, it was an undergraduate department that the administration hoped would draw women students away from competition with men students in the other departments in the College of Arts and Letters at Berkeley. Peixotto and Stebbins nevertheless served on the department's curriculum committee and succeeded in attracting chemist-nutritionist Agnes Fay Morgan to head the department in 1914, a move that increased its emphasis on household science as opposed to household arts.[14]

Morgan and Stebbins and eventually Ruth Okey and others shared a number of characteristics: they were all committed to science as the basis of their research and teaching programs; they worked together to improve the climate for women students and faculty on campus; and they used their research for social improvement. The way one colleague characterized Peixotto's work could apply to them all: "science in the service of humanity."[15] In the case of the early women in the program, particularly Peixotto and Stebbins, their views of social science and academic responsibility were shaped as much by their previous work in settlements and other social service agencies and their direct contact with recent immigrants, people in poverty, and struggling working-class families facing constant economic crises and setbacks as by their commitment to a firm grounding in academic social science research. One could argue that the social service aspect of their experience helped them determine the significant problems to pursue in their research.

Peixotto's place and growing prominence in the economics department lent credibility to her various efforts—in home economics, in civic activities, and in economic research. The department she joined exhibited intellectual as well as social compatibilities. She and her colleagues Adolph Miller and Wesley Mitchell moved in the same circle of friends, attending dinner parties and theater, camping in the Sierra, and sharing manuscripts and professional talk. According to Mary Cookingham, Mitchell, Plehn, and Blum were the economics faculty with whom Peixotto was most involved in her early years as a faculty member. Plehn's interest in government programs, Blum's experience with social work, and Mitchell's work on business cycles were relevant to her own research. The department had been fundamentally shaped by Bernard Moses and then Carl Plehn, both of whom had studied in Germany and witnessed debates about and implementation of social welfare and social insurance programs there. Adolph Miller brought the study of business and commerce into the department. Stuart Daggett in railroad economics, Solomon Blum in labor, Carleton Parker in the psychological elements of economic behavior, Ira Cross in labor and socialism, and Paul Taylor in labor economics, with Peixotto in social economy, shaped the department's programs and research emphases through the 1910s and 1920s.[16]

Among these men, she was considered an intellectual equal in her teaching, program development, and scholarship. Peixotto's work was not as much a break with neoclassical economics as it was a claim that social economy research was important in a field in which the emphasis was on public economic activity and productivity. Her work on women and children in the early years and her later shift to consumer economics represented her efforts to contribute to a research agenda that was largely carried out by women researchers within the economics department.[17]

Peixotto's reputation as a researcher grew in 1906, when she examined the adequacy of relief efforts after the San Francisco earthquake and concluded that assistance was often too meager to lead to full economic rehabilitation of those who lost their homes and jobs. She then explored the role of the state in improving conditions of California's children after the turn of the century, through its juvenile court system, its Board of Control to oversee treatment of indigent orphans, and its widows' pension law, all of which required coordination among local agencies and municipal and county governments. In surveying these, Peixotto developed expertise in state and local government, public welfare, and legislation.[18]

Locally, she served on Berkeley's Commission of Public Charities. At the state level she was a member of the State Board of Charities and Corrections, chairing the committees on children and on research, and wedding her academic and public policy interests by requiring research into children's lives prior to making policies. During World War I, she extended her service to the nation, as a member of the Council of Defense subcommittee on women and children, executive chair of the committee's child welfare section, and chief of the child conservation section of the council. She worked with others to enforce the Federal Child Labor Law by focusing on keeping children in school. Peixotto also organized California's first program of social work training, for Red Cross Home Service workers in 1917. The course eventually moved into the university as part of the graduate training offered in the economics department. These activities and her own research led her to believe that state intervention in the economy to insure public welfare was essential to protect the less fortunate in the United States.

As men and women joined the economics department over the next three decades, they contended as much with Peixotto's interests as with any other faculty member's. Ira Cross, labor economist who joined the department in 1914, remembered Peixotto as "a wonderful, charming, intelligent person," whose shared interests in socialism and social activism placed her on the liberal end of the department, along with Cross himself, Blum, and Carleton Parker. By 1911 when Stebbins joined the department, Peixotto had begun to develop a series of courses, including Contemporary Socialism, History of Socialism, The Control of Poverty, The Child and the State, Household as an Economic Agent, Crime as a Social Problem, and History of Economic Thought, which shaped the program in social economy. Wheeler described this work as "the field of constructive and preventive philanthropy," when he hailed it as one of the two recent major developments in the department by 1912 (the other was railway economics).[19]

The growth of the social economy program opened the doors to women faculty as well as students. Lucy Stebbins's appointment is one such instance. In the 1910s Wheeler allowed Peixotto to seek out and appoint qualified women as assistants and lecturers. These recruits taught courses, graded papers, and, in some cases, finished master's degrees and doctorates. This was an unusual opportunity because the male faculty in the department rarely worked with female assistants. A few women came with a Ph.D. and stayed for a year or more; others came with bachelor's or master's degrees and stayed for a few years, teaching and doing research. Beyond these short-term academic appointments, the next real sign of commitment from the university to women in the program came in 1919, when Barbara Nachtrieb Grimes (later Armstrong) was appointed lecturer in law and economics.[20]

Armstrong was born in 1890 and spent her childhood in San Francisco. An alumna of the university (A.B., 1913; J.D., 1915) she taught for a brief period in a one-room school and then practiced law for a few years. She served as executive secretary of the California Social Insurance Commission from 1915 to 1919. By the time she began lecturing in economics and jurisprudence, she was working on her Ph.D. in economics. From a younger generation than Peixotto's, she was an outspoken feminist, and committed to research into government policies and programs for workers and their families. She finished her Ph.D. in 1921, was promoted to instructor in law and economics, assistant professor, and then associate professor in law in 1928. This was a major milestone for women—Armstrong was the first woman appointed to the faculty of a law school in the United States.[21]

When Armstrong joined the economics faculty in 1919, it had grown considerably and offered "an invigorating intellectual climate" to both faculty and graduate students. As fellow graduate student and faculty colleague Paul S. Taylor noted, Berkeley, though often ignored by economists whose gaze was trained toward the East, was "no educational eddy or backwater." Taylor, like Armstrong, found an "element of tradition" there that confirmed his commitment to situate the study of economics within the real conditions of human activity; he focused on labor economics. In Armstrong's case, her study with Peixotto, Felix Flugel, and Cross helped develop her interest in social economy and labor and social legislation. She taught courses in the history of economics, social insurance, and crime as a social problem, and worked on a massive study that was published after she moved full time to the law school at Boalt Hall. She was succeeded in the economics department by Emily Huntington, but continued her involvement in social economy by serving on committees and teaching graduate courses exploring the relationship between economics and family law, child labor law, and labor relations. Her book *Insuring the Essentials* (1932) was probably as important to the field of economics as Mitchell's *Business Cycles*, because it was a timely and major contribution to the debates over both minimum wage and social insurance legislation in the United States.[22]

Armstrong's study compared United States minimum wage and social insurance policies with those in countries in Asia, Africa, the South Pacific, South America, North America, and Europe. She concluded that "except in the field of industrial accident provision, the United States is in the position of being the most backward of all the nations of commercial importance in insuring the essentials to its workers." In this plea to see all economic activity as part of a global economy, and to deal with the "urgent social problems" generated by "our economic system," she defined the essentials as those programs that provided economic security to workers in the wage system of modern industry. Minimum wage, offering subsistence earnings, and social insurance, compensating for those periods when workers could not perform or find work, were the linchpins of an adequate government social economic program. Economists who made such claims perceived these kinds of programs as both antidotes to unrestrained capitalism and necessary to maintaining a healthy capitalist economy. She found that Germany and Great Britain provided the most comprehensive programs to date, but they, too, had problems. Britain's, for example, offered too little, and were geared only to meet the bare needs of workers, not the needs of their families. Germany's addressed family needs, but were initiated by Bismarck in the 1880s to respond early to Germany's industrialization in an authoritarian, rather than a democratic, political system. Consequently, the twentieth-century programs that evolved out of those offered little choice to workers in such areas as selecting medical providers.[23]

In the United States, minimum wage protection and workmen's compensation legislation had been enacted on a state-by-state basis, leaving many individuals and families dependent on a private charity system woefully inadequate to meet their needs, particularly during an economic depression. Armstrong suggested that one approach in the United States might be to begin by providing constitutional protection of minimum wage legislation for women workers, because they were "underpaid in greater numbers than men" and "even further removed from organized labor help." That effort could "pave the way for the acceptance of the principle of minimum wage for men." This work in social insurance earned Armstrong a national reputation. In 1934 she was appointed to the federal committee on economic security, directing the old-age security study, and working with others to design the collection of laws that became the Social Security Act of 1935.[24]

It is important to note that even as they grew professionally, the women faculty had significant family commitments in addition to their public service. Jessica Peixotto and Lucy Stebbins, for example, lived in Berkeley with their widowed mothers. Armstrong balanced a demanding career as teacher and scholar with the responsibilities of wife and mother in the 1920s and 1930s. Their mutual friendships extended to other women in the university: Agnes Fay Morgan in home economics, Olga Bridgman in psychology, Katherine Felton of San Francisco's Associated Charities and a frequent lecturer in social economy. On campus, the Women's Faculty Club became the hub of their social life. This network not only provided contacts from the university to the city and region, but also yielded research sites for students, a critical mass of men and women interested in social and economic reform, and the kinds of professional support necessary to maintain some power and voice in social and economic research and policy.

The Berkeley women manifested their civic commitments on the campus as well as in the state and nation. When Peixotto and Sprague first joined the faculty, they did not attend faculty meetings, not because they were barred from them, but because they feared they would alienate their male colleagues with their "conspicuous" presence. Sprague remembered that "most of the faculty thought of women frankly as inferior beings," and were "solidly opposed" to women's presence on the faculty. This feeling of separateness or difference based on gender was further evident in the relegation of women to a corner of one room at the university's faculty club, restriction to visits only on special occasions, and admission only if they were accompanied by a male member of the club. Stebbins and Peixotto decided in 1919 that treatment of women at the Faculty Club was intolerable, and collected funds from family and friends to build a club for women faculty and administrators. Barbara Armstrong's sister Florence Nachtrieb Mel left a bequest to the club to help secure a place for professional women on campus. When the Women's Faculty Club was completed in 1923, women faculty and administrators, local professional women, and alumnae joined, and brought their families and friends to parties and other gatherings at the club.[25]

Meanwhile, Peixotto continued working to enlarge the presence of women on the faculty. In addition to Stebbins, Armstrong, and the short-term appointments of research assistants and lecturers, Peixotto was responsible for bringing Emily Noble, Martha Chickering, and Emily Huntington into the department and the university. She did this in two ways, by developing a social work program in the department and by promoting research in social economy. Noble ran the social work program and was succeeded by Chickering. Huntington was appointed as a full-time faculty member and researcher in social economy.[26]

Huntington, the third woman scholar to be appointed to economics by the university, was another Californian. Her father had been a physician on the faculty of the University of California. Against the wishes of her mother, but with the support of her father, she received her A.B. at Berkeley (1917). Two years at the U.S. Bureau of Labor Statistics conducting a cost of living study, and, during World War I, assisting Peixotto when she was the executive secretary of the Women's Committee of the Council of National Defense in Washington, constituted her early experience with government agencies. After study for a year in the graduate department of social economy and social research at Bryn Mawr College and another year at the London School of Economics, she finished her graduate work through Radcliffe at Harvard.[27]

Huntington's research included economics and policy, social insurance, consumer economics, and labor market and employment problems. She recalled that Peixotto, with whom she had studied at Berkeley, was probably the most continuous influence on her professional development—stimulating her interest in economics, particularly in her courses in poverty and household budgets, advising her to pursue graduate study, and helping her to find a position after finishing her Ph.D. in 1928. She worked with Susan Kingsbury and Anne Bezanson at Bryn Mawr, in social economy and industrial relations. Searching for better grounding in economic theory, she chose the London School of Economics, where she found the classroom climate less competitive than in American institutions and was exposed to the current thinking of reformers and social scientists including Beatrice and Sidney Webb and Harold Laski. She earned her doctorate at Radcliffe at a time when women experienced significant hurdles to doctoral study there. She took classes with Frank W. Taussig, who made all the women sit on one side of the room; Charles J. Bullock, who criticized women for being "illogical"; and Allyn Young, who advised women students and maintained a vocal concern for the social and economic complexities of modern industrial society, urging his students to apply economic analysis to real problems, even in statistics courses.[28]

Huntington's dissertation, "Cyclical Fluctuation in the Cotton Manufacturing Industry," only narrowly presaged her various research and policy interests. At Berkeley, she was appointed instructor of economics in 1928, assistant professor in 1930, associate professor in 1937, and professor in 1944. Never married, Huntington had a wide circle of friends in Berkeley. She responded to numerous calls to public service in her professional capacity, as advisor to the California State Relief Administration in the 1930s, senior economist with the Department of Labor early in World War II, and director of Wage Stabilization at the National War Labor Board in San Francisco for the duration of the war. She was advisor to the California department of welfare and member of the California Industrial Welfare Commission, also in the 1940s. After her retirement from the university in 1961, she worked with Barbara Armstrong to establish California's comprehensive health care law and was a member of the governor's Conference on the Aged. At the university, she served on numerous committees and, as a testament to her feminist leanings, was instrumental in gaining the admission of women to the university's Faculty Club.[29]

Her work was, in part, shaped by her commitment to "the problems and deprivations of the low income population," an area of study that held "little interest" for economic analysts "until well into the 1930's." Her research in unemployment and cost of living was well received. *Doors to Jobs*, one of Huntington's most comprehensive studies, examined the organization of the labor market in California, with a focus on how workers found jobs from entry, or in the transition from school to work, to reentry, in the search for jobs after they were laid off. She noted a profound, but largely ignored problem that the depression economy exposed: "one of the most important and difficult problems—that of bringing together jobs and workers, which had "not been attacked with the same vigor and determination" applied to other problems in economics. Upon examining the records of agencies that existed to place workers in the state, trade unions, and schools, she concluded that, aside from centralization of information for some occupational groups, little coordination among them was apparent. In short, after years of attempting to deal with crisis of the Depression, California still did not have state wide mechanisms to assist in placing workers in the state's labor market.[30]

The Heller Committee and Social Economic Research

Where the social economy and social work program created for women students and faculty a place in the economics department's curriculum until the late 1930s, a committee Peixotto formed assured that women doing research in economics were recognized in the department and the university and, as important, could extend their research expertise beyond the campus boundaries. The Heller Committee on Research in Social Economy was a crucial source of support for both Peixotto's and Huntington's work. It provided the funds and internal legitimacy that enabled Peixotto to expand studies in social economics, to contribute to the graduate curricular program in social service, and to employ research and teaching assistants for both programs. The committee allowed them to define projects and carry them forward through the worst years of the Depression. It also helped them acquire an external reputation. As a result of the research she conducted under the committee's auspices, Peixotto was known as one of the pioneers of consumer economics and was elected vice-president of the American Economics Association (in 1928).[31]

The Heller Committee began with a study by Peixotto to determine the adequacy of salaries paid to clerical, wage earning, and executive California state employees. Her close friend Clara Hellman Heller was so impressed with this work that in 1923 she initiated donations to the university for cost of living research. The committee's projects fit into three areas: quantity and cost budgets, published annually; income and expenditure studies; and special studies. The first two comprised cost of living investigations and bore some relationship to the third, research into such areas as care for the dependent, aged, and children, unemployment relief and the unemployed, California's labor market and problems of reemployment, the nutritive value of diets among particular population groups, and standards and methods of relief.[32]

Peixotto's contribution to the studies began with an examination of professional families, challenging the taboo of that "romantic and shadowy domain of home life, 'hopelessly private,' 'sacred'," in which middle-class professional families had been "shut away" making their budgetary decisions. Introducing psychologically and sociologically informed explanations of consumer choice, she presented a case for "the American standard of living." Through this and other studies—of families ranging from lower middle class to those dependent on public assistance—she succeeded in placing economic decisions at the household level squarely within a widely shared social vision of American middle-class life. She used a novel methodological approach, interviewing and distributing questionnaires to housewives, an acknowledgement of their expertise and authority in household consumption. Her research took questions of the social value of "things" out of the realm of theory and into the arena of empirical research. In addition to Peixotto's research, the committee also supported Emily Huntington's in unemployment and unemployment relief and reemployment patterns in the state of California—all in the midst of the depression. As much as the course work in social economy, the Heller Committee research ensured that the economics department continued to foster scholarship in what was considered in mainstream economics less significant (and less masculine) areas of economic study: household income and economic decision making and women's employment and unemployment.[33]

Conclusion

Berkeley afforded Peixotto and her colleagues a unique opportunity to help shape the institution and its programs and to inject their ethical and civic concerns and their scholarship into that process. Between 1900 and 1930, the university made a definite transition in its commitments and its programs—from a largely teaching college of arts and sciences with some agricultural programs under its land grant mandate, to a research university with both state and private funding for faculty inquiry and a diverse range of programs for professional preparation and economic development in the state. The women faculty both rode this wave of change and helped foster it.[34]

It is their contributions to shaping the study of economics as an ethical enterprise concerned with civic improvement that is of interest here. Crucial to this process was creating places for women in the teaching, research, and service programs of the department. Peixotto, Stebbins, Armstrong, and Huntington played key roles as institution and program builders, role models, and scholars. More than their mere presence in the department, their acts and the support they generated among male colleagues defined their impact on the civic sensibilities of the department's work. Those civic sensibilities in turn influenced learning at the state's flagship university for the first half of the twentieth century.

Peixotto created a significant place for women economists at the University of California during the four decades before her death in 1942, a place that expanded women social scientists' capacity to pursue research that influenced public policy debate and reform into the 1960s, when Huntington retired. One might ask: Why was it significant, particularly considering the fact that the University appointed no women to economics between the 1930s and the 1980s? To answer that question, we need to address what these women accomplished at Berkeley, in the field of economics, and in the public policy and reform arenas. Geraldine Clifford has suggested that one important reason for examining the history of women in higher education institutions is to analyze how they changed those institutions. Peixotto and her female colleagues at Berkeley transformed the economics department and the university in a number of ways that not only influenced how they could act on their civic obligations, but also increased the contributions of the university to social and economic research and policy in both prosperous and troubled times. Their presence in economics meant that male and female students had female academic professional role models. This proved to be a decisive influence on men students, like Paul Taylor, Charles Gulick, and others who worked closely with them. Clark Kerr, who took four seminars with Peixotto, recalled that her subject matter was not in the mainstream of classical economics, and that she spent a great deal of time with her students. In the bullpen of faculty desks in economics—open to students and faculty—she was "respected and accepted." Moreover, the economics department was more diverse than most in the 1930s, he noted, in viewpoints and in gender. Their female mentors profoundly affected women who studied at Berkeley, many of whom went on to graduate degrees or social service work.[35]

Emily Huntington remembered that by the late 1920s the department was composed of theorists, applied economists (in banking and finance), and social economists. In the 1930s, the theorists began to assert dominance, denying tenure to at least one social economist, and stressing methodology, particularly mathematically based analysis. Huntington herself carried forward Peixotto's commitment to social problems in economics, problems she had first encountered under the tutelage of Plehn and Peixotto. The women economists at Berkeley, with their male colleagues, balanced the traditional areas, or the canons of economic study—the focus on finance, monetary theory, and processes of production in mainstream economics—with research and teaching in labor, consumption, and poverty, as well as social welfare. This programmatic commitment was shaped by their intellectual interests, but also by their ethical concerns about how economic processes, systems, and effects should be understood. Alice O'Connor suggests that such efforts to develop "poverty knowledge" challenged a fundamental assumption of classical economics: that poverty was a natural outcome of economic processes. The researchers at Berkeley also refused to succumb to the theories developing in the 1920s that offered cultural rationales for group and individual poverty. Instead, they continued to see poverty and unemployment as systemic phenomena that occurred as a result of larger economic and labor market forces, as well as the distribution of wealth—a "problem of political and social economy."[36]

The social welfare program brought more women graduate students and faculty into the department at the same time that it allowed the university to claim that it was responding to local and state demands as a result of the depression. The research in social economics performed a similar function. Both programs, with the Heller Committee support, created a network of women students and researchers devoted to examining how economic and social forces operated together to limit opportunities for single women, working families, the unemployed, and the struggling middle class. President Sproul routinely routed requests for assistance in the domain of social welfare or economic legislation to the women in social economics and to Armstrong.

The social economy program provided an intellectual basis for social work training in the department. When other schools were relying increasingly on psychiatric social work to supply the models of relief and counseling for the dependent, the social workers trained at Berkeley perceived their clients' problems as primarily rooted in larger social and economic contexts, often requiring government intervention and regulation. They derived this understanding of their work from the teaching and research of the social economists. This orientation toward research into and treatment of poverty persisted in the program despite the rise of psychiatric social work in many institutions, which took root in the 1920s and 1930s and gained ground increasingly after World War II, pushing the professional training of social workers toward adjusting clients to their circumstances, rather than examining and attempting to reform the problems inherent in their circumstances. But research and teaching at Berkeley, Chicago, Bryn Mawr College, and a few other programs maintained a commitment to improving clients' circumstances even as they prepared students for individual case work and research in municipal and state agencies.[37]

The women Peixotto brought into economics also influenced their male colleagues. Social economy constituted one of four areas of study in the department, including labor economics, economic theory, and economic history. Those in labor economics found among their female colleagues intellectual support and stimulation in course work and research that was complementary to their own. Added to the curriculum and research program in the department, social economy both broadened and grounded the department's treatment of economics. And it enabled a concern for ethics and civic commitments to balance the growing concern with theory and mathematics in the department's research and teaching, while maintaining the norms of science. Clark Kerr remembered that when most departments were dominated by neoclassical economists, Berkeley's had liberals and radicals, as well as conservatives, more women, and much collegiality.[38]

Finally, Peixotto and her network of female and like-minded male colleagues created spaces in the university in which women faculty and students were welcomed and, in varying degrees, influential. With respect to civic learning, this in itself was a signal contribution. Until the turn of the century, women students had been marginalized and largely ignored (aside from Hearst's philanthropic efforts to create dormitories and a gymnasium) despite making up nearly half the student body at Berkeley. By the 1930s, the university offered women faculty and students opportunities in the regular curriculum and in areas of professional development and civic contributions to the state: home economics, law, social work, and social service, as well as the more traditional, but no less important, field of teaching. Although the university continued to marginalize women in many ways, these programmatic spaces ensured women continuing bases from which to contribute to social and economic reform.[39]

By locating a social economy program within an economics department Peixotto and her colleagues ensured that economics research at Berkeley connected to real problems and issues that affected Californians on a daily basis—how to live on limited income, how to gauge reasonable wages, how to address unemployment and reemployment, how to help the poor become more integrated into local economies, how to develop social legislation not based in prejudice, but in rigorous research, how to understand the struggles of immigrants and other minority groups dealing with an economy that seemed to exclude them. All of these questions are critical to address in a democratic society where political citizenship cannot flower when economic citizenship is denied. The civic and moral implications of these scholars' work were carefully framed and guided by acceptable modes of social science research methods and analysis. But they were also informed by a strong sense of justice and fairness. Those excluded from the economy could not function fully in the political and social sphere. That in itself gave them considerable weight in policy discussions in the state of California and the nation.[40]

Notes

1. Wesley Claire Mitchell, "Foreword," in Ewald T. Grether, et al., eds., *Essays in Social Economics in Honor of Jessica Blanche Peixotto* (Berkeley: University of California Press, 1935), 1.
2. Nancy Folbre, "The 'Sphere of Women' in Early-Twentieth-Century Economics," in Helene Silverberg, ed., *Gender and American Social Science: The Formative Years* (Princeton, NJ: Princeton University Press, 1998), 37. Alice O'Connor, *Poverty Knowledge: Social Science, Social Policy, and the Poor in Twentieth-Century U.S. History* (Princeton, NJ: Princeton University Press, 2001), chapter 1. Mary O. Furner, *Advocacy and Objectivity: A Crisis in the Professionalization of American Social Science, 1865–1905* (Lexington, KY: University Press of Kentucky, 1975). Marianne A. Ferber and Julie A. Nelson, "Introduction," in Ferber and Nelson, eds., *Beyond Economic Man: Feminist Theory and Economics* (Chicago: University of Chicago Press, 1993), 11, on the objectivity question and how it was defined. An early version of this chapter was presented at the History of Education Society meeting in 1994 as "Berkeley Women's Economic Research." The author thanks Anil Belvadi, William F. Tate, and Donald Warren for their insightful comments on an earlier draft.
3. B. Edward McClellan, *Schools and the Shaping of Character: Moral Education in America, 1607–Present* (Bloomington, IN: ERIC Clearinghouse, 1992), 68–72. On women social scientists in a variety of venues, see Robin Muncy, *Creating a Female Dominion of Reform, 1890–1935* (New York: Oxford University Press, 1991); Mary Jo Deegan, ed., *Women in Sociology: A Bio-Bibliographical Sourcebook* (New York: Greenwood Press, 1991); Ellen Fitzpatrick, *Endless Crusade: Women Social Scientists and Progressive Social Reform* (New York: Oxford University Press, 1990); Rosalind Rosenberg, *Beyond Separate Spheres: Intellectual Roots of Modern Feminism* (New Haven, CT: Yale University Press, 1982); Mary Ann Dzuback, "Social Research at Bryn Mawr College, 1915–1940," *History of Education Quarterly* 33 (winter 1993): 579–608.
4. Dorothy Ross, *The Origins of American Social Science* (Cambridge: Cambridge University Press, 1991), 326. The masters and doctoral level dissertations completed at Berkeley in these years explored a range of topics, including labor movements and organization, immigration, history of California industries, agricultural economics, monetary issues, and other areas, but many focused on labor, often from a historical perspective, in line with institutionalist economic research. Of 51 Masters theses finished between 1908 and 1940, 15 were by women; of 28 doctoral theses in the same period at least 3 were by women. In contrast, between 1940 and 1950, only 5 of 33 Masters theses were by women, 3 in Home Economics, and 1 of 22 doctoral theses was by a woman. Thanks to Anil Belvadi for compiling this information for me.
5. See, e.g., Mary Cookingham, "Social Economists and Reform: Berkeley, 1906–1961," *History of Political Economy* 19 (1987): 47–65; Maresi Nerad, *The Academic Kitchen: Gender Stratification at the University of California, Berkeley* (Albany: State University of New York Press, 1999).
6. One exception included women in the School of Social Service Administration at the University of Chicago, but in that case, women faculty economists were in a separate school

rather than integrated into a social science department proper; see Muncy, *Creating a Female Dominion*; Fitzpatrick, *Endless Crusade*; and Folbre, "The 'Sphere of Women,' " on the Chicago social scientists.

7. Jessica Peixotto to Millicent Shinn, July 12, 1896, Millicent Washburn Shinn Correspondence and Papers, Bancroft Library, University of California, Berkeley (BL, UCB).
8. Henry Rand Hatfield, "Jessica Blanche Peixotto," in Grether, et al., eds., *Essays in Social Economics*, 5–14; Mary Ann Dzuback, "Jessica Blanch Peixotto," in John Garraty, ed., *American National Biography* (New York: Oxford University Press, 1999).
9. Lynn D. Gordon, *Gender and Higher Education in the Progressive Era* (New Haven, CT: Yale University Press, 1990), chapter 2; Peixotto, "Phoebe Apperson Hearst," *University of California* Chronicle 21 (1919): 244–247.
10. Jessica Blanche Peixotto, Collected Works, University Archives (UA), BL, UCB; Joyce Antler, *Lucy Sprague Mitchell: The Making of a Modern Woman* (New Haven, CT: Yale University Press, 1987).
11. Wheeler to Miller, May 5, 1903, Box 15, File 103, Presidents' Papers (Wheeler), UA, BL, UCB [hereinafter PP (Wheeler), 15:103]; "Biography," Personnel Files (PF) (Peixotto), UA, BL, UCB. Under "Data concerning marriage. (When, where, wife's name, children, etc)," she noted "Opportunities missed."
12. Folbre, "The 'Sphere of Women,' " 43.
13. "Lucy Ward Stebbins," *University of California In Memoriam, 1951–59*, 110–113, UA, BL, UCB.
14. Nerad, *The Academic Kitchen*, 35; chapter 1 on the creation of the department. See also Sarah Stage and Virginia B. Vicente, eds., *Rethinking Home Economics: Women and the History* of a Profession (Ithaca, NY: Cornell University Press, 1997).
15. Mitchell, "Foreword," 1.
16. Cookingham, "Social Economists and Reform"; Ira Brown Cross, "Portrait of an Economics Professor," University of California Regional Oral History Office (UCROH), BL, UCB.
17. Cookingham, "Social Economists and Reform"; Lucy Sprague Mitchell, *Our Two Lives: The Story of Wesley Clair Mitchell and Myself* (New York: Simon & Schuster, 1953), chapter 9; Folbre, "The 'Sphere of Women.' "
18. Jessica B. Peixotto, et al., *San Francisco Relief Survey: The Organization and Methods Used after the Earthquake and Fire of April 18, 1906* (New York: Survey Associates, 1913); Peixotto wrote Part 5, "Relief Work of the Associated Charities from June, 1907, to June, 1909," pp. 279–318; see also Jessica B. Peixotto, "California's Children: Some Recent Steps in State Child-Welfare Work," *Survey* 36 (1916): 537–540; "The Children's Year and the Woman's Committee," *Annals of the American Academy of Political and Social Sciences* 79 (1918): 257–262; "Minimum Wage for Minors," in *Standards of Child Welfare* (Washington, DC: U.S. Children's Bureau, Bulletin, No. 60, 1919), 118–124.
19. Ira Brown Cross, "Portrait of an Economics Professor," 59, UCROH, BL, UCB; Benjamin Ide Wheeler, *University of California Presidents' Report, 1910–1912* (Berkeley: University of California, 1912), 35.
20. "Lucy Ward Stebbins," PF, UA, BL, UCB; and *In Memoriam, 1951–59*.
21. "Biography," PF, UA, UCB; "Barbara Nachtrieb Armstrong," *In Memoriam, 1977–79*, 11, 13; Roger J. Traynor, et al., "Barbara Nachtrieb Armstrong," *California Law Review* 65 (1977): 920–936. Armstrong was an equality feminist; she believed strongly that women were as capable as men of participation in academic and other professional work and ought to be compensated on an equal basis. She consciously made herself an example and mentor to other women in law.

22. Paul Shuster Taylor, in Irving Stone, ed., *Let There Be Light: Autobiography of a University, Berkeley: 1868–1968* (Garden City, NY: Doubleday & Company, 1970), 34, 35.
23. Barbara Nachtrieb Armstrong, *Insuring the Essentials: Minimum Wage Plus Social Insurance—A Living Wage Program* (New York: Macmillan Company, 1932), 13, 554.
24. Armstrong, *Insuring the Essentials*, 157. Edwin E. Witte, *The Development of the Social Security Act* (Madison: University of Wisconsin Press, 1962), on Armstrong's involvement.
25. Lucy Sprague Mitchell, "Pioneering in Education," 42, UCROH, 1962, BL, UCB, and *Our Two Lives*, 193; Josephine Smith, in Suzanne B. Riess, ed., *The Women's Faculty Club of the University of California, Berkeley, 1979–1982* (UCROH, BL, UCB, 1983).
26. Emily H. Huntington, "A Career in Economics and Social Insurance," 34, UCROH, BL, UCB; Emily H. Huntington, *In Memoriam*, 1989, 61–64; and Emily H. Huntington, PF, UA, BL, UCB.
27. Emily H. Huntington, "A Career in Economics and Social Insurance," UCROH, BL, UCB; Emily H. Huntington, *In Memoriam*, 1989, 61–64.
28. Huntington, "A Career in Economics and Social Insurance," 34. See also Dulles, *Chances of a Lifetime: A Memoir* (Englewood Cliffs, NJ: Prentice-Hall, 1980), 87–103, on their experiences in London and at Radcliffe.
29. Emily Harriet Huntington, "Cyclical Fluctuations in the Cotton Manufacturing Industry" (Ph.D. thesis, Radcliffe College, 1928); PF (Huntington), UA, BL, UCB, on her activities.
30. Emily H. Huntington, "A Career in Economics," 40; *Doors to Jobs: A Study of the Organization of the Labor Market in California* (Berkeley: University of California Press, 1942), v. Huntington, too, was an equality feminist, believing that women should have opportunities equal to men's and be judged equally based on the merits of their performance.
31. Joseph Dorfman, *The Economic Mind in American Civilization*, vol. 5 (5 vols.; New York: Viking Press, 1959), 570–578; Cookingham, "Social Economists at Berkeley."
32. Jessica Blanche Peixotto, et al., *Cost of Living Survey: Report to the California Civil Service Commission Relative to Cost of Living in California for Selected Family Groups* (Sacramento: California State Printing Office, 1923). Peixotto, Annual Report of the Heller Committee for Research in Social Economics, 1929–30, p. 4 (hereinafter HC Annual Report), PP (Sproul), 1930: 248, UA, BL, UCB. See also Huntington, "The Heller Committee for Research in Social Economics," January 20, 1943, PP (Sproul), 1943: 471, UA, BL, UCB. On the committee's work see annual reports of the Heller Committee for Research in Social Economics, PP(Campbell and Sproul), UA, BL, UCB. Other sources are so noted.
33. Jessica B. Peixotto, *Getting and Spending at the Professional Standard of Living: A Study of the Costs of Living an Academic Life* (New York: Macmillan Company, 1927), vii, viii. Emily H. Huntington, *Unemployment Relief and the Unemployed, 1929–1934* (Berkeley: University of California Press, 1939); Huntington, "The California Unemployment Insurance Law," *California Law Review* 24 (1935–36): 288–301, and "The Benefit Provisions of State Unemployment Insurance Laws," *Law and Contemporary Problems* 3 (1936): 20–35; and Huntington, *Doors to Jobs*. See also Morton Keller, *Regulating a New Economy: Public Policy and Economic Change in America, 1900–1933* (Cambridge, MA: Harvard University Press, 1990), 10–11, on the new consumption economics in relation to institutionalist economic theory.
34. On the University of California's history, see John Aubrey Douglass, *The California Idea and American Higher Education, 1850 to the 1960 Master Plan* (Stanford, CA: Stanford University Press, 2000); Henry F. May, *The Three Faces of Berkeley: Competing Ideologies in the Wheeler Era, 1899–1919* (Berkeley: University of California, 1993).

35. Author interview with Clark Kerr, May 14, 1996. Geraldine Jonçich Clifford, "Shaking Dangerous Questions from the Crease: Gender and American Higher Education," *Feminist Issues* 3 (Fall 1983): 3–62; 15.
36. Emily H. Huntington, "A Career in Economics and Social Insurance," v. See essays in *Essays in Honor of Jessica Blanche Peixotto* by former students on topics such as the American Federation of Labor, care of the indigent ill, British health and unemployment insurance, self-help cooperatives, unemployment relief, changing functions of the American family, infant mortality, and historical analyses of various economic reformers. O'Connor, *Poverty Knowledge*, 25, 27.
37. Muncy, *Creating a Female Dominion*; Fitzpatrick, *Endless Crusade*; and Dzuback, "Women and Social Research at Bryn Mawr College" on Chicago and Bryn Mawr's stance on social work professional development. See James Leiby, *A History of Social Welfare and Social Work* (New York: Columbia University Press, 1978); John H. Ehrenreich, *The Altruistic Imagination: A History of Social Work and Social Policy in the United States* (Ithaca, NY: Cornell university Press, 1985); Daniel J. Walkowitz, *Working with Class: Social Workers and the Politics of Middle-Class Identity* (Chapel Hill: University of North Carolina Press, 1999).
38. Author interview with Clark Kerr. See also *Essays in Honor of Jessica Blanche Peixotto* and Cookingham, "Social Economists and Reform."
39. Huntington's work on unemployment and Armstrong's on the Social Security Act are cases in point. Peixotto's commendation on the honorary Ll.D. she received from the university read: "Chosen counselor of the State in matters concerning the protection of children and the care of the unfortunate; social economist marshaling stubborn facts in the service of mankind; comrade among students, inspiring teacher, true lover of humanity" (*In Memoriam, 1941,* 25).
40. Alice Kessler-Harris, *In Pursuit of Equity: Women, Men, and the Quest for Economic Citizenship in 20th-Century America* (New York: Oxford University Press, 2001), 1–18, for the argument about economic, social, and political citizenship.

This page intentionally left blank

Chapter 11

Character and the Clinic: The Shift from Character to Personality in American Character Education, 1930–1940

David P. Setran

Educational historian Sol Cohen has contended that American schools by the 1930s had been captivated by what he termed the "mental hygiene point of view," a confluence of forces that transformed a largely intellectual/moral framework into a framework dominated by therapeutic and psychiatric themes.[1] Bathed in the theories of Freud, Jung, and Adler, this perspective, he noted, shifted the focus of education from the development of character and individual responsibility to the development of mental health: a sense of security, mild extroversion, proper adjustment to others, and overall happiness. In Cohen's estimation, in fact, mental hygiene in this era generated a new "medical" model of education in which the school was portrayed as a child psychiatry clinic, every child was presumed to require treatment, the teacher was billed as a clinician-therapist, and the goal was the adjustment of the child's personality.[2] By altering the very language of educational discourse, this reconstruction, Cohen suggests, resulted in a significant transformation of the school.

Cohen's hypothesis, of course, is intricately related to a broader cultural historiography that has attempted to demonstrate the rise of a therapeutic ethos, often expressed as a shift from concern for character to an obsession with mental health and personality. Twenty years ago, Warren Susman pointed to this reality within American culture at large, focusing particularly on literary sources.[3] Historians E. Brooks Holifield and Heather Warren have described this trajectory in American religious history, both noting the formative nature of the 1930s.[4] More recently, sociologist James Davison Hunter suggested that by this time in the United States, "the classic and religious virtues associated with strong moral character (such as courage, loyalty, truthfulness, and integrity) had ... given way to the grammar of psychological well-being (self-confidence, integration, and social adjustment).[5] Along with a number of others, these scholars have posited a definitive rise in the importance of personality adjustment as a broad educational aim at this time.[6]

Yet, while such trends have been noted in the culture as a whole, few have followed Cohen's call to examine the ways in which this rhetoric became normalized and institutionalized in American educational theory and practice. One interesting means of analyzing the penetration of this perspective in school practice is by surveying the trajectory of American character education in this era. The field of character education, at least through the early 1930s, was the domain that in many ways best exemplified the intellectual/moral paradigm that mental hygienists sought to depose.[7] If indeed there was a broad adoption of the mental hygiene point of view and its attending emphases, one would expect, if not an abandonment of traditional character education, at least a significant syncretism of its principles and practices with these newer ideals. A close analysis of American character education in the mid- to late 1930s reveals that such was indeed the case and that those espousing mental hygiene ideals actually saw this domain as a critical entry point for their perspectives. Exploring the ways in which these themes influenced visions of character training provides a helpful perspective on the tensions between the moral and therapeutic visions of schooling in this era. It also provides a fascinating window into the broader cultural struggle at this time between ideals of citizenship and notions of personal success. In the end, this conflict set the stage for conflicting visions of American "goodness" that remain with us to this day.

Mental Hygiene and the Battle Between Personality and Character

The mental hygiene movement itself actually had its origins early in the twentieth century. Officially inaugurated in 1908 with the formation of the National Commission for Mental Hygiene, this movement was, until the late 1920s, largely devoted to the treatment of mental and emotional disorders and various forms of serious delinquency. By the 1930s, however, the focus upon rehabilitative life adjustment was expanded both in scope and in potential cultural influence. Within the field as a whole, the exclusive concern for individuals with mental and emotional disorders gave way to a concern for the mental health and adjustment needs of the broader population. Leaders of the movement began to speak of mental hygiene as preventative rather than simply curative, a form of inoculation against mental infirmities and personality disorders that might arise if even minor socio-emotional problems were left untreated over time. Recruiting social workers, pastors, and teachers to join them in a crusade for positive mental health at the national level, preventative treatment for normal persons, what one hygienist called the "science of practical living," became the hallmark of the broadened movement.[8] With a comprehensive ideal of capturing all educational institutions with its clinical principles, psychologist and educator Hedley Dimock quipped that the movement aspired for nothing less than, "The world for Freud in this generation."[9]

It was not coincidental, of course, that such an expansion occurred in the wake of the Depression, a time when the emotional pressures on "normal" individuals were quite significant. While there was some debate as to whether the Depression caused maladjustments or simply revealed pre-existing conditions, there was little question that this economic dislocation elevated the importance of mental hygiene on a broad scale. A host of individuals and agencies set out to document the conditions of duress embodied in the lives of 1930s children and youth, resulting in an enormous literature on the physical, educational, economic, and emotional variables at play in their lives.[10] The basic summary of conditions probed in these works was, as expected, quite gloomy. Unemployment was ubiquitous, and young peoples' responses to questions about the future revealed a deep uncertainty regarding the prospects of improvement. Howard Bell of the American Youth Commission estimated the percentage of out-of-school and unemployed youth to be between 40 and 46 percent, an "ominous proportion" for the health of American society.[11] Although church attendance seemed to hold steady and even increase in this period, the insecurity of the population appeared to be on the rise, demonstrated by increasing numbers of suicides among adolescents. Amidst these social variables, youth were proclaimed to be at a point of "crisis," their transition from childhood to adulthood greatly complicated by a rejecting culture that refused to provide ready avenues of sustenance and hope.

Educators waffled between fear and pity for these disillusioned young people. Some, with an eye to Hitler's success among young people, implied that disillusioned youth formed a pliable coterie of "ready recruits" for totalitarian dictators.[12] Most, however, argued that youth had been left emotionally bankrupt. Devoid of secure external foundations and living in a world characterized by growing complexity, they were forced to rely inordinately on dwindling internal resources that were rapidly taxed beyond capacity. Such youth, Maxine Davis noted, were "not radicals ready to remake a faulty society because the problem of making something out of their own lives is a Herculean task in the face of difficulties they must surmount."[13] Rather than enlisting students in social change, as liberal progressives had proposed, a growing number of educators were beginning to argue that life itself had become so emotionally demanding that attention should be given to the internal dynamics of personality in individuals. Although morals were still important, the new burden was for student morale, a sense of confidence and hope that seemed to be lacking in the broader society.

For mental hygiene advocates, traditional character education seemed inadequate as a solution to these problems. The goal of character education, especially in the 1920s, was self-denial for the common good, the development of conformity to national ideals for worthy citizenship. Convinced that the disruptive social changes of this era were creating a climate conducive to moral anarchy, school leaders sought to devise means by which carefully chosen values and behaviors could be inculcated within impressionable youth. Rooted in a keen desire for social stability and efficiency, these educators worked to develop standardized morality codes, ethical anchors designed to fortify a solid stance of character within the tempestuous changes spawned by modern social life. Laced with patriotic fervor and a desire to enhance cooperative citizenship within an emerging industrial order, character education was designed to enhance predictable moral action and to facilitate group-oriented civic virtue. Taught both directly through classroom activities and indirectly through stories and extracurricular clubs, such programs focused upon the development of "good Americans" characterized by the virtues of self-control, duty, industry, honesty, loyalty, kindness, health, reliability, and teamwork.[14]

For many concerned about youth in the post-Depression era, such an approach seemed anachronistic. In interviews with psychologist and progressive educational leader Caroline Zachry in the late 1930s, young people demonstrated a profound disillusionment regarding the prospects of achievement through virtue-centered moral excellence. The ideals of honesty, industry, loyalty, and cooperation did little to buffer individuals against the ravages of economic ruin, thus challenging the cherished American faith in the inevitable link between character and success. Dimock argued that youth were disillusioned about the "ideals of Americanism," noting that "The virtues of thrift and industry and even honesty seem meaningless when they witness or hear about such conditions as: savings being wiped out by the depression, enforced idleness on a gigantic scale; and the exposure of graft and dishonesty in high places and low."[15] As historian Richard Huber has pointed out, there was a growing sense in the 1930s that the virtues sponsored by mainstream character education programs, which had provided both a moral compass and a formula for personal achievement, seemed no longer to guarantee the latter. For many mental hygiene advocates, the moral cynicism produced by economic decline rendered traditional virtue-centered character education less helpful for disillusioned youth.[16]

In addition to such economic and vocational variables, common approaches to character education were also viewed as atavistic because of the growing complexity and fragility of American social institutions. While simple adherence to national virtues might have provided secure guidance for life direction in an earlier era, many were convinced that a new cultural backdrop had greatly expanded the resources necessary for achieving a healthy and successful life. Percival Symonds, a character education theorist with sympathies for mental hygiene, noted that,

> Mental hygiene is of greater importance today than at any other time in the world's history .... With our increasing civilization and industrialism and with the growth of cities, life, particularly social life, has taken on a complexity which makes satisfactory adaptation more difficult .... The high level of stimulation and excitement day after day continues in a way in which it has never done before in the world's history. Social relationships are more complex and their stability less secure than at any time before.[17]

Familiar institutions seemed to be incapable of managing this crisis and in some cases were even cited for exacerbating emotional maladjustments.[18] Economic insecurity threatened family stability and placed strains on marriage and parent–child relations. Schools were thought to be equally troublesome in this regard. Overcrowding and poor building conditions made for depressing accommodations, and many argued that the "custodial" schools of this era were populated by students of lower moral endowment. As character education expert Francis Powers noted, the school had increased in diversity and complexity to the extent that it now required a larger number of adjustments on the part of students. Even worse, while schools were extending personalities in a variety of ways, the Depression-era elimination of many health and recreational activities greatly diminished the institutions' capacities to meet student emotional needs. In the eyes of mental hygiene proponents, the simplistic codes of traditional character education programs were unable to touch these critical realities.[19]

In light of these perceived deficiencies, those espousing the mental hygiene perspective were ready to assist character educators at this critical time. However, it quickly became evident that the goals and rhetoric of mental hygiene differed in significant ways from the core philosophy of American character education. For mental hygiene proponents, character education emphases on self-control, will power, and group conformity were actually destructive to the psychological and personal growth of fragile students. Joseph Folsom, writing for the American Youth Council, noted that teaching students the "where there's a will, there's a way" model of character training was a deeply threatening practice because it denied that many inappropriate behaviors were often linked to the attempt to satisfy real personal needs. By ignoring such needs and focusing simply on personal resolve to abolish behavioral symptoms, teachers were simply setting students up for frustration, disillusionment, and repeated moral failure while they neglected significant maladjustments.[20] In addition, Max Shoen claimed that character education methods were personality-debilitating because they generated self-deception on the part of individuals. Students were never able to confront true feelings and motives because they were always trying to measure up to an external, artificially imposed behavioral standard. In other words, self-actualization and psychological well-being were threatened by an overweaning desire to conform to societal expectations. By forcing students to adopt behaviors without confronting the underlying mental health issues involved, some argued, teachers were producing young hypocrites devoid of a clear sense of self-understanding.[21]

At the root of this critique was a belief that character educators both misinterpreted youthful misbehavior and also neglected the most pressing needs of contemporary students. First, while most character educators attributed negative behavior to willful rebellion, hygienists characterized student misbehavior as an inappropriate means of attempting to satisfy basic psychological needs. The role of the teacher was therefore to diagnose and treat the underlying psychological and environmental issues fueling negative behavior (an indirect approach) rather than directly soliciting behavioral compliance as a first step. As one spokesperson for the new perspective suggested, "Bad conduct, from the point of view of the mental hygienist, is not due to the evil nature of the individual; neither is it sin. It is a symptom of personality ill-health."[22] Second, concern among mental hygiene devotees was much greater for quiet and introverted students than for those who demonstrated more active defiance. Hygienists contended that, while teachers often ascribed a moral "goodness" to shy and reserved children because of their passivity, these "withdrawn" children were the young people most in need of careful attention in order to prevent psychological disorders.[23] Finally, those promulgating mental hygiene perspectives desired to see students reject conformity to externally imposed ideals in favor of an exploration of confident uniqueness, the development of an individualized sense of identity.[24] It was deemed far more critical for students to develop a self-derived life pattern that provided for confidence and proper adjustment than for them to adhere to a teacher's (or a society's) sense of proper decorum. For character educators, conformity to national standards and a developed ability to deny oneself for the common good stood in stark contrast to the hygienists' aims of self-actualization and "happy adjustment." The two movements appeared to have contrary purposes at the very heart of their proposals.

Yet despite these seemingly irreconcilable tensions, many embracing the mental hygiene perspective were increasingly optimistic that hygiene and character education could coalesce in important ways, forging a more holistic form of moral growth linked both to right behavior and heightened mental health. In the 1936 *Fifteenth Yearbook* of the NEA's Department of Elementary School Teachers, one author suggested that,

> [Mental hygiene's] methods are those of carefully studying the individual, attempting to understand his behavior, and producing such changes in his attitudes and his environment as are necessary for the satisfaction of his basic needs. Character education has been traditionally concerned with bringing the individual into conformity with the ideals and behavior patterns of his social group. . . . Fortunately, with the increase of scientific knowledge of child nature, the procedures of mental hygiene and character education are coming to have more in common. Progressive educators realize that adequate training for character must utilize the principles of mental hygiene. . . . That they stress mental and emotional health somewhat more than social conformity is justified by the fact that the latter has been greatly overemphasized in many schools and communities.[25]

Similarly, Joseph Folsom argued that, while the objective of character education was "to develop habits and attitudes serviceable to society" and the aim of mental hygiene was "to develop habits and attitudes making for healthy, well-adjusted, happy individual life," an "increased understanding of human personality" rendered these differences less meaningful. "The basic fact," he suggested, "is that [children] are unhappy or unsatisfied; some 'take it out' on their environment, while others develop neuroses and 'queer' behavior that do not directly menace the social peace and order but which may in the long run constitute a burden and a positive emotional damage to their families and their future offspring."[26] As mental hygiene became more concerned with "normal" children and as character education adopted the Depression-era concern for maladjusted personalities, the two movements, many suggested, could facilitate a unified and broadened perspective.[27]

While such rhetoric implied a blissful marriage of character and personality adjustment, what is clear in these descriptions of compromise is the degree to which themes of morality and character were being enveloped—even eclipsed—by the discourse of mental health and personality adjustment. In fact, the linguistic struggle between the terms "character" and "personality" in the 1930s demonstrated that the former was increasingly subsumed within the vocabulary of the latter. Henry Lester Smith, in his description of trends in character education in the 1930s, suggested that educators now preferred the term "personality" because it was more inclusive, the whole of which character was merely a part.[28] Likewise, in the inaugural issue of the journal *Character and Personality*, psychologist William McDougall suggested that character referred to conduct in keeping with prescribed cultural norms while personality encompassed the whole essence of the individual (intellect, character, temperament, and disposition). In fact, he suggested that the English term "personality" approximated the German word "Charakter," which referred to the sum total of features, properties, and qualities of an individual organism that called out reactions from the environment.[29] Reflecting this perspective, by 1945, *Character and Personality* had changed its name simply to the *Journal of Personality*. Explaining the shift, editor Karl Zener noted that, "The psychological aspects of character are regarded as included within the broader field of personality, and the preservation of the term in the title is thus unnecessary."[30] Rather than focusing on right and wrong, he claimed, "progressive" character educators would be committed to the all-encompassing task of personality development, the building up of "the individual's whole self."[31]

The "Psychologizing" of Character Education

That the proposed merger between mental hygiene and character education was at least attempted is apparent within the character education literature itself. In the *Religious Education* journal, a central source for character education research in the first half of the twentieth century, the term "character" almost disappeared in articles written after 1934. Between this date and 1941, only five articles were written explicitly about "character education" (as contrasted with sixty-five between 1925 and 1934), while fifteen articles mentioned personality and/or mental hygiene in their titles. While the vast majority of character education texts and programs between World War I and the early 1930s revealed an intellectual indebtedness to either conservative theorists like W.W. Charters and Franklin Bobbitt or liberal educators like John Dewey and W.H. Kilpatrick, pieces in the mid- to late-1930s drew heavily on psychologists with affinities for the mental hygiene perspective. Among the most prominent of these were Caroline Zachry, Percival Symonds (author of *The Nature of Conduct*, *Diagnosing Personality and Conduct*, and *The Mental Hygiene of the School Child*), W.H. Burnham (author of *The Normal Mind*), and William McDougall (author of *Character and the Conduct of Life*).[32] These psychologists became the new intellectual leaders of the revised movement, and their scientific posture set the agenda for the expansion and transformation of character education in this era.

The influence of these theorists was readily apparent in both theoretical texts on character education and in state and local programs.[33] Major reports were self-conscious about the heightened emphasis on personality and the ways in which this concept was extending the meaning of character education. This was especially true of the 1934 NEA *Research Bulletin*, which began its 141-page report on character education with a description of the ways in which the meaning of "character" was changing. The authors noted that, while character had been thought of in terms of right and wrong behavior, it now included "practically the entire area of personality," the emotional, mental, and physical factors that contributed to health, well-being, and "happy adjustment." Eschewing a narrow concern for external behavior, educators were now, the report noted, concerned for "the entire emotional makeup of the child, the root issues out of which behaviors emanated and the perceptions of self gained chiefly through the reactions of others to one's unique personality."[34] The

Bulletin noted that the emphasis on personality was an outgrowth of the progressive emphasis on the "whole person." Rather than analyzing the individual as a collection of traits, the report noted that educators were now embracing the "whole individual," one in whom traits, emotions, and dispositions gelled to create a particular "persona" that was more than the sum of its parts.[35] Similarly, despite its significant appeals to social justice themes, the *Tenth Yearbook* of the Department of Superintendence (1934) suggested that character education must account for personality adjustment if it was to exemplify themes of progressive "wholeness" and trace the roots of purported character flaws. The authors contended that the focus on student adjustment was no longer reserved for those dealing with serious disorders. Alternatively, character education for "normal" children was to now encompass personality variables that could lead to personal decay. "The schools' major contribution," the report noted, "lies in promoting vigorous healthy personality growth in so-called normal children rather than in treating personality disorders.... Normal children have personality problems, and the correction of these lesser difficulties may mean the prevention of more serious maladjustments."[36]

By the mid-1930s, character education reports, texts, and programs had indeed adopted many of the central themes and assumptions of this broadened emphasis. For example, the healthy, balanced life was increasingly described as an extroverted life, one dominated by confident, aggressive expression that revealed a strong core of selfhood. Quiet and dutiful children, on the other hand, were viewed increasingly as troubled individuals, lacking self-confidence and withdrawing into a self-absorbed and morbidly introspective world.[37] As Francis Powers, one of the most cited character education theorists of the 1930s, suggested in her work *Character Training*, "Although the extrovert is inclined to be more obtrusive socially, in introversion we are apt to find more dangerous types of mental derangement. Mere quietness on the part of students is not necessarily an indication that they are engaged in some healthful mental pursuit. Part of the teacher's task is to detect an undue amount of introversion or self-centeredness on the part of students."[38] While the concern for the more traditional maladies was never abandoned, the *Tenth Yearbook* proclaimed that character education should concentrate upon, "the girl who is moody and oversensitive, the person who feels himself to be unpopular, the child who does too much daydreaming," and even the child who was "inordinately studious" and interested in isolated reading. In New Jersey, which printed its first state character education bulletin in 1936, teachers were directed to exert the majority of their energy in work with children who were "withdrawn." The timid boy who is "babied," the girl who fails to enter into group activities, and the boy who seemed overly anxious about social interaction were the chief targets of "character" training. The authors of such reports recognized that such concerns were not typical character education fare. One acknowledged that, "Some of the cases listed have no relation to the elements of fine character, narrowly defined." "But," he continued, "every one of them and many others are believed to have decided implications for character when the goals are interpreted broadly."[39]

Perhaps predictably, this "broad interpretation" also led character educators to a disparate perspective on the etiology of misbehavior. While previous texts described immorality as a willful rejection of character traits (conservatives) or weak commitment to democracy (liberals), those embracing mental hygiene saw inappropriate activity as a reflection of personality sickness. This "medical model" placed the emphasis on underlying causes (the illness) rather than on the wrong action itself (the symptom). As character educator Kenneth Heaton put it in his popular 1933 text on moral training, "A deed of misconduct is often only the symptom of an underlying difficulty. When a child has a high fever we do not immediately seek to drive away this symptom, but attempt to find the physical maladjustment which is causing the abnormal temperature. The same is true with the behavior problems of children."[40] Summarizing this perspective, popular spokeswoman Helen Myrick suggested that the character building literature of this era demonstrated conclusively that "We have begun to think not in moral terms but in terms of ill health."[41]

The direct result of this philosophy was a transformed methodology. Because of the concern for underlying causal factors, character educators frequently adopted the clinical case study model as a critical component of moral development.[42] For these theorists, the only way to diagnose underlying causes of misbehavior was through a careful analysis of all of the underlying personal factors that might impinge upon the individual's actions in the social world. As a veritable causal network identifying the chief streams of influence in the individual's life, the case study was to contain information on family background (including records on parental education, marriage relations and child-rearing approaches, sibling relationships, and birth traumas), home environment (including neighborhood characteristics, economic conditions, sleeping arrangements, recreational life), and personal history (health, eating and sleeping habits, social development, sex development, education, vocational ambitions, religious interests, friendships, interests, and hobbies). Such variables, these psychologists proposed, held the key to unlocking the life course of the individual and would explain both potential remedies for maladjustments and preventative measures necessary for those who had not yet manifested maladjustments in their lives.[43]

At its best, the case study was an elaborate and scientific device to determine the root causes of student maladjustment. In New Jersey, the 1936 state-wide character education plan related the account of a seventh-grade girl who was shy and uncomfortable in social situations, sometimes striking out violently at others. By probing into her childhood, they found that the girl had gone through many years of bed-wetting in elementary school and had been teased by classmates who discovered her malady. With this understanding in place, teachers were able to suggest a positive plan emphasizing positive reinforcement and counseling for her problem. In such cases, uncovering the past was indeed a key to unlocking the future. At the same time, case studies were often, in practice, far less scientific than mental hygienists would have desired. In one case study in the same New Jersey plan, for example, a student "John" was known to have a quick temper. Amidst all of the diagnostic issues mentioned, the one highlighted in the study was that, "A study of John's home showed that his parents were both born in Russia and the father had a communistic attitude."[44] The quick attribution of John's problem to ethnic background denied the complexity of causation and further confirmed cultural stereotypes with the authority of scientific analysis. In this sense, case studies often lost their individuality and became reflections of purported group qualities.

In addition to case study methodology, generalized student rating and testing was also adapted to these new emphases. While the character rating of students was certainly not unusual within the character education programs of the previous decade, rating in the 1930s greatly expanded the scope of factors being evaluated by educators. For example, C.H. McCloy at the State University of Iowa character education center suggested in 1936 that rating scales be expanded to include all of the traits necessary for the full-orbed personality. In his own prescribed list, he included many of the traditional character staples—cooperation, self-control, loyalty, and trustworthiness—but also a series of new factors to be measured: enthusiasm, poise, sociability, and self-confidence. In addition, he recommended the use of Edward Webb's scale of "character and intelligence," the chief categories of which were "tendency to be cheerful," "liability to extreme depression," "readiness to become angry," "fondness for large social gatherings," "popularity," and other similar themes.[45] Perhaps the most commonly mentioned scales were the popular Thurstone Personality Schedule and the Benreuter Personality Record. Both tests served to measure the variables critical to the new character education: fear, anxiety, introversion and extroversion, popularity, self-concept, and security. As the authors of a character education program in Cleveland, Ohio put it, such scales could help students and teachers work together for "self-realization, psychical freedom, character, or the achievement of personality."[46]

Perhaps not surprisingly, character education programs also revealed the influence of the mental hygiene perspective in relation to the place of the teacher in the character-building process. While late 1930s character education reports did not discount the importance of instructors' honesty and industry, they certainly did not emphasize these traditional standbys. Instead, the new literature on character education demanded of teachers a new list of personal qualities commensurate with the mental hygiene approach. Reports now urged schools to hire teachers that could serve efficiently as counselors. The *Seventh Yearbook* noted: "The teacher of today must be more than an instructor. He must be to some extent an experimental psychologist, a diagnostician, and a guidance expert. He must be a practicing physician in the realm of personality, interested both in curative and preventative medicine."[47] In addition, teachers were required to possess adjusted personalities themselves. Daniel Larue, in distinguishing between superior and inferior character educators, noted in the *Fifteenth Yearbook* that the best exemplars were less fearful, less angry, more emotionally stable, and less lonesome. Harry Rivlin, also writing for this yearbook, suggested that prospective teachers who were tense, moody or introspective should never be hired, and several authors suggested that student teachers in training schools should be given personality rating tests to determine their potential for leading students to "happy adjustment." By the late 1930s, it seems, character/personality educators were more concerned for teachers' mental health than for the possession of traits revealing strength of character and self-sacrifice.[48]

Yet, even with such exemplar character educators in place within the classroom, many proponents of the new moral training vision made it clear that these changes required a move to heightened vocational expertise and specialization. The authors of character education reports in the 1930s urged schools to construct school guidance clinics, staffed by psychologists, psychiatrists, doctors and nurses, and psychiatric social workers. Since the basic analogy of the movement was a medical one and since plans spoke of determining causal etiology and constructing efficient diagnoses, there was a sense that cases would require advanced specialists with expertise in guidance and psychology. While teachers were still held up as key facilitators in the issues of self-confidence and basic mental health, they were viewed now as just one line of defense against personality difficulties. Thus, while the spread of mental hygiene into the field of character education was a popularization of the mental health agenda, it also had the effect of professionalizing character work in the schools.[49]

The Changing Face of "Goodness"

Through all of these changes, the purpose that was increasingly defined as the "end" of character training was not right behavior or efficient citizenship but "adjustment," the state in which "a person's habits and skills enable him to satisfy his needs, fill his wants, and give him new satisfaction."[50] Finding much in common with the life adjustment emphasis then gaining credence in the schools, the key to such adjustment was to be found in developing personal qualities and a way of life that would generate a harmonious relationship with the environment, particularly one's peers.[51] Symonds's "adjustment questionnaire," utilized in many state and local character education programs in the 1930s, asked children to respond affirmatively or negatively to such questions as, "Do other children let you play with them? Do you get used to new places quickly? Do you have many friends who like you and respond well to you?"[52] When one was able to adjust effectively, the likelihood of misbehavior, many contended, would be markedly reduced. Character education was forced to be remedial so often only because such preventative work was ignored.

Intrinsic to this goal of proper adjustment was the related mental hygiene goal of creating the "attractive" personality. To secure proper emotional adjustments and to overcome the potentially devastating personality flaws of timidity, shyness, seclusion, and depression, character educators spoke directly to the need to make good impressions on other people so as to receive positive reactions. Character educator Powers stated this perspective most clearly:

> Can one have personality if there is no one around to appreciate it? Probably not. This theory has very important educational implications both from the standpoint of general education and the standpoint of character education. For, if personality is the sum total of a certain type of impression which we make upon other people, then by altering the nature of ourselves as a stimulus, we can alter the nature of the response .... And obviously, since most people desire to get along in the world and be happy, we would select those classes of stimuli which produce a happy reaction in other people and thereby cause them to further act in such a way as to increase our well-being.[53]

Cultural changes certainly precipitated this approach, and many saw the social complexity of the culture as an impetus for these new ideals. As character education theorist Harry McKown noted in his widely cited text, *Character Education*, "Where formerly an individual traveled in a small circle, the need for an attractive personality was not very pronounced. Now all of his activities, social, economic, political, religious, etc. have widened, and a fuller personality is required to live successfully in the larger field of his widened activities . . . . So the modern school is making headway in emphasizing training in all-roundedness, and what is all-roundedness but personality and character spelled in a different way."[54] Within a culture characterized by brief and informal contacts with a broad range of people rather than intimate relationships developing over long periods of time, the power of impression through personality was envisioned as the new key to adjustment and success. It was in this sense, in fact, that the mental hygiene movement merged with a more popular conception of personality then superceding the character ethic in American success literature. Rather than cultivating personal virtues through vigorous willpower and discipline, the pathway to success was said to be paved by the ability to make favorable impressions on others. As evidenced by the publication in this era of such best-sellers as Dale Carnegie's *How To Win Friends and Influence People* (1936), individuals were urged to develop strong personal qualities that would elicit the affections of others, crafting a persona that would facilitate personal advance.[55]

In new character education programs designed in the mid- to late-1930s, students were urged to cultivate habits and behaviors that would help them gain esteem in the eyes of peers. Students were repeatedly asked in character education programs to list qualities in people that were either attractive or repellant. Character educator George Herbert Betts asked students, in his *Foundations of Character and Personality* (1937), to list the personal traits of individuals who "make you cross-grained, ready to oppose, overawe you, put you at your worst, make you feel gloomy, depressed or cynical, bore you" and to contrast these with the traits of others who make you feel excited and enthusiastic, worthwhile, cheerful, and important.[56] Students were urged to locate traits that were well received by others, honing such attributes in order to secure personal admiration for self-esteem. Powers, in fact, suggested that the development of character was a process of personal experimentation: "It means trying various possibilities in conduct and judging their effectiveness by the reactions secured through them." Such moral experimentation would help young citizens become exemplary performing selves, generating adjusted and integrated lives. In *Steps Upward in Personality*, an explicit "character education" program designed for the Detroit public schools, author Laura Haddock cited a poem she felt described the new aim:

> You may know just as much as the other man knows,
> You may go just as far as the other man goes,
> You may be just as strong, just as clever, as true,
> Yet some how or other he wins over you.
> The difference is not in the things which you know,
> It is not in the skill or the force of your blow,
> It is not in the work you are able to do,
> It's in the personality labeled as "you."[57]

The poem, she noted, served as a reminder to students that achievement was often dependent on qualities wholly outside the province of character, traditionally considered. Instead, Haddock suggested, "Personality . . . has helped some people to succeed although they had no other justification for success except this one knack for impressing others favorably."[58]

The shift from character to personality in character education programs at this time, mediated by the mental hygiene point of view, thus represented a set of fundamental reorientations in conceptions of moral training. First of all, the personality ethic implied that personal change could come as a "quick fix" rather than through the laborious toil and struggle of prolonged character building.[59] For character educators in the 1920s, the two most representative metaphors for the person growing in character were the farmer and the pilgrim. In both cases, there existed an implicit asceticism, marked by the toil of planting and traveling, and an overwhelming sense of process, characterized by the duration of the germination period and the physical distance of the journey. Within the personality ethic, on the other hand, the salesman was offered as the prototype. Through "market analysis," the individual could assess the desires of "customers" and mold the self accordingly. In this context, the most important factor was not the inherent quality of the product (the self), but rather the ability to make that product acceptable to the consumer (other individuals). As Henry Lester Smith lamented in considering this new paradigm in character training,

> Since the world in general pays such respect to the outward appearance and fails to look intently enough upon the heart why should the individual limit himself or put restraints upon himself in order to build up an inner quality which is invisible and which may be unrewarded. . . . In recent years we have had a flood of advertisements of methods of developing personality. These advertisements make it appear that one can take on personality as readily as he can take on fat. "Acquiring personality" is made almost as alluring to the ambitious climber as is the acquiring of a luxurious growth of hair to the man with a bald pate.[60]

In a world where even lengthy character development did not seem to guarantee success, it is easy to see why this approach had such appeal.

In addition, there was a distinct focus here on individualized character for personal health and self-confidence rather than conformity for the good of the social order. Betts noted that character education, in response to the homogenizing influence of mass culture and the conformist views of many educators, should help people find their "I," the sense of personal uniqueness that distinguished them from every other person.[61] Students were constantly reminded that their own "selves" were unique and personalized, that their "individual differences" created a special and singular persona. America, as opposed to then-forming totalitarian regimes, thrived on the distinct contributions of unique personalities. Betts, in fact, suggested that "This tyrannical insistence by the group that the individual shall conform to established patterns often seems cruel and unnecessary. Especially is this true where refusal to follow prescribed social norms brings no bad results and may even point the way to desirable change." Of course, as cultural historians have also noted, there was a tremendous irony in this process of supposed self-realization. Despite the "inward turn" implied by personality rhetoric, the clear emphasis of personality-minded theorists was to equip students with the personal tools necessary to "fit in," to "adjust" effectively to others.[62] Recognizing this paradox, Susman recognized in the very language of "adjustment" an "obvious difficulty." "One is to be unique, be distinctive, follow one's own feelings, make oneself stand out from the crowd," he contended, "and at the same time appeal—by fascination, magnetism, attractiveness—to it."[63]

Such an irony was pervasive in 1930s character education. Plans regularly pressed students to eschew mere conformity while simultaneously asking them to search out those qualities that would make them most acceptable to their peers. Even Betts, who struck out against conformity, suggested that pupils should select attractive and magnetic personal qualities that would heighten personal "appeal to others."[64] Many authors spoke in terms of personality balance, the ability to avoid extremes so as not to alienate oneself from the "always judging" crowd. Others simply noted quite bluntly that "fit," the ability to continually adjust to one's surroundings, was the most important character trait. For all of its liberating rhetoric, the attempt to foster personality was, no less than character, an appeal to social convention.

While personality-driven character education was directed at individual health and welfare, therefore, it was unequivocally other-directed. Implicit in the mental hygiene approach and blatantly glorified in more popular attempts to develop personality was the notion that individuals were to adjust themselves to the desires of others. Whether the goal of these efforts was conceived as developing wholesome self-concept and personal confidence or as a means of gaining leverage in personal dealings, the ramifications were similar. Students were taught that the essence of their character was to be found in the reactions of other people rather than in an unswerving allegiance to personal conviction. As one critic noted, "The problem for the character ethic was not people, but the individual's own inner resources. The biggest obstacles to be overcome were laziness and profligacy that dragged the individual down to failure. Now the big obstacles were not in the individual himself, though he must overcome his agonies of fear, but in the responses of other people."[65] Because of this, proponents of the new approach never had to fear the ambiguous relationship with success faced by traditional character educators. While character-minded educators in the 1920s recognized that success could destroy the moral qualities of those who achieved because of their honesty, perseverance, and thrift, personality-minded critics had no such fear. Success and self-realization (unlike self-denial) went hand in hand, and prosperity could only enhance the personality qualities listed by these theorists. Here was a movement coming to terms with success as an integral part of the total personal package.

Personality advocates saw themselves as expanding the progressive emphasis on the whole person, bringing into character educators' province the emotions, temperaments, and self-concept of the individual in addition to the intellectual and moral components previously emphasized. In this sense, many saw the growth of this theme as a fulfillment of the progressive vision of organic wholeness. At the same time, the emphasis also led to a narrowing of social vision. Most fundamentally, this new emphasis shifted the center of ethical gravity from civic virtue (self-denial for the common good) to self-realization. Whether compared to more conservative ideals of citizenship training or to liberal social reconstruction, the character education of the later 1930s had lost a sense of scope beyond the individual. While several noted that adjusted personalities would be far less likely to cause social harm and that the emphasis could generate a "kingdom of good adjustment," the programs and plans in this era were highly personal in central focus.[66] Ironically, when morality was reconceived as personal morale, character education succumbed to the disease that mental hygienists most feared: the introverted personality.

Notes

1. Sol Cohen, *Challenging Orthodoxies: Toward a New Cultural History of Education* (New York: P. Lang, 1999); Cohen, "The Mental Hygiene Movement, the Development of Personality and the School: The Medicalization of American Education," *History of Education Quarterly* 23, 2 (1983): 123–149.
2. Cohen, "The Mental Hygiene Movement," 139.
3. Warren I. Susman, *Culture as History: The Transformation of American Society in the Twentieth Century* (New York: Pantheon Books, 1982), 277.
4. See E. Brooks Holifield, *A History of Pastoral Care in the United States* (New York: University of Chicago Press, 1982); Heather Warren, "The Shift from Character to Personality in Mainline Protestant Thought, 1925–1945," *Religion and American Culture* 9, 2 (February 1999): 43–50.
5. James Davison Hunter, *The Death of Character: Moral Education in an Age without Good or Evil* (New York: Basic Books, 2000), 70.
6. See, e.g., Margo Horn, *Before It's Too Late: The Child Guidance Movement in the United States, 1922–1945* (Philadelphia: Temple University Press, 1989); Joel Pfister and Nancy Schnog, eds., *Inventing the Psychological: Toward a Cultural History of Emotional Life in America* (New Haven, CT: Yale University Press, 1997); Theresa R. Richardson, *The Century of the Child: The Mental Hygiene Movement and Social Policy in the United States and Canada* (Albany, NY: State University of New York Press, 1989); Philip Rieff, *The Triumph of the Therapeutic: Uses of Faith after Freud* (Chicago: The University of Chicago Press, 1966).
7. On typical character education approaches in this era, see B. Edward McClellan, *Moral Education in America: Schools and the Shaping of Character from Colonial Times to the Present* (New York: Teachers College Press, 1999), 48–55. For representative state and city plans, see Oregon Office of the Superintendent of Public Instruction, *Character Education: A Manual for Oregon Teachers* (Salem, OR: Office of Superintendent of Public Instruction, 1930); Nebraska State Department of Education, *A Course of Study in Character Education, Supplementary Normal Training Bulletin* (Department of Public Instruction, 1927); J. Cayce Morrison, *Character Building in New York Public Schools: An Analysis of Practices Reported by Teachers and Supervisory Officers for the School Year 1928–1929* (New York: The University of the State of New York, 1929)
8. The best description of the changing perspective of the mental hygiene movement is found in David Foster, *Mental Hygiene and the Rise of the Therapeutic State* (Ph.D. dissertation, University of Oklahoma, 1989). For other treatments, see Susan Riley, "Mental Hygiene and Education, 1900–1930" (Ph.D. dissertation, University of Florida, 1978) and Craig Lockhart, "Personality Guidance for All: Mental Hygiene and the development of Children, 1925–1945" (Ph.D. dissertation, University of Southern California, 1984). For the influence of the movement in education, see Cohen, "From Badness to Sickness: The Mental Hygiene Movement and the Crisis of School Discipline," *Proteus* 24, 3 (1987): 9–14; Cohen, "The Mental Hygiene Movement," 123–149.

9. Hedley Dimock, "Mental Hygiene Attainments Interpreted for Religious Educators," *Religious Education* 25, 7 (September 1930): 677.
10. Perhaps the most important of the survey-minded agencies was the American Youth Commission (AYC), established by the American Council on Education in 1935 in order to provide a tangible data set documenting the "current status of youth in our troubled society." For examples of its work, see Howard Bell, *Youth Tell Their Story* (Washington, DC: American Council of Education, 1938); American Youth Commission, *Youth and the Future: the General Report of the American Youth Commission* (Washington, DC: American Council on Education, 1942); Joseph Folsom, *Youth, Family, and Education* (Washington, DC: American Council on Education, 1941). See also Caroline Zachry, *Emotion and Conduct in Adolescence; for the Commission on Secondary School Curriculum* (New York: D. Appleton-Century Co., 1940); Zachry, "Youth in a Depressed Society," in Harold Rugg, ed., *Democracy and the Curriculum: The Life and Program of the American School* (New York: Appleton-Century-Crofts, Inc., 1939).
11. Bell, *Youth Tell Their Story*, 3; Zachry, "Youth in a Depressed Society," 24.
12. Lawrence K. Frank, "The Reorientation of Education to the Promotion of Mental Hygiene," *Mental Hygiene* 23, 4 (1939): 540.
13. Maxine Davis, *The Lost Generation: A Portrait of American Youth Today* (New York: The Macmillan Company, 1936), 22.
14. National Education Association, Department of Superintendence, *Fourth Yearbook: The Nation at Work on the Public School Curriculum* (Washington, DC: Department of Superintendence, 1926), 264.
15. Hedley Dimock, "Some New Light on Adolescent Religion," *Religious Education* 31, 4 (October 1936): 234.
16. Richard M. Huber, *The American Idea of Success* (New York: McGraw-Hill, 1971), 219–222.
17. Percival Symonds, *Mental Hygiene of the School Child* (New York: The Macmillan Company, 1934), 6–8.
18. See, e.g., Florence Teagarden, "The Effect of Present Conditions on Personality Development," *Religious Education* 31, 3 (July 1936): 54–56.
19. Francis F. Powers, *Character Training* (New York: A.S. Barnes and Company, 1932), 77–80. See also Glen H. Elder, *Children of the Great Depression: Social Change in Life Experience* (Chicago: University of Chicago Press, 1974), 45. For more information on schools and enrollments in this era, see David Tyack, Robert Lowe, and Elizabeth Hansot, *Public Schools in Hard Times: The Great Depression and Recent Years* (Cambridge, MA: Harvard University Press, 1984); David Angus and Jeffrey Mirel, *The Failed Promise of the American High School, 1890–1995* (New York: Teachers College Press, 1999).
20. Folsom, *Youth, Family, and Education*, 45.
21. Schoen, "Personality," 92.
22. Harrison S. Elliott, "Mental Hygiene and Religious Education," *Religious Education* 27, 3 (April 1936): 616.
23. In a fascinating 1928 study conducted by E.K. Wickman of the Child Guidance Center in New York City, teachers and clinicians were polled to determine which behavioral problems were worthy of consideration. The results revealed a sharp discrepancy between the two approaches. Teachers considered transgressions against authority and aggressive violations of classroom order to be most serious, their list including heterosexual activity, stealing, truancy, cheating, and destroying school materials among the top ten. For mental hygienists, the withdrawing behaviors were the most serious, and they listed unsocialness, depression, fearfulness, suspiciousness, and sensitivity among the top ten. E.K. Wickman, *Children's Behavior and Teachers' Attitudes* (New York: The Commonwealth Fund, 1928). See also Horn, *Before Its Too Late*, 187–190; Dimock, "Mental Hygiene Attainments,"

676. See also George Herbert Betts, *Foundations of Character and Personality: An Introduction to the Psychology of Social Adjustment* (Indianapolis: The Bobbs-Merrill Company, 1937), 46–48; Morrison, *Character Building in New York Public Schools*, 86–88.
24. On these themes, see Cohen, *Challenging Orthodoxies* and Richardson, *The Century of the Child*.
25. National Education Association Department of Elementary School Principals, *Fifteenth Yearbook: Personality Adjustment of the Elementary-School Child*, vol. 15 (Washington, DC: National Education Association, July 1936), 235. The reference to character education in the index of the *Yearbook* noted, "See mental hygiene."
26. Folsom, *Youth, Family, and Education*, 66.
27. On this theme, see also Harold A. Anderson, "Character Education or Mental Hygiene—Which Shall it Be?" *Mental Hygiene* 18 (1934): 261–262.
28. William Burnham, perhaps the most renowned hygienist in this era, noted that personality was a description of the individual's basic nature (what the person "is"), of which character (what a person "does") was a partial component. See Burnham, "A Mental Hygienist's View of Character," in David Redding, ed., *Character and Physical Education* (New York: Macmillan, 1937), 15–19.
29. William McDougall, "On the Meaning of the Terms Character and Personality," *Journal of Character and Personality* 1 (April 1935): 1–11.
30. Karl Zener, "A New Direction," *Journal of Personality* 11 (1935): 1.
31. Ibid.
32. Among many sources from these authors, see especially William McDougall, *Character and the Conduct of Life: Practical Psychology for Everyman* (London: Methuen & Co., 1927); Percival M. Symonds, *Diagnosing Personality and Conduct* (New York: The Century Co., 1931); Symonds, *The Nature of Conduct* (New York: The Macmillan Co, 1928); Zachry and Margaret Lightly, *Emotion and Conduct in Adolescence* (New York: D. Appleton, Inc., 1940).
33. The most prominent theoretical pieces included Francis F. Powers, *Character Training* (New York: A.S. Barnes and Company, 1932); Harry McKown, *Character Education* (New York: McGraw-Hill Book Company, 1935); Kenneth Heaton, *The Character Emphasis in Education* (Chicago: University of Chicago Press, 1933). The most prominent national reports included the National Education Association Department of Classroom Teachers, *Seventh Yearbook: Character Education* (Washington, DC: National Education Association, 1932); National Education Association Department of Superintendence, *Tenth Yearbook: Character Education* (Washington, DC: 1932), and National Education Association, *Research Bulletin: Character Education* (Washington, DC: National Education Association, 1934). See also Robert S. McElhinney, Henry Lester Smith, and George R. Steele, *Bulletin of the School of Education, Indiana University: Character Development Through Religious and Moral Education in the Public Schools of the United States* (Bloomington, IN: Indiana University Bureau of Cooperative Research, 1937).
34. National Education Association, *1934 Research Bulletin*, 45.
35. Ibid.
36. National Education Association, *Tenth Yearbook*, 236.
37. McDougall, *Character and the Conduct of Life*, 56–67.
38. Powers, *Character Training*, 100.
39. National Education Association Department of Superintendence, *Tenth Yearbook*, 220. It was not surprising that the plan's bibliography read like a listing of the most highly respected books in the field of mental hygiene, including Symonds's *Mental Hygiene of the School Child*, McDougall's *Character and the Conduct of Life*, and Zachry's *Personality Adjustment in School Children*.

40. Cited in Heaton, *The Character Emphasis in Education*, 99–100.
41. Helen L. Myrick, "Mental Hygiene as a Character Builder: A Commentary on the Current Literature," *Religious Education* 27, 3 (April 1936): 646.
42. Heaton, *The Character Emphasis*, 304.
43. Ibid., 145–152.
44. State of New Jersey Department of Public Instruction, *The Character Emphasis in Public Education*, 40, 43.
45. C.H. McCloy, "A Factor Analysis of Personality Traits to Underlie Character Education," *The Journal of Educational Psychology* 27 (1936): 45.
46. Cited in Heaton, *The Character Emphasis*, 77, 111.
47. National Education Association, *Seventh Yearbook*, 138.
48. National Education Association, *Fifteenth Yearbook*, 89.
49. See, e.g., NEA Department of Superintendence, *Tenth Yearbook*, 244; NEA Department of Classroom Teachers, *Seventh Yearbook*, 143–148.
50. Symonds, *Mental Hygiene of the School Child*, 14–16.
51. Zachry, *Personality Adjustment in School Children*, 14. On life adjustment education, see Herbert Kliebard, *The Struggle for the American Curriculum* (New York: Routledge, 1987), 240–270.
52. Symonds, *Diagnosing Personality and Conduct*, 120–122.
53. Powers, *Character Training*, 96–97.
54. McKown, *Character Education*, 87.
55. By 1969, the book had sold 8 million copies in English, was published in 30 other languages, and was, excluding the Bible, the best-selling non-fiction book in the twentieth century. See Huber, *The American Idea*, 223–239.
56. Betts, *Foundations*, 45.
57. Haddock, *Steps Upward*, 11.
58. Ibid., 8. Interestingly, the emphasis on manners, so prevalent in pre–World War I moral education programs, made a dramatic comeback in the late 1930s. As Huber suggested in relation to the late 1930s, "There was less concern for manners as an expression of morals and character, and more interest in the impression that manners would make on other people. Etiquette consisted of rules to be learned, courtesy possessed a cash value for its own sake and could be employed subtly to manipulate the other fellow." Huber, *The American Idea of Success*, 220. See also Walton Bliss, *Personality and School* (Boston: Allyn & Bacon, 1938), 225.
59. Willis L. Uhl and Francis F. Powers, *Personal and Social Adjustment* (New York: The Macmillan Co., 1938), 56.
60. Henry Lester Smith, *Character Development*, 93; Huber, *The American Idea*, 237.
61. Betts, *Foundations*, 9.
62. For a similar perspective, see Philip Cushman, *Constructing the Self, Constructing America: A Cultural History of Psychotherapy* (Reading, MA: Addison-Wesley Publishing Co., 1995), especially 123–141.
63. Susman, *Culture as History*, 280.
64. Betts, *Foundations*, 17, 25.
65. Huber, *American Idea*, 238; Haddock, *Steps Upward*, 5. As Susman has argued, the vocabulary of character tended to use descriptors like "noble," "citizen," "good," "loyal," and "integrity." The vocabulary of personality, on the other hand, tended to utilize adjectives like "winning," "irresistible," "magnetic," "arresting," "striking," and "attractive," words that connoted an impact on the recipient rather than an internal quality of life. Susman, *Culture as History*, 278.
66. Cited in Cohen, "The Mental Hygiene Movement," 142.

Chapter 12

Sex, Drugs, and Right 'N' Wrong:
Or, The Passion of Joycelyn Elders, M.D.

Jonathan Zimmerman

In 1917, psychologist J. Mace Andress acknowledged the difficulties of teaching about alcohol in a "modern" manner. An instructor at Boston Normal School, Andress was also a national leader in the movement to promote "proper health habits" among American public school children. From diet and fumigation to dental care and physical fitness, Andress maintained, good habits emerged only from continued practice and reinforcement. When it came to alcohol, however, "it is practically impossible to give any kind of training in action," Andress admitted. To teach oral hygiene, for example, instructors could simply drill students in teethbrushing "until the habit has been cultivated." Yet the entire object of alcohol instruction was to *prevent*—not to promote—the "habit" of drinking. Even as it became a standard credo for the rest of the curriculum, Andress conceded, "learning by doing" would never do for alcohol.[1]

A half-century later, Morris Chafetz would try to prove Mace Andress wrong. Like Andress, Chafetz was a mental health expert from New England: a professor of psychiatry at Harvard, Chafetz also directed the alcoholic clinic at Massachusetts General Hospital. In a 1966 address to the New York Academy of Sciences, Chafetz argued that schools should not simply teach *about* alcohol; instead, they should teach the "proper use" of it. Elementary-grade pupils should receive small amounts of sherry in water; as students grew older, the prescribed dose would increase. At every age, most of all, students would learn safe methods for consuming this substance: slowly, in small amounts, and in a social setting. Eventually, Chafetz predicted, such instruction would stem America's rising rate of alcoholism. The best way to lessen "problem drinking" was to show young people a less problematic way to drink.[2]

Chafetz' remarks made national headlines, sparking a mixture of mirth and fury. In the *New York Times*, humorist Russell Baker conjured a future in which parents scolded their children for reading *King Lear* instead of mixing martinis. ("Just as

I thought," cries one father, smelling his son's breath. "You haven't been drinking again!") But to much of America, Chafetz' idea was no laughing matter. Politicians and educators rushed to condemn the formerly unknown psychiatrist as a mortal threat to the body politic. "There is a great danger involved in using alcohol, and children should be taught this," declared Iowa governor Harold H. Hughes, himself a recovering alcoholic. "We teach young people what can happen if they use heroin or marijuana, so why not teach them the effects of liquor?" The president of the National Parent—Teacher Association was more curt—but equally critical—in her assessment of Chafetz: "Outrageous." Indeed, it was difficult to find anyone with a good word to say for Morris Chafetz, who dropped his proposal and dissolved back into obscurity. "The idea of Johnny carrying a copy of the bartender's guide in his school bag apparently was too far out even for the most progressive parents," one reporter observed.[3]

By selecting the adjective *progressive*, the reporter underscored the central irony in the history of instruction about "Bad Habits"—alcohol, sex, and drugs—in American public schools.[4] For more than a century, self-described "progressives" have urged schools to replace sterile, book-centered instruction with activity-based methods that build upon students' own interests and experiences.[5] Yet as J. Mace Andress recognized—and as Morris Chafetz would reconfirm—this paradigm has never fit the nexus of courses surrounding sex, drugs, and alcohol. Whereas most instruction aims to spark student interest, these courses have tried to deflect or suppress it; and while other classes build upon student experience, the sex–drugs–alcohol courses either deny or censure it. Most of all, these courses simply do not lend themselves to "activity" in the classroom—or anywhere else. Courses on Bad Habits seek to *block* activity *before* it becomes a habit.

Nor do the courses leave any doubt about whether the habits are, in fact, bad. B. Edward McClellan has brilliantly chronicled the larger debate between "character" and "critical thinking" in twentieth-century moral education: one side has sought to instill correct patterns of behavior, while the other has emphasized inquiry, reason, and judgment.[6] But our courses on sex, drugs, and alcohol can no more accommodate real moral discussion than they can allow for "activity."[7] Since the 1950s, to be sure, educators have frequently embraced the rhetoric of deliberation—and, especially, of "informed choice"—in their sex–drugs–alcohol classes. Yet, the courses still aim to promote a *single* choice: abstinence, at least during adolescence. "The goal of alcohol education in the school is 'to teach youngsters the facts so that they can make up their own minds—not to drink,'" a Stanford educator frankly admitted in 1964. "Adults want youth to think and to weigh evidence, but they do not consider that any resultant conclusion and behavior is equally good."[8] Raising questions for discussion was a fine idea, so long as everyone came to the same correct answer.

Of course, a genuinely open discussion of sex, drugs, and alcohol would need to acknowledge a simple truth: they make you feel good. But pleasure remains the great taboo in this realm, bridging the two historic poles—activity and discussion—that Ed McClellan has described.[9] We cannot allow children to engage in these activities, which they might find pleasurable; but we cannot discuss pleasure, which might encourage the activities. Teachers steer their classrooms away from the subject of pleasure, and with good reason: in 1994, it got the Surgeon General of the United States fired. Responding to a question about masturbation—an activity devoted entirely to pleasure—Dr. Joycelyn Elders stated: "I think it is a part of human sexuality, and perhaps it should be taught."[10] She did not say that masturbation was "good," or that schools should teach children how to engage in it. Why did so many Americans attach those meanings to her words, forcing President Bill Clinton to remove her from office? Perhaps a brief review of the relevant history can offer a few clues.

Alcohol: From Temperance to "Choice"

America's first system of alcohol education stemmed largely from the efforts of a single activist, Mary Hanchett Hunt, and her local legions in the Woman's Christian Temperance Union. Starting in the 1880s, Hunt and the WCTU pressed state legislatures to require "physiology and hygiene" courses that would examine "the effects of alcohol and other narcotics" on the human body. By 1901, every American state and territory mandated some form of "Scientific Temperance Instruction," as Hunt pointedly called it. Rejecting the "moralism" that surrounded earlier temperance campaigns, she insisted that courses and textbooks provide specific, often lurid accounts of alcohol's dangers to the heart, liver, lungs, and even the eyes. "Do you remember what we said about the red eyes of the hard drinker?" asked one popular turn-of-the-century text. "It is useless for such a person to ask the doctor to cure his eyes so long as he uses strong drink."[11] Books frequently displayed adjacent drawings of "the drunkard's stomach" and a normal one, prefiguring anti-drug campaigns of the 1980s and 1990s.[12]

When physiologists charged that texts exaggerated the ill effects of alcohol, Hunt skillfully mustered her own army of scientists to vouch for the books. She had a harder time answering attacks by psychologists and educators, who complained that Scientific Temperance Instruction was too scientific—and not "moral" *enough*. Instead of harping upon the physical pathology of American drinkers, they argued, schools should praise the ethical integrity of Americans who did not drink. "The trembling hand, the thick speech, the dull senses, the poisoned blood . . . the poverty, crime, and misery of the drunkard are hysterically held up to the gaze of the children," complained one Connecticut school official, "but the steady hand, the distinct speech, the quick senses . . . the success and happiness of the temperate man are scarcely mentioned." Some critics cited new research in child psychology, which supposedly showed that scare-tactic approaches would promote—not suppress—youthful iniquity. But others simply invoked Jesus' Biblical injunction: "He that doeth the will shall know of the doctrine." To learn virtue, in short, students would have to practice it.[13]

But what did it mean to "practice" the "virtue" of temperance? What activity would encourage children not to act? After Mary Hunt's death in 1906, classrooms downplayed temperance lessons in favor of personal hygiene activities that *could* be practiced—especially hand washing and handkerchief use, the two best guards against transmissible disease. Echoing the character-education movement that swept schools during this era, hygienists developed elaborate codes of proper conduct as well as clamorous group rituals to enforce them. Whereas character educators inevitably phrased their goals in broad abstractions such as honesty and diligence, however, the hygiene campaign promoted very specific and observable behaviors. Between 1915 and 1920, for example, more than four million students enlisted as "pages," "knights," or "squires" in a "Modern Health Crusade," vowing their eternal fealty to eleven distinct "health chores." Students could discharge these duties each day, like any other household task; even more, adults—or other children—could monitor them. In high schools, student "sanitary squads" performed periodic hygiene inspections and handed down penalties for pupils who failed them. Significantly, all of these campaigns ignored temperance. Although the WCTU tried gamely to establish its own "Sir Galahad Clubs," a health curriculum that stressed activity simply could not address alcohol.[14]

Theoretically, alcohol *could* fit into America's other model of moral education: group discussion and individual choice. After World War II, schools installed curricula designed to give students "facts" so they could make "informed decisions." Centered at Yale University, a new generation of professional alcohol educators argued that strict teetotal instruction no longer suited the nation's "drinking society." Since the repeal of prohibition in 1933, indeed, more and more middle-class Americans had begun to use alcohol; and, for the most part, they did so in moderation. At the same time, the nation became increasingly aware of a subpopulation that could not drink moderately: alcoholics. Rather than stressing the unequivocal dangers of Demon Rum, educators urged, schools should teach students to recognize the "warning signs" of alcoholism—and, most of all, to make up their own minds about whether to drink at all. "There should be no slant to the presentation of alcohol, as students benefit from honest and serious discussion," declared one spokesman. "Ours is not the task to either encourage or discourage the teen-ager to drink." Anything else would amount to propaganda, a hallmark not of the United States but of its Soviet enemy. "We should see that students get both sides of all issues," a sympathetic journalist wrote about alcohol in 1956, at the height of the Cold War, "not one [side] as is the practice in Russia."[15]

To be sure, millions of Americans continued to abstain from liquor: in the 1950s, the WCTU still boasted more than a quarter million members. Denouncing the "new" approach to alcohol, they evoked the classic idioms of character education: some values are true, now and forever, so we should steadfastly strive to instill them in children. "To attempt to teach [about alcohol] without supporting either wets or drys is like trying to teach American history without driving home the superiority of democracy over dictatorship or communism," one WCTU author declared, invoking her own Cold War metaphor. In private, temperance leaders admitted that the nation was much more divided about the morality of alcohol than it was about the Soviet Union. Significantly, however, even parents who drank cocktails over dinner supported—or, at least, did not denounce—total abstinence lessons in the classroom. "When children are taught at school . . . that all drinking is wrong, there are seldom any complaints from parents who approve of and practice social drinking," wrote one observer in 1961. That same year, a frustrated alcohol educator estimated that 90 percent of instruction in the subject still aimed at abstinence. However "wet" Americans had become, it seemed, they still wanted their schools to stay dry.[16]

Drugs: From Just Say Nothing to Just Say No

America's first great anti-drug warrior was also an enemy of drug education. In 1951, on the eve of a dramatic youth narcotics expose in New York, U.S. Commissioner of Narcotics Harry J. Anslinger urged city school officials to avoid the subject altogether. "We find that most young people who have become addicted, acquired this evil habit not because of ignorance of consequences, but rather because they had learned too much about the effects of drugs," Anslinger wrote. "I cannot overemphasize the folly of letting children know too much about the use of narcotics." A few weeks later, New York school superintendent William Jansen told a packed hearing that the city's 300,000 students included 1500 narcotics users—a "1-in-200 ratio," as front-page headlines blared. Ten months after that, state governor Thomas E. Dewey signed a bill requiring instruction on "the effect of habit-forming narcotics"; by 1953, nine other states had followed suit. Yet most educators—and, probably, most citizens—agreed with Harry Anslinger: drug education did more harm than good. Especially after a 1956 Congressional subcommittee concluded that the subject "would tend to arouse undue curiosity" in students, schools generally ignored it.[17]

A decade later, a second set of youth drug exposes would bring this silence to an end. Newspapers carried reports of widespread drug use among young middle-class whites: even in Greenwich, Connecticut, a national symbol of suburban affluence, nearly half of high school seniors in 1970 reported that they had tried marijuana. Such reports spread panic among well-to-do parents, who had grown up regarding drugs as the exclusive province of black jazz musicians, sandal-clad Beatniks, and other bohemian outcasts. Sponsoring rallies and study groups, they soon brought drug education into every American school. As late as 1966, Bureau of Narcotics officials responded to public inquiries about drug education with a form letter warning that such instruction "should be undertaken only with extreme caution." By February 1968, however, the letter itself bore a warning, scrawled in pencil across its top: "no longer used." Students need "*more* information," one official stressed, quoting a recent statement by President Richard Nixon. Nixon went on to sign a 1970 bill authorizing $58 million over three years for drug education, the nation's first federal commitment to the subject.[18]

As in the case of alcohol education, however, Americans could never agree on *which* information to provide—or how to present it. Flush with federal dollars, school districts purchased films depicting the physiological dangers of drug use. Like Mary Hunt's temperance textbooks, however, some of these movies exaggerated the effects of drugs—so much so, critics charged, that they made these substances *more* alluring rather than less so. "Most films . . . offer a virtual how-to kit of techniques for shooting heroin, sniffing glue, downing goofballs, or using aerosol cans," declared one observer. Echoing mid-century alcoholism experts, then, drug educators began to suggest that schools teach "responsible decision-making" rather than the simple dangers of drugs. "The teacher cannot afford to become a preacher," explained one champion of this technique. "He must be prepared to take a flexible approach, maintaining . . . an open mind to the range of student feelings and attitudes." Previous approaches presumed that "people are basically bad," another advocate explained, "so they have to be controlled." But the responsible-decision model assumed just the opposite: that "given the chance, an intelligent human being will make the right decision."[19]

When it came to drugs, clearly, there was only one "right decision": to avoid them, at all times and at all costs. "Programs may go by various names . . . but, fundamentally, drug education is little more than a frantic search for the 'best method of persuading youths to abstain,' " wrote one scholar in 1981, reviewing a decade of reforms. "[T]he hidden agenda is that once a young person learns about the health hazards inherent in drugs, he or she will decide against drug use." But even the rhetoric of neutrality and "choice" was too much for American parents, who mounted a second drug-education revolt in the late 1970s. The movement began when Atlanta native Marsha Schuchard hosted a party for her daughter's 13th birthday—and many of the guests arrived "stoned." Afterwards, she found roach clips and bags of marijuana that they had left behind. Visiting local schools, Schuchard saw that many of their books contained what she called "mixed messages"—especially the idea of "responsible decisionmaking." Whereas the champions of this approach viewed it as the best way to prevent the use of drugs, Schuchard saw it as a subtle mechanism for promoting them. Schuchard started the Parent Resource Institute for Drug Education (PRIDE) in 1978, which helped local parents purge "mixed messages" from their schools. It also urged federal drug officials to bar such phrases from their own directives and publications.[20]

The strategy bore fruit immediately. By 1982, an astounding 4,000 anti-drug parent groups would dot the American landscape. In Washington, meanwhile, drug administrators began to take notice. Schuchard found an important ally in Robert L. DuPont, director of the National Institute on Drug Abuse (NIDA). "When it came to drugs, the 'experts' whom I had come to rely on . . . were just as vulnerable to fad and fashion as everyone else," DuPont recalled. "It was the American parents—not the scientists and certainly not the drug bureaucrats such as myself—who had seen the devastating effects of marijuana on their children and who played Paul Revere waking up the nation." DuPont even commissioned Schuchard to author NIDA's 1979 handbook, *Parents, Peers, and Pot*. Written under the pseudonym of Marsha Manatt (to protect Schuchard's daughter from teasing, she said), the booklet and its 1983 second edition would become the single most requested resource in NIDA history.[21]

Although the parent antidrug movement was often credited to First Lady Nancy Reagan, then, it predated her own efforts by several years. She apparently embraced the issue in 1981 at the behest of Presidential advisor Michael Deaver and pollster Richard Wirthlin, who hoped to temper the First Lady's opulent image by providing her with a political "cause." Reagan's astrologer concurred, instructing her to "get involved in a volunteer project" and "play down all her privileged social connections." The First Lady would visit 64 American cities and eight foreign countries over the next seven years on behalf of the antidrug movement, lending it an enormous boost of publicity and morale. She also gave the campaign its most memorable slogan, advising an Oakland elementary school child in 1984 to "Just Say No" when a peer asked her to try drugs. The First Lady directed her strongest fire at so-called "casual" drug users, whom she deemed "accomplices to murder." Most famously,

Reagan even encouraged children to report their drug-using parents to law enforcement officials.[22]

Here Nancy Reagan was echoed—and, frequently, applauded—by African-American activists, who forged their own, mostly independent antidrug network. As early as 1983, for example, United Black Fund president Calvin Rolark asked schoolchildren in Washington, D.C. to tell the police about parents or other relatives who used narcotics. On most social and economic questions, of course, black voters diverged sharply from President Reagan and the First Lady. On the drug issue, however, they often acted as the Reagans's strongest supporters. The irony was captured by community organizer and erstwhile Presidential aspirant Jesse Jackson, who praised the White House's "Just Say No" campaign and blasted its welfare cuts in the same breath. "I am concerned about the collapse in morality and moral character," Jackson declared in 1986, during his own antidrug tour through American schools. "Reagan's budget . . . can only be fought by people who are alert and sober and sensitive." The spread of crack cocaine across the inner cities made antidrug messages especially urgent for black youth.[23]

African Americans also played a key role in winning passage of the 1986 Drug-Free Schools and Communities Act, which marked the next great escalation in the federal commitment to drug education. Up until then, blacks noted, Congress and the White House had failed to match their drug-fighting rhetoric with commensurate resources. "President Reagan proclaims how terrible drugs are and Nancy Reagan does TV commercials," noted one skeptical black spokesman in July of 1986. "This sounds good but Reagan Administration policies have crippled drug enforcement and education programs." Three months later, Reagan signed into law the single-greatest increase in drug-education funds in American history. Earmarking $700 million for school-based drug-prevention programs over the next three years, the measure also mandated that materials purchased under the law condemned all illegal drug use as "wrong and harmful." Finally, it assigned 10 percent of its state grants to projects that sent uniformed police into classrooms. At the time, only one nationwide antidrug program met that standard: Project Drug Abuse Resistance Education (DARE), the brainchild of Los Angeles police chief Darryl Gates. A decade later, more than three-quarters of the nation's school districts had adopted DARE.[24]

Sex: From the "Birds and Bees" to the "Sick Sixties"

Like drug education, sex education began after middle-class Americans realized that their own children were engaging in an allegedly working-class vice. It started 60 years earlier, at the dawn of the twentieth century, when a sensational series of exposes revealed that men across the social spectrum patronized prostitutes, contracted venereal disease, and—most alarmingly—transmitted the affliction to their wives. Led by New York dermatologist Prince Morrow, a small group of physicians pleaded with schools to teach "sex hygiene" to American children, especially to boys.

Men who visited prostitutes might be irredeemable, both physically and morally. Surely, though, schools could help save young innocents before it was too late.[25]

But how? Condemning the "conspiracy of silence" that had long shrouded the subject of sex, Morrow and his colleagues were less clear about what—precisely—schools should say. For the first two decades of the century, as "sex hygiene" spread slowly into American classrooms, it focused mainly upon the dangers of communicable disease. Prefiguring Harry J. Anslinger, however, critics complained that these lurid warnings would lure young people into evil. "Just at present our ears are dinned with the fad of sex hygiene," fumed a New Jersey clergyman in 1913. "If ever there was a system diabolically devised to injure our youth, and to make them voluptuaries, this is by far the most effective." Indeed, the first generation of sex educators were themselves profoundly ambivalent about their danger-centered approach. Even Harvard ex-president and sex-education stalwart Charles Eliot worried that continual admonitions about venereal disease might "invite youth to experiment in sexual vice."[26] Starting in the 1920s, then, sex educators would seek to develop "positive" rather than "negative" curricula. But they also had to make sure that any new approach was not so positive that it promoted sex. "In most biology work, one of the most important aims is to awaken interest to lead to experimentation," explained a New York science teacher. Yet "the aim of sex instruction" was "the exact opposite": to teach children without "exciting curiosity." Educators seized upon the study of nature, soon known as "the birds and the bees," which seemed to demonstrate the biological basis of monogamous marriage but skirted the sticky question of what monogamous human beings actually did. By dissecting a lily, for example, students learned that "all life comes from eggs," and that eggs must be "fertilized"; but they did not discuss the ways that people might accomplish this feat. After World War II, sex educators supplemented or replaced the nature-study approach with units that focused directly upon "family life" in the United States. But here, too, they downplayed or ignored the sexual act itself. When California teachers discovered a chapter about sex in their 1947 textbook, *Marriage and Family Relations*, they carefully cut out the chapter before distributing the book to their students.[27]

By the 1960s, however, sex educators could no longer keep sex out of their textbooks—or their classrooms. The topic seemed to saturate every other American institution, from literature and film to fashion and music. Educators needed an approach that would acknowledge this "Sexual Revolution" but also tame its excesses, particularly pre-marital intercourse. They found a champion in Mary Calderone, founder of the Sex Information and Education Council of the United States (SIECUS). A physician and former Planned Parenthood official, Calderone insisted that sex was a normal and even beautiful dimension of the human experience. But she also sought to channel it into its traditional venue, the marriage bed, condemning "casual" heterosexual relations as well as homosexual activity of every kind. In their denigration of human sexuality, Calderone argued, previous educators had sought in vain to "impose" an ethical code; in the future, she hoped, schools would lead "open discussions" that let children reach their "own decisions." Like sex and alcohol educators, however, she never doubted that truly open discussions would confirm her ethics—especially her commitment to monogamy. Out in the schools, teachers who conducted these dialogues inevitably directed them toward a similar conclusion. "We don't lecture or give sermons," explained one school official in 1968. "The truth is, though, we *are* selling middle-class morality."[28]

For a large sector of the American middle class, however, the mere mention of "discussion" in this realm conjured a world *without* morality and a society crazed by uncurbed sex—the "Sick Sixties," as critics called it. As in the case of drug education, then, a mostly rhetorical campaign for value-neutrality spawned an enormous grassroots revolt. Sex education promotes a "pluralistic viewpoint" by refusing to "take sides," complained a California minister in 1969. When it comes to sex, however, "we *must* take sides," he underlined. "Who among us will be so foolhardy as to say of our children . . . that they are fully equipped to decide their own basis for morality?" Indeed, another Californian added that the entire social order rested upon absolute standards of behavior. "There is an authoritarian element in moral education, training, and discipline," he emphasized. "The fact that truth telling and respect for the person and property of others is a virtue should not be subjected to 'open discussion.' To teach a youth that theft is wrong [is] to relate a fact which *does indeed* foreclose 'discussion.'" Whereas sex educators instructed students to "set their own standards of conduct," a third critic noted, the Bible laid down "a set of inflexible rules"—including, of course, a prohibition upon extra-marital sex.[29]

Worst of all, these foes alleged, the very impulse to discuss the rule encouraged children to flout it. Even as they blasted sex education for abandoning fixed codes of behavior, then, critics also contended that it promoted its own preferred behavior: sex itself. "Sexucators [sic] claim if you 'understand' sex, it will lose its compulsive power—which is just like saying if you understand nutrition, you won't get hungry," wrote one activist in 1969. "The sexologists' creed is 'Learn by doing.'" Across the country, armies of activists spread sensational but apocryphal tales about the ways that sex education put theory into practice. One teacher disrobed at school; another had sex with her students, while the class watched; another herded children into a closet so they could fondle each other; and so on. The far-right John Birch Society even claimed that sex education was a "filthy Communist plot," designed to keep young Americans obsessed with fornication. The charge caught the eye of bemused Chicago columnist Mike Royko, who suggested his own titles for subversive literature: "Want to Know? Ask Ho," "Hit the Hay, by Fidel and Che," "The Birds and the Bees—Who Gives Them Their Orders?," and "Let Mao Tell You How."[30]

To date, no solid evidence has ever shown that sex education promotes sex. Yet we also have very little data to suggest—as did Mary Calderone—that sex education can *prevent* sex or channel it into desirable forms.[31] To its foes, sex education reflected an extraordinarily naive view of human nature as well as a dangerous underestimation of physical temptation. Why presume that children—if confronted with a wide array of choices—would arrive at abstinence? Wouldn't they just as likely yield to their urges? However fabricated their charges against sex education ("Now, children, go fondle each other in the closet while I finish disrobing"), critics correctly identified a huge tension in the subject—indeed, in the entire panoply of courses on sex, drugs, and alcohol. Lest students engage in their own brand of learning-by-doing, educators eschewed graphic descriptions of the dangers inherent in sexual or drug-related activity. They turned instead to "discussion," where they struggled to avoid any mention of the pleasures linked to these activities.

Symbolizing a decadent culture that had lost its moral compass, sex education would become a lightning rod for the rise of the New Right in the 1960s and 1970s.[32] This coalition would score its first and greatest victory in 1980, helping the GOP capture both the White House and the Senate. Just one year later, Congress passed a measure mandating "abstinence only" messages in all federally funded sex education programs. Sex education already aimed at abstinence, of course, if only indirectly: by "discussing" sex, educators presumed, children would be swayed against it. But under the Adolescent Family Life Act of 1981—nicknamed "The Chastity Act"—nothing would be left to chance.[33] Like drug education curricula, sex education programs would have to eliminate even the patina of value-neutrality if they wished to feed at the federal trough.

Conclusion: The Passion of Joycelyn Elders, M.D.

The problem of pleasure returns us to Joycelyn Elders, who had the temerity to mention it. As Surgeon General under Bill Clinton, Elders had already offended the Right with her views on AIDS and drug decriminalization. Significantly, however, it was her remark on masturbation that led to her dismissal. Elders made the comment at a 1994 AIDS conference, where a psychiatrist asked her if other methods of sexual release might be encouraged in order to fight the disease. "What do you think are the prospects for a discussion and promotion of masturbation?" he inquired.[34]

The psychiatrist's serendipitous choice of terms—"discussion and promotion"—encapsulated the two central poles in twentieth-century American moral education, as well as the central dilemma surrounding sex, drugs, and alcohol. As Ed McClellan has taught us, Americans have long debated whether children should practice righteousness or inquire into it. Yet neither model fits the sex–drugs–alcohol arena, where "practice" is verboten—and inquiry might provoke it. To millions of Americans, indeed, "discussion" and "promotion" in these subjects are one and the same. Although Elders simply said masturbation "should be taught," then, listeners presumed that she was encouraging schools to teach children how to do it—and Clinton fired her. On its face, the decision seemed absurd: as *New York Times* columnist Frank Rich quipped, "the President knows that anyone who needs masturbation lessons is unlikely to meet the minimal intelligence requirement for school attendance anyway."[35] But at the level of culture—and, especially, of history—it made sense. A model based on individual decision-making simply cannot accommodate pleasure, which might cause individuals to make the wrong decision.

Into the present, our sex and drug programs continue to maintain the fiction of independent choice. Yet, curricula in both areas have moved steadily *away* from choice, presenting only those facts and arguments that would tend to discourage activity. Even more, many of the "facts" are simply false. With only the flimsiest of evidence, for example, federally funded sex education programs in the 1990s told children that the HIV virus could pass through condoms. Hence, using a condom to guard against AIDS "is like playing Russian roulette," declared one curriculum, entitled—without irony—*Choosing the Best*.[36] Meanwhile, drug education programs like DARE continued to warn children that all illegal drug use put them in mortal danger—an easily refutable claim.[37] Faced with strong evidence that this approach did not deter drug use, DARE changed its approach in 2001 to emphasize what it called—again, without irony—"responsible decision making." Instead of lecturing on the evils of narcotics, police officers and classroom teachers would conduct "honest discussions" about them.[38]

Of course, a truly honest discussion would have to acknowledge the potentials for pleasure as well as peril that lurk within sex, drugs, and alcohol. But any such discussion in the foreseeable future is probably a pipe dream, to borrow a term from twentieth-century drug culture. In the late 1990s, a Philadelphia teacher was transferred from her school after an allegation that she told students she had experienced her best orgasm while reading a book under a tree. Like all such fabrications, the story contained a small kernel of truth: the teacher had told her students that sex was "fun." Yet she went on to emphasize that it was "dangerous fun." Indeed, she told her class, "[t]here are other things you can do, you can go for a walk together, go roller skating, *read a book*." Even in a plea for abstinence, it seemed, the mere mention of pleasure in American schools was simply too hot for Americans to touch.[39]

Notes

1. J. Mace Andress, *The Teaching of Hygiene in the Grades* (Boston: Houghton Mifflin, 1917), 87–88.
2. "School Drinking Urged," *New York Times*, January 13, 1966: 41.
3. Russell Baker, "Observer: Bad News for the Old Booze School," *New York Times*, January 18, 1966: 36; "Idea of Drinking in Schools Scored," ibid., January 14, 1966: 41; "School Daze," ibid., January 16, 1966, IV, 2.
4. I have borrowed this rich phrase from John C. Burnham, *Bad Habits: Drinking, Smoking, Taking Drugs, Gambling, Sexual Misbehavior, and Swearing in American History* (New York: New York University Press, 1993). Especially after the repeal of national prohibition in 1933, Burnham shows, these formerly tabooed habits became increasingly "normalized" for middle-class Americans. As I argue below and elsewhere, however, the middle class continued to insist that *schools* forbid these behaviors. Jonathan Zimmerman, " 'One's Total World View Comes Into Play': America's Culture War Over Alcohol Education, 1945–1964," *History of Education Quarterly* 42 (Winter 2002): 486n42, 492n63.
5. Lawrence A. Cremin, *The Transformation of the School: Progressivism in American Education, 1876–1957* (New York: Vintage, 1961), esp. 127–176, 274–327; Arthur Zilversmit, *Changing Schools: Progressive Education in Theory and Practice. 1930–1960* (Chicago: University of Chicago Press, 1993), 19–36; Diane Ravitch, *Left Back: A Century of Failed School Reforms* (New York: Simon & Schuster, 2000), esp. 162–201. As Larry Cuban and other scholars have reminded us, the vast majority of actual classroom instruction in the United States has hewed to teacher-centered "traditional" methods rather than to child-centered "progressive" ones. Yet the persistence of "reform talk" in most academic subjects—that is, the perpetual demand to make these subjects more activity-based—differentiates them sharply from the sex/drugs/alcohol nexus, where (as Morris Chafetz would discover) the mere suggestion of "learning-by-doing" is enough to provoke a scandal. Larry Cuban, *How Teachers Taught: Constancy and Change in American Classrooms,*

1890–1980 (New York: Longman, 1984); Linda M. McNeil, *Contradictions of Control: School Structure and School Knowledge* (New York: Routledge, 1986), esp. 157–190; David K. Cohen, "Teaching Practice: Plus Que Ca Change...," in Philip W. Jackson, ed., *Contributing to Educational Change: Perspectives on Research and Practice* (Berkeley, CA: McCutchan, 1988), esp. 44–47.

6. B. Edward McClellan, *Moral Education in America: Schools and the Shaping of Character from Colonial Times to the Present* (New York: Teachers College Press, 1999), 46–61.
7. We should note that both sides of our debate on moral education have embraced the "activity" mantra at the heart of twentieth-century school reform. Condemning the didactic, book-centered style of nineteenth-century pedagogy, most famously associated with *McGuffey's Readers*, moral educators aimed to construct lessons that vigorously engaged children in their own learning. But one camp emphasized group activity as a route to proper habits and character formation, while the other stressed intellectual discussion and individual decision-making. Compare Edward A. Wynne, "For-Character Education," *The Construction of Children's Character*, 96th Yearbook of the National Society for the Study of Education, Part II (Chicago: University of Chicago Press, 1997), 67–68 and Alfle Kohn, "The Trouble with Character Education," ibid., 158.
8. Robert D. Russell, "Alcohol," *NEA Journal* 53 (1964): 66.
9. The now-classic article on the neglect of pleasure in sex education is Michelle Fine, "Sexuality, Schooling, and Adolescent Females: The Missing Discourse of Desire," *Harvard Educational Review* 58 (Feb. 1988): 29–53. Since mid-century, to be sure, some curricula and even some textbooks have included frank passages about sexual instincts and pleasure. Yet pleasure is almost never mentioned in the day-to-day practice of American sex education, as Fine and other ethnographers have documented. In classes about drugs and alcohol, meanwhile, schools teach that peer pressure and low self-esteem cause youngsters to ingest dangerous substances. But rarely do curricula cite the most obvious cause of all: alcohol and drugs can bring feelings of euphoria to the human psyche—in a word, pleasure. Bonnie K. Trudell, "Inside a Ninth-Grade Sexuality Classroom: The Process of Knowledge Construction," in James T. Sears, ed., *Sexuality and the Curriculum: The Politics and Practices of Sexuality Education* (New York: Teachers College Press, 1992), 221, 223; Jonathan Zimmerman, "Our Blind Spot About Drugs," *Washington Post*, April 12, 2002: A31.
10. Joycelyn Elders with David Chanoff, *Joycelyn Elders, M.D.: From Sharecropper's Daughter to Surgeon General of the United States of America* (New York: William Morrow, 1996), 331; Thomas W. Laqueur, *Solitary Sex: A Cultural History of Masturbation* (New York: Zone Books, 2003), 416.
11. Charles H. Stowell, *A Primer of Health: Practical Hygiene for Pupils in Primary and Lower Grades* (New York: Silver, Burdett and Co., 1906), 123. The information about Mary Hunt in this paragraph and the ensuing ones comes from Jonathan Zimmerman, *Distilling Democracy: Alcohol Education in America's Public Schools, 1880–1925* (Lawrence: University Press of Kansas, 1999).
12. I am thinking, of course, about the television campaigns by the Partnership for a Drug-Free America, showing a young man with an egg and a frying pan. "This is your brain," he says, holding the egg aloft. "And this," he adds, as he cracks the egg into the pan, "is your brain on drugs. Any questions?" In 1998, the Office of National Drug Control Policy reintroduced the egg-and-frying-pan concept to kick off a $2 billion, 5-year campaign against youth drug use. Mathea Falco, *The Making of a Drug-Free America: Programs That Work* (New York: Times Books, 1992), 166; Michael T. Stephenson and Kim Witte, "Creating Fear in a Risky World: Generating Effective Health Risk Messages," in Ronald E. Rice and Charles K. Atkin, eds., *Public Communication Campaigns*, 3rd edn (Thousand Oaks, CA: Sage Publications, 2001), 90.

13. W.B. Ferguson, "Temperance Teaching and Recent Legislation in Connecticut," *Educational Review* 23 (1902): 242; "Discussion," *NEA Proceedings* 39 (1900): 256. Of course, Mary Hunt and the WCTU could also cite Scripture—*against* the doctrine of learning by doing. When God handed down the Ten Commandments, Hunt argued, He never paused to consider that His "Thou Shalt Nots" would encourage people to steal, murder, or commit adultery. "How unfortunate," quipped one of Hunt's supporters, "that the Bible is so unpedagogical as to teach the Decalogue as well as the Beatitudes." Mary Hunt, "These Are the Commandments," *School Physiology Journal* 6 (January 1897): 84–85; Macy A. Smith, "Some Untenable Criticisms on the Temperance Education Laws," ibid. 12 (February 1903): 92–93.
14. McClellan, *Moral Education in America*, 50–52; Zimmerman, *Distilling Democracy*, 131, 130, 133.
15. Gail Milgram, "A Historical Review of Alcohol Education Research and Comments," *Journal of Alcohol and Drug Education* 21 (1976): 4; "All Views Necessary," *Stillwater [OK] News-Press*, February 9, 1956, "1956" folder, box 9, Marty Mann Papers, George Arents Research Library, Syracuse University, Syracuse, New York. For an overview and interpretation of alcohol education in the postwar period, see Zimmerman, " 'One's Total World View Comes Into Play.' "
16. Catherine Gilbert Murdock, *Domesticating Drink: Women, Men, and Alcohol in America, 1870–1940* (Baltimore: Johns Hopkins University Press, 1998), 156; "A Call for Mark Hopkins," *Union Signal* 81 (1955): 235, quoted in Raymond G. McCarthy, *Teen-Agers and Alcohol: A Handbook for the Educator* (New Haven, CT: Yale Center of Alcohol Studies, 1956), 63; Ralph W. Daniel, "Alcohol Education and a Social Hangover," *PTA Magazine* 56 (December 1961): 32; Gilbert M. Shimmel, "Content and Method in Controversial Areas," *Journal of School Health* 31 (1961): 231; Zimmerman, " 'One's Total World View Comes Into Play,' " 475.
17. "A Message from Commissioner Harry J. Anslinger" (ms, n.p. [1951]), "Education—History" vertical file, Drug Enforcement Administration Library, Pentagon City, Virginia; "High School Users of Narcotics at 1-in-200 Ratio," *New York Times*, June 13, 1951: 51; "Three Narcotics Bills Signed by Dewey," *New York Times*, April 4, 1952: 13; Mrs. Lynn Straton Morris, "Should Narcotics Education be Extended to the Juvenile?" *Congressional Digest* 33 (December 1954): 312; *Report to the House Committee on Ways and Means From the Subcommittee on Narcotics on the Illicit Traffic in Narcotics . . .* (Washington, DC: Government Printing Office, 1956), 15, "Education—History" vertical file, DEA Library. On America's widening "drug crisis" during the 1950s, see Jill Jonnes, *Hep-Cats, Narcs, and Pipe Dreams: A History of America's Romance with Illegal Drugs* (Baltimore: Johns Hopkins University Press, 1999 [1996]), chapter 7, esp. pp. 137–140; on Anslinger, the most complete source is John C. McWilliams, *The Protectors: Harry J. Anslinger and the Federal Bureau of Narcotics, 1930–1962* (Newark, DE: University of Delaware Press, 1990).
18. "The Drug Scene: High Schools are Higher Now," *Newsweek* 75 (February 16, 1970): 66; *Congressional Record*, November 19, 1969: H12809-10, "Education—1952–1969" vertical file; David C. Acheson to William Haake, n.d. [January 1966], enclosed with Henry L. Giordano to Acheson, January 14, 1966, "Education—History" vertical file; John Finlator, "Educational Aspects of the Drug Problem—Education the Key?" *I.N.E.O.A. 9th Annual Conference Report* (1968): 42–43, "Education—1952–1969" vertical file; idem., "The Drug Scene: The Scope of the Problem Faced by the Schools" (ms, 1970), 2, "Education 1970–1972" vertical file; "What the U.S. Office of Education is doing about Drug Education," *Today's Education* 61 (February 1972): 37, "Education 1970–1972" vertical file, all in DEA Library.
19. Bernard Bard, "The Shameful Truth and Consequences of School Drug Programs," *Parents Magazine* 49 (September 1974): 50; Donald J. Wolk, "Four Rules for Teaching

About Drugs," in Donald J. Wolk, ed., *Drugs and Youth* (Washington, DC: National Council for the Social Studies, 1971), 76; "Dr. Helen Nowlis Named to Head U.S. Drug Education," *Drugs and Drug Abuse Education Newsletter* 2 (September 1971): 1, 6.

20. Chwee Lye Chng, "The Goal of Abstinence: Implications for Drug Education," *Journal of Drug Education* 11 (1981): 14; Dan Baum, *Smoke and Mirrors: The War on Drugs and the Politics of Failure* (New York: Little, Brown & Co., 1996), 88–90, 99. See also Marsha Manatt, *Parents, Peers and Pot* (Rockville, MD: National Institute on Drug Abuse, 1979), chapter 1.

21. Peggy Mann, *Marijuana Alert* (New York: McGraw-Hill, 1985), 413, 416; David F. Musto, *The American Disease: Origins of Narcotic Control*, 3rd edn (New York: Oxford University Press, 1999), 265; Jonnes, *Hep-Cats, Narcs, and Pipe Dreams*, 393; Baum, *Smoke and Mirrors*, 122; Marsha Manatt, *Parents, Peers and Pot II: Parents In Action* (Rockville, MD: National Institute on Drug Abuse, 1983), 36.

22. Richard A. Hawley, "The Bumpy Road to Drug-Free Schools," *Phi Delta Kappan* 72 (December 1990): 312; Kitty Kelley, *Nancy Reagan: The Unauthorized Biography* (New York: Simon & Schuster, 1991), 368–371, 389; Baum, *Smoke and Mirrors*, 200; "Drug Education Gets an F," *U.S. News and World Report* 101 (October 13, 1986): 64.

23. "Antidrug Rally Draws 150 Southeast Youth," *Washington Post*, November 20, 1983: 133; "Jackson's Ambitious Drug Crusade," ibid., March 17, 1986: A1; Nadine Brown, "Kids on crack need adults," *Michigan Chronicle*, October 18, 1986: A7.

24. Ed Towns, "Crack: We Need Cabinet Official," *Amsterdam News*, July 27, 1986: 30; D.M. Gorman, "The Failure of Drug Education," *Public Interest* 129 (Fall 1997): 57; Peggy Mann, "We're Teaching our Kids to Use Drugs," *Readers' Digest* 131 (November 1987): 109; Jeff Elliott, "Just Say Nonsense," *Washington Monthly* 25 (May 1993): 20; "Just Say Life Skills," *Time* 148 (November 11, 1996): 70.

25. The most complete and judicious account of sex education in the United States is Jeffrey P. Moran, *Teaching Sex: The Shaping of Twentieth-Century Adolescence* (Cambridge, MA: Harvard University Press, 2000). I have also benefited from two subsequent works, which build but also expand upon Moran's interpretation: Julian B. Carter, "Birds, Bees, and Venereal Disease: Toward an Intellectual History of Sex Education," *Journal of the History of Sexuality* 10 (2001): 213–249 and Janice M. Irvine, *Talk About Sex: The Battles over Sex Education in the United States* (Berkeley and Los Angeles: University of California Press, 2002).

26. Moran, *Teaching Sex*, 25; "Sex Education," *Vigilance* 27 (1913): 6, quoted in John C. Burnham, *Paths Into American Culture: Psychology, Medicine, and Morals* (Philadelphia: Temple University Press, 1988), 163; Charles W. Eliot, untitled remarks, *Social Hygiene* 1 (1914): 2, quoted in Carter, "Birds, Bees, and Venereal Disease," 225.

27. Edgar F. Van Buskirk, "How Can Sex Education be Made a Part of Biology?" *School Science and Mathematics* 19 (1919): 336, quoted in Philip J. Pauly, "The Development of High School Biology: New York City, 1900–1925," *Isis* 82 (1991): 684; Carter, "Birds, Bees, and Venereal Disease," 244; *Third Report of Joint Fact-Finding Committee on Un-American Activities* (Sacramento: California Senate, 1947), 324, California State Archives, Sacramento, California.

28. "Playboy Interview: Dr. Mary Calderone," *Playboy*, April 1970, reel 9, Women and Health Collection, microfilm edn. (Berkeley: Women's History Research Center, 1975); Marjorie F. Iseman, "Sex Ed," in Stewat E. Fraser, ed., *Sex, Schools, and Society: International Perspectives* (Nashville: Aurora Publishers, 1972), 159. For an expanded version of the interpretation presented here, see Jonathan Zimmerman, *Whose America? Culture Wars in the Public Schools* (Cambridge, MA: Harvard University Press, 2002), 186–211.

29. Statement of Reverend W.B. Woodard (ms, April 10, 1969), Legislative Papers 175: 231; H. Edward Rowe, "Statement Concerning Moral Guidelines Rough Draft" (ms, July 24, 1972), folder 442, Department of Education Records; statement of M.H. Reynolds, Jr. (ms, April 16, 1969), Legislative Papers 175: 231, all in California State Archives.
30. Tom Anderson, "Straight Talk," *Southern Farm Publications* (June 1969), "Sex Education" folder, box 7, William Ford Papers, Bentley Historical Library, Ann Arbor, Michigan; Irvine, *Talk About Sex*, 55–57; "Sees Reds Under Beds," *Leawood Sun* [Shawnee Mission, Kansas], February 6, 1969; Mike Royko, "The New Peril: A Red in Bed," *Chicago Daily News*, February 24, 1969, both in folder 46, accession 73-150-81 M35, Mary Steichen Calderone Papers, Arthur and Elizabeth Schlesinger Library, Radcliffe College, Harvard University.
31. Even the most zealous advocates of sex education have acknowledged that they simply do not know if it "works." See, e.g., the 1997 report by the National Campaign to Prevent Teen Pregnancy: "It is not likely that there are any simple, easy-to-implement prevention programs . . . that will substantially change adolescent sexual behavior." Douglas Kirby, *No Easy Answers: Research Findings on Programs to Reduce Teen Pregnancy* (Washington, DC: National Campaign to Prevent Teen Pregnancy, 1997), 14, quoted in Irvine, *Talk About Sex*, 237n3.
32. On sex education and the rise of the New Right, see Moran, *Teaching Sex*, 178–193; Zimmerman, *Whose America?*, 193–206; Irvine, *Talk About Sex*, 35–80.
33. Irvine, *Talk About Sex*, 90; Moran, *Teaching Sex*, 204.
34. Elders, *Joycelyn Elders, M.D.*, 331.
35. Frank Rich, "The Last Taboo," *New York Times*, December 18, 1994: 15, quoted in Laqueur, *Solitary Sex*, 416. All of these events transpired before President Clinton's own well-publicized sexual escapades, of course, in which masturbation—not to mention a cigar—played leading roles.
36. Irvine, *Talk About Sex*, 121.
37. David Wagner, *The New Temperance: The American Obsession with Sin and Vice* (Boulder, CO: Westview Press, 1997), 73–78; Jonathan Zimmerman, "Amotivation and Other Syndromes," *Baltimore Sun*, June 14, 1991.
38. "DARE Checks Into Rehab: A New Strategy for the Popular Anti-Drug Program," *Newsweek*, February 26, 2001: 56; Jonathan Zimmerman, "Our Duplicitous Drug Dialogues," *Washington Post*, February 26, 2001: Al 9.
39. Irvine, *Talk About Sex*, 124.

This page intentionally left blank

Chapter 13

Monuments and Morals: The Nationalization of Civic Instruction

John Bodnar

Modern nations emerged in the West in the late eighteenth century as the power of religious authority declined. Benedict Anderson has explained well how these nations created new visions of human destiny that were pointed more in the direction of happiness on earth than in eternal salvation in heaven. The power of God on earth and of kings gave way to rising expectations of human happiness in the here and now. As subjects became citizens, the source of moral authority changed as well. Human nature and individual happiness were now recognized as rationales for judging what was right and proper to a greater extent. This did not mean that calls were no longer made for individuals to sacrifice their self-interest or submit to higher authority. For now people also talked increasingly about what was good for the nation or for society. The nationalist revolutions in eighteenth-century America and France brought about the promise of citizen rights but they also would encourage calls for patriotic service and sacrifice for the public good. These new nations faced the task of trying to reconcile dreams that were both personal and national.

Over time this shift in the center of moral authority would have profound consequences. As human liberty and reason were seen as keys to happiness on earth, the power of churches, patriarchs, and sacred scriptures declined. It was not that the nation replaced God as a source of moral authority. It was more that they now had to co-exist. The discussion of what was right and proper became more contested. Tensions emerged along lines of thought that might be characterized as sacred and secular. The idea that moral virtue was a fixed notion easily transferable between generations was challenged. Since the nation, in fact, was imagined to stand above various forms of sectarian and political outlooks, it took on the task of trying to contain and merge such differences. And, inevitably, it mounted its own campaign to define a new form of moral virtue that was worldly in tone. Public or national virtue brought to human life a greater sense of social rather than sacred time and a feeling that life was to be lived more intently in the present. And yet it demanded its own degree of loyalty and created its own set of hallowed texts and ideals. Anderson explains well how nations inspired love because they seemed to stand above any special group or interest. As he says, citizens came to accept generally the idea that, for instance, dying for one's nation had a tone of "moral grandeur" whereas sacrifice of one's party or church did not. This is not to say that religious belief never served the need for national sacrifice or the pursuit of the common good. Rather it is to suggest that by the twentieth century the locus of power and obligation had shifted so strongly to nations that millions were willing to die for their defense.[1]

Although the quest for individual happiness was part of the rhetoric of the American Revolution, at the heart of the movement for independence was an explicitly moral vision that scholars have defined as civic republicanism. As Gordon Wood has observed, this ideal was essentially the "ideology of the Enlightenment" and a source of "public morality and values." In this view men found their greatest fulfillment not in following the sacred scripture but in participating in the governing of a republic. Such a position was clearly meant to erode the power of hierarchy and monarchy and offer (influential) men the major share of political power. But republicanism was no mere rationale for a simple quest for influence. It was also a broadly based outlook that placed a sense of responsibility on all men who aspired to pursue their happiness and to participate actively in national life. Such men had an obligation to be virtuous, willing to sacrifice purely private interests for the common good. The republic—and the pursuit of happiness by free citizens—could only be sustained if its public life were shaped by men of character who could temper their personal drives with a sense of obligation to others. Wood has argued that the revolutionaries who helped to form America had a utopian dream that the moral and social order would be led by (white) men of virtue. The future of the nation was contingent, in other words, not so much on religious faith or divine rule but on the exercise of human reason and character. It was a matter of personal and public morality. The power of monarchs was consigned to the past. A hierarchical society would be supplanted by a more egalitarian society where men drew upon the better side of their nature and were selfless and benevolent. Wood sees in this certainly a sense of "radical individualism." But he affirms as well a strain of selflessness and the secularization of the Christian belief in the equality of all souls before God. For Wood, society could not survive if citizens did not have a sense of obligation to the common good and the needs of others. He writes that "virtue became less the harsh self-sacrifice of antiquity and more the willingness to get along with others for the sake of peace and prosperity." The hope was that if one wanted to be free to exercise their rights and pursue happiness, they would have to respect the rights and happiness of others.[2]

The tensions inherent in the nationalization of moral thought soon manifested themselves in the experience of the new nation. The work of Edward McClellan, for instance, reveals well how extensive and contentious were debates in America over moral instruction and ideals. In his particular focus on public schools, he is able to document a long-term transformation in the goals and objectives of moral standards. In the early nineteenth century, before the idea of the new nation was firmly entrenched, it was the rise of public schools themselves that actually helped to erode an older locus of moral authority that was centered in families and households and designed to regulate the moral behavior of household members. By extending his story into the later stages of the twentieth century, moreover, he is able to show that eventually even the power of the public schools waned, challenged by both a continuation of traditional religious interests and a growing (and highly secular) fascination with personal growth and success. One of his central conclusions is absolutely indispensable for understanding the history of moral instruction in America. "As Americans gained confidence in their society," he argued, "many of them lost their hard-edged religious orthodoxy and moral rigidity."[3]

McClellan's baseline for examining the transformation of moral education in America is the colonial society. In this eighteenth-century world, moral instruction served the needs of households and small locales to preserve their adherence to patriarchy and doctrinal teachings. Personal desire—especially for women and children—was tightly governed. He notes how parents were particularly central to this exercise and often conducted family devotions, offered theological training, and used severe discipline to make their points. Moral visions seldom extended horizontally to strangers or to a larger society. It was nationalism that introduced the concept that individuals were bound to others in a society moving through time toward earthly ends.[4]

The growing power of the nation over ethical thinking was dramatic. McClellan shows how political leaders like Thomas Jefferson, Benjamin Franklin, and others grew concerned over the ability of early national society to withstand the divisive pressures of sectarianism and parochialism. One response they had to this problem was the creation of state systems of pubic schools that would offer not only instruction in practical subjects but also teach "republican values" and encourage loyalty to the new nation. The privileged place of the household and the small community was suddenly disrupted by secular and national projects that promoted not only a greater sense of individualism but submission to national authority. McClellan also noted the increasing mobility of early American society as another factor that tended to erode household authority and foster a desire for public schools. These institutions received increasing public support not only because they appeared to offer large numbers of young citizens skills they would need to survive, but also because they appeared to offer them training as well in forms of public virtue and patriotism as they were leaving the "protective environment" of the home and the small community. If a society that was increasingly egalitarian and mobile offered new opportunities for personal success, it also required in the eyes of many a more vigorous public effort at moral instruction. Now citizens worried over the moral learning of people they did not know. But the concern was not eternal salvation but the health and order of the nation itself.[5]

Certainly religious instruction continued in nineteenth-century churches and families, but the ethical teaching of civic virtue and national loyalty was rapidly becoming the only uniform and standardized form of moral instruction. Woman, often seen as inherently moral creatures, dominated the ranks of teachers and were central to this public effort. And throughout the century there was an increase in the use of standardized textbooks that stressed obedience to the laws of men, civic obligation, and patriotism. McClellan astutely points out as well that the thrust of this instruction was aimed not so much at fostering personal adjustment and happiness but at building character and restraining unbridled individualism.[6]

As American society became more complex and diverse in the twentieth century, educators had to broaden their approach. The older emphasis on character and civic obligation was retained, but it was joined by a more diligent effort to recognize the personal aptitudes. Tensions evident in national culture from the beginning of the nation between the quest for personal happiness and civic duty were more apparent. Advocates of "progressive" education attempted to both discover and reinforce the pursuit of individual interests on the part of students and, at the same time, sustain the more traditional effort to instill patriotism and civic obligation. Progressive educators, from time to time, even arranged for religious instruction outside of schools to be part of a daily schedule. And almost invariably they were interested in order and efficiency, seeking to impart practical skills to fit people into a new urban and industrial work structure as much as they were to encourage the quest for personal fulfillment. As McClellan argues, the proponents of progressive education were tied less to any specific moral principles and more interested in cultivating a flexible approach to morality by which individuals would learn to make "moral judgements" through the use of reason in particular situations. He observes that the progressive educators did not abandon the concern for a ordered national community but their path to order and stability was less reliant on imparting character traits and more reliant on "one's ability to foster the creation of a more humane and democratic society." In a sense this newer approach—which proved influential well into the twentieth century—was an extension of the basic faith of the Enlightenment in human reason to improve life on earth.

The end point for McClellan's history of moral instruction is not, however, the triumph of progressive views but their demise after World War II. In the postwar era Americans tended to favor forms of instruction that advanced the cause of individual success in society; the study of civic obligation and character building took up less classroom time. Certainly there was considerable discussion about the need to temper individual forms of hatred and create a more just and tolerant society. But the progressive hope for a balance between social and individual forms of morality seemed to be leaning more in the direction of the latter.[7]

McClellan has made it clear that the progressive moral vision was attacked eventually by a highly developed sense of individualism and careerism. But it was also challenged continually by a set of traditional values that blended the timelessness of religious dogma with an undying faith in the solitary individual. This is made clear in Jonathan Zimmerman's study of "culture wars" in American schools. In part, progressive perspectives were always open to the critique of traditionalists because they were contingent upon a malleable sense of morality. They were designed to be flexible in order to solve social problems as they were identified and, consequently, more likely to be based in social science than in longstanding dogma. Traditional moral outlooks, however, remained riveted to a curious blend of religious faith and the romance of individual freedom and national greatness. God and nation were joined in the minds of traditionalists as venerable concepts. Traditionalists attacked school textbooks that stressed economic and social analysis over the celebration of national greatness. They favored a form of moral and civic education that has been described by Morris Janowitz as "uncomplicated religious ritual" such as the Pledge of Allegiance and an "uncritical sense of patriotism," a position that made them anti-progressive. Zimmerman shows, for instance, how patriotic societies in the 1920s joined forces to bar any textbook that "defames the nation's founders." And patriotic societies were vehement in their critique of social studies in the 1940s and 1950s. But traditionalists who linked the idea of the nation to a divine plan were no civic republicans. The moral vision of the founding generation was more profane and benevolent toward those who held different beliefs, and staunch in its defense of the separation of church and state. A moral outlook embedded in the concept of a nation under God was more intolerant of diverse faiths and state regulation of society.[8]

As moral debate became more secular and more connected to the ideal of the nation, citizens were forced to construct new images and symbols that addressed this vast public discussion. Flags, oaths, and monuments came to dominate public spaces considerably more than crosses and saints. Indeed, saints became more secular. Public architecture adopted forms and styles from antiquity in order to reach back to a time before the power of the Church had taken hold in the Western world. Scholars have often noted debates over moral values in schools. Less appreciated has been the vast discussion over the design and use of public symbols and the manner in which they have contributed to the larger debate over national values. These images and icons were very much a part of the long-term project to nationalize moral life and, as such, were inevitably inscribed with the crosscurrents of patriotism, religion, progressivism, and individualism. Jenny Franchot has written about the ways the status of religious images and texts have declined in the culture of modern nations. Only recently, however, have scholars paid attention to the iconography that emerged in their place. The remainder of this essay will attempt to explore two of the most important public monuments in American national life—the Statue of Liberty and the Lincoln Memorial—as a way to understand the role the new public icons played in discussions over civic and moral teachings.[9]

The Statue of Liberty

The Statue of Liberty aspired to venerate the central ideal of the American Revolution—human liberty. In the purest sense it ignored moral standpoints of religions, kings, or even nations. It was not progressive or civic-minded in the sense that it hoped to blend individual or societal needs; it was a statement of a timeless virtue to be sure, but one meant only to serve the individual not the state or God. Since its dedication in 1886, it has served as an icon of American political culture and has been a central part of the moral vision of American nationalism. Although Americans and others have interpreted the ideal of human freedom in many ways, this ideal was firmly inscribed in founding documents of the new nation such as the Declaration of Independence and the Bill of Rights. People were no longer considered to be subjects of a monarch but citizens imbued with rights by virtue of their being human. The great revolutions in America and France—imbued with an optimistic faith in human nature—not only sought to end the rule of monarchs and clerics but were determined to replace existing forms of authority and place the future into the hands of citizens who would be free to pursue their desires. At the moment of its birth, the national society contained the seeds of rebellion toward efforts to preach restraint of any sort to individuals in families and communities.

Certainly there were limits in the early nation to the idea of who was free and who was a citizen. Women and racial minorities did not enjoy the same level of rights as powerful white men who manifested a continued attachment to patriarchy. Clear limits existed to moral visions of the time. But in creating a new political society called a nation and placing human liberty at its core, the stage was set to alter public discussion of moral behavior. The frame now moved slowly not only from the needs of the monarchy but from the needs of patriarchs who headed households and led the Revolution to the specific interests of individuals. The upshot of this transformation was that moral debate now centered mostly on how much individual freedom could be tolerated. Efforts to expand the circle of those who enjoyed the full fruits of human rights and liberty continued to move forward. But always there was a counterthrust to limit freedom for reasons that were at times reasonable and at times unjust. Calls for national order and individual sacrifice pervaded moments such as wartime; there were always illiberals who sought to turn some people into second-class citizens. One person's freedom was often achieved at the expense of another. The moral debates grounded in this tension are well known—debates over racism, women's rights, and labor justice. Over two centuries, however, a pattern became clear: the scope of personal rights was continually expanded in American society. In the 1930s ten percent of the courses before the U.S. Supreme Court involved individual rights. Today the figure is seventy percent.[10]

The idea for the Statue of Liberty served the American dream of personal independence but came from France. The original inspiration came from a French liberal, Edouard-Rene Lefebvre de Laboulaye in 1865. French liberals in the mid-nineteenth century believed deeply in principles such as universal manhood suffrage, a free press, and representative government. Laboulaye was displeased by the actions of the government of Emperor Napoleon III in his home country which he felt was moving too far in the direction of a monarchy and away from the liberal ideals of the French Revolution. The eventual effort to place a statue in New York entitled "Liberty Enlightening the World," was meant not only to sustain a moral ideal in the world but to send a message to conservatives in Laboulaye's native land.[11]

Laboulaye also had other considerations in his take on liberty. He was supportive of Abraham Lincoln's emancipation of the slaves, but, at the same time not ready to turn political life over to the masses. He was a true believer in the ability of the free individual to make his way in the world, but that individual should in his estimation be a man of learning like he was. In fact, Laboulaye was an admirer of Horace Mann and was fascinated with his life story of rising from poverty through education. He fully supported Mann's ideas for public education as an ideal form of preparation for effective citizenship. The final design of the statue ultimately was meant to articulate an ideal of liberty achieved not through revolutionary uprisings but through the exercise of legal procedures. Laboulaye had no sympathy for the type of radical protest depicted in a famous French painting by Eugene Delacroix—"Liberty Leading the People, 1830." In Delacroix's rendition of political change, angry citizens demanding rights are led by a bare-breasted woman wearing a "liberty cap." It is not an accident that the statue one sees in New York harbor today is fully clothed and topped by a halo instead of a cap. Laboyale wanted to proclaim the timelessness of universal liberty for all but not at the expense of investing political power in all of the people—or certainly the king.[12]

Discussions of human liberty were also quite rampant in early nineteenth-century America, and they would have some impact on the final image that was erected in New York harbor in ways that have not always been fully appreciated. From the very beginning of the new American nation, citizens sought to personify both this fundamental ideal and the nation itself. Citizens needed ways to represent the nation and think of what it meant. In America's first century, two female symbols—Columbia and Liberty—performed much of the cultural work of representing the meaning of the nation. These classical female forms adorned monuments, works of arts, and were even immortalized in song. John Higham has argued that there was never any question that America would be personified through classical female forms because of the "immense authority" that classical images such as the Roman "Goddess of Liberty" exercised over the eighteenth century. Higham explains also that these images served different ideals. Columbia was preferable to images of an "Indian princess" that was frequently used in a pejorative way to characterize North America as uncivilized when compared to Britain. After the revolution it came to serve the interests of those who wanted to affirm the power of the new nation as an equal to England. It was the American version of the English goddess Britannia and the dream of national power. "Liberty," however, signified less the authority and power of the new nation and, as Higham says, more the transnational symbol of human rights. Liberty held more firmly to the romantic ideal of freedom for all men.[13]

In the culture of the early United States the meaning of freedom or liberty was closer to the universal symbol Higham discussed than it was to a specific invocation of all things American. It stood more for a rejection of absolutism and slavery but over time it would become associated to a greater extent with the ideal of a powerful American state. Moral authority would move back and forth between the individual and the nation and, in that struggle, the parameters of a nationalist discourse over morality would be carried out. This tension was already apparent in 1792 when Congress decided to put a neoclassical picture of a female named "liberty" on American coinage instead of the image of the president. The fear was that the office of the chief executive was growing too powerful. In the early nineteenth century the growing defense of slavery further diminished the dream of human freedom and equality. In the 1850s, two sculptors vied for a government commission to create a figure of Columbia atop the dome of the U.S. Capitol building. Due to the influence of Jefferson Davis, who chaired the Capitol Building Program, the final selection was one consciously stripped of a liberty cap and broken chairs meant to signify the triumph of liberty over despotism. Davis had complained that such features reminded him of antislavery sentiment and preferred a design with an eagle's head on top instead of a cap associated with popular uprisings. The assassination of Abraham Lincoln and the emancipation of slaves were certainly events that promoted a greater acceptance of the ideal of human equality. Yet, as we will see it was never easy to simply proclaim freedom and equality for all races as a moral vision of American society before modern times without jeopardizing the stability of the American nation itself.[14]

By the time of the dedication of the Statue of Liberty in the 1880s, however, the close association between liberty and antislavery had subsided somewhat, although there is evidence that African-Americans supported the fund drive to build a pedestal to receive the gift from France. Black newspapers such as the *Cleveland Gazette* published poetry in connection with the dedication ceremonies and linked the event to the long-term assault on slavery throughout the nineteenth century. Some even editorialized that the statue's torch should not be lighted until this country becomes "a free one in reality." Yet, it was really the upper-class businessmen and industrialists in France and the United States who led drives to finance the statue and build a pedestal in New York to serve as a foundation. These men—sharing a vision with French entrepreneurs who came to back the statue project in hopes of expanding trade with the United States—saw liberty in terms of unencumbered economic activity and the free pursuit of wealth more than they saw it as a renunciation of despotism and slavery. Men such as Gustave Eiffel, who designed the inner structure of the statue, had complete faith in their abilities and their sense of individualism and saw the statue and the Eiffel tower in the following decade as a reaffirmation of that confidence. This is why many of the organizers of the dedication ceremony shared Laboulaye's aversion to mass protest as a vehicle for change.[15]

The struggle against slavery and despotism and the veneration of human freedom were central to the political morality of much of the nineteenth century. As American society evolved in the twentieth century, however, this ideal was recast more specifically into a celebration of personal fulfillment and individual acquisitiveness. In the Revolutionary era of expression of the ideal of human freedom, there was an implicit call for a new state to defend this belief. In the nineteenth century it took state action to extend its benefits and eradicate its opponents. And there were heightened expectations that citizens would be willing to serve the public good from time to time in order to limit excessive individualism. In the modern manifestation of freedom that came to dominate the twentieth century, liberty came to be more about personal freedom and less about the need to expand state power or promote calls for civic obligation. One variant of the ideal never replaced the other, but the trend was clear. Walter Gray has argued that liberty in our times came to serve the imperatives of a commercial and manufacturing society. It was based less in opposition to slavery and despotism—although anti-totalitarian impulses were expressed in times of war—and more on the pursuit of private pleasures and wealth. In the era of the Revolution there was a sense that the free individual needed to be subordinate to newly created states. In our times the individual came to be seen as preeminent and states as merely guarantors of individual rights.[16]

The Statue of Liberty managed to serve this transformation well. Consider the way it was linked throughout much of the twentieth century to the story of American immigration and capitalist success. This link went through two basic stages. In the 1880s, newspaper editor Joseph Pulitzer, an immigrant himself who fashioned a successful career in America, started a national campaign to raise money to build a base for the statue. His newspapers led the campaign in which countless numbers of Americans contributed donations to ensure that the statue would stand in New York harbor. Illustrations in popular magazines and emigrant guidebooks distributed throughout Europe portrayed steerage passengers in peasant garb saluting the statue.

It is true that at times the monument was used by nativists interested in restricting the immigrant flow into America. At the 1886 unveiling the president of the New York Central Railroad qualified any thought of an open door for the "huddled masses" by suggesting that poor newcomers were welcome as long as they did not hold any radical or alien political beliefs. By the twentieth century, however, the statue stood as a beacon for the poor and unfortunate who desired to come to America and make their own way to financial and political freedom. In the 1950s efforts were made to create a museum of immigration at the statue's base that celebrated the achievement of "liberty" for those who came to the United States and worked diligently. In the 1986 celebration over the restoration of the statue, the meaning of liberty was cast decidedly in the direction of free-wheeling and free spending capitalists and consumers. Long forgotten links to anti-slavery and civic obligation were seldom heard or seen. Magazine covers with images of the Statue of Liberty also proclaimed the revival of American economic growth after the doldrums of the 1970s. A fund raising drive led by a corporate leader of a distinctive immigrant background—Lee Iacocca—reinforced the connection between the nation, the idea of liberty, and moral goodness of the unfettered pursuit of self-interest. Thousands of Americans bought products stamped with the statue's image and wore on their heads "cheap, sponge tiaras" that replicated the headdress of Lady Liberty.[17]

Not only did the statue in the later part of the twentieth century associate individual freedom more with capitalism than civic republicanism or progressivism but the image of the statue simply became a commercial product used in countless ways. It would be hard to recall the original dream of human freedom and the attack upon slavery and despotism in items such as "halo hats" that tourists could buy in New York or in the advertisements of a zipper manufacturer that showed the back of the statue's toga as having a zipper. The caption in this depiction read: "We hold America together." Similar trends toward the trivialization of older form of political morality are evident in products such as liberty pears, liberty cigars, and liberty cloth dolls.

The Lincoln Memorial

Public symbols—consider the American flag—are nearly always ambiguous in their meanings and subject to many uses. Victor Turner has shown how the most important symbols in a culture derive their power from the fact that they restate social contradictions and remain ambiguous and multivocal in meaning. This was certainly true of both the Lincoln Memorial and the Statue of Liberty, two public symbols evaluated here. They both shared a classical form of architecture that represented the sense of their creators that they aspired to reinforce the massive project to create the modern nation and tap the potential of human emotions as a source of moral and social behavior. And they both expressed central ideals and values associated with the American national experience. But clearly the statue was less bound by the specifics of American history than the memorial. It tended to retain a more universalist than nationalist appeal. Thus, it was more likely to be replicated at places like Tiananmen Square in China than an image such as the Lincoln Memorial that was so much more nationally specific. Yet variability was at the heart of the conception of public morality in liberal nations. It was that characteristic that not only accounted for the popularity of these icons but also set them apart from older forms of morality that were based in specific texts and dogmas. The hope for timeless moral values that drove traditionalists in American culture was always undermined by public moral discussions of earthly ideals.

Dedicated in 1922, the Lincoln Memorial resembled a Greek temple, a symbol of sacredness and timelessness. We know that the men who promoted its construction and design had very clear ideas of the values they wanted to enshrine and, by implication, the ones they wanted to erase from public view. In fact, both the statue and the memorial were the result of projects began by powerful elites who hoped to, in the words of Kirk Savage, "mould history into its rightful pattern." They never succeeded. As Christopher Thomas has observed for the Lincoln Memorial, it became "many things at once—a war memorial, a monument to a national hero, a temple to American ideals, and a national stage." And Thomas astutely observed that its "generality was intentional." That is to say that as a national icon it needed to reach across society and its sectional, denominational, and class interests in order to serve the interests of national society and the desires of powerful white leaders. It had to appear more democratic than its specific origins might suggest.[18]

Abstract classical images have long been used to bring a sense of order to society and to an understanding of its political values. Images that are more realistic—one might think of the realism of a novel or a film—tended to portray society and the experience of individualism in more convoluted and cynical terms. They seldom offered pure and simple prescriptions of how life was to be lived or what the future might hold. And as such it threatened depictions of the nation, its leaders, and its future in ideal or optimistic terms. In the aftermath of the Civil War and Reconstruction—with its lessons of brutality, racial strife, and sectionalism—many felt that the most urgent national need was the reunification and reification of the Union itself. In the late nineteenth century Republican elites, especially in the North, mounted an effort to construct what Thomas called "idealizing civic monuments" and programs to Americanize "workers and immigrants" by celebrating high-minded, patriotic ideals of "civic and national harmony."[19]

There is much to admire in the design of the Lincoln Memorial. By reproducing both the text of the "Gettysburg Address" and Lincoln's "Second Inaugural Address" the monument signaled its intention to affirm the sacredness of national unity and the connection between national loyalty and democratic forms of government. There were silences in all this—including the omission of the Emancipation Proclamation. National reconciliation could not be advanced at the time if the Northern triumph over the South was memorialized in an explicit way or if the emancipation of African-Americans were vividly recalled at the site. In fact, the memorial that stands in Washington, DC today originally constituted a rejection of the ideal of racial equality that had been discussed in earlier designs for memorials to Lincoln. In the 1860s plans were put forward by some Republicans to build a monument to the sixteenth president to honor the idea of "universal liberty in America." In this plan a figure of Lincoln as patriarch seated in the act of signing the Emancipation Proclamation would be mounted on the top of the memorial. Below him would be figures of war generals and below that "allegorical" figures of the "Negro" progressing from slavery to freedom but, as Savage suggests, removed from the "civic realm of the hero." The Greek temple-like monument we see today represents a rejection of this level of realism. Later in time a plan for a Lincoln Memorial that would include more populist sentiments of a log cabin and faith in the people—with less reference to classical design—was also rejected.[20]

The final design attempted to transform Lincoln and the nation into a timeless and sacred image of high virtue—but one that placed more faith in the ideal of an ordered nation under the leadership of heroic and benevolent men than in the simple declaration of human freedom. Lincoln himself was a symbol of national order and power more than he was a representation of a self-made man. As such he kept alive the Revolutionary ideal of civic obligation attached to human freedom. Thomas makes the good point that a Greek temple in antiquity may have served as a sign of the dwelling place of a god or a goddess. In the modern liberal nation, however, it was the morally perfect and patriotic man that was celebrated. He was god-like while still retaining the citizen's commitment to public order and some national political ideals. The monument drew upon civic republicanism in its aspirations for a vital national society but it backed off a full-fledged faith in the actions and thought of all citizens. The overall memorial was very much a part of the type of iconography that dominated America in the late nineteenth and early twentieth century that was heavily infused with sacred and patriotic imagery and highly supportive of powerful men. This view was also seen in the public veneration of veterans from both sides in the Civil War and in the celebration of the flag in U.S. schoolrooms.[21]

The anti-democratic impulses pervading the minds of the original designers were effectively contested over time. The memorial came to serve, in effect, as a site of debate over the moral vision of the nation. The key moment in revising some of the authoritarian and racist aspirations associated with the original plan came in 1939. In that year Marian Anderson, a black singer who was refused permission to sing in their hall by the Daughters of the American Revolution, was granted the same privilege at the Lincoln Memorial. Anderson's powerful rendition of the National Anthem not only inspired blacks and whites, but generated a renewed sense of activism on the part of African-Americans. Her 1939 concert, in fact, was carefully organized by Walter White, a leading official of the National Association for the Advancement of Colored People. White, angered by the DAR's rejection, sought to reinforce the broad sense of national symbolism associated with the Lincoln site in a way that consciously invoked the image of Lincoln not so much as the savior of the union but as the "Great Emancipator." The NAACP's moral vision was of a nation free of racial prejudice and tolerant of people with varying characteristics and background more than it was of a strong and powerful national idea. Those who heard Anderson's inspired performance, according to historian Scott Sandage, remarked that it was "like a religious service" and "a great spiritual experience of common sympathy and understanding." Sandage shows how this concert led to a long sustained effort on the part of African-Americans to overturn the system of white supremacy that pervaded American society and culminated in Martin Luther King's speech at the memorial in front of 400,000 Americans in 1963. America's secular memorials could have many meanings and could evoke alternative visions of an ideal and just society. At times the power of the nation was imagined to be more important than an explicit defense of a fair and cooperative society. But the desire for a good society continually reasserted itself.[22]

Conclusion

In intent and in use these two public monuments served the needs of the nation for moral instruction. They did this in different ways, however, because the secular project of creating and sustaining a liberal nation was based on ideals and values that were inherently contradictory. A deep commitment to individualism and equality continually collided against more dogmatic dreams of national order, patriarchy, and elitism. At times unity and national power were invoked to ratify the aspirations of powerful men. At other times state power was called upon to promote justice for all citizens. Overall the Statue of Liberty served primarily the dream of the free individual. The Lincoln Memorial took up the question of how best to sustain the power of the nation and how best to use that power. The nationalization of moral life—promoted by these public icons—meant, however, that moral issues would never be settled. Thus, the meaning of both national icons discussed here was transformed over time and in dramatic ways. Traditions did not go away. Patriotic rituals and sentiments of America being a nation under God continued in the centuries after the Revolution, but the debate over moral authority in American life was centered not in the past or in some conception of an afterlife but in the tumultuous pursuit of both liberty and power in the present.

Notes

1. Benedict Anderson, *Imagined Communities: The Origins and Spread of Nationalism* (Ithaca, NY: Cornell University Press, 1983), 6–26, 141–145.
2. Gordon Wood, *The Radicalism of the American Revolution* (New York: Vintage, 1991), 95–105, 214–217, 229–234.
3. B. Edward McClellan, *Moral Education in America: Schools and the Shaping of Character from Colonial Times to the Present* (New York: Teacher's College Press, 1999), 10.
4. Ibid., 9–12.
5. Ibid., 17–23.
6. Ruth Elson, *Guardians of Tradition* (Lincoln, NE: University of Nebraska Press, 1964), 338; McClellan, *Moral Education in America*, 56–57.
7. See Ronald D. Cohen and Raymond A. Mohl, *The Paradox of Progressive Education: The Gary Plan and Urban Schooling* (Port Washington, NY: Kennikat Press, 1979), 3–7; McClellan, *Moral Education in America*, 73.
8. Jonathan Zimmerman, *Whose America? Culture Wars in the Public Schools* (Cambridge, MA: Harvard University Press, 2002), 2–3, 26–32, 138–158; Morris Janowitz, *The Reconstruction of Patriotism: Education for a Civic Consciousness* (Chicago: University of Chicago Press, 1983), 59, 192–195. Janowitz called for new forms of national service as a way to restore a sense of civic obligation rather than simply social analysis of problems or faith in God and character.

9. Jenny Franchot, "Unseemly Commemoration: Religion, Fragments and the Icon," in Larry J. Reynolds and Gordon Hunter, eds., *National Imaginaries, American Identities* (Princeton, NJ: Princeton University Press, 2000), 211–212.
10. Mary Ann Glendon, *Rights Talk: The Impoverishment of Political Discourse* (New York: The Free Press, 1991), 3–14.
11. Albert Boime, *The Unveiling of the National Icons: A Plea for Patriotic Iconoclasm in a Nationalist Era* (Cambridge, UK: Cambridge University Press, 1998), 86–103; Marvin Tractenburg, *The Statue of Liberty* (New York: Viking Press, 1976), 17–37.
12. Boime, *The Unveiling of the National Icons*, 94–98; Boime, *Hollow Icons: The Politics of Sculpture in Nineteenth-Century France* (Kent, OH: Kent State University Press, 1987), 120–125. Walter D. Gray, *Interpreting American Democracy in France: The Career of Edouard Laboulaye, 1811–1883* (Newark, DE: University of Delaware Press, 1994), 67–74.
13. John Higham, "Indian Princess and Roman Goddess: The First Female Symbols of America," *Proceedings of the American Antiquarian Society*, 100, I (1990), 45–79.
14. Jean Fagan Yellin, "Caps and Chains: Hiram Powers' Statue of Liberty," *American Quarterly*, 38 (Winter 1986): 798–826.
15. Gray, *Interpreting American Democracy in France*, 28–29; Tractenburg, *The Statue of Liberty*, p. 186; Rebecca M. Joseph, "The Black Statue of Liberty Rumor: An Inquiry into the History and Meaning of Bartholdi's *Liberte eclairant le Monde*" (New York: National Park Service, Unpublished report, 2000), 63–68.
16. Gray, *Interpreting American Democracy in France*, 36–94.
17. Kathy Evertz, "The 1986 Statue of Liberty Centennial: Commercialization and Reaganism," *Journal of Popular Culture*, 29 (Winter 1995): 214–219.
18. Christopher Thomas, *The Lincoln Memorial and American Life* (Princeton, NJ: Princeton University Press, 2002), xix–xx. Kirk Savage, *Standing Soldiers, Kneeling Slaves* (Princeton, NJ: Princeton University Press, 1997), 3–7; Victor Turner, *The Ritual Process* (Ithaca, NY: Cornell University Press, 1977).
19. Thomas, *The Lincoln Memorial and American Life*, xxiii–xxiv.
20. Ibid., 1–6. Savage, *Standing Soldiers, Kneeling Slaves*, 106.
21. Thomas, *The Lincoln Memorial and American Life*, 23. Stuart McConnell, "Reading the Flag: A Reconsideration of the Patriotic Cults of the 1890s," in John Bodnar, ed., *Bonds of Affection: Americans Define their Patriotism* (Princeton, NJ: Princeton University Press, 1996), 102–118.
22. Scott A. Sandage, "A Marble House Divided: The Lincoln Memorial, the Civil Rights Movement, and the Politics of Memory," *Journal of American History*, 80 (June 1993): 135–167.

This page intentionally left blank

Afterword

Donald Warren and John J. Patrick

Civic and Moral Learning in America offers a sample of studies meant to expand the pool of resources for public and scholarly discussions and for educational planning. In the tradition exemplified by the work of B. Edward McClellan the editors and authors have approached the topic of civic and moral education analytically, while keeping it near the heart of narratives on where we have been as American people and how we got there. When given curricular forms, this tradition of inquiry expresses optimism and intentionality with regard to the nation's future as a democratic society. Multiple research perspectives generated in a variety of disciplines, fields of study, and professions (represented here by history, philosophy, and education) can help build confidence that the research itself and resulting curriculum projects can escape the taint of cultural imperialism. Establishing that confidence is a necessary step. From its beginnings, U.S. history has presented numerous examples of civic and moral imposition by reform groups, committees, or movements determined to enforce their norms on others. Relegated to the social margins, some religious persuasions have faced pressures to conform to more prevalent doctrines and codes, war protesters and civil rights advocates have found themselves labeled unpatriotic, immigrants have experienced demeaning quarantines, and factory workers have suffered demands to rest satisfied with the status (and income) bestowed on them by owners and managers. To the extent that formal moral and civic education has been an instrument of encoded goals to tame legitimate political and religious expression and to stifle appreciation for the cultural diversity long ago woven into the country's fabric, curriculum projects have been rightly greeted with suspicion by affected communities and families. But this sort of disengagement from the official curriculum has merely reinforced the process of civic and moral learning in places and on occasions beyond the reach of classrooms and majoritarian convictions. The relevant question thus becomes where, not whether, it has occurred. Answers provide resources for curriculum planners who want to design programs that engage children and adults meaningfully and publicly with civic and moral issues. When asked, we Americans seem to agree that our society requires educational initiatives of this quality and purpose.

The needed research falls well beyond the exclusive purview of academicians. Using inquiry as a teaching tool can engage students of any age in formal moral and civic learning. We underestimate the capacities and curiosities of children if we assume they cannot join the quests. A similar devaluation of experience can undermine civic and moral learning in adult literacy programs and in advancing the goals of professional development for teachers. Consider the interests aroused as young and old enrollees conduct inquiry on their family's or community's history or on actual moral dilemmas like the distribution of relief to the victims of hurricanes. Such investigations establish a continuing link of personal engagement with the study of documents and ideas commonly associated with civic and moral learning. They can equip students to find evidence leading to their own answers to the fundamental question: Why should I care that from the nation's inception citizens of the United States have debated, often fiercely, their aspirations to function as a democratic society?

The authors and editors of this book have intended to illustrate the research agenda following in the wake of this question and some of the funny and sad, exhilarating and infuriating answers that result from it. We have also tried to demonstrate that significant inquiry remains to be done. Filling the gaps may reveal the necessity of more basic new constructions of national narratives, reconsiderations of our public philosophies, and acknowledgement that a canonical account of such matters—a uniform and sanctioned mode of thinking and acting as moral citizens—may be wrong-headed educationally. Each of the topics dealt with in this book warrants further and more extensive investigation. Trying to keep the book to a reasonable length, we omit other relevant topics entirely. Art, literature, music, architecture, and popular culture play roles in the formation of political and moral sensibilities that we have not examined. Nor have we explored the specific influences of poverty, war, and natural disasters on the sense of national membership among those most affected and on the broader public's commitment to the general welfare. Several of our chapters speak to the relationships of organized Christianity and personal spirituality to the preparation of good citizens, but none extends the analysis to American Jews or Muslims, to cite two glaring omissions. Our one chapter on immigrants leaves untouched the detailed experiences of other newcomers to the United States, notably the great number of recent arrivals from other parts of the Americas and from Asia. Then there is the matter of indigenous and inventive developments in the western regions of the United States, where only fragments of eastern seaboard ingredients can be discovered in the social glue of civic and moral learning. Finally, to underscore a point made in the Introduction, the global interest in civic and moral learning suggests a wide array of pertinent research issues in international and comparative studies. The examples remind us that an important and inviting agenda awaits the attention from diverse perspectives that it is due.

We are writing this at the end of August 2005, one week after Hurricane Katrina laid waste to New Orleans and much of the Gulf Coast's northern rim. News reports have moved quickly from descriptions of devastation to fury at the delayed, halting responses of federal, state, and local officials. Proving to be an intersection of issues related to race, social class, reduced investment of public funds in services and infrastructure, long-practiced abandonment of our most vulnerable citizens, and leadership failures, the storm's aftermath has presented an image of the nation's character that Americans now seem determined to reject as unacceptable. The picture does not reflect the fair-minded, generous, and problem-solving society we envision ourselves to be. Katrina's lessons will emerge more sharply over the months ahead, and they may be different for the members of various communities, but among those lessons are sure to be many about our civic and moral obligations to one another.

Index

Abbott, Edith, 154
Abbott, Jacob, 140
Abbott, Lyman, 124
Adams, David Wallace, 60
Adams, John, 36, 38, 44
Adolescent Family Life Act, 200
African American educators, 104, 107–109, 114
African Americans
  black churches, 105, 107–108, 112
  black identity, 109
  moral and civic learning and, 105–111
  women and moral learning, 112–113
agriculture, 4, 52, 71, 77–78, 82, 87–95, 97–98, 100, 125, 131, 165
Alabama Penny Loan & Savings, 110
Alaska
  importation of reindeer to, 63–64
  and Protestant moral education, 57–64
  and Russian Orthodox moral education, 52–57
alcohol education, 191–195, 198–201
Aldridge, Derrick, 110–111
Alien and Sedition Acts, 44
Amarok, William, 63
American Home Economics Association
American Indians, *see* Native Americans (AHEA), 158
American Missionary Association (AMA), 109
American Youth Commission, 175
Americanism, 145–146, 176
Anatoli, Archimandrite, 62
Anderson, Benedict, 207–208
Anderson, James, 109
Anderson, Marian, 217
Andress, J. Mace, 191–192
Anslinger, Harry J., 195, 198

Armstrong, Barbara Nachtrieb, 155, 160–163, 165–166
Armstrong, Samuel Chapman, 109
Atkins, J.D.C., 125
Ayers, Edward, 79

Bailyn, Bernard, 54, 100
Baker, Russell, 191
Bancroft, Hubert Howe, 61
Banner, James M., 44
Bell, Howard, 175
Bennett, William J., 14
Benreuter Personality Record, 182
Berkeley, University of California at, 153–163, 165–167
  social economic research and, 164–165
  social research and policy reform, 156–164
  women economists and, 153–155, 157, 159, 161, 163, 165–167
  Women's Faculty Club, 162–163
  see also Heller Committee
Betts, George Herbert, 184–186
Bezanson, Anne, 163
Bidwell, Charles, 80–83
Bishop, Abraham, 35
Bishop Innocent
  see Veniaminov, John
Blackstone, William, 39–40
boarding schools, 59–60, 62, 130
Bobbitt, Franklin, 179
Bollman, Lewis, 96
Boone, A.J., 94
Boyer, Ernest, 15
Breckinridge, Sophonisba, 154
Bridgman, Olga, 162
Brown, Austin H., 135

Brown, Ignatius, 95–97
Bryn Mawr, 154, 163, 167
Bureau of Indian Affairs, 61, 121–123, 125–126, 130–131
Burgh, James, 35
Burnham, W.H., 179
Bush, Edgar D., 146
Bush, George W., 7–10, 12–13, 16
  agenda for education, 7–12
  faith-based initiatives and, 12–14

Calderone, Mary, 198–199
Candler, Allen Daniel, 103
Cannon, Katie, 105, 113
Carlisle Indian School, 124, 126–130
Cato's Letters, 39
Cavanaugh, Sean, 13
Chafetz, Morris, 191–192
Character and Personality, 178, 184
character education, 9, 14, 142, 147, 173–187, 194
  "goodness," and, 183–187
  "psychologizing" of, 179–183
Character Training, 180
Charters, W.W., 179
Chickering, Martha, 162
civic education, during Revolutionary period, 41–43
Civic Ideals (Smith), 119
civic ideals, 21–23, 25, 27–30, 119, 131
civic virtues, 14–16, 18, 33–35, 69, 119, 186, 209
civic vision, 87–88, 99
civil rights, 12, 106, 111, 114, 221
Civil War, 28–29, 95, 98, 106, 108, 137, 142, 147, 156, 216–217
CIVITAS, 15–16, 18
Clinton, Bill, 14, 193, 200
Coffroth, John R., 138
Cohen, Sol, 173–174
Coleman, James, 69–71, 74, 79–80, 82–83
Collins, Patricia Hill, 112–113
common schools, 8, 16, 45, 69–72, 91, 111, 137
  curriculum, 80–82
  differences in Northern vs. Southern, 77–80
  historical circumstances of, 72–77

Cone, James, 106, 120
Constitution, 12, 14, 16, 34, 36, 38, 40–42, 104, 120, 125–126
Cook, Joseph T., 123–124, 159
Cookingham, Mary, 159
Cooper, Anna Julia, 103–104, 112–113
Coram, Robert, 39–42
crops, 79, 88, 90, 96–97
Cropsey, Nebraska, 135
Cross, Ira, 159–161
Cubberley, Ellwood, 54
Curti, Merle, 74–75
Curtis Act (1924), 131

Daughters of the American Revolution (DAR), 217
Davis, Jefferson, 213
Davis, Maxine, 173, 175, 213
Davis, Michelle, 13
Dawes Act, 63, 123, 128
Dawson, Michael, 114
Deaver, Michael, 196
Declaration of Independence, 1, 33, 36, 40, 104, 211
Delacroix, Eugene, 212
Democratic-Republican Societies, 33–36, 40, 44
Depression, 164, 175–176, 178
de Tocqueville, Alexis, 14, 99
Dewey, John, 54, 147, 179
Dewey, Thomas E., 195
Dimock, Hedley, 174, 176
Dingeldey, 138–139
Donskoy, Vladmir, 62
Doors to Jobs (Huntington), 163
Douglass, Frederick, 106
Drug Abuse Resistance Education (DARE), 197, 201
drug education, 191–193, 195–197, 199–201
  see also narcotics
DuBois, W.E.B., 3, 104, 108–112, 114
DuPont, Robert L., 196

Eastman, Charles, 125
education
  Bush's agenda for, 7–12
  and civic virtue, 14–18
  court cases regarding, 17

faith-based, 9, 11–14
   parental involvement in, 12, 17,
      74–77, 181
   public, 11, 14, 16–17, 25, 29, 33, 41, 79,
      104, 115, 137, 143, 212
   teacher, 9–11, 16–18
Elders, Jocelyn, 191, 193, 200
Eliot, Charles, 198
Ellsworth, Henry, 89
Emancipation, 107–109, 111,
   212–213, 216
Emmerich, Charles, 139–140, 142–144
Enlightenment, 34–37, 60, 119, 208, 210
enrollment, school, 52–53, 71–73, 77–78,
   80, 82–83
Etzioni, Amitai, 14

Federalists, 10, 33–34, 37, 39, 44–45
Felton, Katherine, 162
First Amendment, 12–13
Folbre, Nancy, 154, 157
Folsom, Joseph, 177–178
Foster, Charles, 61
Frazier, E. Franklin, 108
freethinkers, 139–142, 147
Fuller, Wayne, 69, 73, 75–76

Galvin, John, 144
Garland, Hamlin, 73
Garrett, Philip, 121
Gates, Darryl, 197
Gates, Henry Louis, 106
Gates, Merrill, 63, 122, 124–125
General Allotment Act (1887), 63, 122
Goethe, Johann Wolfgang von, 141–142
Goldin, Claudia, 71–73, 77
Golovin, Gregory, 53
Gookins, S.B., 89

Haddock, Laura, 184–185
Hampton Model of education, 109, 111
Harris, William Torrey, 61, 63, 126, 142
Haskell Institute, 125–126, 129–131
Haughey, Theodore P., 144
Haycox, Stephen, 59
Hearst, Phoebe Apperson, 156–157, 167
Heaton, Kenneth, 181
Heller, Clara Hellman, 164–166
Heller Committee, 164–165

Hewes, Amy, 154
Hickok, Gene, 13
Higgenbotham, Evelyn B., 112
Higham, John, 213
Holifield, E. Brooks, 173
Howe, Julia Ward, 61
Huber, Richard, 176
Hughes, Harold H., 192
Hunt, Mary Hanchett, 193, 195
Hunter, James Davison, 173
Huntington, Emily, 155, 161–166
Hyat, Ezra, 122

Indian before the Law, The (Pancoast),
   121–122
Indian Helper, 126
Indian Leader (Haskell), 130–131
Indian policy, 59, 63, 120–121
Indian schools, 61–62, 124–126, 128, 130
Indiana
   agricultural improvement in, 88–90
   Boone County, 93–94
   civic learning, 95–100
   institutionalization and transformation in,
      90–95
   State Fair's role in growth of, 90–98
Indianapolis Public Schools (IPS), 135–147
   German-American education in,
      137–140, 143–145
   German freethinkers and, 140–143
   growth of, 137–140
   nativism and, 143–146
individualism, 35, 63, 98, 121, 125, 127,
   208–211, 214, 216, 218
Insuring the Essentials (Huntington), 161

Jackson, Andrew, 37, 45
Jackson, Jesse, 197
Jackson, Sheldon, 57–64
Janowitz, Morris, 210
Jefferson, Thomas, 1, 16, 36–37, 41–42,
   44–45, 87–88, 209
Jim Crow, 112
John Birch Society, 199
Jordan, David Starr, 61

Kaestle, Carl, 75–76, 82–83
Kan, Sergei, 130
Kant, Immanuel, 21, 29, 106

Katz, Lawrence, 37, 71–73, 77
Kendall, Calvin N., 136, 143, 145–146
Kilpatrick, W.H., 179
Kingsbury, Susan, 154, 163
kirchendeutsche, 139
Knortz, Karl, 145

Laboulaye, Edouard-Rene, 212, 214
Lake Mohonk Conference, 63, 121–122, 124–126
Lamar, Lucius Q., 121
Lane, Franklin, 123
Larkin, Jack, 73, 75
Larue, Daniel, 182
Laski, Harold, 163
Last Arrow Ceremony, 123–124, 129
  see also Native Americans
Lemann, Nicholas, 8
Leupp, Francis, 123, 129
Levine, Arthur, 10
liberalism, 21–22, 30–31, 119
Lincoln, Abraham, 4, 109
Lincoln Memorial, 215–218
literacy, 2, 9, 44, 53, 57, 69, 75, 78, 106–109, 114, 222
Locke, John, 21, 36, 40–41
Loop, W.T., 64
Loven, Jennifer, 13

Madison, James, 37, 44
Maine, Henry, 54, 77–78
Mann, Horace, 57, 212
Marshall, John, 120
McClellan, B. Edward, 1, 18, 69, 98, 105, 136, 154, 192, 200, 208–210, 221
McCloy, C.H., 182
McCray, Franklin, 146
McDougall, William, 178–179
McGuffey readers, 42, 69
McKinley, William, 127
McKown, Harry, 183
Menand, Louis, 141, 147
Mencken, H.L., 140
mental hygiene, 173–179, 181–185
  and personality vs. character, 174–179
Mill, John Stuart, 18, 21, 157
Miller, Adolph, 157, 159
Milton, John, 35, 39

Mis-Education of the Negro, The (Woodson), 111
missionaries, 52, 54–56, 60–61, 106, 109, 124
moral authority, 21–22, 207–208, 213, 218
Moral Education in America (McClellan), 57, 105
Morgan, Agnes Fay, 158, 162
Morgan, Thomas J., 121, 126–127
Morrow, Prince, 197–198
Moses, Bernard, 156–157, 159
M Street School Controversy, 113
Murray, C.L., 91
Myrdal, Gunner, 104
Myrick, Helen, 181

narcotics, 193, 195, 197, 201
  see also drug education
Nat Turner rebellion, 78
National Council for the Social Studies (NCSS), 10
National Education Association (NEA), 178–179
  Yearbook of Department of Elementary School Teachers, 178, 180, 182
National Institute on Drug Abuse (NIDA), 196
nationalization, 207–208, 218
Native Americans, 3, 127, 129
  citizenship, 119–121, 123, 131
  reservations and, 120, 122–124, 126, 130–131, 139
nativism, 59, 136, 143–147, 215
New Jersey, 180–181, 198
newspapers, as educational source, 43–45
Nix, Robert, 136, 140–142, 145–147
Nixon, Richard, 195
No Child Left Behind Act, 9–11
Nordlander, David, 57
Notes on the State of Virginia (Jefferson), 87
Nunn, Sam, 14

Oberly, John, 63, 122, 124
Okey, Ruth, 158
Oleksa, Michael, 63
Orcutt, Hiram, 75–76
Orthodox missionaries, 55–56

Paige, Rod, 10, 13
Paine, Thomas, 37, 40–41
Pancoast, Henry, 121
Pan'kov, Ivan, 53
Parent Resource Institute for Drug Education (PRIDE), 196
Parker, Carleton, 159–160
patriotism, 14–15, 38, 73, 127, 129, 131, 145–146, 209–211
Payton, Philip, 110
Peaslee, John B., 145
Peirce, Charles, 135, 147
Peixotto, Jessica, 155–167
Pennsylvania, 13, 33, 36, 43, 79
personality, 156, 173–174, 177–187
Pettiford, William, 110
Phoenix Indian School, 127, 129
Political Liberalism (Rawls), 22
political participation, 43, 45
Powers, Francis, 180, 183–184
Pratt, Richard, 127, 130
Presbyterian, 57–60, 64
Price, Richard, 36, 43, 91
Protestantism
  Alaska and, 51–52, 55, 57–60, 62
  common schools and, 73, 75, 77–78
Putnam, Robert, 71, 82

racial justice, 103–104, 106–107, 111–113
Rawls, John, 22–25, 29–31
  Principles of Justice, 22
  principles of liberty, 23–24
Reagan, Nancy, 196–197
Reagan, Ronald, 8, 12
reflective equilibrium, 22–27, 29–30
reformers, 73, 75, 87–92, 96–99, 121–126, 158, 163
Reisman, David, 54
republicanism, 119, 121, 208, 215, 217
  enlightened interpretations of, 35–41
Republican Society, 33, 35, 38
Ridpath, John, 141
Rivlin, Harry, 182
Roman Catholic Church, 51, 59
Rothstein, Richard, 9
Rousseau, Jean-Jacques, 43
Royko, Mike, 99
Rush, Benjamin, 41–42
Russian American Company, 52–53, 56

Russian Orthodox Church, 52–57, 59–62, 64
Russian Revolution, 63–64

Sanborn, Franklin, 157
Savage, Kirk, 216–217
Schuchard, Marsha, 196
sex education, 191–193, 195, 197–201
Sex Information and Education Council of the United States (SIECUS), 198
Sheldon Jackson, 57–58, 63
Shelikof, Grigor and Natalya, 52
Shevzov, Vera, 55–56
Shoen, Max, 177
Shurz, Carl, 121
slavery, 1, 3, 23, 78–79, 105–109, 113, 212–215, 217
Smith, Roger M., 119
Smith, Ronald, 131, 178, 185
social capital
  common schools and, 72–82
  moral education and, 82–83
  past and present, 70–72
social Darwinism, 60, 121
social stratification, 38, 42, 56, 73, 82
Souls of Black Folk, The (DuBois), 108, 110
South, 59, 77–80, 88, 103, 106–109, 111–112, 156, 161, 216
Sprague, Lucy, 157–158, 162
Statue of Liberty, 211–215, 218
Stebbins, Lucy, 156, 158, 160, 162, 165
Stempfel, Theodore, 137–138
Supreme Court, 7, 13, 17, 131, 144, 146, 212
Susman, Warren, 173, 186
Symonds, Percival, 176, 179, 183

Taussig, Frank W., 163
Taylor, Paul S., 159–160, 166
temperance, 91, 142, 193–195
  see also alcohol education; Woman's Christian Temperance Union (WCTU)
Ten Commandments, 12
Theory of Justice, A (Rawls), 22–23
Thomas, Christopher, 216–217
Thomas, Clarence, 13, 16
Thomas, William III, 79
Tönnies, Ferdinand, 54

Truth, Sojourner, 106
tserkovnost, 54–56, 62
Tubman, Harriet, 106
Turner societies, 139–140, 142–143

Ueda, Reed, 71
unemployment, 12, 163–167, 175
United States v. Nice, 131
University of California, 154, 156–157, 162
Updegraaf, Harlan, 64

Veniaminov, John, 53, 55, 57
Voice from the South, A (Cooper), 112
Vonnegut, Clemens, 140–142, 144

Ward, Janie, 104
Warren, Heather, 173
Washington, Booker T., 104, 109–112
Washington, George, 34, 37, 42
Webb, Edward, 182
Webb, Sidney, 163
Webster, Noah, 42
Weir, James, 60
Wheeler, Benjamin Ide, 157–158, 160
Whigs, 34–35, 38–39, 43, 45

Williams, Heather, 106
Williams, W.H., 61
Willson, Marcius, 140
Wirthlin, Richard, 196
Woman's Christian Temperance Union (WCTU), 193–194
  see also temperance
Wood, Gordon, 34, 37, 208
Woodburn, James, 146
Woodson, Carter G., 104, 111
Worcester v. Georgia, 120
World War I, 129, 131, 146–147, 159, 162–163, 167, 179, 194, 198, 210
Wortman, Tunis, 38, 43
Wright, Elizabeth, 110

Yonge, Charlotte, 141
Young, Allyn, 163
Young, S. Hall, 60

Zachry, Caroline, 176, 179
Zener, Karl, 179
Zimmerman, Jonathan, 210–211
Znamenski, Andrei, 56–57

GPSR Compliance

The European Union's (EU) General Product Safety Regulation (GPSR) is a set of rules that requires consumer products to be safe and our obligations to ensure this.

If you have any concerns about our products, you can contact us on

ProductSafety@springernature.com

In case Publisher is established outside the EU, the EU authorized representative is:

Springer Nature Customer Service Center GmbH
Europaplatz 3
69115 Heidelberg, Germany

www.ingramcontent.com/pod-product-compliance
Lightning Source LLC
LaVergne TN
LVHW020344260326
834688LV00045B/1515